CONTEMPORARY SOCIETY: TRIBAL STUDIES

VOLUME SIX
TRIBAL SITUATION
IN INDIA

CONTEMPORARY SOCIETY: TRIBAL STUDIES

Edited by

DEEPAK KUMAR BEHERA
and
GEORG PFEFFER

VOLUME ONE	—	STRUCTURE AND PROCESS
VOLUME TWO	—	DEVELOPMENTAL ISSUES, TRANSITION AND CHANGE
VOLUME THREE	—	SOCIAL CONCERN
VOLUME FOUR	—	SOCIAL REALITIES
VOLUME FIVE	—	THE CONCEPT OF TRIBAL SOCIETY
VOLUME SIX	—	TRIBAL SITUATION IN INDIA

The Editors

Deepak Kumar Behera is Professor and Head of the Department of Anthropology, Sambalpur University, Sambalpur, Orissa (India).

George Pfeffer is Professor and Head of the Department of Ethnology, Freie University of Berlin (Germany).

CONTEMPORARY SOCIETY: TRIBAL STUDIES

VOLUME SIX

TRIBAL SITUATION IN INDIA

Edited by

DEEPAK KUMAR BEHERA
Department of Anthropology
Sambalpur University
Sambalpur-768 019
Orissa
India

GEORG PFEFFER
Freie Universität Berlin
Institut für Ethnologie
Drosselweg 1-3
D-14195 Berlin
Germany

CONCEPT PUBLISHING COMPANY, NEW DELHI-110 059

Cataloging in Publication Data—DK
Courtesy: D.K. Agencies (P) Ltd. <docinfo@dkagencies.com>

Contemporary society : tribal studies : Professor Satya Narayana Ratha felicitation volumes / edited by Georg Pfeffer, Deepak Kumar Behera.
v. cm.
Vols. 3-6 lack part of subtitle.
Satyanarayana Ratha, b. 1936, Indian anthropologist; contributed articles.
Includes bibliographical references.
Includes indexes.
Contents: v. 1. Structure and process — v. 2. Development issues, transition and change — v. 3. Social concern — v. 4. Social realities — v. 5. Concept of tribal society — v. 6. Tribal situation in India.
ISBN 8170226406 (set)

1. Tribes—India. 2. India—Scheduled tribes. 3. Ethnology—India. 4. India—Social conditions. I. Ratha, S. N. (Satyanarayana), 1936- II. Pfeffer, Georg, 1943- III. Behera, Deepak Kumar, 1956-

DDC 307.772 095 4 21

Associate Editor
Nibedita Nath

ISBN 81-7022-640-6 (Series)
ISBN 81-7022-984-7 (Vol. VI)

First Published 2005

Published and Printed by
Ashok Kumar Mittal
Concept Publishing Company
A/15-16, Commercial Block, Mohan Garden
New Delhi-110059 (India)

Phone: 25351460, 25351794
Fax: 091–(11)–25357103
E-mail: publishing@conceptpub.com

ACKNOWLEDGEMENTS

We are grateful to all the contributors to the volume. Their academic generosity has enabled us to complete this work successfully. We offer our special thanks to Nibedita Nath for her untiring help and cooperation all through the project. Without her cooperation the volume could not have seen the light of the day. We also thank all others who helped us directly or indirectly for bringing the volume to its present shape. Last but not least, we are thankful to Concept Publishing Company for publishing this volume.

DEEPAK KUMAR BEHERA
GEORG PFEFFER

CONTENTS

SECTION IV
HEALTH ISSUES

TRIBAL SITUATION IN INDIA: An Introduction

GEORG PFEFFER and DEEPAK KUMAR BEHERA

Indian society is generally associated with the unique caste system, which implies endogamous social categories within an overall social order that is ranked and based upon religious principles. Caste society is centralized. Under the political authority of the king spiritual leaders have devised a moral order frequently coinciding with professional specialization of farmers and cattle-herders, sweepers and salesmen, artisans and fishermen. Today a secular constitution may have abolished the formal influence of kingship and priesthood, of discrimination and specialization, and yet political leaders pose in the royal role, priesthood is wielding mass influence, and caste discrimination continues to be the central political topic.

Outside of India, very few people are aware of a major Indian societal type not included in the order of caste: tribal society. In fact, the boundaries between the two types have been blurred and the coexistence between caste and tribe has regularly been viewed as a continuum linking two extreme forms. Both systems are indeed based on the organizational structure of kinship and marriage, both recognise status differences and apply rules of commensality, both avoid a fixed canon of religious commandments, both operate with units marked by fuzzy boundaries.

The tribal political order, however, is not centralized, not devised and legitimized by religious intellectuals and not characterized by economic specialization. Different tribal units may follow different callings which may even be complementary to a certain degree, but the system as such is neither defined by this complementarity and hierarchy, nor by a certain nature of religious and political leadership. Indian tribes are acephalous, or "without a head," thus resembling those of other countries and continents. Their social order is not-as is that of caste - unique to the subcontinent. Furthermore, tribal issues rarely figure in debates of public media. They may create major conflicts at times, but they do not qualify for the routine of political discussion. Urban intellectuals, always well-versed in matters of caste, are frequently absolutely unaware of tribal categories and values, vaguely conceiving tribes as units of equally "backward" and "exploited" fellow citizens — and nothing more. Tribes are "remote" from the centres.

This general lack of awareness is certainly not due to a lack of literature. Numerous government and university departments in almost all Indian states have published monographs and overviews without end, just as they have brought out problem oriented studies on development and change. The circulation of this literature has been parochial, however. Books on the tribes of Malabar, or a specific district of Malabar, are unavailable and unread anywhere else in the country, in case they are not just produced to fill libraries. If generalization and comparison has been attempted at all in this literature, administrative rather than sociological criteria have been considered. Throughout the 20th century, tribal issues in India appear to have been administrative issues, with the major directions coming from the central administration, to be practically applied by the local officers. Vast funds have been channelled into an equally vast bureaucratic machinery of "tribal development" that has grown from decade to decade, supplemented by numerous Non-Government Organizations in the last twenty years, but such an expansion not necessarily coincided with an improved condition of the tribal people or and improved knowledge of their socio-cultural order. The tribes have always been an administrative problem. Only very few individuals, e.g. Sarat Chandra Roy, have seen problems (plural form) among several aspects of a rich and fascinating tribal culture.

The problem of the tribes may have existed since millennia. Asoka, in the third century BC, uses his important administrative tool of rock inscriptions to demand peace in the tribal borderland of his empire. Tribal society of the highlands has never been isolated from caste society in the lowlands. Connections, exchanges and mutual influences must have existed since time immemorial. Some unique aspects of caste and Hinduism, i.e. the central and multidimensional concept of a ritual pollution or the doctrine of transmigration of souls, may have been adopted from tribal society, since these are common features of Indian as well as many overseas tribes. Indian tribes are very much exemplified a part of Indian culture, even though these commonalities are rarely recognized in the anthropological literature. In case they are, the simplistic formula of "Hinduization" — of one version or the other — is applied.

The modern problem of the tribes was discovered at the end of the 18th century in the southeast of the Bengal Presidency. The British colonial power had, so far, managed to occupy a major tract of India without any significant opposition of the peasant population. The latter, as is well known from numerous historical research projects, simply conceived themselves as being shifted from one type of autocratic rule to another. In the Rajmahal Hills, however, the

British met with armed resistance by the ordinary people. Not a regular army, but local villagers fought against the invaders with bows and arrows, being well aware of their dim chances of success. Throughout the 19th century, the tribes of Chhota Nagpur rose in similar style. The "Great Kol Rebellion", the "Great Santal Rebellion" and the drawn-out revolt under the leadership of Birsa Munda were never planned campaigns with specific strategic aims but regularly outbursts of protest that had been smothering for longer periods under the European colonial rule with its tendency to "open" the region by modern means of communication, thereby initiating the mass influx of adventurous immigrants from the plains. The "Kondh Rebellion" and many other tribal protest movements against the British were the outcome. So the administration reacted. By the end of the 19th century, special rights and reservations were introduced everywhere on the Subcontinent to protect "Hill Tribes", "Primitive Tribes," or "Forest Tribes" against land-grabbing peasants from the lowlands.

In the course of the Census of India, members of the Indian Civil Service, as Census Officers, also became ethnographic specialists around the turn of the century, publishing innumerable volumes on the "Tribes and Castes" of one region or the other. They followed a pragmatic approach, giving accounts of local groups, legends and customs in the shape in which they had been discovered on the ground. Categories of social units were listed in alphabetical order. Under each heading, the author accumulated whatever information the local officers had gathered in the course of the decades. Theorising or even empirical exactness was avoided. Until the time of John Hutton - who was the last great Census Ethnographer in 1931 - the volumes were to be used as handbooks on local mores and superstitions, in case the administration was facing any of such issues.

The constitutional reforms of 1936 witnessed a unification of "the tribal problem" in administrative terms. Thereafter, highlanders in "remote areas" enjoyed their "protective discrimination" under the labels of Scheduled Tribes (ST) and Scheduled Castes (SC) and the constitution of independent India continued this tradition, until, during the 1980s, the so-called Other Backward Classes (OBC) were added. Some details of this new classification will be added in the following articles, and the particular history of the Criminal Tribes, a very dark spot of colonial history, will not be discussed here, since the category was abolished in the early 1950s. Nevertheless, the drawing of these new administrative boundaries had far-reaching consequences for the people concerned, the most obvious one being the separation of ST and SC. The latter were artificially opposed to the former by the fact that, practically over night, they were disallowed to purchase land in the tribal belt. Much of the transactions that had been legal to that date were shifted to the realm of illegality ever since, resulting in the usual hazards of the black market and not in added protection of the ST landholders. While the latter retained their status in case they became Muslims or Christians, the SC, on conversion, lost their claim to special governmental benefits, since "caste" was supposed to be an essential of Hinduism and Non-Hindus were thus freed from caste discrimination. Such was the sophistry of the new order. Similarly, the new SC of the highlands had very little in common with the SC of the lowlands. The administrative segregation of the former — forcing them into an opposition to the ST in the context of several politico-economic issues — had the effect of dividing the loyalties in the tribal zone and — at face value — minimising the sheer size and importance of the tribal society. The same consequence was achieved with the introduction of the OBCs. Local tribes who were very similar in socio-cultural terms were suddenly graded and opposed to one another in terms of a new administrative hierarchy that linked them with culturally quite different entities of the lowlands and covered up the real numeric and political dimension of tribal society.

Thus in India, tribal society was mistakenly equated with that of the ST only. The administrative category was taken as an anthropological one, which, in fact, was the outcome of the initial British pragmatism. Because of this confusion and because of the general lack of acquaintance with the social structure of Non-Indian tribes, modern authors like Beteille (1998) find it easy to "deconstruct" the category of tribe as such. The Indian ST, however, must only be seen in the light of administrative history and should never be equated with "tribes" in anthropological terms. The Indian constitution reserves the right of selection to the President of the Republic who, in defining a unit as ST, is not bound by any criteria whatsoever.

Thus the tribal situation in India confuses as ST "tribes" in the anthropological sense as well as hunter/gatherers and other marginal groups, and the present volume has taken into account this situation. Similarly, numerous OBC of the tribal area are completely ignored by the debates on tribal issues, because of the artificial administrative segregation. Furthermore, major cultural differences are observable between different southern ST such as the Yanadi and the Naiken, even though both would equally qualify as hunter/gatherers in anthropology and all southerners have very little in common with the ST of Central India, of the Northeast or of the Himalayan region, the latter being cattle-raising nomads, while the North-easterners roughly belong to the same great cultural complex as their neighbours in Bangladesh, Burma and southwest China. Of the Central Indian complex, everyone who has eyes to see would notice the dividing line between cattle-herders and shifting cultivators somewhere in Rajasthan and Gujarat. In short, the Indian administrative term of ST is excluding numerous tribes (in the anthropological sense) found under the headings of SC and OBC, and including numerous hunter/gatherer groups, just as the ST include people with diverse technical specializations, leave alone socio-cultural values. Whereas anthropology defines tribes as acephalous social categories of people, organized along the lines of kinship and marriage in the "domestic mode of production" (Sahlins, 1968) without specialized institutions, the Indian administration follows some vague idea of "backwardness." While in Africa, the term "tribe" has become disreputable and in Arabia (or indeed the whole of West Asia), it is a marker of honour and status (see Pfeffer & Behera, 2002), some 70 million members of the Indian Scheduled Tribes seem to be associated only with remote villages and reserved constituencies.

The volume consisting of seventeen chapters presents a picture of contemporary tribal situation in India. It primarily focuses on (a) definitional problem (b) development issues (c) changing cultural patterns and social networks (d) health issues, in the context of tribal society. A total number of twenty-five social scientist (mostly anthropologists) from India and aboard have made important contribution to this volume.

The first chapter by Peter T. Suzuki deals with definitional problem of the term "tribe." He critically examines different definitions of "tribe," given by various anthropologists from India and aboard. The postmodernists and the deconstructionists are very critical of the use of the term "tribe." In the absence of any suitable term Suzuki suggests "ethnic group" as a substitute to tribe. He feels that his article would stimulate others to re-examine the term "tribe" in order to further our understanding of the concept.

The second chapter coming under section II deals with planned change among the Andaman Islanders. Sita Venkateswar, the author of the chapter, is critical about the policies of planned change introduced by the government among the tribal islanders in recent times. The paper giving an introductory note on Andaman Island analyses the policies introduced by the government in the islands in the post-independence era. The critical assessment of welfare measure is the most significant aspect of the paper. K.K. Mishra's chapter deals with Island cultures and approaches to tribal development in India. The paper provides a general picture of the tribal islanders, viz. the Sentinelese, Jarwa, Onge, Great Andamanese and Shompen. The endangered tribes in the Andaman Islands now face some unique problems, which are closely linked to their peculiar cultural history. The paper analyses the problems faced by the tribal and the developmental interventions in the Andamans. The development programme among the tribal should aim primarily at confidence building. Any attempt to overburden and confuse the tribal with multifarious schemes of development is bound to fail. The very first step in this direction should be the formulation and implementation of legislative measures to restore tribal customary rights over the natural resources.

In the following chapter, Fernandes makes an effort to study multifarious impact of displacement on tribal women. He strongly argues that in the National Policies on Rehabilitation and various resettlement packages, the women are by and large ignored. The status of tribal women has changed during the decades of planned development. To a tribal woman displacement has meant the loss of the very foundation of her power and privilege. Fernandes argues that displacement has resulted in economic subordination and marginalization of tribal women. He has analyzed impact of loss CPRs on tribal women. He concludes that displacement is not a one-time event but it includes a number of processes.

S.N. Ratha's contribution on tribal welfare administration in Orissa is based upon a review of secondary literatures. He makes a critical assessment of tribal development efforts in Orissa, the administrative set up for the welfare efforts and the outcomes of welfare efforts. Ratha opines that the investments including the cost of tribal administration are massive whereas the achievements are negligible. While dealing with the concept of development he concludes that all development strategies must be related to the organizational values of the community, socio-cultural environment and community resources.

In the sixth chapter Kumkum Bhattacharya looks at the Santal from different angles, viz. plurality, socialization, religion and identity. The chapter highlights Santal identity vis-à-vis common perceptions. Bhattacharya explores the concepts of adjustment, perceptions, attitudes and prejudices in the light of Santal identity formation. Santal live in a world of limited dependencies and they are contained within the limits of their culture. The author argues that development as a process offers scope for the loosening of the bindings of tradition, however what items of culture are to be retained and what to jettison, is often taken out of the control of the target group. This results in feelings of discomfort in the targeted population.

Viswajit Pandya's chapter dealing with the Ongees of Andaman Islands reveals that dreams are not entirely subjective, private and illusionary but aspects of real and community life. Ongees are concerned with meaning of what the image is symbolizing within the dream as well as what reality may be attributed to the dream. Before falling asleep they tell their dreams and the intertextuality of the dreams presented gets located within the collectivism. Pandya discusses how dream telling and interpreting is culturally constructed within the society and changing times unfolding the logic that different places generate different ways to sleep and dream. Dreams are different not because of individuals but because of the places and smells that individuals are subject to.

The chapter by Arima Mishra deals with the informal process of land transfer in the Kutia Kandha community in Lanjigarh block of Kalahandi district, Orissa. The informal practice of mortgaging of land is known as *Kado Bikri*. *Kado* refers to the land at a particular stage in the agricultural cycle, when the land is ploughed and ready to be sown. The poignancy of the transaction in *Kado Bikri* needs to be understood in the context of economic, social as well as religious factors. Mishra agrues that it is not suffice to know how does the informal transactions on land take place but it is important to unveil the ways and means of sustenance and legitimization of these transactions. Land transactions are not simple one to one transaction. It is complex processes, which can be examined in relation to a network of credit transactions often laying bare the nexus between land, cultivation and credit transactions. The analysis of credit transactions needs to be linked to the phenomenon of time.

In chapter ninth Vijoy Sahay has made an attempt to understand the significance of Gharwa art in the tribal life of Bastar. He tries to find out the causes of decline of the quality of Gharwa craftsmanship. The Gharwas, a little known community in Bastar, have influenced the tribal life in general and religion of Bastar tribes in particular by their ancient art of bell metal craftsmanship. The tribal religion of Bastar revolves round the concepts of *matas* and *devas*, which are the anthropomorphic forms of female and male deities respectively. During crisis, the deities are offered sacrifices and propitiated by the tribesmen with the help of a *sirha* (witch doctor/shaman). The Gharwas make bell metal images of all the deities of the Bastar tribes. Besides the images, they also make the ornaments and other items of daily use by the tribesmen. After the recognition of folk art of Gharwa at the national and international level, the demand of Gharwa artifacts has increased, but the quality of craftsmanship has decreased for some obvious reasons.

The chapter by Hota and others deals with gender issues in a changing tribal context. The study primarily focuses on the Munda women of a fringe village of Sambalpur town. The authors argue that the changes brought about by some external forces have drastically altered the gender equation in the community. Munda women in this changing situation now shoulder up additional physical and social responsibilities both in household and extra-household spheres. The changing situation forces women to work as men's substitutes. The analysis revolves round three key incidents that have brought about a chain reaction in the life of Munda women in the studied village, viz. growth of bidi industries in the region, construction of a link road to highway, land transfer from the Munda to the other groups. Analysis of gender bias in a changing context is the most fascinating part of this chapter.

In the following chapter N.K Behura discusses about kinship, marriage, family and descent in tribal and rural Orissa. Behura argues that there exists a continuum between tribal and caste socio-cultural systems. Caste and tribe in Orissa have many common features, viz. common descent, rules of exogamy and endogamy, principles of classification and grouping of kin, existence of polytheism, corporate socio-cultural references to religion, believe in supernatural powers, collectivism, village solidarity, etc. He opines that tribal communities and caste societies together constitute a unique socio-cultural universe, each representing a different stage in the scale of social evolution.

In the twelfth chapter R. Vashum presents a background of the Naga movement. The struggle of the Nagas for self-determination is one of the most fascinating, enduring and active ethnic assertions in the Indian sub-continent. Though it took long for the Nagas to organize themselves for launching a mass movement for national independence, yet there were resistance movements of the various Naga tribes at the individual group level against the outsiders, particularly the British colonialists. On the eve of the British departure from the Indian sub-continent, the Nagas under the aegis of the Naga National Council (NNC) somehow organized themselves and declared Naga independence on 14 August 1947. Vashum examines various factors that gave rise to the Naga national movement.

The following chapter by Sunita Bharati Reddy explores the general health of tribal women in India and specific to Konda Reddi women of Kamman district. Konda Reddi is a Primitive Tribal Group of Andhra Pradesh. The author gives a detailed ethnographic description about the beliefs and practices related to childbirth and child rearing among the tribe. Reddy has also discussed the availability and utilization of health care services and other alternative folk medicines among the Konda Reddis. Reddy feels that maternal and child health care is an important aspect of health seeking behaviour, which is largely neglected among the tribal popuation.

Veena Bhasin gives a description of the ecology and economy of the study area and people. She discusses about the occupational structure and coping mechanism of the Saharias in the background of different developmental schemes. The efforts of government and other agencies to raise the economic standards of Sahariyas have been critically evaluated by Bhasin. Various schemes of development among the Saharias have not been able to bring the expected results. The Saharias with high level of ignorance and poverty are caught in a deprivation trap. Bhasin suggests that the government effort for raising the living standards of the Saharias needs to be restructured in the light of the ecology, economy and culture of the people.

Fertility is the actual reproductive performances, whether applied to an individual or a group. The chapter by S.S. Guru and others highlights the factors that influence the differential reproductive performance in a primitive tribe of Madhya Pradesh. They argue that a number of biological and social variables affect the reproductive performances among the Kamars. Against this backdrop, they have tried to test some hypotheses. The influences of age at menarche, age at marriage, age at first live birth, education of women, structure of family, etc. have been discussed. The authors opine that composite family structure, lack or low level of education, marriage at an early age and reluctance to accept family planning methods jointly contribute to the high fertility among the Kamars. They suggest that suitable steps should be taken to educate the women folk, motivate them to adopt family planning method, ensure regular visit of health workers to provide health education in order to ameliorate the situations.

Mishra and Kapoor write about socio-cultural and environmental factors affecting health behaviour among the Saharias of Rajasthan. They try to show that the health seeking behaviour of this primitive tribal group (Saharias) is rooted in their immediate environment. Health and culture are very much connected with etiology of diseases. The traditional health care system is based upon people's understanding of nature and culture. The authors make an attempt to study the socio-cultural and environmental factors of health seeking behaviours among the Saharia. Saharias believe that most of the diseases are caused by evil spirits. They worship different benevolent deities and spirits in order to protect them from the wrath of supernatural. They comment that lack of socio-psychological reinforcement is one of the important reasons of unpopularity of modern treatment systems in the tribal world. Saharias who live in interior areas mainly practice ethno-medical system. However in more exposed villages different kinds of treatment go side by side and people have faith in all those treatments.

The last chapter by R.S. Balgir deals with the emergence of biomedical anthropology in India. Biomedical anthropology is a newly emerging discipline, which combines the theoretical and methodological concepts of physical anthropology and medical anthropology in the study of diseases and health of human (tribal) populations. He suggests that a biomedical anthropological approach to the tribal health is the best when it emphasizes the biological basis of health and disease incorporating understanding of the socio-cultural nature of the sickness process in the tribal society. He is of the opinion that the strength of anthropology lies in its analytical potentials, constructive suggestions and practical applications in the contemporary tribal society.

The present edition is a continuation of the earlier published volumes under the series *Contemporary Society: Tribal Studies.* It is hoped that the volume will further our understanding on the tribal situation in India.

REFERENCES

Béteille, André. 1998. "The Idea of Indigenous People," *Current Anthropology*, 39 (2): 187-222

Pfeffer, Georg & Deepak Kumar Behera. 2002. "Introduction," (pp 9-31) in G. Pfeffer & D.K. Behera (eds.), *The Concept of Tribal Society. Contemporary Society: Tribal Studies*. Vol. 5. New Delhi: Concept Publishing Company.

Sahlins, Marshall D. 1968. *Tribesmen.* Englewood Cliffs: Prentice Hall.

SECTION I

DEFINITIONAL PROBLEM

SECTION I

DEFINITIONAL PROBLEM

ONE

TRIBE: Chimeric or Polymorphic

PETER T. SUZUKI

Given that this series is entitled Tribal Studies, it would make sense to examine the concept of tribe. Accordingly, what follows below is an attempt to do just that. Because, to some extent it is an enigmatic topic, this essay is not offered as anything but one that, hopefully, will stimulate another re-examination of a traditional term in anthropology.

It would be fair to state that anthropology appears to be burdened with a four-letter word and a five-letter word, both of which have caused consternation and heated discussions. The former is "race." It seems to be agreed that there is no agreement on what constitutes race, and perspectives on the concept have often changed with the political and economic times, not to mention advances in science and technology. A term almost as elusive, but perhaps not quite as contentious, is "tribe," the five-letter word, except that in examining this concept one is at a disadvantage because one cannot fall back on the rigorous techniques of biology and chemistry such as in the field of genetics, DNA, and the like to back up the arguments.

One of the clearest definitions and delineations of tribe that I have come across happens to be in a book by two Indian social anthropologists who authored a textbook that was widely used (and its revised version might still be in great use) in India as an introduction to the field. It is Ram Nath Sharma and Rajendra K. Sharma's Social Anthropology and Indian Tribes (1983). They characterize tribes as having these eleven features: 1) Definite common geography; 2) consciousness of unity; 3) common language; 4) endogamous group; 5) ties of blood relationship; 6) experience of need for protection;

7) political organization; 8) importance of religion; 9) common name; 10) common culture; and 11) organization of clans (1983: 177-178).

On its surface, their definition seems to be not only comprehensive but also reasonable and acceptable. However, eight years earlier, Morton H. Fried of Columbia University had written what I consider to be a seminal study on the notion of tribe (Fried, 1975).[1] As though anticipating the approach to the concept of tribe by the Sharmas, and, incidentally, of many American anthropologists as well in coming to grips with this concept in general anthropology textbooks, Fried first carefully examined the etymology of the very term, tribe, a term that came into use in the English speaking world during the 17th and 18th centuries to designate "the other." Then he examined tribes as: "breeding populations," linguistic groups, named groups, economic and political systems, "ideological" groups, and cultural units. In his analyses, he found much wanting in each of the categories owing to such things as the interminglings of peoples, fuzzy boundaries both geographically and linguistically, the ever dynamic situation in which the world operates, which includes impacting those "tribes" supposedly quite isolated from the nation-state in which they are found, etc.

Although it is fashionable now to attribute many phenomena (including the term tribe) to Western imperialism/and or colonialism, as an expert on Chinese history and culture, Fried ably pointed to eras when China as an expansionist state the peoples conquered were given pejorative terms on par with "tribe" (Fried, 1975: 36-38). The same may be said of other empires (e.g. The Roman Empire, The Ottoman Empire, etc.) but also of stronger groups conquering weaker ones where state systems were non-existent or were in their nascent state conditions (cf. Suzuki, 1973).[2] Indeed, this seems to have been and continues to be a near universal phenomenon of the human condition.

Fried's words in the penultimate paragraph of his last chapter bear quoting because they summarize admirably his conclusion.

> "there is one usage that is in excellent accord with our knowledge and experience; this is tribe as a secondary sociopolitical phenomenon, brought about by the intercession of more complex ordered societies, states in particular. I call this 'secondary tribe' and I believe that all the tribes with which we have experience are this kind. The 'pristine tribe,' on the other hand, is a creation of myth and legend, pertaining either to the golden age of the noble savage or romantic barbarism" (Fried, 1975: 114).

Thus, his "pristine tribe" is the chimeric tribe, and the "secondary tribe," it can be recognized, are those that anthropologists have been studying, and the ones that lay people often can also readily identify in terms of named units. And this is what the Sharmas had in mind in their delineation of tribe but, technically speaking, to the degree that they were positing the ideal situation, had a chimeric tribe in mind. Parenthetically, as regards India, the magisterial volume by Moonis Raza and Aijazuddin Ahmad, An Atlas of Tribal India (1990), which focuses on "Scheduled Tribes," makes a formidable point in the following sentences.

> "It is, however, interesting to note that tribal studies [in India] have been generally considered to be the preserve of the anthropologists or the sociologist only. Social scientists from other disciplines have tended to accord too much respect to this colonial tradition and have generally shied away from an analysis of the tribal ethos" (p. 5).

They might have also added that they themselves were embedded in a colonial frame because many of the peoples they designate as tribes were originally identified as such by colonial administrators.

However, the problem that anthropologists have frequently encountered or have not duly noted adequately in their publications are the dynamically changing situations each group has been undergoing and the relationship of the group to the larger whole, which, in modern times has been the nation state. Often implicit in this, too, is their failure to recognize the units they are studying or have studied are what Fried calls secondary tribes, which, he feels, is a sine qua non.

Although Fried takes cognizance of the term tribe as being a pejorative, the irony is that he himself cannot escape this term but tries, by virtue of simply adding a modifier before the term, i.e. secondary tribe.

Now, anyone who is familiar with even a smattering of United States history knows that the native populations were subjugated and the vast majority put on special lands, reservations (or in places like California, termed rancherias, or in the Southwest, pueblos), with a long history that can be traced to the eighteenth century. Today there are more than five-hundred officially recognized Indian tribes, meaning that the U.S. Government through its Bureau of Indian Affairs (BIA) makes available to them certain goods and services, jurisdiction, and duties that tribes not officially recognized would not receive or have (e.g. Castile & Bee, 1992). Accordingly, one could not find a more clear-cut case of secondary tribes as in the situation that obtains among American Indians.

In most cases, owing to specific boundaries established for reservations and the equally specific tribes placed on them (however, in places like Oklahoma, rather than reservations, those areas inhabited by Indians are simply designated as Indian Country), there are thus identifiable geographic units. Nevertheless, many of the reservations were established on arbitrary bases so that those within given linguistic groups, or cultures were separated in a willy-nilly fashion. As an example, the Omaha and Winnebago Reservations in Nebraska share a common border. However, the latter, speaking Chiwere Sioux, originally from Wisconsin, some 600 miles away, historically were a Woodland culture people while the Omahas, speaking Dhegiha Sioux, were part of the Northern Plains culture.[3] (Because of their close proximity to each other, there have been many intermarriages). And thanks to rapid mobility through transportation or communication, along with the migration of reservation Indians to urban places since the BIA encouraged the movement through its 1952 Voluntary Relocation Program (VRP), resulting in more Indians in cities than on reservations, the criteria cited by the Sharmas, and the commonly held constituent features about a tribe that Fried has effectively desolated, the concept of tribe nevertheless prevails.

In part this is because the BIA has not abandoned this term (and the BIA gets its marching orders from the U.S. Congress, which is the only body that can legislate affairs pertaining to Native Americans) and, most importantly, the Indians themselves have not yet abandoned it, although there is a small movement away from it, which will be brought out below.

The power of the modern state and tribes within its borders can also be brought out in two other U.S. examples. The first has to do with Indian identity and definition of Indian. In 1887, the U.S. Congress passed the Allotment Act, by which Indian land (typically 160 acres) was parceled out to individuals but only those who had one half or more Indian blood. Then this blood quantum approach and mentality carried over into the Indian Citizenship Act of 1924 that made Indians U.S. citizens, but only those that met the blood quantum criterion (Jaime, 1991: 124-127). Such moves have necessitated the establishment of enrollment offices by tribes. The official assigned to run the office records the blood quantum of tribal members and when births occur, the parents register children at such an office. Here too one receives an enrollment card that looks like a typical driver's license that an American might hold except it contains the quantum blood of the card holder, his/her enrollment number, tribe name, picture, official seal and signature, birth date, etc.[4]

The second and equally cynical approach to Indians was in the Termination Act of 1953 that literally "detribalized" 109 officially recognized tribes so that all of the services and benefits that they had enjoyed prior to detribalization were immediately withdrawn. More tribes would have come under this ax had not the tragic consequences of this movement not been brought out, perhaps most dramatically in the case of the Menominee of the State of Wisconsin (1982).[5]

That a modern nation state such as the U.S. can also create a non-Indian tribe out of a group of widely scattered people but racially from one stock with literally a stroke of pen is evidenced in Executive Order 9066 signed by President Roosevelt on February 19, 1942. This executive order, which by-passed the U.S. Congress, enabled the removal of some 120,000 people of Japanese descent from their homes on the West Coast into camps (initially 16 temporary camps). The permanent camps, "relocation centers," were the equivalents of Indian reservations. Indeed, one of the largest, Poston, Arizona, was on an Indian reservation despite the protest of the Tribal Council of the Colorado River Indian Reservation because the Council did not want the Japanese to be meted out the same treatment that Indians had received, but was overruled by the BIA. The ten internment camps, all situated in isolated parts of the states in which they were placed (Arizona, Arkansas, California, Colorado, Idaho, Utah, and Wyoming) differed from Indian reservations because each camp was surrounded by barbed wire fences and guarded by armed U.S. Army personnel, and ingress and egress were possible only by special permission. If one were to examine the criteria established by the Sharmas, many would accord with their list (this named tribe, the internees, became commonly known as "The Japs").

Like reservations, anthropologists and sociologists were based in the camps, but hired by the War Relocation Authority, to study the inmates. And one large research project, based at the University of California at Berkeley, the Japanese Evacuation and Resettlement Study, a covert research project, had its own anthropologists in several of the camps. To the ever-lasting shame of American anthropology and sociology, many of these professionals - which included some of the most prominent figures in their field - turned out to be informers and intelligence gatherers for U.S. Government agencies such as the FBI and the Office of Naval Intelligence (Suzuki, 1976, 1981, 1986a, 1986b, 1989).[6]

Returning to the case of American Indians, as can be imagined, many American Indian tribes' names were assigned to them by Whites. Also as has been the experience in the majority of the cases throughout the world where a dyadic relationship existed between stronger groups against weaker ones (not necessarily Whites on one side and natives on the other), the weaker groups became the recipients of new names. Not surprisingly, the assigned names have often been inaccurate, less than flattering, derogatory, or innocuous but just plain wrong. Ethnographically speaking, one of the most well known peoples throughout the world among both social scientists and lay people must surely be the Eskimos because of their traditional culture. Anthroponymically, it is interesting that it was the Cree and Abenaki Indians who labeled them Eskimos, a name which has stuck, but in reality, means "those who eat raw meat." Incidentally, I believe Fried cited this example because of the degree to which these people are known throughout the world (1975: 34); but, of course, they were never viewed nor analyzed as a tribe because of their traditional nomadic culture and the fact that they moved about as a single family or small groups of families. It must be noted too that in Canada they are officially referred to as Inuit ("Human Beings") a self-designated term. In the U.S., although the term is not official, increasingly Inuit is being used instead of Eskimo.

As a follow-up on the issue of assigned tribal names, a national policy for American Indians could be implemented to rectify any anthroponymic injustices by the following proposed method (with the backing of the U.S. Congress, of course, because it could be an expensive program). A name-changing program would ask each tribe by which name they would like to be known. After a consensus has been reached by the tribes, the new names would then be officially changed by edict. Some of these changes have been going on informally among some tribes. For example, the Oglala Sioux now prefer to be known as Lakota. There are several signs that the Winnebago Tribe of Nebraska are going to start referring to themselves more and more as Hochungra ("People of the Parent Speech") vs. Winnebago ("People of the Salt Water"; one interpretation of salt water is "dirty water"). Equally important, the term tribe is being substituted for "nation" (e.g., The Winnebago Nation; The Omaha Nation, etc.) because the U.S. Government made treaties with tribes as sovereign entities, and under President Ronald Reagan, affirmed a "nation to nation" relationship. Even with such changes, commonly used terms, as tribal council, tribal police, tribal office, etc., would experience a slow death.

Following Fried, if one accepts, as I do, his position that secondary tribes are the only "real" tribes (and those few anthropologists who do not, in a manner of speaking, would be dealing with "chimeras"), we will not "...

succumb to an easy, conventional use of the concept of tribe" (Fried, 1975: 114). In other words, anthropologists may still use the concept of tribe provided that cognizance is taken of the primacy of another, larger political entity, the modern nation state. In the words of Fried again, "...you may still use the term tribe...but it will be with a twinge of alarm and a new shock of recognition" (1975: 114).[7] Hence, beyond accepting the concept of secondary tribe, is the acceptance of tribal polymorphism, which has long been in each anthropologist's "tool kit," as it were, anyway. That is to say, for the most part, anthropologists indeed have been circumscribing carefully the groups ("tribes") that they have studied by delineation of their geographic, linguistic, population, cultural, etc. boundaries because they know that secondary tribes come in all shapes, forms, and sizes and do not fit any one particular mold.[8]

A vigorous and stimulating attestation to what has been stated in the previous paragraph may be found in a set of essays between the covers of Tribes and State Formation in the Middle East (Khoury and Kostiner, 1990). Six of the thirteen (46.2%) contributors are anthropologists; the others represent political science and history. Although it would be beyond the scope of this paper to go over each article, because of the salience of Iran in contemporary world affairs, a precise of the contribution by the anthropologist Lois Beck follows. After a long and detailed discussion of the characteristics and categories of tribes in Iran - which includes definitions - that occupies almost 16 pages, the author encapsulates Iran's history with reference to state and tribal relations. One would be hard put to find a more apposite statement on what I have attempted to get across, in part, in this essay than the following paragraph by Becker, although she has Iran in mind.

> Many social scientists and others have traditionally viewed tribes as bounded, self-contained, autonomous, often isolated entities created by autochthonous factors. Tribes, however, were formed and sustained within the context of broad external forces. The resulting tribal formations [i.e. "secondary tribes"] were ways of integrating people into state structures, while at the same time preventing these peoples' subordination to, or assimilation into, the state (Becker, 1990: 215; also, cf. Hart, 2000).

In a brief but incisive overview of tribe, Gingrich after having duly noted the most recent critics of the term - feminists, postmodernists, deconstructionists, post-colonial theorists, et al. -- by taking into account the turmoil in such places where the state has become weakened (e.g. Afghanistan), arrives at a most interesting conclusion.

> It would amount to a strange paradox if anthropologists limited themselves defensively to deconstructing completely the concept of tribe, while many parts of the world in fact go through retribalization (sic) of some sort. In view of these developments, an active reformulation of the concept seems to be a more productive alternative. With this alternative, ideological movements of "tribalism" will have to be distinguished more clearly from "tribe," parallel to concepts of nationalism and of nation. (Gingrich, 2001: 15908)

To this observer, it is apparent that anthropologists for some time indeed have been "reformulating" the concept of tribe by virtue of rigorous and meticulous definitions that critics would find difficult to fault (for example, see the article by Gellner (1990) in the same collection that contains Beck's). (Nevertheless the critics might not be satisfied insofaras tribe implies the Other.) If, however, he means by this coining a new term or using another term, I would suggest looking at the concept of "ethnic group."

This term has no pejorative implication, can transcend racially based groups, and yet can be defined in a way that would satisfy traditional anthropological concerns. Elsewhere, I have applied this concept to the Omaha and Winnebago Indians of Nebraska owing to their growing sense of ethnicity (vs. "tribalhood") (Suzuki, 1996, 1999). In many respects, anthropologists seem to be hesitant in using this term and appear to leave this term to sociologists because it is the latter who, historically, "discovered" it and have continued to use it to good advantage to analyze situations in modern society.[9] As globalization, urbanization, and modernization march on, should a time come when "tribe" becomes totally anathema to anthropologists, it might make sense to substitute ethnic group for tribe or to at least examine this concept.

However, until such time arrives, it is my opinion that the concept of tribe can be productively used with certain strictures such as the recognition of tribes as secondary phenomena and of the total neutrality of the term. Of course these would go in tandem with careful circumscriptions of the constituent elements that are being examined as a tribe. But then, for the most part, anthropologists have been doing these things all along anyway.

Conclusions

It is my view that the following conclusions are warranted

- Historically, tribe was used to designate The Other, especially during colonial expansion. This phenomenon, however, was not restricted to Western colonialism/imperialism in that non-Western empires have used its equivalent to designate those not of their kind. This labeling appears to be a human universal because of simple contact (e.g. the Algonkian Cree and Abenaki Indians in labeling the Inuits Eskimos) or by conquest.
- Tribes are chimeric when, in the minds of anthropologists they conceive of an "ideal" in circumscribing the concept of tribe.
- In recognition of the roles of states and tribes, Fried's concept of "secondary tribe" is important but this does not obviate the use of the word "tribe." It does, however, take cognizance of the polymorphic nature of tribes.
- The situation of the U.S. and its America Indians is instructive in showing the power of a modern nation-state and its relations with its native peoples. However, certain remedies can be corrected such as name changes of tribes. The proposal presented for the U.S. could also be a template for other nations with tribes within their borders.
- The internment of people of Japanese descent by the U.S. Government during WWII created a tribe in the technical sense and clearly limns what Fried has termed the concept of tribe as a secondary phenomenon.
- Although anthropologists have been troubled by the concept of tribe, with some of the severest criticisms coming from postmodernists, deconstructionists, et al., a satisfactory substitute term has not been preferred.
- It is quite possible that "ethnic group" might be a viable substitute.
- There is no reason to shy away from using the term tribe provided that the user takes into consideration some of the caveats noted in this essay.

NOTES

1. Fried was my instructor for several of my graduate courses at Columbia. Although labeled a Marxist by Gingrich (2001: 15908), all his writings indicate that he was a neo-evolutionist, who was greatly influenced by Julian H. Steward, under whom he studied at Columbia.
2. Although identified as miniature Nias states with virtually all of the features of a regular state, Fried perhaps would have seen them as "communal" (Fried 1975: 105).
3. Siouan is a large language family somewhat parallel to Indo-European.
4. An enrollment card gains entry to any Indian Health Service hospital in the U.S. Some tribes have lowered their blood quantum requirement to 1/32; another, the Lakota, have abolished it. As more and more intermarriages take place among members of various tribes and with non-Indians, a logical progression of such events would seem to indicate that the blood quantum criterion of other tribes would eventually have to be lowered. The Onandega of New York, on the other hand, historically a matrilineal society, in the 1970s expelled all those who had married members other than their own tribe, as a measure to keep the tribe "pure." In reaction to all this, one of my Winnebago informants, a lady of 55 in an interview that tookplace in July 2002, put it this way as a negative reaction to the demands of blood quantum: "I'm not a measuring cup."
5. Fried cites the Menominee case while the tribe was seeking restoration as an officially recognized tribe (1975: 112).
6. The anthropologist Weston LaBarre after only ten days in the camp in Utah as Community Analyst, came up with a list of 19 neurotic features of the Japanese; he then sought and found all 19 features among the internees of that camp. His total stay in the camp was 42 days (+ 2 days; the day of arrival and the day of departure). In his way, he justified the internment to policy makers because, after all, the internees were mentally ill anyway (Suzuki, 1980).
7. Gingrich makes a similar point (2001: 15908).
8. Fried describes secondary tribes as being "heterogeneous" (1975: 103).
9. Fried gingerly mentions ethnic group but does not delve into its implications (1975: 104).

REFERENCES

Beck, Lois. 1990. "Tribes and the State in Nineteenth-and Twentieth Century Iran," (pp. 185-225) in P.S. Khoury & J. Kostiner (eds.), *Tribes & State Formation in the Middle East*. Berkeley: University of California Press.

Castile, George & Roland L. Bee (eds.). 1992. *State & Reservation: New Perspectives on Federal l Indian Policy*. Tuscon: University of Arizona Press.

Fried, Morton H. 1975. *The Notion of Tribe*. Menlo Park: Cummings Publishing Co.

Gellner, Ernest. 1990. "Tribalism and the State in the Middle East," (pp. 109-126) in P.S. Khoury & J. Kostiner (eds.), *Tribes & State Formation in the Middle East*. Berkeley: University of California Press.

Gingrich, A. 2001. "Tribe," in Neal Smelser & Paul Balter (eds.), *International Encyclopedia of the Social and Behavioral Sciences*. 23: 15906-09. Amsterdam: Eslevier.

Hart, David M. 2000. *Tribe & Society in Rural Morocco*. London: Frank Cass.

Jaimes, M. Annette. 1991. "Federal Indian Identification Policy," (pp. 123- 40) in M. A. Jaimes (ed.), *The State of Native America*. Boston: South End Press,

Khoury, Philip S. and Joseph Kostiner (eds.). 1990. *Tribes & State Formation in the Middle East*. Berkeley: University of California Press.

Peroff, Nicholas C. 1982. *Menominee Drums: Tribal Termination and Restoration, 1954-1974*. Norman: University of Oklahoma Press.

Raza, Moonis & Aijazuddin Ahmad. 1989. *An Atlas of Tribal India*. New Delhi: Concept Publishing Co.

Sharma, Ram Nath & Rajendra K. Sharma. 1983. *Social Anthropology & Indian Tribes*. West Sussex: J.K. Publishers.

Suzuki, Peter T. 1973. "Autochthonous States of Nias, Indonesia: Extinct or Extant?", *Urgent Anthropological and Ethnological Research*, 15: 27-49.

____. 1976. "The Ethnolinguistics of Japanese Americans in the Wartime Camps," *Anthropological Linguistics*, 18: 416-27.

____. 1980. "A Retrospective Analysis of a Wartime 'National Character Study' [written by Weston LaBarre]," *Dialectical Anthropology*, 5: 33-45.

____. 1981. "Anthropologists in the Wartime Camps for Japanese Americans: A Documentary Study," *Dialectical Anthropology*, 6: 23-60.

____. 1986a. "When Black was White: Misapplied Anthropology in Wartime America," *Dialectical Anthropology*, 12 (1 & 2): 1-13.

____. 1986b. "The University of California Japanese Evacuation & Resettlement Study: A Prolegomenon," *Dialectical Anthropology*, 10: 189-213.

____. 1989. "For the Sake of Inter-University Comity: The Attempted Suppression by the University of California of Morton Grodzins' Americans Betrayed," (pp. 95-123) in Y. Ichioka (ed.), *Views from Within: The Japanese American Evacuation and Resettlement Study*. Los Angeles: UCLA Asian American Studies Center.

____. 1996. "Pan-Indianism, Ethnicity, and the Omaha Tribe of Nebraska," (pp.103-114) in Deepak Kumar Behera & Georg Pfeffer (eds.), *Contemporary Society: Tribal Studies*. Vol. 1. New Delhi: Concept Publishing Company.

____. 1999. "The Rebirth of a Nation: The Winnebago Tribe of Nebraska & Managed Ethnicity," (pp.71-83) in Deepak Kumar Behera & Georg Pfeffer (eds.), *Contemporary Society: Tribal Studies. Vol. 4.* New Delhi: Concept Publishing Company.

SECTION II

DEVELOPMENT ISSUES

TWO

AN ETHNOGRAPHIC OVERVIEW OF POLICIES OF "PLANNED CHANGE"

SITA VENKATESWAR

"It is flat, bright and very hot. Like everything that has happened at Dugong Creek. All the trees are gone, the forest is disappearing, everything will become flat and hot. Everything will dry up like death" (Totanange, commenting on the solar plant installed at Dugong Creek).[1]

This paper provides an ethnographic overview of the policies proposed for the assimilation of the Andaman Islanders after these islands became a part of the Republic of India. I argue that the situation of the islanders and other "tribals" in India can be characterized as internal colonialism. The policies of planned change for the "uplift" of "primitives" initiate a process of ethnocide, erasing a sustaining life-way as it divests them of their resource base.

The "Independent" Andaman Islands

In 1947, when the British transferred control[2] of the Andaman Islands to the newly installed Indian government in mainland India, these islands were designated as "Union Territories." "Union Territories" are administered by the central government from New Delhi, and does not exist as a separate "state" with its autonomous bureaucratic structure. The administration within the islands, as in mainland India, maintained the bureaucracy inherited from the British, with minimal alterations to the structure of government.

In the years preceding independence from the British, as the nationalist movement gathered momentum in India, many of the "freedom fighters," i.e. those most radical and active in their opposition to colonial rule, were incarcerated in the Cellular Jail[3] in Port Blair. At independence, the "liberation" of these "heroes" received wide publicity from the press in India, with several months of newsprint devoted to the story of each "hero." The Andaman Islanders themselves did not get much attention from the government headed by Jawaharlal Nehru in New Delhi after independence. However, Nehru traveled extensively to other "tribal"[4] areas in mainland India, to make himself known to the indigenous[5] peoples in these regions, and discuss his plans for assimilating them as citizens of India.

With independence in 1947, the former British colonial territory was partitioned into two nations, India and Pakistan. Pakistan was further divided into into an eastern and western block, each located across the diagonal extent of India. Many thousands of displaced refugees had to be accommodated in the newly independent country of India. This situation coincided with the emerging plans for a policy of strategic colonization of the Andaman Islands, with the objective of attaining self-sufficiency in terms of food. Displaced Hindu families from East Pakistan (now Bangladesh) were sent to the Andaman Islands and allotted tracts of land on South and Middle Andaman in the vicinity of Jarawa territory. The large-scale deforestation, as land was cleared for agriculture, villages and roads constructed, with a greater influx of people entering the remaining forest cover for hunting and firewood, led to a marked increase in the frequency of "Jarawa incidents" (Pandit, 1989; Sarkar, 1990).

Post-independence Anthropology

During this phase, Lidio Cipriani was commissioned by the Indian government to set up a substation of the Anthropological Survey of India at Port Blair. A sub-regional office of the Anthropological Survey of India (ASI) was established at Port Blair in the early fifties. It included plans for a special unit on Little Andaman, to gain more knowledge of the Onge and "to assist them in any manner desirable and feasible" (Pandit, 1989: 88). In 1953, on advice from ASI, a substantial coconut plantation was established at Dugong Creek, a large Onge camp on Little Andaman.

Cipriani was the first anthropologist to conduct fieldwork among the Onge. The English translation of Cipriani's *The Andaman Islanders* was published posthumously in 1966, the material having come into the publisher's hands only after Cipriani's death. The book represents a brief account of his observations during a period of nearly two years between 1952 and 54 that he spent on Little Andaman with the Onge.

According to Cipriani, he was beckoned by the mystery of the unknown interior of the island, as well as the prevailing lack of information of any kind about the Onge. One of his first tasks was to establish contact with the Onge and survey Little Andaman, marking the routes that the Onge took through the forest, and locating the territorial divisions of the various communal huts dotting the length and breadth of the island. Cipriani admits to a longstanding interest in the question of the origins of the pygmies. He spent some years studying them in Africa and Asia. He arrived at the conclusion that the peoples of the Andaman Islands represented the "purest" living example of Negrito stock and culture, having remained in complete isolation until very recently. He makes frequent comparisons with the Semang of Malaya, the Aeta of the Philippines, the Mbuti of Africa, as well as the "Bushmen" of the Kalahari, in terms of their somatic and cultural characteristics.

Based on conclusions derived from his excavations of the kitchen middens in the different islands, Cipriani viewed the islanders as "involuted" rather than primitive, having regressed culturally, physiologically and psychologically. According to Cipriani, because of their prolonged isolation from the outside world, "they now represent the last and decadent expression of a very lengthy stage of biological and cultural development, a point of arrival, and not one of departure" (1966: 67), a process that inevitably leads to extinction. As a self-professed humanitarian, Cipriani sought to avert this inevitable decline through "scientific" intervention.

Cipriani set up camp close to the communal huts of every territorial group that he visited on the island. Since the island was teeming with game, wild fruit and edible roots, food was never a problem, and it was even unnecessary for Cipriani to bring with him any provisions. He appears to have partaken of everything that the Onge ate since he is able to vividly describe these culinary experiences. Living so close to the Onge, he was in a position, (unlike Radcliffe-Brown, who conducted much of his investigation on the Andamanese who lived close to the civilized center of the colonial administration), to witness intimate details of their everyday activities.

Shocked by "the rampant homosexuality" of the Onge men when they travelled in the forest, he went on to view the Onge as "decadent," and also attempted to ensure that the Onge men who accompanied him brought their wives with them. But their unabashed and unbridled sexual activities with either sex, led him to label the Onge as "child-like" with a child's lack of shame, or the absence of any sense of modesty, the complete lack of hygiene, "an infantile vanity," a child's thoughtless cruelty, and a child's abounding pleasure in obscenities. Extending such a view, he believed the Onge had remained virtually unchanged since Paleolithic times.

A number of parallels can be drawn between Man and Cipriani. Man, too, had an obvious affection for the Andamanese, which was both paternalistic and condescending. He viewed the Andamanese as "wayward but attractive children" (Prain, 1932: 21), conforming to the prevailing ideas about primitive races as embodying the childhood of mankind. But more importantly, both Cipriani and Man played significant political roles, in the ways in which their scholarly work served to endorse official policy. In the period after the departure of the British from the islands, and the transfer of the Andaman Islands to the newly installed Indian government, Cipriani's research with the Onge, together with his appointment as director of the research sub-station of the Anthropological Survey of India at Port Blair, paved the way for the colonization of Little Andaman and the confinement of the Onge in permanent settlements.

Two Decades of Policy

The old British tradition of inviting parties of Onge to pay periodic visits to Port Blair and call on the Chief Commissioner was encouraged. In turn, the Onge were given gifts of tobacco, tea, sugar etc. and "offered official hospitality" (Pandit, 1989: 88). A Chief Commissioner during the fifties, Mr. A.K. Ghosh remarked at the time, "If this continues, they will go the same way as the Andamanese" (cited in Whittaker, 1985: 10).

Of the 23 Andamanese enumerated in the Census of India 1951, the first census operation in independent India, the adult men retained their earlier occupation from British days in the "Bush Police" force, stationed in and around the forest in Jarawa territory. The "Bush Police," originally created to protect the British settlement from the Jarawa, performed the same function after independence, and remained a potential employment option for male Andamanese.

The sixties and seventies marked a turning point for the islands, with a large influx of settlers from mainland India, comprehensive schemes for the development of the islands, and the first enunciation of plans and policies for the islanders. Venkatesan (1990) traces the contours of land allotment on Little Andaman from the late sixties, when the government of India passed a resolution under the Special Area Development Programme to resettle refugees[6] on Little Andaman. Almost 30,000 hectares of forest was cleared by the early seventies for settler villages, most of it encroaching on the territories of the remaining Onge groups in the island. Through the seventies, intensive clearance and commercial exploitation of the forest was initiated under the supervision of the Andaman and Nicobar Forest and Plantation Development Corporation (ANFPDC), encouraging private traders to extract timber, with no effort made to control illegal tree cutting. In an attempt to restock the cleared forest, a regeneration project called Red Oil Palm Plantation designated 2400 hectares for regeneration with red oil palm monocrop species. The construction of roads, government offices, private industries, a harbor, a subnaval base, an agriculture farm and a helipad all added to the large-scale deforestation, pushing the Onge into ever-smaller pockets in the northern and southern parts of the island. Bodley (1988) observes that:

> "The most intense arenas of conflict between tribals and national governments involve the development of natural resources on tribal lands by outside interests. Tribal populations invariably occupy territories that are but lightly exploited and then only for local, tribal use. National governments... are understandably eager to extract as much wealth as possible from their entire national territory. Thus we see highways, mining operations... lumbering, agri-business, and planned colonization projects, all intruding on tribal territories" (p.135).

The rationale for such a course of events is provided for in the ambiguous status of "tribal" peoples in the Constitution of India. On the one hand, according to Article 46 of the Constitution of India:

> "The State shall promote with special care the educational and economic interests of the weaker section of the people, and in particular of the Scheduled Castes and Scheduled Tribes,[7] and protect them from social injustice and all forms of exploitation" (cited in George, 1991: 22).

But on the other hand, the constitution also maintains that the traditional rights of "tribals" over natural resources and forest lands, is a privilege or a concession granted to them, and can be "terminated at the will of the Sovereign" (ibid: 22). Thus, as George (ibid.,) points out with some irony, while "India would like to see her tribal people retain their religion, culture, ethos and institutions," the conditions that would ensure their distinct identity, namely, the guarantee of a stable resource base, is imperiled by the terms of the same constitution. Bodley's survey on "tribal" peoples notes that:

> "[T]he most obvious detrimental impacts are caused by a weakening of the subsistence base due to resource depletion and/or breakdowns in the social organization of subsistence activites. Pressures on natural resources may increase immediately as outsiders begin to compete for them or as tribal peoples themselves begin to harvest for the market. The territorial base may be drastically reduced as official policy restricts tribal access to make tribal resources directly available to outsiders" (p.209).

The strategic monopoly over forestlands is clearly a legacy from British days. Guha (1991) notes that a prolonged debate had ensued within the colonial bureaucracy, over the customary use of forests that is based on "rights" as opposed to "privilege." The debate was settled by an ingenious use of precedent, by citing the principle that "the right of conquest is the strongest of all rights—it is a right against which there is no appeal" (Amery, 1876 cited in Guha, 1991: 38).

This language, formulated in the context of colonial rule, was carried over without any alteration into the constitution of the "independent" India, as it defined the status of the "tribals" within the country. As regards "tribal" access to forests and traditional rights of use, the policies of the British and the Indian government are formulated identically—the forest is always perceived as "virgin terrain," available for alternative commercially profitable use. Such sharply opposed perceptions of the forest was perceptively framed by a colonial officer in mainland India as:

> "[T]he struggle for existence between the villagers and the Forest Department; the former to live, the latter to show a surplus and what the department looks on as efficient forest management" (Percy Wyndham, 1921 cited in Guha, 1991).

The special provisions for the protection of the "tribals" were also inherited from the Government of India Act of 1935, Articles 91 and 92. By this Act, "enclaves" were produced, i.e. areas in which the "tribals" were concentrated, outside of ordinary administration, where they would be "insulated" from "exploitation or demoralizing contact with sophisticated outsiders" (Galanter, 1984: 147). Concurrently, the colonial government maintained rigorous control over the forests customarily available for "tribal" use.

Such a paternalistic framework for the treatment of the "tribals," first drafted during British colonial rule, then further elaborated by the Indian government, lends some salience to a recognition of the situation of "tribals" in India as one of "internal colonialism." Colby and van den Berghe (1969) as cited in Blauner (1972), distinguish as "internal colonialism," a situation where an independent country has, within its boundaries, given special legal status to groups that differ culturally from the dominant group, and created a distinct administrative machinery to handle such groups. Such groups are usually referred to as "tribes" by the state for administrative purposes.

It is not coincidental that the plans for the re-population and development of the Andaman Islands were repeatedly alluded to as a program for "colonization" by the Indian government. With their long experience of colonial rule, it is curious (or revealing) that the term should be brought back into administrative currency promptly after shaking off the shackles of colonial dominance. It does suggest that the former colonial subjects have flipped the situation over, and in turn, become the colonizers.

For the Andaman Islanders, it was merely a transfer of power between two colonial regimes, with very little to differentiate the two, except perhaps, the colour of the skin. The colonizer changed from the "white man" to the "brown" one after 1947, who, like the former, proceeded to shoulder the "the white man's burden" of undertaking to "uplift" the "backward" "primitives."

The significant factor to be noted here is that, when schemes were proposed on behalf of the islanders, there was concurrently a second agenda implicated. Of development plans for the mainland Indian population, which involved the increased clearing of the forest for agriculture, forest-based industries, villages, roads, etc. Thus plans for the islanders did not occur in isolation, but were mobilized within a larger context that was contingent on reducing the extent of forest available to them. The strategy for colonization of Little Andaman with settlers from mainland India, coincided with the program for sedenterization of the Onge.

The Situation of the Jarawa

As in the earlier British period, the specific situation of the Jarawa presented a set of conjunctures that was not as readily resolved as in the case of the Onge or the Andamanese. When the British left the islands, about 765 sq km of South and Middle Andaman were decreed as Jarawa Reserve forest. I have noted earlier that when displaced refugees were resettled on South and Middle Andaman, it led to a marked increase in the frequency of "Jarawa incidents." According to the Census of India, 1961, there were as many as 89 cases of raids between 1946 and 1963 (cited in Sarkar, 1990: 48).

The 340 km construction of the Andaman Trunk Road through South Andaman, linking Diglipur in North Andaman with Port Blair, brought large numbers of laborers into Jarawa territory, and disturbed the area by way of felling of trees, blasting by explosives, the construction of labor camps etc. The entry of large numbers of people into the area also resulted in an increase in the incidence of poaching (Sarkar, 1990). The road building was brought to a halt in 1976, when several members of the road-building crew of the Public Works Department died from arrow wounds. The engineers had aligned the road well into the eastern edge of the reserve (Whitaker, 1985). Recently, the road construction was resumed from a different section, suggesting the possibility of renewed conflict with the Jarawa in the near future.

> "In the last 20 years, the Andamans have been increasingly ravaged for resources and used as a dumping ground for the landless; since 1960, the population has expanded from 50,000 to about 180,000, and over 100,000 hectares of forest have been cleared and 600 km of road constructed" (Whitaker and Whitaker, 1984: 16).

Whitaker (1985) goes on to assert that the most serious threat to the Jarawa in the present is the increasing human pressure on the islands, and the continued encroachment into their territory which is prime hunting and fishing land. He observes that the Jarawa now use metal for their arrowheads and are willing to undertake considerable risks to obtain it, raiding road-building camps, forest ("Bush" police) camps and farms. As the number and scale of "Jarawa incidents" indicate, receiving media attention only if there are deaths on the Indian side, the settlers, illegal encroachers and the "Bush" police, without formal government approval, take it upon themselves to launch a mini-war against the Jarawa. In this connection, a former Lieutenant Governor was heard to remark that the Jarawa "menace" could be ended once and for all, by rounding them up, and holding them in some place where they would be unable to "cause trouble." Meanwhile, the administration continues to allot land to settlers, or legalize encroachments along the borders of the contested forest tract. For the Jarawa too, as Mukerjee (1995) recognizes, it is a declaration of war. She reports of an incident when "the tribe attacked a forest outpost, impaling a woman and slaying a calf" (p.20). Dogs and elephants, which are associated with settlers are regularly killed, but "in the process they have protected the pristine forests of their territory, along with its unique wildlife" (p.20).

The "Breakthrough"

The following are a series of commentaries made by anthropologists and other observers, on the perceived major turning point in the ongoing ambivalent relations with the Jarawa. The continuities with earlier British policies are remarkable. More astonishing is that these connections are cited as an affirmation of present policy.

> "In 1968, 3 Jarawa boys were captured...and brought to Port Blair, where they were kept for a month under the observation of 2 anthropologists of the Anthropological Survey of India. They were treated well and then set free near their area with a large quantity of gifts" (Pandit, 1974 cited in Sarkar, 1990: 51)...*In fact, the method adopted by Portman 1879-1894 was followed"* (Sarkar, 1990: 51) (my emphasis).

Sarkar (1990) describes the "momentous" occasion when some kind of "connection" seemed to have been made with the Jarawa.

> "There was a major breakthrough in February 1974 when a few Jawawa made friendly gestures towards a contact party led by members of the Bush Police, who used to visit the area from time to time. A Jarawa man swam across and came on board the dungi[8] and collected the gifts...*Perhaps this had some positive impact and thereafter the Jarawa came forward on their own to greet the Contact Party, as happened in the case of Colebrooke during the first penal settlement"* (Sarkar, 1990: 51) (my emphasis).

Whitaker and Whitaker (1984) are more wary, urging caution in considering the utility of these developments.

> "From 1974 onwards regular contact has been made with the Jarawa at their coastal camp at Chotaling Bang (Middle Andaman). In 1981, another group in South Andaman was contacted using the Chotaling Bang Jarawa as go-betweens. The latter were taken to Strait Island and shown[9] the Andamanese settlement there" (ibid: 13) (my emphasis).

A more critical assessment of these policies is drowned in the flood of acclamatory comments on the government's breakthrough efforts. The health hazards of such contact with outsiders is blithely ignored, and the enormity of the risk of taking the Jarawa to Strait Island where one or more Andamanese chronically suffer from tuberculosis, is alarming. As Whitaker (1984) urgently points out, "even an influenza virus could prove fatal to people with no immunity to civilization's diseases" (p.70). She goes on to remind those who have become rashly forgetful of the tragic consequences of such imprudent tactics in earlier times:

> "The post-independence policy toward the Jarawa mimics that of the British administration in trying to appease and buy the Jarawa's friendship. In a typical display of bureaucratic shortsightedness, we have yet to learn our lessons from the tragedy of the Andamanese extermination. Regular patrols are still sent out with gifts such as cloth, plastic buckets and matches; one group of Jarawa has been in contact with these parties for 10 years, and another group has now joined in. These "gift patrols" may spell the end of the Jarawa; the government should take heed and leave them alone. Isolation is apparently the best policy in the delicate Andamans situation until we can be sure our friendship won't kill them...The government's maneuvers look alarmingly like the practice of scattering rice to attract birds to the snare" (ibid: 16).

On the flip side of the "breakthrough in the situation," are the continuing sequence of "Jarawa incidents," when trespassers or poachers encountered in Jarawa territory are usually attacked and killed. Or the periodic raids that are made on nearby villages every month around full-moon, for metal implements and utensils, bananas, coconuts and cooked rice (all of which are now customary gift items carried by the "contact" team). Vishwajit Pandya (1992) with some amusement refers to these incidents as "the bad guys riding into town, to raise hell, and engage in some duty-free shopping."

Some salutary lessons may be drawn from recalling the early days of British contact with the Andamanese, when similar "plundering" by night, and acceptance of gifts by day were regular occurrences. Portman cherishes no illusions when he observes, "we must admit the unflattering fact that it is not any particular love of us, but chiefly the greed for [goods and] food which tempts them to the Settlement" (Portman, 1899: 412).

"Retrieval from Precipice"

The following is a close reading from a document entitled "Retrieval From Precipice," published by the Andaman Adim Janjati Vikas Samiti (AAJVS), the Committee for the Enlightenment of Primitive Peoples. The document is a compilation of cumulative reports and the measures adopted for a programme of "planned change," that was proposed for the islanders by the Andaman administration in 1976. The "exciting experiment" also named "Retrieval from Precipice," to "retrieve these rare racial groups from the path of extinction down the precipice of death" was conceived as an endeavour that was in keeping with "the noblest tradition of the Indian Civilization."[10] The document gives insight into the strategies followed in the "unique experiment," as well as an explicit rationale for the undertaking.

A committee named "The Andaman Adim Janjati Vikas Samiti" was constituted to monitor the project, with the help of an advisory "Committee on Primitive Tribal Groups" comprising of "experts," mainly anthropologists, an eminent geneticist, and other government officers. These were heady days for the group, as they responded to the "clarion call" of the former Prime Minister Indira Gandhi, in her "20-Point Economic Programme" which laid "great emphasis on the weaker section of society." With immense faith in the possibilities offered by the advances in science and medicine, buoyed up by good intentions and the excitement of "experimenting" on human subjects, the committee set about their task.

The preface lays out the framework for the project "for the amelioration of the tribes," the "purest forms," of the "few endangered remnants of the negrito race" who "still survive in their stone age glory," are "not cannibals or inhuman," but are "weak, hapless," and in need of the Indian government's "magnanimity and protection." The AAJVS is therefore:

> "[E]ngaged in a task which shows that they can be befriended, their health and life protected and their living conditions gradually developed into an economic pattern which can, at appropriate stage, merge with the economic and living patterns of these islands. In the years to come they will survive, develop confidence and a will to live and become useful citizens of India."

In contradiction to the agenda stated here, the former Prime Minister[11] Morarji Desai's message registers a different intent:

"It should therefore be our duty to let these tribes live their lives as they would like to while providing them with such of the amenities of life to which all citizens of our country are entitled. We do not want the tribes to be ethnological exhibits; nor do we want to lose their distinctive personality under pressure. We need imaginative policies rooted in wider sympathetic knowledge of the tribes."

These two mutually contradictory strands alternate in the document with respect to the policies to be followed, i.e. whether to permit the islanders to maintain their distinctive lifestyle or to integrate them with the other populations. Although the former is asserted at the level of political statements, the latter is the program that is in operation.

The strategies to achieve these projected goals required that:

"These remaining specimens of bygone races...be looked after closely, watchfully and carefully in their small population if their survival is to be ensured. Their future can now only be nurtured in a sort of controlled demographic laboratory till they have been regenerated to come once again into their own" (p.31) (my emphasis).

In the case of the Andamanese, described as "all intermixed and indistinguishable in their ethnic identity," the criteria by which their success as a population was to be assessed included: literacy which was "practically absent," work participation rate "as low as 8.3 per cent (13.3 per cent among the males and practically nil among females)," and a dismal reproductive rate as a consequence of "their males having lost their vitality and the females their fertility" (ibid: 30) (my emphasis).

The Onge "are a shade better off than the Andamanese," but persist at a "pre-agricultural stage of food gathering in jungles and pig hunting" (ibid: 31). In contrast to the Andamanese and the Onge are the Jarawa "who retain their virility and vitality and are of excellent physique" (ibid: 32). The future envisaged for the Jarawa through the "goodwill" generated by the "plan-of-action" proposed for them: "survi[val] as fully conscious Indian citizens in not too distant a future" (ibid: 32). As for the Sentinelese, who "appeared beyond doubt to be fully virile" (p.32), apart from the "occasional dropping of gifts to augment their resources" and to "infuse goodwill," there was little else that was planned.

The programme included plans for the appointment of a "suitable, senior and experienced social worker who could exercise his good judgement[,] and a medical officer preferably gynecologist together with a lady doctor[,] preferably wife of one of the workers" (AAJVS, 1978: 39).

There were small modifications in the details of the program as it related to the Andamanese and the Onge, based on their separate historical circumstances. In the case of the Andamanese, the primary task at hand was the recuperation of a group of derelicts existing in a state of utter degradation and ill health. But, after rehabilitation of "these children of nature" and providing the "grown-ups" with a "modest pocket-money allowance" (AAJVS, 1978: 36), other schemes were proposed to inculcate useful work habits. It was resolved that the Andamanese should be engaged in making canoes and ropes. All the necessary tools and materials would be supplied to them free of cost. It was matter of some excitement for the committee that soon the Andamanese would be "busy in their traditional vocations" (p.45). In addition, a "piggery unit" was set up, and a calf for breeding purposes. Vegetable and fruit seeds were provided free of cost to help raise kitchen gardens.[12] A system of "passes"[13] was instituted, which meant that the Andamanese could leave Strait Island only when they obtained a pass issued for a specific purpose. A report that was submitted a year after these schemes were underway concludes:

> "The impact of all these welfare activities initiated by the Samiti has been very encouraging. Not only the Andamanese who used to loiter in Port Blair and other places have gone back to their settlement in Strait Island, there are visible signs of their being hopeful to live. A sense of belonging is more dawning on them. No wonder, if the tempo of developmental efforts is further stepped up with more welfare amenities, the Andamanese may again turn out to be a thriving community as they were a century before" (AAJVS, 1978: 46).

With the Andamanese satisfactorily re-settled, it was next the turn of the Onge. In 1976, development plans with the professed intention of providing the Onges with "mainstream amenities" were set in motion. The scheme involved the "rehabilitation and resettlement" of the Onge, in the north-east corner of Little Andaman known as Dugong Creek.

The "self-contained settlement" that was constructed for the Onge, included individual houses for each couple, with asbestos, corrugated roofs constructed by the Public Works Department. The Public Works Department is responsible for government sanctioned constructions in India. They have several categories of "quarters" that are determined according to the official status of the government officers who will live in these houses during the tenure of their appointment. These are classified as Type I, Type II, etc. For the Onge, the lowest of these categories was considered appropriate. An interesting additional influence determined the design of the houses intended for the Onges. The Commissioner of the Andamans at the time, who was also the director of the welfare scheme, had returned from an appointment in the remote North-East region of India, in the state of Manipur. In that region, the people lived in raised houses, built on four posts that functioned as stilts. The Commissioner was much taken with this design, and decided to transplant the homes of one group of "tribals" to a different one—after all, there was not much to distinguish one "tribal" from another.

Other "civic amenities like medical care, water hygiene, general provisions, marketing, recreation, etc.," were part of the "Package Scheme" (ibid: 39). Here too, "a piggery unit" was established, and "goat rearing" was to be attempted. And, to underscore the sincerity of these intentions, a reward of Rs.500 was offered to those who acquired a working knowledge of the Onge language.

Food for the Islanders

Food aid in the form of rations is distributed to the Onge and the Andamanese every month. Rations[14] were started as an emergency measure after a cyclone in 1976 when the forests of Little Andaman were ravaged by storms, but was continued subsequently as an important element in the administrative strategy for sedenterization.

A striking feature of the ration items is the inherent ethnocentrism with respect to food. It was unthinkable that a people could survive on a diet devoid of rice and wheat staples or spices. These introductions have been extremely deleterious to a people who had subsisted on a predominantly meat/protein diet, and for whom the question of preserving or storing[15] food was never an issue. The introduction of milk-powder may have contributed to the unabated infant mortality even after settlement, and the periodic deaths of children from diahorrea/dysentry.[16] A connection can be made between sedenterization, and the introduction of foods without associations or learned rules of consumption. Fischler (1980) suggests the term gastro-anomie[17] to describe the characteristic state of normlessness and ignorance about food selection and food use in situations of rapid change. The outcome is illnesses[18] and maldigestion of a kind not previously encountered and hence not treatable in known, traditional ways.

The Power of Representations

It is obvious from the discussion so far that national discourses which medicalize the islanders as "rare" and "endangered" contribute to the formulation of government policies, which seek to either "preserve" an "authentic" way of life, or a unique people. These discursive formations are problematized by the contradictory policy options that follow from such representations. Since the islanders have been labeled as "rare," the administration is compelled to make available a substantial forest resource base for the islanders' use, to maintain their unique life way. But, because the Onge are also designated as "endangered," they are considered in need of administrative protection. This is to be delivered in the form of medical care, aid in food and reproductive incentives. All this is only possible if they are located within a circumscribed area[19] for the efficient functioning of the medical staff appointed to oversee their health. The representations have legitimized the Indian government's attempts to deploy a policy of sedenterization overseen by social and medical welfare providers. Thus, the medicalization of the islanders reinforces the necessity to sedenterize them, eliding the primary fact that these people are endangered only through the encroachment into their territory.

As past events have demonstrated with the Andamanese, when the British extended their colony across North, Middle and South Andaman and the neighbouring islands, there is a recurrent pattern to these shifting representations of the islanders and the policies that follow thereafter. As soon as plans are finalized for large-scale utilization and a more commercially profitable use for the islanders' territory, government policies are clearly resolved in favor of sedenterization of the islanders. After independence, the forests of Little Andaman became the target for another round of development efforts. And, at present, the same process is visible with the Jarawa: the administration periodically proclaiming them as a rare people, and espousing the unique way of life of the Jarawa, while in the same breath declaring their intentions of including the Jarawa as "full-fledged citizens of the country." The Sentinelese are assured of a certain degree of security, by occupying a small, isolated island, access to which remains difficult.

Berkhofer (1978) examines how imagery conflates with policy in the case of the Native American Indian, particularly in the context of arguments over rights to land. It mattered little whether the efforts were towards reform of the "deficient" Indian, or the taming of the "bloodthirsty savages." Or whether the policies followed were the General Allotment Act or the New Deal for

Indians. The ultimate consequence for the Native Indian was the loss of land held collectively by them. Reiterating the justification that what was good for the whites was also good for the Indian, the general perception was that any policy followed had mutually beneficial outcomes.

Likewise, in the Andaman Islands no matter how the policies are framed, for the islanders the consequences are a steady dwindling of territory under their control. This is particularly noticeable in the case of the Onge and Jarawa. But the few, remnant Andamanese are the exception to this norm. Barely surviving in the appalling conditions that they were reduced to by the time the British left the islands, the government's plan did result in an improvement of the material conditions of their existence.

An Assessment of the Welfare System

The "welfare" programme was ostensibly designed to benefit the islanders, to arrest their mortality, assure them of health and gently assimilate them into the dominant population. In the intervening years since the programme went into operation, these ideals have given way to disillusionment and cynicism. Foucault's comment made in an entirely different context is as apt here: "far from precipitating their breakdown [the failure] acts instead as the impulse for a perpetual effort to reform...reinvok[ing] the model of its original aborted programme" (1994: 215). The essential features of the system is presented as I observed its operation between 1989-1992. The general organization of the programme is similar for the Onge and the Andamanese, but at the time, the Onge appeared mostly unaware of the exploitation that they were subject to, while the greater worldliness and sophistication of the Andamanese made them active collaborators in a system, which they used and bent according to the situation.

An assessment of the programme requires a dismantling of its constituent parts, to permit an analysis of the different levels at which it operates. The first level of appraisal is the primary level at which the programme exists, i.e. in the person of the implementers, those who mediate between the islanders and the policy-makers, translating the policies on paper into quotidian practice. These are the welfare personnel who are appointed by the Andaman administration, to oversee the scheme to assimilate the islanders into "fully conscious citizens" of the country. The various positions created for this task include a social worker, a teacher, an auxiliary nurse cum midwife, a medical attendant, a wireless operator, a generator operator, and two guards (a euphemism for "all-purpose functionaries" who are expected to make themselves available for any kind of work). Their term of appointment varies from anywhere between 3 months to 8 years.

The distinctive personalities of individual members of the welfare staff have been significant in determining the ups and downs, swings and shifts in the fortunes of the Onge and the Andamanese, ever since their destinies were placed under the control of the Indian bureaucracy. Most of the welfare staff manage these settlements as if it was their private fiefdoms. Their lowly, ill-paid status in the hierarchy of government office, undermines the lofty ideals attributed to their assigned duties. This means that the general attitude of these "government servants" is to appropriate as much as possible during their tenure and "to hell with the junglees." Most feel that the islanders are beneficieries of a largesse that is undeserved, and therefore, it is only just that they direct a share to themselves.

In addition to the welfare staff there is a medical officer who is a separate appointee of the Directorate of Health Services. At Dugong Creek, the medical officer is the highest paid functionary in the settlement, usually fresh from medical school, and has a term of appointment of 6 months. Every medical officer who has left Dugong Creek at the end of his tenure has made a small fortune from varied means. The medications sent for the Onge, the milk powder, rations[20] and the wages that he is responsible for distributing in conjunction with the other welfare staff.[21] From the coconuts collected by the Onge, and last but not the least, the ambergris that washes up on the shores of Dugong Creek during the monsoons. At least two former medical officers have been held responsible by Onge elders, for introducing alcohol to other Onge as inducements for procuring ambergris for them.

In their defense, it is usually conceded that it is the officers' inexperience, together with the loneliness and isolation of the appointment at Dugong Creek that makes the situation difficult to cope with. Hence all succumb to the blandishments of corruption, which is equated as justifying the hardships endured at Dugong Creek. But the situation has proven no different even when senior, more experienced officers are appointed along with their families, so that this particular line of reasoning loses any credibility.

Apart from the long litany of vices of the welfare staff implementing the program, they are as callous in the actual discharge of their duties. Infants continue to die at regular intervals. Most of the Onge and Andamanese are under treatment for tubercular and other respiratory diseases. And every adult and child suffers from anemia and recurring skin infections. Thus, the most conspicuous feature of the welfare system in terms of its execution, is that all the personnel are in cahoots with each other, to prosper from the varied means available to amass wealth during their appointment.

A government appointment in India is a permanent position, with minimal risk of dismissal. There is no penalty for an unsatisfactory discharge of responsibilities or reprehensible conduct, especially in places as remote as the Andaman Islands. Because of this lack of accountability, and the large sums allocated for "tribal welfare," corruption is an endemic feature of government bureacracy.

To illustrate these assertions, I will offer some examples of inappropriate conduct by the welfare personnel that came to my attention during the period of my research. The first one occurred at Strait Island where I ascertained the reasons for the odd behaviour of Pejeye, one of the Andamanese men. His behaviour was the manifestation of symptoms of extreme addiction to a "cocktail" of sedatives, with a shot of methylated spirit for good measure, given to him over several months by the "compounder,"[22] as inducement for procuring "birds-nest" and ambergris for him. This discovery led to the transfer of the "compounder" to a different "tribal" posting in the Nicobar Islands, but there was no question of the termination of his employment. The explanation offered was that the "compounder" would be coming up for retirement shortly,[23] and it was "unethical" to deprive him of his job at this stage of his employment.

Similarly, the medical attendant at Dugong Creek had a stash of alcohol, regularly replenished during her visits to the nearest town, in exchange for honey, ambergris and incense from the Onge. She too was transferred elsewhere, and this time the justification was the large family she supported. Hence, although her conduct was not to be condoned, it was to be forgiven.

Finally, the medical officer at Dugong Creek assaulted a young, attractive Onge woman, who defended herself with a knife. His behaviour was simply laughed away, to the outrage of other Onge. When I queried the Onge as to why they did not take matters into their own hands, they indicated their tenous control over any situation by confessing their inability to take any strong action against the officer.

This diatribe against the welfare personnel with respect to their dealings with the Onge or the Andamanese has to be juxtaposed against my own personal experience of them during the period of my reseach in the islands. My memories of the exchanges of hospitalities, small courtesies, the many kindnesses that went a long way towards mitigating the loneliness and hardships of life in these remote outposts, are to be included in my inscription of these people here. These disjunctions problematized day-to-day practices, and the only means out of the impasse was to finally separate (as I did), the sphere of my own interactions with the welfare staff from their conduct with the islanders. It did not make my own daily existence any easier as I negotiated these disjunctions, but such contradictions constituted my positionality in the islands and forged the framework for my research there.

It can be argued, as it is by "higher" authorities in the government, that corruption in the lower ranks has deviated the original intent of the programme. But the extent of corruption cuts across all levels of the hierarchy as a consequence of the inherent structure of government, and the large profits at stake. Such a situation is typical of government bureaucracies across south and South East Asia. In my presentation of the contemporary situation of the Andaman Islands, I do not assert that the forms of bureaucracy or scale of corruption is unusual to the islands. It is a feature of nation/states across the world. But that does not make a discussion of such characteristics, or its inclusion here any less pertinent. The point is to delineate the ways the islanders are inextricably linked to larger processes that are globally widespread.

The programme as charted by several anthropologists, the eminent geneticist, and some idealistic "top" officials had very little bearing on the reality of its implementation. But what of the original intent of the programme? Can it pass muster without comment? The well-intended policies for the "uplift" of the "primitives" can also be viewed as a charter for the ethnocide of a distinct group of people, albeit, a benevolent ethnocide.

The Content of Policies: Ethnocide/Benevolent Ethnocide

In recent years, the term ethnocide has increasingly come into prominence as a framework for describing the condition of indigenous peoples across the world (Barabas and Bartolemé, 1973; Lizot, 1976; Whitten, Jr., 1976; Ehrenreich, 1985; Escobar, 1989; George, 1991). As defined by Whitten, Jr. (1976: 24):

> "[T]he concept of ethnocide is taken from genocide, and refers to the process of exterminating the total lifeway of a people or nation, but in the ethnocidal process many of the peoples themselves are allowed to continue living" (p.24).

The starting point for this process in contemporary nation/states, is very often a situation that I have defined earlier as internal colonialism. By that process, indigenous peoples are deprived of any control over a traditional resource base, are sequestered within "enclaves" where they are rendered dependent on a dominant majority who have taken over their lands, and are left without any alternative means for survival. The dominant majority then proceeds to improve the condition of such "hapless" "primitives" by destroying all the elements of their "backward" lifeway, thus resulting in the ethnocide of a distinct group of people.

Ehrenreich (1985) offers a more nuanced understanding of the ethnocide of contemporary indigenous peoples by associating two apparently irreconciliable terms, namely that of benevolent ethnocide. His conceptualization of "benevolent ethnocide" is drawn from his work with the Coaiquer of Ecuador, and in large measure, denotes the condition of indigenous peoples in varied parts of the world. While on the surface policies of "planned change" "are propelled by positive and 'enlightened' humanitarian concerns," Ehrenreich demonstrates how the process is "steeped in racism and basic contempt for indigenous tribal peoples, no matter how well-intended particular proponents in any given case might prove to be" (p.17).

An examination of such policies reveals that they are premised upon the assumption that the lifestyle of indigenous people is inherently inferior, and hence must be supplanted by a different and better one. Moreover, it is also presumed that indigenous peoples are incapable of envisioning or planning their own future, therefore it is "outsiders" who know what is best for them (ibid: 17).

But, a careful scrutiny of the entire context in which such policies are formulated reveals that the motives for the amelioration of the condition of the "tribals" is usually suspect. As the example of the Andaman Islanders suggests, the assimilation of the islanders into "the mainstream" benefits primarily the well-intentioned "outsiders." In view of the ambiguous intent underlying policies of "planned change," despite their well-meaning appearance, their ultimate objectives distinguish them as sanctioning a process of ethnocide.

The initiation of ethnocide through policy intersects with a different process, that of "subjection," whereby the islanders become increasingly enmeshed in a trend that effaces their existing way of life. The consequence of such a two-way sequence of events is the destruction of a viable life way, and the induction of the islanders into the swelling ranks of other dispossessed marginal of mainsland Indian society.

A Matrix for Subjection: Individual Autonomy

Biolsi (1995) traces the history among the Lakota of what Foucault (1983) calls "subjection," which Biolsi interprets as the process that constituted the

Lakota "as social persons who could fit into the American nation-state and the market system of metropolitan capitalism" (Biolsi, 1995: 30). The series of administrative techniques deployed to construct these "new individuals," share a startling resemblance to the welfare programme administered by the Indian government, which too is intended to assimilate the Andaman Islanders with the dominant population.

Like the Lakota, the Onge are a particularly individualistic society "in which political power [is] not centralized but tend[s] to cohere around self-made leaders...[b]ut this form of individuality emerged in the context of social relations profoundly different from those of...industrial capitalism" (ibid: 29). Individualism[24] as understood in the context of the Onge should be regarded as a marked self-sufficiency. Each individual is autonomous, free to pursue his or her self-interest, and is not subservient to any structure of authority within the community. Therefore the relationship between each individual is that of equality regardless of age or gender.

The Onges' relationships with each other manifests itself on a day-to-day basis in the form of sharing of food, of which the most overt example is the sharing of pork. It is this transaction between individuals that maintains the notion of a "community." Therefore, the atomistic, fissioning tendency as a result of each individual's freedom to pursue his or her self-interest, in whichever direction he or she chooses, is countered by the strong pull inwards towards the community, which is reinforced everyday by the sharing of food. This is what has maintained the integrity of the community despite the heavy mortality and the disruptions of settlement.

The same characteristic is visible among the Andamanese as well, who can also be described as individuals who are self-sufficient and free to pursue their interests. But in contrast to the Onge, they live in an environment alien to them, a universe that has lost all meaning and significance, and hence there is no possibility of any relationship with and within this universe. Having lost their focal center, and without any basis for transactions between themselves, the Andamanese have splintered into individuals moving outwards and away from each other.

Other reports on the Onge (Basu, 1990) have interpreted this quality of individualism as a form of selfishness, where no one goes to the aid of another person. But as early as 1952, Cipriani comments on the Onge attribute of self-sufficiency as characteristic of other foraging groups as well, while noting the help and generosity extended if a man is injured or his wife is ill. All food is provided for and the person relieved of any duties. I concur with Cipriani that it is more accurate to describe the Onge as self-reliant, an attribute that is inculcated at an early age. Children are allowed to play with knives and other implements and become proficient in handling them. Even infants are permitted to clamber about the scaffolding of the tokabe, the Onge communal huts while their fathers are engaged in the construction.

The issue is one of labor. No Onge gives nor expects to receive help in the form of labor, i.e. an activity that can be included within the range of domestic responsibilities, for someone else. In this context, the nuclear family unit is very important in the sharing of labor. It is essential to have an husband or wife and children to complement one's tasks in the quotidian round of activities.

The distribution of domestic tasks is both shared and divided along lines of gender and age. The condition of Nabekutti and Shiela (both recently widowed at the time of my research), was illustrative of the importance of first, a spouse, and next in order of importance, children, to keep the "home fires burning." Nabekutti, who lost his wife some years ago, and without any surviving offspring, had abandoned his house in the settlement. He roamed around the forest and the nearby Bengali villages, selling everything that he gathered from the forest for alcohol. During the entire period of my stay in Dugong Creek, even when he occasionally stayed in the settlement, he never cooked in his house, but partook of food in other peoples homes.

Shiela, on the other hand, with six children to care for, even with the help of her older children, had difficulties organizing her household. She could not count on assistance from her male kins, since they were responsible for their own homes. The specific tasks that a husband would have shared with her remained undone with nobody else who could permanently take over those responsibilities.

It is against such a "matrix of individualism" that the "subjection" of the Onge through the welfare efforts be assessed. The most significant development that has emerged over the years is the notion of individual property—objects that are not a product of an Onge's singular effort are now accomodated within the frame of individual ownership. Money accumulating in the bank the real value of which is still unintelligible. Locks placed on doors and suitcases—this is an impressionistic rendering of a trend that is at odds with other values of sharing, the open give and take, also observable among the Onge. The new attribute of ownership is ascribed by the Onge to objects that they have purchased with money—transistors, tape-recorders, watches that they cannot read etc. But objects that have been given or gifted to them including their rations of food, as well as things that they have made themselves, still freely circulate between them.

More important, however, are the conflicts over power that have hardened over the years, as a consequence of the individual relationships that have been struck with the welfare staff and other officials of the administration. These in turn, have opened up "avenues for enablement" and privileges not available to everyone else.

Subjection and Power

In my discussion elsewhere of the Andamanese during the period of British control of the islands (Venkateswar, 1997), I noted the incidence of specific individuals who were singled out by the British officers and conferred certain privileges. Similar observations have been made in the case of the Ik, the !Kung or Native Americans (Turnbull, 1972; Wilmsen, 1990; Berkhofer, 1978). Drawing on Foucault's work, Biolsi (1995) further elaborates the process by which individuals are linked with structures of power. According to Biolsi:

> "Subjection is the construction by the powerful of spaces in which human beings are enabled to participate in the social life of public institutions, in the economy, and in the body politic of the nation. It involves the official promulgation of fundamental social classifications, through which individuals are to be known (by themselves, by other individuals, and by the officials) and allowed to act. Subjection also involves the linkage of these social classifications to power, both negative and positive: not only can individuals be punished by the officials for violating the social classifications, they quickly come to find that abiding by them opens up new avenues of enablement. Thus subjection is not absolutely imposed from above; it also seduces the subaltern to live by its rules, and thereby shapes new and predictable self-interests, outlooks, and behavior patterns" (Biolsi, 1995: 30) (my emphasis).

I retrace the trajectory of a similar process as it developed in the case of the Onge in my discussion below. Until the breakwater was constructed in the sixties, Little Andaman was surrounded by notoriously rough seas, making landing on the island a risky and difficult undertaking. Dugong Creek was one of the routes to easy access because of the deep, tidewater creek that opened out to sea. Hence the territorial groups of Onge who lived in the Dugong Creek area and its vicinity,[25] have historically had more access to outsiders than the groups living in the more interior and other coastal parts.

When the settlement at Dugong Creek was constructed, there were a number of different territorial groups of Onge who were accommodated in that space, including all the groups around Dugong Creek itself. Typically, when the welfare program was initiated, Tambolai,[26] an intelligent and personable young man fluent in Hindi, was appointed Raja. The other[27] territorial groups around Dugong Creek were allied through affinal relations with Tambolai's group. As a result of their longer duration of "contact," first with the British and then the Indians, members of these groups were more proficient in Hindi than the Onge from the more distant regions of Little Andaman. Young men drawn from these groups were appointed as "helpers"[28] to the welfare staff. Thus, Berogegi, Tai and Totanange were the next rung[29] of Onge with structured links with the Indians. Tambolai was also appointed as member of various executive bodies of the Andaman administration, received a large salary, and had to appear for periodic "meetings" in Port Blair. He was flown in as a special guest of the Prime Minister for Republic Day parades in New Delhi and was exempt from all wage-work. The exemption from the tedious, grind of wage-work also extended to the other "helpers," who over the years have learned to negotiate their duties with the entale.[30]

In view of the lack of any permanent, institutionalized structure of authority prior to these events, a three-tiered, hierarchical structure was installed on a purported decentralized, pluralistic and egalitarian[31] people. The rumblings of dissent soon became apparent as members of the other[32] territorial groups voiced their claims to the same privileges. Nabekutti from Deshenghri, with the support of all his affinal allies, sought to replace Tambolai as Raja. But Nabekutti did not have the same presence of personality nor the linguistic abilities of Tambolai. As a gesture of appeasement by the Andaman administration he was made co-Raja, but the position did not carry the same weight—he was only a "titular head" in the sense that the welfare personnel referred to him as Raja together with Tambolai.

There was yet another basis for the shifting of power over to Tambolai's group. The torale or the spirit communicators are purportedly very powerful figures for the Onge, since they alone have the ability to mediate between the human and spirit realms (Pandya, 1992). The two extant torale are Kwerai of the Chamale group, and Moroi. Moroi is territorially allied with the rival camp, but is married to a Chamale woman. Tambolai claims both as his allies to endorse the position of authority conferred on him by the Andaman administration.

Meanwhile, over the years, another contender to the position of Raja has emerged from the rival camp, in the person of Bara Raju. The route that he chose to follow was as a hard-working, reliable recruiter of labor for wage-work. The welfare personnel can always depend on Bara Raju to round up the men required to perform any work in the settlement. Bara Raju has dreams of flying to Delhi for Independence Day or Republic Day parades, attending meetings in Port Blair, and having the ear of the Lieutenant-Governor of the Andamans. The increasing trust placed on him by the authorities in Port Blair, has enabled him to use it as a lever to negotiate with, and check the excesses of the welfare personnel at Dugong Creek. Bara Raju is also proficient in Hindi with an appreciation for the colloquialisms and the flavor of invectives in that language. His claim that he should rightfully displace Tambolai as Raja finds a growing body of support at Port Blair, since Tambolai has, over the years, also acquired a reputation for drinking. More pertinently for my purposes, was Bara Raju's agreement to work with me based on his appraisal of the extent to which I could influence the direction of his aspirations, by endorsing his claim to Rajaship with the right authorities.

Alongside these power moves constituted by the entry of the welfare system into Dugong Creek, and the incorporation of the Onge within relatively new dimensions of privilege, the "traditional" structure of authority remains invested in the person of Tilai, the last of the "oldtime" Onge. He remains distant from the maneuverings of either Tambolai, Nabekutti or Bara Raju, although both Nabekutti and Bara Raju can claim him as a territorial and an affinal ally.

The narrative above clearly illustrates the process of "subjection" that has "seduced" some Onge, by offering to them certain privileges that are available by taking the routes to power opened up by the Indian government. The process described here demonstrates the ways in which informal modes of authority have been recast into more permanent, hierarchical structures of power endorsed by the Indian government. The situation exhibits many similarities to Biolsi's work with the Lakota, as they moved into the spaces of power made available by the administration.

But the Andaman administration has met with little success in the other schemes that were also initiated at Dugong Creek, namely, the attempts to direct the Onge away from subsistence practices rooted in the forest. "Piggery units," vegetable gardens, diary cows, goat-rearing projects—have nourished and sustained the welfare personnel. For many years they presented these programs as a great success, until some higher officials came to investigate. The Onge have remained indifferent to these particular efforts to "civilize" and lure them from the forest.

Some Alternatives?

Tennant and Turpel (1986) point out that the post-war process of decolonisation has passed over the claims of indigenous peoples. They stress the fact that the claims of indigenous peoples for sufficient autonomy to ensure their continued existence as culturally-distinct collectivities is a political claim that challenges the territorial sovereignty and nationality of a state. As Maybury-Lewis (1981) notes:

> "Land, and the struggle for it, is at the heart of the problem of cultural survival, for the guarantee of their lands is what tribal peoples need most" (p. 73).

Since indigenous claims pose a challenge to the state, they have met with little success in resolving their claims domestically, where such claims are both decontexualised and depoliticised into questions of minority rights, language rights, etc. International human rights fora, however, provide an environment in which the political aspects of indigenous claims can be discussed. But here too, claims to collective existence as a people, cannot be readily accommodated within the existing human rights norms and tend to become fragmented and decontextualized. Falk (1988) suggests that what indigenous peoples can hope to achieve through international human rights norms and procedures is to expand the discussion of their claims, and to underscore the unfinished nature of the decolonization effort.

Arguably such a scenario is not relevant to the existing condition of the islanders, because of their inability or inarticulacy to participate to any significant degree in the public institutions of civil society. But the significance of international fora like the United Nations is to provide the space for developing alternative standards, which can then serve as a point of reference in policy initiatives. The politicization of the islanders, if ever, to avail of such standards and make a bid for an opportunity to define their own rights is a later phase.

Lesser (1968, cited in Ehrenreich, 1985: 324) argued in the context of the assimilation pressures on the Native American Indian that the "decision to become fully assimilated and to give up Indian identity and community life was not for the nation or the government to make, but the Indians to make for themselves" (1968: 591). Such a statement succinctly challenges the patronizing presumptions behind much of the decisions made on behalf of people like the Andaman Islanders. The first step then, as an alternative mode for policy initiatives at the local level, is to acknowledge that the islanders are capable of envisioning their own future, whatever its configuration and trajectory of unfolding.

Conclusion

This chapter traces the development of policies proposed for the assimilation of the islanders after the Andaman Islands became incorporated into the newly independent nation of India. The contentious issue of the presumed "failure" of the welfare system merits further discussion here. Steeped in the paternalistic, linear, evolutionary and economic rationality characteristic of development interventions everywhere (Escobar, 1995) the welfare system had other "side effects" that should be made "legible." Drawing on his research in Lesotho, James Ferguson (1994) notes that development projects, "while "failing" on their own terms, nonetheless have regular effects, which include the expansion and entrenchment of bureaucratic state power, side by side with the projection of a representation of economic and social life which denies "politics" (xv). Hence:

> "[A]n unsuccessful attempt to engineer an economic transformation becomes legible in another perspective as unintended yet instrumental elements in a resultant constellation that has the effect of expanding the exercise of a particular sort of state power while simultaneously exerting a powerful depoliticizing effect" (p. 21).

I have shown how the medicalization of the islanders is an integral element in a profoundly political process that divests a people of their land, but is simultaneously depoliticized by the deployment of representations that elides the fact that such a process is underway. Moreover, despite the lamented "failure" of the welfare system, and its deviations from the purported "ideals" as originally formulated, for all the reasons discussed above, it has ensured the incorporation of the Onge and Andamanese into the bureaucratic structures of the state, with the entrenchment of state power into their daily lives.

NOTES

1. The comment was made during a discussion between Totanange, Vishwajit Pandya and me at Dugong Creek. Totanange was asked about his views on the new solar plant that was being installed at the time.
2. A recent newspaper article discusses the prolonged negotiations between Britain and the new national governments of India and Pakistan over rights and control over the Andaman and Nicobar Islands (Singh, 1995).
3. The Cellular Jail which grew out of the former penal colony is a landmark and a major tourist attraction in the Andaman Islands.
4. In India,"tribe" is a legal referent rather than a social category, to designate those groups who are believed to be indigenous/autochthonous to a region. It also serves to distinguish such people socially and economically from the "caste" society characteristic of settled agriculture.
5. Here indigenous is understood as original inhabitants of their territories. In the Andaman Islands it can be more precisely used in this sense than in mainland India, where such a definition of indigenous becomes problematic. As George (1991) observes, every Indian could claim to be indigenous if that meant "a native of the soil" as defined by the Webster's New Dictionary. A large majority of Indians could also claim indigenous state by following ILO Convention 169, which defines indigenous as "peoples in independent countries whose social, cultural and economic conditions distinguish them from other sections of the national community and whose status is regulated wholly or partially by their own customs or traditions or by special laws or regulations." However, a definition of indigenous inclusive of its negative connotations of "primitive" and "backward," would reduce the numbers of claimants willing to be identified in this way. Thus, in India, "aboriginal" or "tribal" is the preferred term of reference for people like the Andaman Islanders.
6. The issue of refugees crossing over into India from Bangladesh (formerly East Pakistan) has been a matter of some concern since independence. With the increasing violence between the Sinhalese and Tamil populations in Sri Lanka, there is another continuous source of refugees. The Andaman Islands is perceived as the last bastion where all such displaced people can be accommodated.
7. Scheduled tribes are defined as those groups who are characterized as "primitive," isolated, and "backward," thus making them deserving of special treatment (Galanter, 1984).
8. Dungi, which is a modification of dinghy, is the Andaman word for a boat with an outboard motor.
9. These gestures are reminiscent of Portman's or other British officers' policy of taking the Andamanese and Onge to Port Blair or Calcutta to impress them with the "wonders and pleasures of civilization."
10. This is a part of the congratulatory message sent to the Andaman administration from Charan Singh, the Home Minister at the time, which

appeared in the published version of the document "Retrieval from Precipice" 1978.

11. The political situation in India was tense at the time, and there were a number of quick turnovers of the government, headed by the leaders of different political parties.
12. All this is reminiscent of the schemes set up for the Andamanese in the Homes that were created for them by the British. See discussion in chapter 2.
13. The system of "passes" was discontinued some years later and did not exist at the time of my research in the islands.
14. Tobacco was included as one of the ration items and was eliminated recently. However, tobacco, areca nuts and alcohol continues to be used as bribes by the welfare staff and others to obtain forest products from the Onge or as an inducement for extracting labor from the Onge.
15. The tropical climate and the necessity of transporting all ration items by sea, hastens the process of spoilage and vermin infestation in the sodden sacks that arrive at the settlement. Moreover, analogous to the earlier British period, the most inferior quality supplies are obtained for the islanders. This is true even in the case of the edible "gifts" carried during "Jarawa" contact.
16. Besides the possibility of lactose intolerance, there is also the issue of awareness of the importance of hygienic practices, proper sterilization of milk bottles etc.
17. The situation assumes tragic proportions when such anomie means that potentially harmful substances are offered to children. There is no cognizance of the detrimental effects that alcohol or tobacco can have, and everything that adults like and enjoy is also considered good for children.
18. See Joos (1984) for a discussion on obesity and diabetes among the Florida Seminole Indians, and Fitzgerald (1980) for the effects of dietary change on Cook Islanders.
19. During the early years of the settlement at Dugong Creek, when their houses were still in the process of construction, the Onge continued to roam about at will in the forests of Little Andaman. The first few medical officers appointed to the post at Dugong Creek refused to search for the Onge in the forest. They insisted that they could not fulfill their medical responsibilities until it was ensured that the Onge were accessible within a circumscribed area.
20. Many Onge and Andamanese nowadays have taken to selling their rations to obtain cash for the purchase of alcohol.
21. Conflicts between the welfare personnel arise when one or more feel they that they have been left out of their due share of the pickings.
22. The "compounder" is an appointee of the Directorate of Health Services, usually with some pharmaceutical training.
23. Here, "shortly" should be read as a few more years to perform his nefarious activities elsewhere.
24. See Gardner 1991 for a discussion on current theories to account for foragers' individual autonomy.

25. Dugong Creek and its vicinity is referred to as Lebanare by the Onge.
26. From the territorially defined group belonging to Dugong Creek.
27. The Tokebui, Chamale and Titaje groups.
28. The term "helper" is a euphemism for a domestic servant for the welfare staff. The appointment has undergone some modifications since it was first conceived by the formulators of the welfare sytem. These assignments were to enable the Onge to receive training in the specific areas of appointment of the welfare personnel. At present, the duties of a "helper" include the transport and storage of water for daily use, the collection of firewood, scouring of vessels and scrubbing the lodging where the particular staff member is housed.
29. At present there is a back-up crew of other Onge, Ramesh, Chogegi, Kimboi, Kokegile to take over the more disagreable tasks from this rung of appointees.
30. The Onge word for "officer."
31. Previous reports on the Onge (Portman, Cipriani, Basu, etc) especially those prior to their settlement, endorse the egalitarian quality of their social relations.
32. The Tochieddi and the Togalange groups.

REFERENCES

A.A J.V.S. 1978. *Retrieval From Precipice.* Port Blair: Andaman Adim Janjati Samiti.

Barabas, A. and Bartholeme. 1973. *Hydraulic Development and Ethnocide: The Mazatec and Chinantec People of Oaxaca, Mexico.* Copenhagen: International Working Group for Indigenous Affairs (IWGIA).

Basu, B. K. 1990. *The Onge.* Calcutta: Seagull Books.

Berkofer (Jr), R.F. 1978. *The White Man's Indian: Images of the American Indian from Columbus to the Present.* New York: Alfred A. Knopf.

Biolsi, T. 1995. "The Birth of the Reservation: Making the Modern Individual among the Lakota," *American Ethnologist,* 22 (1): 28-53.

Blauner, R. 1972. "Internal Colonialism and Ghetto," (pp. 82-110) *in Racial Oppression in America.* New York: Harper Row.

Bodley, J. H., *(ed.).* 1988. Tribal Peoples *and* Development Issues: A Global Overview. *California: Mayfield Publishing Company.*

Cipriani, L. 1966. *The Andaman Islanders.* New York: Frederic A. Praeger.

Escobar, A. 1995. *Encountering Development: The Making and Unmaking of the Third World.* Princeton: Princeton University Press.

Escobar, T. 1989. *Ethnocide: Mission Accomplished?* Copenhagen: International Working Group for Indigenous Affairs (IWGIA).

Falk, R. 1988. *The Rights of Peoples (In Particular Indigenous Peoples).* Oxford: Clarendon Press.

Ferguson, J. 1994. *The Anti-Politics Machine: Development. 'Depoliticization' and Bureaucratic Power in Lesotho.* Minneapolis: University of Minnesota Press.

Fischler, C. 1980. "Food Habits, Social Change and the Nature/Culture Dilemma." *Social Science Information,* 19 (6): 937-953.

Fitzgerald, T. K. 1980. "Dietary Change among Cook Islanders in New Zealand." *Social Science Information,* 19 (4/5): 805-832.

Foucault, M. 1983. "The Subject and Power," (pp. 208-226) in H. L. Dreyfus and P. Rabinow (eds.), *Michel Foucault: Beyond Structuralism and Hermeneutics.* Chicago: University of Chicago Press.

Galanter, M. 1984. Competing Equalities: Law and the Backward Classes in India. Delhi: Oxford University Press.

George, R. 1991. *Ethnocide: The Cost of Development.* LL.M Dissertation. Boston, Massachussetts: Harvard Law School.

Guha, R. 1991. *The Unquiet Woods: Ecological Change and Peasant Resistance in the Himalaya.* Delhi: Oxford University Press.

Hechter, M. 1975. *Internal Colonialism: The Celtic Fringe in British National Development,* 1536-1966. Berkeley: University of California Press.

Joos, S. K. 1984. "Economic, Social and Cultural Factors in the Analysis of Disease: Dietary Change and Diabetes Mellitus among the Florida Seminole Indians," (pp. 217-237) in L. K. Brown and K. Mussel (eds.), *Ethnic and Regional Foodways in the United States: The Performance of Group Identity.* Knoxville: University of Tennessee Press.

Lizot, J. 1976. *The Yanomami in the Face of Ethnocide.* International Working Group for Indigenous Affairs (IWGIA). Copenhagen.

Man, E. H. 1885. "On the Andaman Islands, and their inhabitants," *Journal of the Anthropological Institute,* 14: 253-272.

Maybury-Lewis, D. 1981. "Some Lessons in Cultural Survival," *Odyssey Magazine.* Boston: Publishing Broadcasting Association.

Mukherjee, M. 1995. "Tribal Struggle. Stone Age Guardians of the Andaman Islands Fight to Survive, " *Scientific American,* 272 (5): 17-20.

Pandit, T. N. 1989. "Tribal Policy in the Andaman and Nicobar Islands: The Impact of Nehru's Philosophy," (pp. 83-92) in Jawarharlal Nehru (ed.), *Tribes and Tribal Policy.* Calcutta: Anthropological Survey of India.

Pandya, V. 1992. Personal Communication.

Portman, M. V. 1899. *A History of Our Relations with the Andamanese.* Compiled from histories and travels and from the records of the Government of India. New Delhi: Asian Educational Services.

Prain, D. 1932. "Memoir: Edward Horace Man C. I. E. 1846-1929," in E. H. Man (ed.), *The Nicobar Islands and their People.* London: Royal Anthropological Institute (RAI).

Radcliffe-Brown, A. R. 1964. *The Andaman Islanders.* New York: Free Press.

Sarkar, J. 1990. *The Jarawas.* Calcutta: Seagull Books.

Singh, S. 1995. "The Treasured Islands," *Indian Express*, Sunday, December 3.

Tennant, C. C. and Turpel. 1986. "A Case Study of Indigenous Peoples: Genocide, Ethnocide and Self-determination," *Nordic Journal of International Law,* 59 (4): 287-319.

Turnbull, C. M. 1972. *The Mountain People.* New York: Simon and Schuster.

Venkatesan, S. 1990. "Ecocide or Genocide," *Cultural Survival Quarterly,* 14 (4): 49-51.

Whitaker, R. 1985. *Endangered Andamans: Managing Tropical Moist Forests: A Case Study of the Andamans*. Environmental Sevices Group. India: WWF-India and MAB India, Dept. of Environment.

Whitaker, R., and Whitaker. 1984. "The Andaman Tribes---Victims of Development," *Cultural Survival Quarterly,* 10 (2): 13-18.

Whitten, J. N. E. 1976. *Ecuadorian Ethnocide and Indigenous Ethnogenesis: Amazonian Resurgence Amidst Andean Colonialism.* Copenhagen: International Working Group for Indigenous Affairs (IWGIA).

Wilmsen, E. N. 1989. *Land Filled with Flies: A Political Economy of the Kalahari.* Chicago: University of Chicago Press.

THREE

ISLAND CULTURES AND APPROACHES TO TRIBAL DEVELOPMENT IN INDIA

KAMAL K. MISHRA

Introduction

For two major reasons, development planning in India for the indigenous and tribal peoples has been a highly contentious issue since the independence. Firstly, the planning process in the country is largely centralized, most often undermining the cultural values and social priorities of the beneficiary tribal communities. Secondly, these communities themselves inhabit many different geo-ecological settings along the length and breadth of the country; they are ethnically divided into more than 400 distinct cultural groups; they are culturally heterogeneous, and are at different levels of socio-economic integration. This is the reason why any common development intervention for these communities proves to be inadequate and ineffective (Sarkar, 1993: 1-2). Since the indigenous and tribal peoples were nearly 68 million when the last Census was taken in 1991, constituting about 8.08 per cent of the total Indian population, their development at par with other non-tribal communities is an urgent priority in this largest democracy. Although the Indian Constitution has made ample provisions for the overall social and economic progress of these communities, it is no secret that nothing significant has been achieved so far in ameliorating them from many of their plights and tribulations (Misra, 1995: 159-173). This has resulted in the expression of discontent by the tribal communities from time to time, culminating in sporadic tribal movements in different pockets of the country (see for details, Singh, 1982; Sinha, 1993).

The problem of tribal development is still more pressing for those communities living in islands in a state of complete or near-complete isolation and registering violent protest against intervention of any kind with a gesture of hostility. Their number remains very small for many biological disabilities and cultural isolation. Therefore, anthropologists and development administrators often face the dilemma as to how constitutional rights and privileges could be extended to these endangered and very small populations, without eroding their cultural beliefs and social values (Sarkar, 1993: 1-45). This dilemma has come up also with regard to the development of the tribal populations in the Andaman islands. It is well known that the Andaman group of islands have been frequently visited since 1858 with the establishment of the Second Penal Settlement by the British Raj in India, thereby exposing the local Negrito tribes to outside contacts (see for details Singh, 1975: 66-91; Singh, 1978). After the Independence in 1947, constant efforts have been made by the Indian Government and the Andaman administration to protect these small and endangered communities from extinction, and to establish regular contacts with them (Pandit and Chattopadhyay, 1993: 169-178). It is no wonder that the results are not very encouraging. On the contrary, some of these communities are now on the verge of extinction, and some others still resist outside intervention with violent hostility. They prefer to defend their territories and cultural practices from external invasion. In this paper, we shall contemplate on the special biological and socio-cultural problems these Negrito tribes in the Andaman islands encounter, and to introspect why many of these developmental programmes initiated by the Indian Government for the last five decades for their welfare have not been as successful as envisaged. But before that, we need to acquaint ourselves with the islands and the indigenous groups living there.

The Andaman and Nicobar Islands

The Andaman and Nicobar groups of islands are located more or less as an arch towards southeast of the Indian peninsula and appear as a pearl necklace in the Bay of Bengal, which constitute a Union Territory of the Republic of India. These islands are 319 in number, big and small, and are situated between 6^0 and 14^0 North latitude and 92^0 and 94^0 East longitude with the 10^0 channel separating the Andaman group of islands from the Nicobar group (Das and Rath, 1991: 1). The Andaman group of islands is about 1255 km from the Eastern Indian city of Calcutta and about 1190 km from the Southern Indian city of Chennai. Its eastern most point, the Indira point, is just about 154 km from the island of Sumatra. The total area of the Andaman and Nicobar group of islands is about 8293 sq. km. spread over a length of approximately 700 km. Out of these 319 big and small islands, only 38 are inhabited by the human populations; 26 of them being in the Andaman and 12 in the Nicobar group (Sarkar, 1993: 2).

The topography of these islands is generally hilly and undulating. The main hill range runs from north to south. Saddla Peak in the North Andaman is the highest point in the islands with a height of 732 metres above the sea level. Flat lands are comparatively scarce in these islands. Long, narrow stretches of sandy beaches are the significant aspect of the topography here. The soil is usually infertile with low moisture retaining capacity. It consists of soft and deep sandy loam. The soil variation in the islands is from fine texture of the alluvial flats to the gravel soil of the low hills (Das and Rath, 1991: 3).

The Andaman and Nicobar islands experience both southwest and northeast monsoons with an average rainfall of about 320 cm. Rainfall varies from about 300 cm in the north to about 380 cm in the south. February to April every year is the relatively dry period in these islands. Temperature here varies from 23^0 to 29^0 C with the humidity as high as 80 per cent throughout the year. Mean wind speed is about 10.6 km per hour (Das and Rath, 1991: 4).

Abundant rainfall helps in luxurious growth of tropical forests in the islands, which occupy nearly 90 per cent of the total land area. The vegetation of these islands can be classified as mangrove forests, deciduous forests and tropical evergreen forests, showing distinct floral affinities with Assam and Burma in the north, Thailand and Malaysia in the east and Indonesia in the south. These islands are rich with varieties of timber yielding plants with the growth of palms, bamboo and canes in abundance (Balakrishnan and Nair, 1977: 638-40).

Out of the 38 human inhabited islands, only 4 are populated by 5 very small tribal communities in the Andaman and Nicobar islands. They are the Great Andamanese, the Onge, the Jarawa, the Sentinelese and the Shompen. Except the last one, which has marked Mongolian features, the rest 4 tribal groups represent the Negrito ethnic stock. An anthropometric survey among the Negrito tribes of the Andamans reveals that they are the smallest (in stature as well as in number) among all human races. An average Andamanese woman has a height of 137 cm and weighs 43.4 kg while their men have an average height of 148.5 cm and weigh about 39.5 kg. They have very dark skin colour and the hair is of peppercorn variety, unlike the curly hair of the African populations. Some Andamanese women however show the trait of steatopygia like the Khoi (Hottentot) of southern Africa (Weber, 1998: 18). Linguistically, the Andamanese is an "enigmatic" family, as it shows no relationship with any other language grouping, except the extinct Tasmanian language family, as hypothesized by Greenberg in 1971 (Weber, 1998: 19).

The Negrito tribes of the Andaman islands, although commonly referred to as "Andamanese", are the descendants of as many as 12 different tribes; each one once occupying a distinct territory and speaking a distinct dialect (Mann, 1976: 37-50). They could be divided into 3 broad divisions, such as, the Yerewa group, the Aka Bojigyab group and the Onge-Jarawa group. Out of these 3 groups of Negritos in the Andaman, the Aka Bojigyab group is now completely extinct, which was consisted of 5 different tribes. The Yerewa group, which had 4 different tribes, is now represented by the Aka-Toda and Aka-Yere (commonly known as the Great Andamanese and resettled in the Strait Island). The other living tribes include the Jarawa of the Middle and South Andaman, the Onge of the Little Andaman, and the Sentinelese of the North Sentinel Island. So, out of the 12 original Negrito tribes of the Andaman, we can now find only 5, the rest 7 tribes being extinct (Mann, 1976: 38).

Although these islands were mentioned by the Arab travelers as early as 871 A.D (Singh, 1975: 70) and were known to the people of the Malay peninsula, China and Japan much before, it was the British, who tried to establish a settlement here in 1789 at Port Cornowallis (now known as Port Blair, the capital of the Andaman and Nicobar islands, after Capt. Archibald Blair). The British administration in colonial India used the islands to force the convicts from the Indian mainland for exile. But the practice was abandoned in 1796, as the climate was very unsuitable for human habitation, and consequently, all the prisoners died in tropical diseases. Till 1858, when the Second Penal Settlement was established by the British Raj in India, these islands were only occupied by the indigenous populations without much of outside intervention, except occasional raids by the Malayas and the Chienese to capture Negrito slaves. The Andaman islands were then considered as the best option for the British administration, as it was looking for an inaccessible and escape-proof place to lock up Indian freedom fighters after the historic "Great Mutiny" of 1857 (Das and Rath, 1991: 121-122; Sarkar, 1993: 10; Weber, 1998: 21 etc.). In 1874, the Cellular Jail with 698 cells was constructed for solitary confinement of the freedom fighters from the mainland of India. This was the beginning of exodus of large hordes of population from Indian mainland and Burma into the hitherto serene islands of the Andaman and Nicobar.

Indigenous Tribal Groups in the Islands

As mentioned earlier, the indigenous groups of the Andaman and Nicobar islands is constituted by 4 Negrito and 1 Mongoloid tribes. All these tribes are by and large semi-nomadic hunter-foragers. But insofar as their degree of acculturation, they stand at different levels. Before embarking upon their very special problems and welfare measures, it is imperative to look into their typical way of life.

The Sentinelese

The Sentinelese are considered to be an offshoot of the Onge, who inhabit the Little Andaman (Bhat, n.d.: 84). According to the degree of contact with the outsiders, the Sentinelese occupy the very last position among all the tribes of Andaman and Nicobar islands. Even now, they live in complete isolation in the North Sentinel island, an isolated island surrounded by a nearly unbroken line of dangerous reefs (Weber, 1998: 22), and at a distance of about 60 km southwest of Port Blair. This Negrito tribe is still hostile to the contact parties sent by the Andaman administration from time to time since the establishment of the Second Penal Settlement in 1858. It is recorded that M.V.Portman landed up on North Sentinel island in 1880 and stayed there for a fortnight. Subsequent visits by Col. Ferrar, Mahabir Singh, Ramkumar Ohri and other parties could not apparently befriend the Sentinelese (Bhat, n.d.: 84). Their number is expected to be around 100, as the exact number is difficult to count (Sarkar, 1993: 17). Their number was estimated as 117, as per the Census of 1901 (Bhat, n.d.: 84). The Sentinelese are still at the stage of hunting-foraging, and subsist on wild pigs, sea shells, molluscs, fish, berries, tubers and raw honey. Some adult males seem to have used bark waist guard, while the children remain naked. For food collection, they use small cane baskets. They use iron arrowheads, trident arrows and harpoons with cane heads for hunting and fishing. They lead a semi-nomadic life and live in small grass thatched huts with all sides open in the shore area. They can manufacture small dug out outriggered canoe for plying on shallow water with the help of long poles (Sarkar, 1993: 3).

The Jarawa

The Jarawa is another Negrito tribe in the Andaman islands, who originally lived on the southern tip of South Andaman, and now spread out in the dense forests along the west coast of South and Middle Andaman (Weber, 1998:

22). Their number is estimated to be less than 200 (ibid.) or about 250 (Sarkar, 1993: 4). Very little is authentically known about them, as until recently they resisted any kind of contact with outsiders. However, Weber's account states that two small Jarawa local groups have since been contacted, who have started receiving small gifts from the visiting parties without the traditional bloodbath (Weber, 1998: 22). They also lead a semi-nomadic life with hunting, foraging and fishing as the major means of livelihood. They are divided into local groups and live in large semi-permanent community huts, where 50-60 persons can easily sleep. But when they move out in search of games or food, they live in small family huts deep in the forest. They live on wild pigs, big monitor lizards, fish, molluscs, honey, fruits and tubers. They use small fishing nets along with bows and arrows. Leaf ornaments and bark chestguards are still used by the Jarawa (Sarkar, 1993: 3-4). The first successful contact with the Jarawa could be made in March 1979 at Chota Ling Bang in the Middle Andaman. The contacted Jarawa group consisted of 35 persons, including men, women and children. Out of them, 25 persons including 12 men had come to spend some time in *Adi Basera* in Port Blair (Bhat, n.d.: 83). But such contacts with the Jarawa living in Jirktang and Tirur area of south Andaman is yet to be established (Sarkar, 1993: 4). Even where contact has been established, it is not uncommon to come across reports of frequent encounter between the Jarawa and others.

The Onge

The Onge also belongs to the Negrito stock and inhabit the island of Little Andaman, situated towards the southern most part of the Andaman group of islands and at a distance of about 66 nautical miles south of Port Blair (Sarkar, 1993: 4). Their number has shrunk from an estimated 700 in the 1860s, to 150 in 1951 and just under 100 at present (Weber, 1998: 22). They came into contact with outsiders way back in 1886. In 1890s M.V.Portman could manage to pacify them and establish contact, since when the Onge are mostly peaceful. Until 1967 they were the sole occupants of this tiny island with an area of about 731 sq. km. But the resettlement of Bengali refugees from erstwhile East Pakistan, Tamils from Sri Lanka, and Nicobarese from Car Nicobar pushed them into the interior. Before their resettlement in 1974 in Dugong Creek and South Bay regions by the Andaman Administration, they were divided into three distinct local semi-nomadic groups. Similarly, they had divided the island into three distinct resource zones with natural boundaries like small rivers or creeks, and were operating in their respective zones without encroaching into other's territories (Danda and Mukherjee, 1993: 49). All the territorial groups were headed by their respective leaders. The community life was very much democratic with utmost respect for individual freedom. Advice of the leaders and not the order was sought only at the time of acute necessity (Cipriani, 1966: 18). Their main food consisted of pork, turtle, dugong, fish, crabs, molluscs etc. besides tubers, berries and raw honey. Cooking of fish, meat, roots and jack fruits is done by putting them on fire. They learned domestication of dogs, which help them in chasing the game. During rainy season members of each local group were returning to their large semi-permanent community huts. In other seasons, they were moving with their families in the forest or near the seashore in search of food, when they were living in very small temporary thatched huts. The Onge men usually go for hunting, fishing and engage themselves in construction of huts and preparation of dug out canoe. Their women go to the forest for collecting roots, tubers and fire wood, besides their responsibility of rearing the young children (Sarkar, 1993: 5). Both men and women among the Onge shave their heads. The body is painted with white clay to get rid of the insect bite. Red paints on the body are for medicinal purpose. The Onge women wear a fibrous tassel made out of fine germinal apex of a particular plant. It hangs around the waist and over the hips (Das and Rath, 1991: 25). Ever since their resettlement by the Andaman Administration, their traditional food habit has undergone profound changes. They mostly subsist on Government supply of ration like rice and flour, but occasionally go for hunting and collecting to supplement their diet. They collect honey mostly to sell in the co-operative societies for an additional cash income. Because of their contact with outsiders for a relatively long time, their level of acculturation is higher than that of the Sentinelese and the Jarawa (Sarkar, 1993: 5).

The Great Andamanese

Another indigenous Negrito group in the Andaman islands is that of the Great Andamanese. Originally they were divided into 10 local groups and were scattered all over the Andaman islands from the North to the South. They are now about 25, divided into only 3 local groups, although at the time of first contact during the establishment of the Second Penal Settlement in 1858, their number was about 3500 (Sarkar, 1993: 6). The Andamanese literally became extinct with the establishment of the penal settlements. As per 1981 Census, their number was reduced to 28. Now they are all intermixed, while the 10 original local groups are lost in oblivion. They have a short stature and extremely frizzly hair with bronze or sooty black skin colour (Das and Rath, 1991: 20). Before their resettlement in 1970 on the Strait Island, their local groups were independent and autonomous. Within their territories of operation, they were living a semi-nomadic life searching for food. They were depending on hunting, fishing, collection of shells etc. for sale or barter. They did not practice agriculture, horticulture or had proficiency in craft of any kind. Even they did not know domestication of dogs, which was introduced to them in 1658 (Das and Rath, 1991: 22). After the contact, they took up menial jobs and inter-community marriage increased. They are largely dependent upon Government supply of ration food materials, although occasionally they set out for hunting or fishing.

The Shompen

The Shompen is an indigenous group, which has kept itself away from the invaders thus maintaining its separate existence, inhabits the Great Nicobar Island and is believed to be the last survivors of the Malay race (Das and Rath, 1991:40). Its members are racially and linguistically different from the Andaman tribes, about whom we discussed above. The Shompen inhabit the interior forest area of the island and are constantly in touch with the Nicobarese of coastal Great Nicobar. Their living area could be divided into 4 distinct geographical zones within the island, such as, (a) Northern zone covering Trinket Bay, Laful Bay and Zhabu Nalla, (b) Northwestern zone covering the Dogmar and the Alexandra river basins, (c) Southwestern zone covering Kokean, Koshintown and Pulobha regions, and (d) Central region covering the Galathia river basin and camps around Shompen hut complex (Awardi, 1990: 28). These groups show some variations in their material culture (Awardi, 1993: 149) and are at different levels of contact with the outsiders. They prefer to live close to the source of fresh water, where they grow pandanus (Palmyra palm), arecanut, citrus, coconut, betel leaves, sweet potato, banana, papaya, tobacco, yams etc. However, pandanus is their staple food. They rear pigs and hunt wild boars. They also fish with the help of spear type harpoons. They are divided into small local groups of 5-6 families and resort to semi-nomadism for food. The resource area for each local group varies from 5-10 km and they live in community huts. Each settlement with a few families owns a fruit garden and it is the common property of the settlement. They live both in permanent pile dwellings and in temporary small huts. With the resettlement of the families of the ex-service personnel in Great Nicobar and consequent clearing of large patches of forest, the traditional resource zones of the Shompen have been greatly curtailed. Since the Shompen did not like to move towards the coast due to the presence of the Nicobarese there, they are now most susceptible to outside intervention with the reduction of the forest coverage (Sarkar, 1993: 7-8).

Problems of the Andaman Tribes

The year 1858 A.D. has a special significance in the history of the Andaman islands, in which isolation of these islands was broke open and the first outsiders made their presence felt in the pristine habitats of the indigenous communities (Sarkar, 1993: 9; Singh, 1982; Weber, 1998: 21 etc.). When the pro-independence movement in India began with the historic "Sepoy Mutiny" of 1857 A.D., there was no room in the existing jails in the Indian mainland to house thousands of freedom fighters from different parts of the country. Therefore, the British colonial Government looked for an isolated place away from the Indian mainland to drive away these jailed fighters. At that time, the Andaman islands were found to be most suitable place with their "... hostile natives, atrocious climate, surrounded by reefs and a large expanse of stormy seas" (Weber, 1998: 21) for solitary confinement of the convicts. The convicts were sent out to these islands and the British problem was temporarily solved; but that was the beginning of the end of the world from the point of view of the Andamanese indigenous communities and cultures. According to Sarkar (1993), the typical problems these island communities face since then could be broadly divided into two types. The first is the socio-economic problems consequent upon waves of migration into these islands and establishment of new settlements on the hitherto exclusive tribal territories; and the second is the problem of population decline or depopulation among the native inhabitants. A third problem could be added to the above two, namely, the psychological problem, which relates to the cultural invasions by the non-indigenous communities and retention of ethnic and cultural identities of the indigenous populations in these islands.

As discussed earlier, the most pressing problem that the small indigenous populations of the Andaman and Nicobar Islands face today is the large-scale migration of people from the Indian mainland, which continued since 1858 with the establishment of the Second Penal Settlement. First, it was the convicts of both the sexes and the jail staff who began populating the islands and efforts to contact the native Andamanese also began. There are also evidences that tribals from Chotanagpur and adjoining areas migrated into the islands from 1906 onwards. The migration was under the patronage of the R.C. Missionary with the Head Quarters at Ranchi; and these Ranchi labourers, as they were popularly called, were used to work in the forest, P.W.D., marine and wood industries located in these islands (Verma, O.P., 1976: 114). Their number was more than 15000, when Vidyarthi (1976: 8) visited the islands in February 1976 and named them as "builders of the modern Andaman". The Ranchi labourers were drawn from the tribes of the Oraon, Munda, Kharia and others, who continued to retain their traditional social and religious practices in the Andaman islands (see Verma, 1976: 114-123 for details).

Although the penal settlement was abolished sometimes after the independence, Government of India used these islands for resettling the refugees from the erstwhile East Pakistan and Sri Lanka. In fact, resettlement of Begali refugees started in the South Andaman since 1949 and in the Middle Andaman since 1964. In Little Andaman the refugees from these two countries were resettled in the year 1967 in Hut Bay and in neighbouring settlements. In the early 1970s the Great Nicobar island was occupied by 303 families of ex-service personnel of the Indian Armed Forces along the east-west road from Campbell Bay to Indira point (Sarkar, 1993: 13).

In the 1970s, Government of India recognized the strategic importance of these islands, which are mid-way between South Asia and Southeast Asia, with the establishment of the Indian Air Force Base on Car Nicobar and Indian Navy Base on different islands. This period also witnessed the establishment of Satellite Training Stations and setting up of joint military command for use by the Indian defense forces. The potential of the bay islands as strong naval bases and for the promotion of naval, fishing and associated industries were particularly recognized (Das and Rath, 1991: 13). The personnel required for these establishments gradually populated large and small islands of the Andaman and Nicobar groups. This is in addition to the Government employees to take charge of all the Departments and their families.

Migration of people in the post-independence period and development of infrastructure for them resulted in further migration of labourers and reduction of the forest cover in the islands. With the new settlements coming up, the traditional resource areas for the tribal communities reduced drastically, making their traditional practices of hunting and foraging no more sustainable. Wild pig populations, on which some of these tribes depended to a large extent, declined considerably due to uninhibited poaching by the outsiders, thus denying natural food supply to them. This problem is in sharp contrast with that faced by the tribes in the Indian mainland. In case of the latter, the tribes moved further into deep forests and mountains to continue with their traditional means of subsistence. But in case of the islands, there was no more vacant forest left for the tribes to get pushed into.

In the pre-independence period, convicts from the Indian mainland, the jail staff and other supporting population in the service sector were resettled in the Andaman islands, causing colossal loss to the natural resources in the islands. The convicts in the islands were involved in clearing land and cultivating them, lumbering, fishing and building roads. In fact, most of them settled in the islands on completion of their sentences (Singh 1975-76). The prisoners were encouraged to marry the fellow female convicts and settle, as the tribal women were not preferred for marriage. On completion of certain number of years in confinement with the demonstration of good behaviour, the convicts were allowed to settle down permanently in the islands, and they were popularly called as "free ticket holders" (Majumdar, 1975: 29). "Thus, the Pathans from North-West Frontier Province, Bhatus from M.P., Mopla rebels from Kerala, Burmese rebels from Chingurin (Upper Burma), Afghans and a host of others became the compatriots of this natural prison house and eventually settled down in various settlements around Port Blair ..." (Das and Rath, 1991: 11-12).

In the post-independence period, the magnitude of migration was still more, because of setting up of administrative offices, accommodating refugees from other countries and creating infrastructure for them. Migration of these people had a spiralling effect, which resulted in further migration of labourers. The gravity of this problem can be realized from the population variation in each decade in the islands from the table 3.1 given below.

Increase in the island population by more than double between 1951 and 1961 (+105.19%) is evidently due to large-scale exodus of refugees from other countries. The settlements of the Bengali refugees in the South and Middle Andaman were established in the traditionally inhabited Jarawa territories. Construction of Andaman Trunk Road connecting North Andaman with the South forced them to get further pushed inside. Construction of labour camps, clearing forests and blasting of explosives must have created a state of panic among the tribes. Consequent upon these developments, Jarawas now live in an area of about 309 sq. miles in the Western coast, which is declared by the Government as "Reserved Area" under tribal regulations, into which entry of the non-Jarawas is strictly prohibited (Chanda, 1976: 64). In 1967, when the Tamil refugees from Sri Lanka poured into these islands, they were also resettled there. Non-tribal settlements came up in the Little Andaman, which was the original abode of the Onge. Sarkar

Table 3.1: Population of Andaman and Nicobar Islands from 1901 to1991

Year	Total Population in the Islands	% of decadal variation
1901	24649	+7.34
1911	26459	+2.37
1921	27086	+8.78
1931	29463	+14.61
1941	33768	–8.28
1951	30974	+105.19
1961	63548	+81.17
1971	115133	+63.93
1981	188741	+48.70
1991	280661	+44.33
2000*	405100	——

* Projected Populations
Source: Gazetteers of India

notes that in Middle Andaman about 200 Jarawas live amidst 31,359 population, and in Little Andaman about 100 Onges live with 7,114 other population, indicating their minority status in their own habitat which they were inhabiting since generations (Sarkar, 1993: 11). This situation led to very unhealthy competition between the non-tribals and the tribes. The latter with very simple technology had to compete with the people from outside, equipped with better technology in utilizing the forest and marine resources for subsistence. This was a competition between unequal technologies, putting the Onge and the Jarawa in great disadvantage. Similarly, resettlement of 303 families of ex-service personnel at the fringe of the Shompen territory on the Great Nicobar not only squeezed the tribal resource base, but also created an unhealthy competition between the tribals and the non-tribals (Sarkar, 1993: 16 17).

More than the problem of overpopulation and resulting loss of resource base of the tribal population, there is the problem of depopulation among the tribes. The Great Andamanese are the worst sufferers in this respect. At the time of the establishment of the Second Penal Settlement their number was about 3500, which is reduced to just 28 at the end of 1987 (Sarkar, 1993: 17).

Table 3.2: Population decline among the tribes

	1901	1911	1921	1931	1941	1951	1961	1971	1981	1995•
Tmanese	625	455	209	90	—	23	19	24	27	37
anelese	572•	631•	346•	250	—	150•	129	112	97	99
pen	468•	114•	114•	70•	—	50•	500•	275•	200•	>200
	117•	117•	117•	50•	—	—	50•	82•	100•	80
	348•	375•	375•	200•	—	20•	70	92	214	—

• Indicates estimated population figure *(Source:* Sarkar, 1993: 17)
•• Estimation by Weber (www.andaman.org).

The above Table 3.2 is the testimony of the gloomy picture of depopulation among all the Negrito tribes and the Shompen. Mann (n.d) has attributed several reasons for this problem. One of the reasons of depopulation is because of numerous encounters between the tribals and the armed forces from outside, frequently killing the ill-equipped young natives. Another reason of depopulation, as proposed by Mann is the induced habit of addiction to opium and alcohol. Probably the most dreadful reason of depopulation is sterility among the native women, for most of them being the victim of veneral diseases contracted by the outside population. There is also another hypothesis that consumption of Discorea tubers by the natives could be contributing to the loss of fertility among the women (Das and Rath, 1991: 25), which needs thorough probing. The natives, however, have the belief that a barren woman faces the wrath of different spirits. Environmental changes also contributed to the susceptibility of the tribals to various diseases. For example, forest clearance led to high incidence of Malaria. Because of their low immunity to diseases, the tribals have been suffering from bronchial-pulmonary infections, measles and smallpox etc. Foregoing their customary diet and accepting the ration food provided by the Government is also one of the reasons for high mortality rate among the Andaman tribes (Mann, 1976: 37-46).

Cipriani (1966) draws our attention to the problem of infertility among the Andamanese tribes, which has since been proved wrong. For example, Malhotra and Awaradi (1981) estimate that mean fecundity among the Andamanese mothers is 3.5 per mother, when the All India average stands at 3.76 pregnancies per mother, as per the Census report of 1971. But it is observed that there is more casualties in later infancy or early childhood than during the neo-natal period. Although there are conflicting views based on micro studies among selected tribal populations regarding demographic problems, there is not much room for cross-examining these findings, as the tribes are apprehensive of the research teams and are hostile towards them.

Problems of health and nutrition are not less alarming among the tribal populations of the Andaman and Nicobar islands. It is found that the Great Andamanese and the Onge suffer from Tuberculosis. Cases of anemia are not rare to find with hemoglobin value less than 9 g/dl. Studies, however, do not show deficiency of Vitamins. But the situation is very different among the resettled population, which depend upon the supply of ration by the Government. In their natural environment while for the hunter-foragers the dietary intake per day is 2618 calorie and the daily consumption of protein is 136.5 gm (Verma, 1976: 20), the resettled population do not get adequate protein in ration food, although milk powder is regularly supplied to them (Jain, 1981). In one of the surveys among the Onge, Venkatesan arrives at a similar conclusion. Venkatesan is of the opinion that "Their (the Onges') traditional dietary pattern deteriorated with the advent of 'resettlement' and introduction of cash economy which led (to) an inadequate protein intake" (Venkatesan, 1993: 514). He also opines that significant age difference between the Onge husband and the wife also contributes to depopulation among the tribals (ibid.). Rapid encroachment into the food reserve areas of the tribes by the non-tribal outsiders and their very traditional level of technology to cope up with new challenges literally push these already endangered tribes into a state of extinction, which is a matter of concern for all.

Inter-tribal and tribal-nontribal hostilities in the Andamans have been endemic. Inter-tribal hostility is probably due to competition for scarce terrestrial and marine resources, and due to proximity of the Great Andamanese to the outside population. From the British period till recently, the Great Andamanese have been the guides to locate and make contacts with other tribal groups. However, it is said, "For the past 1300 years and possibly much longer, the Andamanese have been hostile to outsiders. Ships trying to replenish their fresh water, looking for wood to make repairs or just seeking shelter from storms, were attacked just as was any mariner unfortunate enough to be wrecked on one of the many Andamanese reefs" (Weber, 1998: 21). The reason behind hostility seems to be nothing other than psychological and to show the tribal disapproval of the presence of outsiders. Until about 130 years ago, raid for Negrito slaves in these islands was not uncommon by traders from outside, which is why the fear psychosis is still in the tribal mind. When the British established the Penal Settlement and thereafter, many Negritos were killed in encounters or were captured alive. This must have sent shock waves among the tribes to keep away from the outsiders. During the Second World War, these islands were under the occupation of the Japanese forces from 1942 to 1945, till they came under the British. Towards the end of the Japanese occupation, there is evidence of mass killing (Vidyarthi, 1976: 1), further shocking the tribes to face the outsiders, much less to consider them as friends. There was indiscriminate bombing during the War, killing the innocent tribals and devastating their natural eco-system. After independence, there were waves of migrations, the immigrants forcibly occupying tribal resource bases and establishing their settlements at the cost of the tribal livelihood. Therefore, there is every reason for the tribals to resent and become hostile not to allow the outside population to enter into their places of habitation. Precisely for these, the Jarawa and the Sentinelese continue to defend their respective territories against the colonisers by expressing their hostility. Even when the intention of the contact parties is to befriend the tribals, the latter are still suspicious of others, because of these historical reasons, and the physical, cultural and mental shocks they had to undergo all these years.

Developmental Interventions in the Andamans: Problems and Possibilities

Recently, an enthusiastic lawyer has initiated a public litigation case against the Government alleging that there is lack of efforts all these years in bringing these endangered tribes in the islands into the national mainstream (as reported by Survival International, London). Anthropologists, however, advise to move cautiously in the matter of tribal development and administration. This is keeping in mind the tactics of forcible capture of the natives, housing them in Port Blair and releasing them with huge gifts, adopted by the British. This has proved disastrous as one of the champions of this tactics, M.V.Portman, has confessed that forcible capture of the Sentinelese by him in 1880 was "… hardly the right way to go about establishing friendly relations" (Weber, 1998: 23). Therefore, they suggest that at least the tribal right over resources be restored as a first step, honouring the U.N. Resolution 47/135 of December 1992, and I.L.O. convention No. 169 etc. (see Bhengra et al., 1999), and they be allowed to lead their own life the way they like. They invoke the policy of "Tribal Panchasheel" as suggested by Late Pandit Nehru for the preservation of tribal culture and heritage (see Misra, 1995). At best, they opine, let the Government act as the catalyst in the process of development of these tribes, while the latter decide their own course of action. But the question remains whether the role of the Government should be paternalistic as it has been since the independence, or there ought to be some kind of voluntary participation by the indigenous communities.

At this point, it is appropriate to look at the post-independence development programmes for the tribes in the Andaman and Nicobar islands. Since all the Negrito tribes in the Andaman islands are primarily hunters and gatherers, including a fair percentage of the Nicobarese, the Andaman and Nicobar Administration has envisaged to have a single Integrated Tribal Development Project for all these island populations together. Although Nicobar district is the area of operation for the sub-plan schemes, special care is being taken for the Negrito tribes, making financial provisions under the State Plan and under Special Central Assistance of Government of India. Since the 6th Five-year Plan, a separate Five-year Sub-plan is being implemented for the primitive tribes of the islands (Das and Rath, 1991: 60-61).

The process of post-independence welfare measures for tribal development in the Andaman and Nicobar islands began in 1949, when the Forest Department of Andaman took the initiative of putting the Andamanese together on the Bluff Island to protect them from the hostile Jarawa and other non-tribals. In order to protect the tribals from the exploitation of the non-tribal outsiders, the Andaman and Nicobar Islands (Protection of Aboriginal Tribes) Regulation was promulgated in 1956, under the provision of which the areas inhabited by the tribes were declared as "Primitive Tribes Reserve Areas". No non-tribal, under this Regulation, is supposed to enter into the reserve areas without prior permission of the Deputy Commissioner of the district concerned (Das and Rath, 1991: 61-62). Under this provision an area of about 206 sq. miles has been reserved for the Jarawa on the West Coast, based on the recommendations of a study team of the Planning Commission. However, there was no welfare scheme proposed for these areas (Sarkar, 1993: 27).

The welfare measures during the earlier Five-year Plans were mostly confined to contact the hitherto secluded tribes by offering them food and other material gifts. During the 2nd Five-year Plan period (1956-60), a fair weather dispensary was established in the Little Andaman. During this period, food packets were dropped for the Jarawa and the Sentinelese and preliminary attempts were made to contact the Shompen. In the 3rd Five-year Plan (1961-65), 100 acres of land were brought under coconut plantation for the benefit of the Onge. In the 4th Five-year Plan, provisions were made to resettle 19 Great Andamanese on the Strait Island in 1970 with all modern facilities. Gradually, they were employed in non-technical jobs. A transit home for them was set up in 1976 in Port Blair to accommodate them during transit. Until 1975, these welfare activities were formulated and implemented by the Tribal Welfare Department of the Andaman Government. But since 1976, an NGO, Andaman Adim Janajati Vikas Samiti (AAJVS), is looking after the welfare schemes in the islands. The objectives of AAJVS are: "(1) To protect the health and prevent the extinction of the primitive tribal groups, the Great Andamanese, the Onge, the Shompen, the Jarawa and the Sentinelese, inhabiting Andaman and Nicobar islands; (2) To promote the economic and social development of the said primitive tribal communities; (3) To take a comprehensive view of the problems of these tribal welfare programmes in pursuance of the national policy for their development; and (4) To develop measures for coordination of Governmental, institutional and voluntary action for protection of their economic and social environments, essential for their survival and growth" (Sarkar, 1993: 28).

During the 7th Five-year Plan, provisions have been made for basic tribal welfare in the islands. "Apart from the efforts of the Andaman and Nicobar Administration and Central Government for modernization of tribals especially the primitive ones, much work is being done by Andaman Adim Janjati Vikas Samiti for promoting the welfare of the tribals. The Samiti is trying its best to prevent the extinction of the remaining Negrito primitive tribes in Andaman" (Das and Rath, 1991: 62).

Although huge expenditure is made towards development of these endangered tribes, problems still continue even now. Depopulation and high rate of infant mortality are haunting these people. They still suffer from anemia, tuberculosis, malaria, sex-born diseases etc. They do not care much for the coconut gardens, and dairy and piggery units established for them. Adult education centres and balwadis are being closed down. The psychological trauma and apprehensiveness against the outsiders still continue, which are reflected in their non-acceptance of any body from outside in their islands.

Why is it that despite a huge budgetary allocation and sympathy of the local administration and NGOs, the Negrito tribes of the Andaman islands lead a life of alienation and desperation? Why hostility still continues notwithstanding the intention of the contact parties to befriend the Jarawa and the Sentinelese? Why there is no perceptible change despite five decades of "careful" tribal development plans for these groups of Negrito tribes? There is obviously no single answer to these questions.

It is established from the development trends that mere paternalistic attitude of the non-Andamanese for the development of these indigenous populations will not bring about any desired result, no matter what amount of money is pumped into the tribal development budget. What is foremost is to rid them off their psychological problems of fear and suspicion, which gained ground over centuries of exploitation by different groups of people. But how to go about with making the tribes more confident of themselves and others? The first step in this direction should be to restore the equilibrium between community life of the tribals and their ecology. It must be admitted that the tribals are minorities in their own habitats. A recent estimate suggests that "... for each Onge, there are at least 120 outsiders here and this imbalance is rapidly increasing. What more needs to be said?" (Sekhsaria, 2000: 41). In order to overcome this problem, there should be sufficient legislation to restore the lost land by outside encroachment to the tribals and to allow them to continue with their traditional economic activities and community life. Establishment of colonies for labourers and refugees should be done away with, and legislation should be made to ban outsiders from entering into the tribal reserves without a valid permission, where it does not exist. Only after these confidence-building steps are taken, concrete developmental programmes could be formulated and implemented with the participation of the local communities. Mutual trust and cooperation is most essential for saving these communities from extinction and making them gradually developed.

There is an urgent need to strengthen the tribal institutions and empower them to effectively participate in the development processes. Their knowledge of environment should be utilized for the furtherance of the economic well-being. A gradual withdrawal of the gift culture or free food supply is essential to make them feel independent. This could be done by providing them with adequate moral and technical support. As education is the basic foundation of development, efforts should be made to spread education by mutual consent and convenience rather than by forcing the tribals to adapt to the formal schooling system all of a sudden. In the health front, a lot has to be done. In a recent report, it is stated that Tuberculosis is still a persistent problem with the Jarawa and other tribes (see the reference to the Jarawa Conference of 1999 in the Andaman website). Health care for mother and children could be ensured by regular visits of health workers to the tribal settlements. All the development programmes need to be monitored and evaluated on a regular basis by an autonomous research body, which should advise the administration regarding the implementation of the development programmes. Development of the tribes should be measured in terms of improvement in the quality of life rather than by the amount of money spent in the programmes. Since all these tribes live at different levels of acculturation, there is a need to devise suitable development programmes for each one of them, instead of a single overarching one that might contradict their basic values. It is most important to assure them that their traditional culture and community life do not get completely annihilated by the development interventions (Sarkar, 1993; Sharma, 1976; Vidyarthi, 1976 etc.). Although tribal problems in the Andaman and Nicobar islands is not entirely different from those elsewhere in the Indian mainland and hence cannot be delinked entirely, because of their extreme sensitiveness, development interventions among these endangered tribal communities need to be done with caution and care.

REFERENCES

Awardi, S.A. 1990. *Computerized Master Plan (1991-2021) for the Welfare of the Primitive Tribes of Andaman and Nicobar Islands*. Port Blair: Andaman-Nicobar Administration.

_____. 1993. "People of 'Wood-Age' - Crafts and Material Culture of the Shompen of the Great Nicobar Island," (pp.149-162) in Basu, Arabinda *et al.* (eds.), *Andaman and Nicobar Islanders: Studies on Small Populations*, Calcutta: Indian Anthropological Society.

Balakrishnan, N.B. and N.G. Nair 1977. "New Records of Plants from Andaman and Nicobar Islands," *Indian Forestry*, 103: 638-640.

Basu, Arabinda *et al* (eds.). 1993. *Andaman and Nicobar Islanders: Studies on Small Populations*. Calcutta: Indian Anthropological Society.

Basu, B.K. (1990) *The Onge*, Calcutta: Seagull Books.

Bhat, V.V. (n.d.). "Hostile Jarawas and Sentinelese of Andaman," (pp.75-84) in G.P.Reddy and V.Sudersen (eds), *Studies in Island Cultures of India*, Secunderabad: Gautami Education Society.

Bhengra, Ratnakar *et al.* 1999. *The Adivasis of India*. London: Minority Rights Group International.

Chanda, Sudhendu. 1976. "The Hostile Jarawa of Andaman and the Semi-Hostile Shompen of Great Nicobar Islands," *Journal of Social Research*, XIX (2): 64-73.

Cipriani, Lido. 1966. *The Andaman Islanders*. London: Widenfeld and Nicolson.

Danda, D.G. and Sumit Mukherjee. 1993. "A Study on Onge Population," (pp.47-68) in Arabinda Basu *et al.* (eds.), *Andaman and Nicobar Islanders: Studies on Small Populations*. Calcutta: Indian Anthropological Society.

Das, Hari Hara and R. Rath. 1991. *The Tribals of Andaman and Nicobar Islands*. New Delhi: Ashish Publishing House.

Jain, T.S. 1981 *Recommendations of the Research Team on Action Oriented Research of Primitive Tribal Communities*. New Delhi: ICMR.

Majumdar, R.C. 1975. *Penal Settlement in Andaman*. New Delhi: Ministry of Education, Government of India.

Malhotra, R. and S.A. Awardi. 1981. Socio-demographic Studies in Andamans (unpublished report). Calcutta: Anthropological Survey of India.

Mann, R.S. (n.d). *The Bay Islanders*. Bidisa: ISRAA.

_____. 1976. "Depopulation among Andaman Aborigines - An Analysis," *Journal of Social Research*, XIX (2): 37-50.

Misra, K.K. 1995. "Tribalism and National Integration," (pp.159-173) in A.K.Singh and M.K.Jabbi (eds), *Tribals in India*. New Delhi: Har-Anand Publications.

_____. 2000. "Indigenous Peoples and Development Interventions in the Andamans," (pp. 234-242) *Proceedings of the International Conference on Sustainable Development for Island Societies*, Taiwan.

Mouat, F.J. 1995 (1863). *The Andaman Islanders*. New Delhi: Mittal Publications.

Pandit, T.N. and M. Chattopadhyay. 1993. "Meeting the Sentinel Islanders: The Least Known of the Andaman Hunter-gatherers," (pp.169-178) in A. Basu *et al.* (eds.), *Andaman and Nicobar Islanders: Studies on Small Populations*. Calcutta: Indian Anthropological Society.

Radcliffe-Brown, A.R. 1922. *The Andaman Islanders*. Cambridge: Cambridge University Press.

Reddy, G.P. and V. Sudersen. (eds.). (n.d.). *Studies in Island Cultures of India*. Secunderabad: Gautami Education Society.

Sarkar, Jayanta. 1987. "Befriending the Jarawa: A Challenging Task," *Human Science*, XXXVI (1).

Sarkar, Jayanta. 1993. "Endangered Tribes and their Development in Andaman and Nicobar Islands," (pp.1-46) in A. Basu *et al.* (eds.), *Andaman and Nicobar Islanders: Studies on Small Populations*. Calcutta: Indian Anthropological Society,

Sekhsaria, Pankaj. 2000. "A History of Alienation," *The Hindu Folio*, 16 July, 40-41.

Sharma, B.D. 1976. "Approach to the Development of Onges of Little Andaman," *Journal of Social Research*, XIX (2): 25-36.

Singh, K.S. 1982. *Tribal Movements in India*. New Delhi: Manohar.

Singh, N. Iqbal. 1978. *The Andaman Story*. New Delhi: Vikas Publishing House Pvt Ltd.

Singh, Raghuvir. 1975. "The Last Andaman Islanders," *National Geographic*, 148 (1): 66-91.

Sinha, S.P. 1993. *Conflict and Tension in Tribal Society*. New Delhi: Concept Publishing Co.

Venkatesan, D. 1993. "Ecology, Food and Nutrition: The Onge Foragers of the Andaman Tropical Forest," (pp. 505-514) in C.M.Hladik *et al.* (eds.), *Tropical Forests, People and Food*. Paris: UNESCO and The Parthenon Publishing Group.

Verma, I.C. 1976. "Health Problems of Tribal Communities in Andaman and Nicobar Islands," *Journal of Social Research*, Special Number, XIX (2): 16-24.

Verma, O.P. 1976. "The Working Composition of the Ranchi Tribal Labourers in Andaman and Nicobar Islands," *Journal of Social Research*, Special Number, XIX (2): 114-123.

Vidyarthi, L.P. (ed.). 1976. "The Tribes of Andaman & Nicobar Islands," *Journal of Social Research*, Special Number, XIX (2)

Weber, George. 1998. "The Andamanese Language Family: A Contribution to the Centenary of M.V.Portman's Work," *Language Today*, October, 18-23.

FOUR

THE IMPACT OF DISPLACEMENT ON TRIBAL WOMEN

WALTER FERNANDES

An estimated 300 lakh persons have been displaced in India since 1951 in the name of national development. But a national policy on rehabilitation is being formulated only now and is yet to be promulgated. The 1998 draft has many positive points but it is weak on questions concerning women. Most projects that have a resettlement package show the same weakness. In most of them the displaced persons (DPs) are taken as a homogeneous category. Recent projects give some importance to categories like the tribals. But women are by and large ignored. And yet, studies indicate that they pay a higher price of development than men do. It is true about all ethnic groups. But their situation is the worst among the marginalized categories. In this paper, therefore, we shall make an effort to study the impact of displacement on women from these groups, with specific focus on tribal women. This paper is based mostly on the studies we have completed on development-induced displacement in Orissa, Andhra Pradesh and Goa.

Tribal Women: Tradition and Modernity

We choose to analyse tribal women's status because the estimates available till now show that not fewer than 40 per cent of the DPs/PAPs of the last four decades are tribals who form only 8.08 per cent of the country's population (Fernandes, 1998: 265). Three aspects concerning them are rarely attended to while discussing deprival by development projects and in policy making. The first is that the natural resources from which the tribals are alienated through displacement are the very foundation of their economy, culture, social systems and political structures. Secondly, they are common property resources (CPRs), not individual property before their alienation from the tribals. Thirdly, the tribal woman had a higher status than her high caste counterpart had. Both her status and children's upbringing depended on abundant resources and the partial control she exercised over them. Alienation from them results not merely in economic impoverishment but also in deprival of community support, i.e. weakening of their community systems. The downward social mobility follows. But the few rehabilitation packages that exist do not go beyond the economic factor to community and cultural support.

To understand it, we repeat that the tribal woman owed her relatively high status both to the abundance of resources and the clear division in their societies between the family and social spheres. The family was traditionally her sphere of influence. The man represented it in the social sphere. The mother had more decision-making power in the family economy, production and social relations than her upper caste counterpart did. For example, she took the decision concerning children's upbringing and marriage. The boy or girl after choosing a life partner first approached her. Only after she agreed to the match could the father approach the village council made up of men, for its consent. An example of her control over the family economy is shifting cultivation that was traditionally the sustenance of about 25 per cent of Indian tribals. In settled agriculture the man owns the plot and takes most decisions about production and division of work. In shifting cultivation, on the contrary, men and women share the burden. Traditionally the village council took a decision on which area the village was to cultivate during the year and how much was to be allotted to each family according to the number of mouths to feed. After it the man as the head of the family chose the plot it would cultivate. The woman then took charge of it and organised production and work (Fernandes and Menon, 1987: 72-90).

The fact that she controlled the family economy is the main reason why her status depended on abundant resources. That was also the basis of the family's sustenance. It also meant that the woman depended more on these resources than the man did, as such she had a bigger vested interest in treating them as renewable, i.e. in their sustainable use. This vested interest, her relatively high status and the control she exercised over the family economy depended on the resource as a community asset, not on individual property (Pathy, 1988: 26).

Much of it has changed during the decades of planned development. Displacement has resulted in the family being alienated from the resource, its sustenance. From the economic point of view it involves impoverishment. But because the community had built its culture and identity around these resources, their alienation also results in the weakening of the community support systems and the culture of sustainable development and mutual dependence that was dependent on it. To the woman it has meant the loss of the very foundation of her higher status.

Women's Subordination in the Economic Sphere

Women's situation is aggravated not merely by the fact of displacement but also because despite claims to the contrary, rehabilitation of the DPs has been extremely limited. Some (e.g. Hansda, 1983: 23) state that fewer than 25 per cent of those displaced during the first three decades of the country's planned development have been rehabilitated. Recent studies show that the situation has not changed substantially since then (e.g. Mahapatra, 1990: 90; Fernandes, 1998: 251). To the tribal and other assetless rural poor communities who have traditionally depended on the CPRs or have been surviving by rendering services to the village as a community, the first result of this neglect is economic impoverishment, followed by loss of social status. Since these resources are a source of nutrition for the family, they have traditionally been the basis of the family economy, of the woman's work outside the family and of her social relations. With their alienation from the family, the woman is unable to work outside. But the project that deprives her of these resources, does not give her a job. Thus she is reduced to being a housewife alone, unable to make an economic contribution to the family economy.

Displacement and the Tribal Woman's Economic Status

The tribal woman's status change is not limited to displacement without resettlement. Even when resettled, she cannot hope to continue the economic autonomy she had in the past. If resettlement is land-based, it is allotted in the name of individuals, invariably men, considered heads of families, except in women-headed households. She had decision-making power in the family as long as the resources belonged to the community as a whole. She as the main decision-maker in the family, controlled production as part of the family. With individual *patta* becoming the only form of land ownership after resettlement, this power is transferred to the man and from him to his son. The woman ceases to be the main decision-maker in the family economy and becomes dependent on men (Thekkekara, 1993).

Moreover, the tribals receive very low compensation. Much of what the tribals live on is CPRs. For example, among the 11 representative projects we studied in Orissa, two were plants owned by the National Aluminium Corporation (NALCO), one in the tribal majority Damanjodi in Koraput district and the other in the upper caste dominated Angul district. In the former 58 per cent of all land taken over, and more than 65 per cent of what was acquired from the tribals, was CPRs. In the latter it was only 18 per cent. The CPRs that are tribal sustenance, are considered State property according to the principle of eminent domain that governs land laws. So they received no compensation for it. The tribal areas are administratively neglected, are considered backward. Compensation is based on the market price. So they receive very low compensation for the little individual land they own. For example, those who lost land to the Damanjodi plant received an average of Rs. 2,700 per acre while in Angul it was Rs 25,000 (Fernandes and Raj, 1992: 90). The same is seen in our study in AP. The tribals who are a little over 6 per cent of the State's population, are 27 per cent of its 32 lakh DPs/ PAPs, 1951-1995. Most of them being CPR dependants received no compensation. In our sample of 627 from 14 representative projects in AP, all those who had to resettle themselves are tribals and Dalits (Fernandes *et al.*, 2000: 79 and 93). Besides, the CPRs the very source of their livelihood are not replaced. The woman whose task it is to ensure regular food supply to the family, is left without this sustenance.

The tribals are thus forced to spend much of the compensation received on daily needs with no possibility of long-term investment. It also leaves very little for the woman to maintain the household. In Table 4.1 we give the manner in which 562 out of the 800 respondent families in our study of 11 representative projects in Orissa spent their compensation. The situation is similar in all the States we studied. So to make comparison easy, in all four Tables we give data only from Orissa. One can see that the Dalits (SCs) and tribals (STs) are forced to spend most of it on daily consumer needs and in the case of those who have not been resettled, on house building. On the other hand the "others," i.e. persons belonging to the middle and upper castes, use it for long term investment. Most of the "others" who spend it on house building are in Angul district where their land was acquired but were not displaced. As such, investment on the house is for its improvement with a higher status in view. The DPs are mainly Dalits and tribals and they have to invest on a house for survival, not for a higher status.

Table 4.1: Caste/tribe-wise difference in spending compensation by district in Orissa

Sl. No.		Angul				Koraput			
		SC	ST	Oth	Total	SC	ST	Oth	Total
01	Land Purchase	14	12	36	62	7	11	11	29
02	Land Development	3	—	19	22	—	4	1	5
03	House Building	14	2	31	47	39	99	21	159
04	Purchase Gold	3	—	3	6	17	23	5	45
05	Household Art	10	—	2	12	58	180	45	283
06	Consumer Art	18	8	26	52	47	138	40	225
07	Social Function	30	6	68	104	20	46	34	—
		Keonjhar				Whole Sample			
		SC	ST	Oth	Total	SC	ST	Oth	Total
01	Land Purchase	—	—	1	1	21	23	48	92
02	Land Development	0	7	5	12	3	11	25	39
03	House Building	—	42	12	54	53	143	64	260
04	Purchase Gold	—	—	1	1	20	23	8	51
05	Household Art	1	56	20	77	69	236	67	372
06	Consumer Art	1	44	11	56	66	190	77	333
07	Social Functions	6	—	6	6	50	58	102	210

N.B.: This refers to 562 respondents who have received compensation

Additional Work Less Food

Displacement and deprival of the resource, more often than not result in additional workload for the woman, with less food made available to the family. For example, in a study on the role of tribal women in the forest economy we saw that consequent upon deforestation the situation of women had deteriorated more than that of men even among the tribals. While tribal women have a relatively high status in their traditional society, their gender-based division of work between the social and family spheres and the higher status than what the high castes enjoyed was centred on the natural resources. While conferring a higher status on them, it also made them more dependent on these resources. Consequently, when alienated from the forest and other resources their situation deteriorates more than that of men.

One sign of this deterioration is the distance of forests and extra workload. In Orissa and Chattisgarh it had increased from around one km from the village in the 1960s, to more than five km in the 1980s (Fernandes and Menon, 1987: 72). This resulted in more hours of work, less food and greater malnutrition since children and older women are today unable to help the housewife to collect the forest produce like fruits that are basic to their nutrition. So she works more than in the past to gather less food. Deforestation also deprives her of medicinal herbs. But she is unable to visit the health centre since it is open only during the day when she has to be working in the fields or forests. Because of the extra workload, in parts of India the pregnant forest dweller woman is forced to work till a week before child delivery and begin to work within a week after it (Agarwal and Narain, 1985).

Lack of Skills and Impoverishment

Till 1986, industries and mines came under the T. N. Singh Formula 1967 that stipulated that the displacing public sector industry or mine should give a job to every family it displaced. One of its shortcomings was that it did not take women into consideration. Jobs were normally given to men, considered heads of families (Fernandes and Ganguly Thukral, 1989: 5). The tribals in general and women among them in particular, living in secluded and administratively neglected regions had less exposure to the external world than most other social groups did. In the Koraput district of Orissa, for example, the literacy of tribal men in our sample was around 20 per cent and that among women 2.3 per cent. Similar is the situation in our sample of 618 from 14 projects in AP, of 800 from 15 projects in Kerala and of 900 from 18 projects in Jaharkhand. As a result, most jobs given were unskilled and often temporary or on daily wages. Despite its shortcomings, it was a step in the right direction. But it was abandoned in 1986 because very few jobs were created after mechanisation.

But the woman could not hope to get even these unskilled jobs. On the other side she has lost access to the land and forests that provided her with the economic opportunities. So she is reduced to being a housewife alone with no opportunity to work outside the house and make a contribution to the family economy. She thus becomes dependent on her husband's income for a living. One may add that even this possibility has disappeared with the public sector enterprises abandoning the T. N. Singh Formula. It has meant further impoverishment of the tribal and other rural poor families and further marginalization of women among them.

If some skills are imparted, focus is invariably on men. For example, in our sample of 800 respondents in Orissa, 189 had a job in the project area, though not all of them in the project. 27 of them were semi-skilled. Of the 162 unskilled jobs, 79 were on a monthly salary and the rest on daily wages. Only 49 women were employed, all of them in unskilled jobs. 30 of them were on daily wages and only 19 on a monthly salary—all of them in women-headed families. Till March 1992, NALCO, Damanjodi had provided one job each to 443 families out of the 602 they had displaced in 1986. Only 25 of them were to women, all of them in women-headed families (Fernandes and Raj, 1992: 141-142). In AP only NTPC and Vishaka Steel have given some jobs, all of them to men. These data confirm our earlier findings that where a job per family is provided, almost invariably it goes to men.

Besides, in most cases women get only low status unskilled jobs because of their very poor literacy status them and much lower exposure to the external world. As stated above, literacy among tribal women in Koraput was as low as 2.3 per cent. In the Angul unit, on the contrary, most upper caste persons were deprived of land without being displaced. They have prospered after loss of land because their somewhat infertile land had fetched a higher price than what the tribals in the "backward" districts had got, as we know already from the example given above. Besides, many of their sons got semi-skilled jobs since literacy was higher among them than among the tribals and they could afford to get technical training which was not accessible to the others. In other places, for example in the Jagannathpur mines of Talcher and the Piparwar mines of Palamau in Jharkhand, a family is entitled to a job for every three acres of land it owns. At Piparwar it comes down to two acres in the case of matriculates (Sherman, 1993).

Thus those who are better off get all the benefits. They are also the village leaders. Through this measure the project gets their co-operation in displacing the rest without any protest. But very few women even of this class get many project benefits. The difference between them and tribal women is that the former are kept down by their gender-based lower status among the dominant castes. The latter experience downward social mobility because they are deprived of the natural resources that are the basis of their relatively high social status.

Displacement and Women's Social Status

Thus with the alienation of the natural resources, the woman ceases to be an economic asset to the family. Its impact is felt not in the economic field alone but also in the social arena. She ceases to be autonomous and becomes only a housewife. This change is often legitimised by the subaltern classes internalising the upper caste ideology of the woman's subjugation.

Loss of Autonomous Status

We have already stated that as a result of the loss of the assets on which their status depended, women are forced to remain at home and only look after the household, without any productive work outside. In our earlier study on the impact of deforestation on women, we had said that tribal women had complained of overwork because of the distance of forests. But in our studies on displacement 1951-1995 (which we have completed in AP, Goa, Jharkhand, Kerala and Orissa, they complain about decrease in their workload which affects their morale just as much as additional workload did (Fernandes and Raj, 1992: 155). The fact of being forced to remain at home also lays the foundation to their being reduced to the role of housewives alone. In other words, it results in their status deterioration since their relatively high status depended to a great extent on the contribution they made to the family economy.

They become dependent on men to run the family since they are the only income earners. However, even when men among them get a job, one is not certain that the woman is able to run the family properly. Men and children often absorb the value system of the dominant culture to which they are exposed through the migrant workers in the new industrial townships. So they spend more than in the past on clothes, entertainment and other trivia, thus making a relatively small amount available for the woman to run the household. In other words, social factors like such cultural contact affect women more than men. Another example is drunkenness. The traumatic experience of displacement and changeover to a new economy and culture result in a great amount of tension among men as well as women. Accepting status symbols like expensive clothes and other trinkets is one way of coping with it. Another mode is drunkenness, and we found that it is very common among the displaced whose status we studied in Orissa, Andhra Pradesh and Jharkhand. It is true mainly but not exclusively of men. In the resettlement colonies where most women have become only housewives, we found several of them getting drunk even during the day. It was obviously a coping mechanism, meant to get over the trauma of displacement and the cultural, social and economic changes that are intrinsic to it.

Many other cultural changes too have greater impact on women than on men. So mainly women complained about them in Orissa as well as in other States. After displacement they experienced changes such as tribals beginning to cut forests for firewood, changes in the food habits of men and children that make it difficult for women to maintain the family, men's drunken behaviour and more wife beating, changes in the religious practices and children abandoning their traditional practices on which depended their sustainable culture and the relatively high status women had in their community (Table 4.2).

Table 4.2: Cultural changes and women's status after displacement

Sl. No.	Problem	Males	%	Females	%	Total	%
01.	Cutting Forests	16	03.33	34	10.63	50	06.25
02.	New Clothes	31	06.46	51	15.94	82	10.25
03.	Different Food	22	04.58	42	13.13	64	08.00
04.	Drunken Behaviour	23	04.79	63	19.69	86	10.75
05.	Wife Beating	14	02.92	46	14.34	60	07.50
06.	Gambling	13	02.71	43	13.44	56	07.00
07.	Religious Practices have changed	11	02.29	36	11.25	47	05.88

N.B.: Many are multiple responses got from the 320 female and 480 male respondents in Orissa.

The nature of resettlement causes other problems. For example, very few projects provide common facilities like a place for hygienic needs. Women are expected by cultural norms, to observe greater privacy than men. Their traditional society provided proper spaces and environment for these needs. Since these spaces are not replaced in the new situation, they are unable to attend to the needs of nature. This was seen in our earlier studies too, for example the one on the working conditions of Asiad construction workers in 1982. The contractors had not provided proper housing and toilet facilities to the labourers. So about 500 families had to use a small plot for their hygienic needs. So hygiene was deplorable, and women were unable to ease themselves during the day (Fernandes, 1986: 277). We observed a similar situation in the Delhi slums (Fernandes, 1990: 97) and in many resettlement colonies in Orissa and Andhra Pradesh. For example, at Damanjodi, Koraput, NALCO has provided to the DPs, houses without toilet facilities. But no other place is available for this purpose. So the people use a plot that the neighbouring village had set aside for pasture. Quarrels are frequent and they are mainly between women (Fernandes and Raj, 1992: 135-136). The main reason for it is that while planning the project that displaces people, the project authorities bear almost exclusively economic aspects in mind. They ignore the needs of the subaltern groups and of women. They forget that actions like the morning ablutions and collecting water in the evening also have a social meaning. That is when women meet one another and share confidences. Apart from causing conflicts, not taking these aspects into consideration adds further to the woman's isolation.

Upward Mobility, Sanskritization and Women's Status

It is not merely that cultural changes are introduced. More important is the fact that as a mode of upward mobility, the family with the man as its head, adopts the mainstream upper caste customs to which women's subordination is basic. M. N. Srinivas (1966: 52) calls it Sanskritization. As a mode of upward mobility, the low castes adopt over a generation or two, upper caste gods and customs such as vegetarianism. Many go beyond adopting individual customs to internalise the dominant ideology. John Gaventa (1980: 7-30) thinks that such internalisation is the third step in the maintenance of an unequal society. The first is for the decision-makers to declare all equal before the law. Institutions are made legally available to all but access is denied to many classes by fixing the norms for access that are beyond their reach. The second step is to provide access to a few individuals of the subaltern class. For example, the school meant for the rich may admit a few from the poorer classes. But because of the cultural gap and the economic need of the child's work, most of them drop out. The dominant classes attribute it to their intellectual inadequacy, not to the economic and cultural factors, thus finding a victim blaming justification. The third is for the subaltern classes to internalise the dominant ideology. This has been substantiated in studies on caste, colonialism, women etc.

A good example of internalization is the reasons our male as well as female respondents gave to explain why women get only low paid unskilled jobs. Once again we give data (Table 4.3) only from our Orissa study though we heard these statements elsewhere too. Justifying their status as housewives alone, time and again several men as well as women justified the subordinate status of women as being natural. They stated that the woman's place is in the house and that she should not aspire for anything else. Some men insisted

Table 4.3: Attitude to women getting unskilled jobs or remaining at home

Sl.No.	Problem	Males	%	Females	%	Total	%
01.	Women Not Intelligent/interested	48	10.00	22	21.88	70	08.75
02.	Women Not Educated	34	07.08	27	08.44	61	07.63
03.	Not Capable	44	09.17	49	15.31	93	11.63
04.	Discriminated against	227	47.29	153	47.81	380	47.50
05.	Give Any Job, We need to live	25	05.21	17	05.31	42	05.25
06.	Not Applicable	67	13.96	33	10.31	100	12.50
07.	Not Available	35	07.29	19	05.94	54	06.75
	Total	480	60.00	320	60.00	800	100.00

that women did not contribute to the household since they worked neither on land nor in the project. So they should obey men who alone earned their livelihood. Some men who held even grade 4 jobs like peons did not want their wives to work as unskilled manual labourers, since it went against their status of "workers in an office." Women get only unskilled jobs though they too would be able to do skilled work with better access to education. As many as 163 (more than 25 per cnet out of the 648 respondents to whom the question was applicable and who answered it) stated either that women are not intelligent, as such not capable of being trained for skilled jobs, or that they were not interested in acquiring the skills these jobs required. So they should be satisfied with unskilled jobs. They included 71 out of 268 women, many of them tribal, who responded to this question (Fernandes and Raj, 1992: 154).

Outmigration and Women's Status

Forced outmigration is intrinsic to displacement and deprival of resources. In some cases men migrate alone, leaving women behind in the village. In other cases the whole family migrates to the urban slums. In either case, the woman feels its negative impact more than men do. To begin with outmigration of men, most scholars assume that it is exclusively economic i.e. that poverty forces them to leave their village and go in search of jobs elsewhere. But after she gained their confidence tribal women told one of our researchers that the change in men's social status is basic to it. In their traditional society, men were hunters, guardians and village council leaders. These roles have now been taken over by the State, without providing any alternative to suit their lost status. Security has been taken over by the police and the role of the village council by the panchayat. Hunting is all but banned. Men are, therefore, left with no status in the village. They try to compensate for it by migrating to another place, improving their economic status and getting absorbed into another value system and society (Menon, 1995).

As a result of outmigration, the housewife is of forced to look after the household all alone. Other men, particularly moneylenders and merchants, exploit her powerlessness by occupying her land, thus depriving her of her livelihood (Menon, 1992). Often the husband absorbs the value system of another society and returns with a second younger wife. In the traditional tribal system in which divorce was allowed, the woman would have walked out of the house and got married again. But being deprived of sustenance, she has no choice but to put up with this deviation and accept her subordinate status as *de facto* second wife (Menon, 1995).

Things do not improve much even when the whole family migrates to the urban slums. Because of their low exposure to the external society, the tribals are able to cope with migration much less than other social groups can do. The woman, being illiterate and less exposed to the external world, is forced to accept only very low status jobs at exploitative wages. Our study in the Delhi slums, for example, showed that around 97 per cent of the urban slum women belong to the informal economy, against around 55 per cent among men. Besides, as mentioned above, often they internalize upper caste customs. One of them is that of the housewife eating last, after feeding the elders, husband, his brothers, boy children and girl children, in that order. In a context of food shortages, the woman has to starve every now and then. As many as 164 women in our sample of 400 (320 women and 80 men), lived on gruel for at least three days in a week. As upward mobility many also adopt the high caste custom of dowry in the place of bride price. 82 of our 400 respondents 80 were tribals or others who had paid a bride price at their marriage. 55 per cent of them said that after moving to the city they had either given or will give dowry at their daughter's marriage. 70 per cent wanted to receive dowry for their sons (Fernandes, 1990: 148-149).

In our study in Goa we found that nutrition of girl children in particular was adversely affected as a result of displacement. In the displaced families we studied in that State, the proportion of girl children below the age of 9 was only 632 for 1,000 boys. Goa and Kerala are two States that have attended to the social sector. As a result of education and health care of women in particular, they have been able to ensure the small family norm, not through force but through the social process of women's empowerment. But it seems to be of no avail when their nutritional status deteriorates after displacement and more girl children than boys die as infants. That has serious implications for their status (Fernandes and Naik, 1999: 71).

Displacement as a Process

Most of these problems begin already from the first announcement of the project, and continue to have an impact on them for many years after their resettlement. Most official schemes stop as soon as the project is announced, so do loans from financial institutions. This lays the basis for moneylenders and other outsiders to start exploiting them. These problems impinge more on the woman's sphere than that of the man. With them begins the attack on the natural resources on which she is fully dependent to play her role as the caretaker of the family. The man can carry on for some more time, with his work in the social sphere. But restrictions are put on shifting cultivation and other sources of livelihood. These and other cultural changes that are introduced at this stage in the form of cutting trees and stealing result in insecurity that is felt primarily around this resource and affects her sphere more than that of men.

This situation continues throughout the process of land take over, compensation, resettlement and for many years after that. Economically often it leads to impoverishment. Socially the woman's status deteriorates more than that of men. And yet, policy makers pay very little attention to her situation. They take her subordinate role for granted even in the few rehabilitation schemes that have been drawn up. The Narmada Award, for example, states that adult men above 18 years of age are to be treated as a family and allotted two hectares of land each. No such provision is made for women above 18. The Orissa policy of 1994 treats men above 18 and unmarried women above 30 as separate families. No such provision is made in the Rajasthan policy or in the three rehabilitation laws that exist in Karnataka, Maharashtra and MP. Thus displacement runs the risk of playing the double role of weakening the tribal society and further marginalizing women within this community.

Table 4.4: Major problems after the first announcement, by village number

Sl. No.	Project	Devt progr. Stop	Loans stop	Restriction on ploughing land	Lose interest in improving assets	Theft of property	Outsiders interfere in local affairs	NAP
01	NTPC	1-3	1-3	—	1-3	—	—	—
02	THERMAL	4,5	5	4	—	4	—	—
03	FCI	6	6	6	6	—	—	—
04	COAL	7-9	7,9	9	7,9	7	7	—
05	SANCT	—	—	—	—	—	—	10-13
06	TALCHER	14,15	14,15	—	14	14,15	15	—
07	DAMAND	16,19,-	16-25	16-25	—	—	—	2025
08	MINES	—	—	26	26	—	—	—
09	U. KOLAB	28	—	28	27-29	—	—	—
10	MCHKND	—	—	31,32	30-32	31,32	—	—
11	SALANDI	33,34	35-37	34-37	33-37	—	—	—

N.B.: Village Nos. 1 to 15 are non-tribal in Angul district. 10 to 13 are tribal, but belong to a future project. No. 3 is *dalit.* Nos. 16 to 32 are in Koraput. 16, 19, 20, 25 and 28 were on the roadside and the rest in the interior before displacement. 33 to 37 are in Keonjhar, the first two predominantly non-tribal and on the roadside, the rest tribal and in the interior before deprival.

Conclusion

The above somewhat sketchy discussion on the tribal woman's status change by forced deprival of resources, focuses on the fact that displacement and rehabilitation are not a one time event but are a process that begins long before land is acquired and continues much after physical resettlement. So one should take a new look at the process of displacement as well the rehabilitation policy. Much greater attention than hitherto has to be paid to the informal economy to which most tribal communities belong. Compensation cannot be according to the market principles. The people lose their whole livelihood, not merely individual assets. One has to move away from the principle of eminent domain that takes all the CPRs as State property. One has to recognize that the CPRs are the tribal livelihood. As such they have a right to its replacement. The people have to be involved in the decision concerning the project and not merely in rehabilitation (Sharma, 1993).

Finally rehabilitation has to be total. Their CPRs have to be replaced, so also their community systems and cultural structures they need for survival.

These issues are of importance to the tribals in general but of much greater relevance to women who have traditionally had a higher socio-economic status than their high caste sisters did. It depended on the partial control they exercised over the natural resources. Their alienation deprives women of their economic sustenance as well as the social status they enjoyed in their society. This has to be a major area of concern to persons involved in human development. Unless precautions are taken, it can result in the woman being marginalised completely.

That requires much investment to prepare them for the encounter with a different society. The cost of preparing them for it has to be built into the cost of the project. Some think that it may make the project economically non-viable. The studies on rehabilitation show that it is not the case. Even if it were true, that would be no reason to exclude these costs because development is for the people, not merely the profit of a few. An important social component in the cost has to be women's status. Social investment to help them in the transition from their informal to the formal economy is integral to it. If this cost makes the project economically non-viable, then it is reason enough not to ignore it but to search for alternatives to the project.

REFERENCES

Agarwal, Anil and Sunita Narain. 1985. "Women and Natural Resources," *Social Action*, 35.(4): 301-325.

Dhagamwar, Vasudha. 1989. "Rehabilitation: Policy and Institutional Changes Required," (pp. 171-184) in Walter Fernandes and Enakshi Ganguly Thukral (eds.), *Development, Displacement and Rehabilitation: Issues for a National Debate.* New Delhi: Indian Social Institute.

Fernandes, Walter. 1986. "Construction Workers, Powerlessness and Bondage: The Case of the Asian Games," *Social Action,* 36: 264-291.

____. 1990. *Women's Status in the Delhi Bastis: Urbanisation, Economic Forces and Voluntary Organisations.* New Delhi: Indian Social Institute (mimeo).

____. 1998. "Development-Induced Displacement in Eastern India," (pp. 217-300) in S.C. Dube (ed.), *Antiquity to Modernity in Tribal India, Volume I: Continuity and Change among Indian Tribes.* New Delhi: Inter-India Publications.

Fernandes, Walter and Geeta Menon. 1987. *Tribal Women and Forest Economy: Deforestation, Exploitation and Status Change.* New Delhi: Indian Social Institute.

Fernandes, Walter and Enakshi Ganguly Thukral. 1989. "Introduction: Questions on Development, Displacement and Rehabilitation," (pp.7-28) in Walter Fernandes and Enakshi Canguly Thukral (eds), *op. cit.*

Fernandes, Walter and S. Anthony Raj. 1992. *Development, Displacement and Rehabilitation in the Tribal Areas of Orissa.* New Delhi: Indian Social Institute.

Fernandes, Walter and Niraj Naik. 1999. *Development-Induced Displacement in Goa 1965-1995.* New Delhi: Indian Social Institute.

Fernandes, Walter *et al.* 2000. *Development-Induced Displacement in Andhra Pradesh 1951-1995.* New Delhi and Guwahati: Indian Social Institute and North-Eastern Social Research Centre.

Ganguly Thukral, Enakshi. 1992. "Introduction," (pp. 7-28) in Enakshi Ganguly Thukral (ed.), *Big Dams Displaced People: Rivers of Sorrow Rivers of Change.* New Delhi: Sage Publications.

Gaventa, John. 1980. *Power and Powerlessness: Quiescence and Rebellion in an Appalachian Valley.* Oxford: Clarendon.

Hansda, Subotu. 1983. "Agricultural Development in Tribal Areas," (pp. 21-26) in S.N. Mishra and Bhupinder Singh (eds.), *Tribal Area Development.* New Delhi: Society for the Study of Regional Disparities.

Mahapatra, L. K. 1990. "Rehabilitation of Tribals Affected by Major Dams and other Projects in Orissa," (pp. 85-99) in Aloysius P. Fernandez (ed.), *Workshop on Rehabilitation of Persons Displaced by Development Projects.* Bangalore: Institute for Social and Economic Change and MYRADA.

Menon, Geeta. 1992. "Tribal Women: Victims of the Development Process," (pp. 208-225) in Walter Fernandes (ed.), *National Development and Tribal Deprivation.* New Delhi: Indian Social Institute.

____. 1995. "The Impact of Migration on the Work and Tribal Women's Status," (pp. 79-154) in Loes Schenken-Sandbergen (ed.), *Women and Seasonal Labour Migration.* New Delhi: Sage.

Pathy, Jagannath. 1988. *Ethnic Minorities in the Process of Development.* Jaipur: Rawat Publicatiions.

Sherman, Carol. 1993. *The People's Story: A Report on the Social Impact of the Australian-Financed Piparwar Coal Mine, Bihar, India.* AID/WATCH.

Thekkekara, Stan. 1993. "Historic *Adivasi Sangamam* at Mananthavady," *Social Action*, 43 (1): 88-92.

FIVE

TRIBAL WELFARE ADMINISTRATION AND DEVELOPMENT IN ORISSA

S.N. RATHA

The Tribal Situation in Orissa

Orissa has 70,32,214 persons marked as Scheduled Tribe (ST) contributing 22.21 per cent to the state population of 3,16,59,736 (1991 census). They are drawn from 62 communities and are at various stages of socio-economic development. 10.38 per cent of India's Scheduled Tribe population is in Orissa, the third in terms of tribal concentration, only next to Madhaya Pradesh and Maharashtra.

The size and distribution of these communities vary widely. At the lowest, there is the Chenchu with only 100 members and at the highest, the Kandha (Khond) numbering more than a million. About three-fourth of the Scheduled Tribe population of the state live in 10 districts: Malkangiri, Nabarangpur, Koraput, Rayagada, Gajapati, Phulbani, Nuapara (in the southern Region), Sundargarh (in Western Region). The proportion of the tribal population to the total population of the district is highest in Malkangiri (58.54%) and lowest in Puri (0.27%). 94.86 per cent of the tribal area is largely hilly and forest clad.

During the decade 1981-1991, the tribes registered a growth of 18.89 per cent. The sex ratio in 1991 is 1002 females for 1000 males for the tribal as against 971 for the total population of the state.

22.21 per cent among the tribal of the state are reported to be literate, lower than the Scheduled Caste (SC) figure of 36.78 per cent and the non-SC/ST figure of 49.09 per cent. The drop out rate is said to be as high as 72 per cent.

Nearly 90 per cent of the tribal population of the state is locked up in the agricultural sector (50.70%) as cultivator and 38.30 per cent as agricultural labourer. However, dependence on the forest still continues. The Birhor, Mankirdia and Hill Kharia are primarily forest collectors and hunters. The Juang, Hill Bhuyan, Lanjia Saura, Kandha, Bondo, Didayi are shifting cultivators, supplementing their living through forest collections and hunting. The Ho, Saura, Oraon, Kisan, Santal and Khadia are settled cultivators with marginal dependence on hunting and forest collection.

These inadequacies find their expression in glaring poverty. Poverty, however, should not only be measured in terms of inadequate food in quantity and quality, but also in terms of such other parameters as non-literacy, immobility, unhygienic living conditions, suffering from easily curable diseases, early death and the like.

II
Tribal Development Efforts in Orissa

In exercise of powers conferred by subparagraph 6 of the fifth schedule to the constitution of India, the revised Presidential Order titled "the Scheduled Areas (State of Bihar, Gujarat, Madhaya Pradesh and Orissa) Order, 1977 (Constitutional Order, 109 dated 31.12.1977 has declared three full undivided districts, viz., Mayurbhanj, Sundargarh and Koraput (Now Koraput, Rayagada, Malkangiri, Nabarangpur), Kuchianda tahasils of Sambalpur district, Keonjhar, Telkoi, Champua, and Barbil tahasils of Keonjhar district, Khandamal, Balliguda and G. Udayagiri tahasisls of Boudh- Kondhamal district, R.Udayagiri tahasil Gumma and Rayagada Blocks of Gajapati district, Suruda tahasil (excluding Gazalbadi and Gochha Grama Panchayats), of Ganjam district, Thuamul Rampur and Lanjigarh Blocks of Kalahandi district, and Nilgiri Block of Balasore district as Scheduled Areas. Now, the Scheduled Area of the state is spread over 6 full districts and 6 districts in part, out of a total of 30 districts in the state.

The Scheduled Area covers 69613.80sq km (about 44.70 per cent of the total area of the state). Its total population is 88,71,071, where the population of the Scheduled Tribe is 47,62,207 (53.68% as per 1991 census).

The Scheduled Area in Orissa is nearly conterminous with the Tribal Sub-plan area of the state. Suruda tahasil (excluding Gazalbadi and Gochha Grama Panchayats) of Ganjam district, does not come under the Tribal Sub-plan.

The welfare of the Scheduled Tribes of the Scheduled Areas in the state is being looked after by the State Government in pursuance of Article 46 of the Constitution of India. Schemes and programmes and being drawn up since the fifth five year plan for the development of the tribal and to bridge the gap between the socio economic conditions of these communities and those of others.

Article 46 of the constitution of India envisages that the state shall promote with special care the educational and economic interests of the weaker sections of the people, and in particular that of the Scheduled Tribes and Scheduled Castes and shall also protect them from social injustice as well as exploitation. In keeping with the aforesaid constitutional obligations, due attention is being paid to ameliorate their conditions and protect them from exploitation by framing various anti exploitative regulations and providing educational facilities. The various development initiatives taken for the all-round development of the tribal include adoption of the Tribal Sub-plan (TSP) approach, development of the tribal through the Integrated Tribal Development Agencies (ITDA), Micro Projects for the development of Primitive Tribal Groups (PTG), Dispersed Tribal Development Programme (DTDP) for the development of the tribal living outside the gamut of special project areas, the International Fund for Agricultural Development (IFAD) assisted Orissa Tribal Development Project (OTDP) for the all-around development of Kashipur Block of Rayagada district, antipoverty programmes and other programems that have a bearing upon the economic development of Scheduled Tribes and Scheduled Areas of the state.

Tribal Sub-plan

The Tribal Sub-plan is a special and separate plan/programme within the state plan, which caters to the special needs of the area, having majority tribal population by employing an integrated area approach as development strategy. The Tribal Sub-plan approach was evolved and made effective during the fifth five-year plan, which resulted in speedier development of Scheduled Tribes. The objective of the Tribal Sub-plan approach is the combined development of the area and tribal population living there in. The strategy of development was oriented within the frame work of the Five Year Plan towards taking up individual and family benefit oriented income generating schemes in spheres of agriculture, horticulture, animal husbandry and human resources development through educational training and infrastructure development programmes.

Financial Framework of Tribal Sub-plan

The Tribal Sub-plan approach to development envisages an integrated development of the tribal area and, as such, every programme, irrespective of their source of funding functions in unison, achieving the general objective of bringing the area at par with the rest of the state.

The various sources of funding for the development of TSP areas are:

- State Plan
- Special Central Assistance (SCA)
- Central and Centrally Sponsored Scheme (SCP)

Salient Features of the Tribal Sub-plan Approach

- Quantification of funds from different sectors and fixation of physical targets to be achieved under different sectoral programs for speedier development of tribal areas.
- The quantum of budgetary allocation earmarked for tribal development should be equivalent to the population percentage of the scheduled tribes and should not be diverted for other purposes. The quantification of flow of funds to TSP areas aims at realistic presentation of the amount actually spent in TSP areas and working out the percentage of the amount spent, out of the total budget provision of the State.

Only such schemes and programs, which are relevant and beneficial to the tribal should be reflected in flow of funds to the Tribal Sub-plan.

Integrated Tribal Development Agencies (ITDA)

21 ITDAs have been established in the state to function as nodal agencies for plan formulation, implementation of programs and to make the Tribal Sub-plan concept effective.

Micro Projects for Development of Primitive Tribal Groups (PTG)

The Primitive Tribal Groups (PTGs) are found in remote areas of the state. These tribal groups are selected on the basis of the guidelines issued by the Government of India. They have been identified on the basis of their pre agricultural level of economy, low level of literacy and diminishing population. Keeping this in view, 17 micro projects are functioning in the state for all-round development of 13 Primitive Tribal communities out of which 13 projects are inside the Scheduled Areas. The communities covered are: Birhor, Bondo, Didayi, Dongaria- Khond, Juang, Kharia, Kutia Khond, Lanjia Saura, Lodha, Mankirdia, Paudi Bhuyan, Saura, Chuktia Bhunjia

The Primitive Tribes are given 100 per cent subsidy for individual family benefit oriented schemes. The projects aim at the development of the core economic sectors like agriculture, horticulture, soil conservation, animal husbandry, besides providing facilities for drinking water supply, education and health. About 61,000 Scheduled Tribe people are covered under the scheme of Micro Projects. The primary object of the government is to ensure all-round development of the tribal so that they develop an institution of their own which will keep the development efforts alive even after the assistance of government is withdrawn.

Orissa Tribal Development Project (OTDP) in Kashipur Block of Rayagada District is assisted by the International Fund for Agricultural Development (IFAD). The total outlay of the project was initially Rs.31.70 crores to be implemented over a period of 14 years in 2 phases of 7 years each. The outlay of the first phase from 1988-89 to 1994-95 was Rs. 24.70 crores and that of the second phase from 1995-96 to 2001-2002 was Rs.7.00 crores. The project cost of the first phase was revised to Rs.43.26 crores due to the devaluation of the rupee. The project envisaged an integrated and multi-pronged development of the area including development of natural resources, communication, human resources and survey and settlement operations.

Anti-poverty and Legal Aid Programs

The Scheduled Tribes are assisted under various anti poverty programmes, like Integrated Tribal Development Program (ITDP), assistance to Small and Marginal farmers, etc. Special Central Assistance is also given to the ITDA for implementation of income generating schemes for Scheduled Tribes.

Legal Aid is given to deserving STs for establishing, enforcing and maintaining their rights, title of possession of landed poverty in Civil or Revenue courts provided that the opposite party is a non ST. Legal Aid is also admissible for cases under Sec.379 IPC, 447. IPC and 107,144,145 cr. PC involving land dispute cases provided the opposite party is not a member of ST.

III

Administrative Set-up for Promoting the Welfare of Scheduled Tribes in Scheduled Areas

According to the proviso to Article164 (I) of the Constitution of India, there shall be, in the state of Orissa, a Minister of Cabinet rank in charge of the portfolio of Tribal Welfare.

The Central and the State Governments are jointly responsible for framing legislations for peace and good governance of Scheduled Areas and framing programs for their all-round development. The Welfare Department functions to discharge its own administrative and developmental functions besides acting as a liaison and coordinating department for the Scheduled Areas.

The Department of Welfare functions under the direct supervision of a Principal Secretary. He is assisted by three Directors, one in charge of Tribal Welfare, one in charge of Harijan Welfare and one in charge of Welfare of Other Backward Classes, Deputy Secretaries, a Financial Advisor cum Deputy Secretary, etc., along with other ministerial and technical staff.

Field Organization

The field organization is based on a four-tier system of administration at Block, Sub-divisional, District and Divisional levels.

- The welfare schemes at the divisional level are administered under the supervision of the Revenue Divisional Commissioner (RDC). The Joint Director, Tribal Welfare, assists the RDC in execution of Welfare Schemes for development of Scheduled Tribes.
- The Scheduled Areas are spread over 13 districts of the state, either fully or in part. The District Welfare Officer of every district works under the direct supervision of the District
- Magistrate and Collector and is in charge of execution of welfare schemes and programs for the Scheduled Tribes.
- At the sub divisional level, Assistant District Welfare Officers function under the direct supervision of the Sub-Collector of their respective sub-divisions.
- Two Welfare Extension Officers are posted in each Block of the Tribal Sub-plan area to function under the control of the Block Development Officer. Besides two, another officer is posted in every Block having MADA pockets. These officers monitor different schemes and programs at the grass root.

Tribal Sub-plan (TSP)

There are 21 ITDAs and 13 Micro Projects in the Tribal Sub-plan areas. Each ITDA is headed by a Project Administrator (PA). The PAs work under the immediate control and supervision of the concerned District Magistrate and Collector. In each ITDA there is a Project Level Committee (PLC) constituted under the Chairmanship of the Collector. The PA is the member secretary while the local MPs, MLAs, Chairman of Panchayat Samities and other District Level Officers in charge of developmental works are members of the said committee. Similarly, each Micro Project is headed by a Special Officer under the immediate control and supervision of the concerned District Magistrate and Collector. In each Micro Project there is a Governing body constituted under the Chairmanship of the concerned Project Administrator of ITDA.

Research

An institute named as Scheduled Caste and Scheduled Tribe Research and Training Institute (SCSTRTI), an organization of the Welfare Department, functions with the primary objective of conducting research and survey as well as imparting training to the in-service officers, preparation of action plans on tribal and other scheduled communities.

IV

A Glance at the Outcome of the Development Efforts

Investments, including the cost of administration in these projects, are massive. But the achievements are greatly uneven. For example, over a 30-year period (1961-91) the literacy among the tribal of Orissa improved only by 10.74 per cent. As it stood in 1991, only 27.93 per cent of the tribal male and 8.29 per cent of the tribal female in Orissa are reported to be literate (1991 census).

Some progress is, no doubt, made. In many cases, however, the difference in the level of development of the tribal areas and the remaining regions in the states are even accentuated. A Government of India document issued by the Ministry of Home Affairs "for official use only" laments: "in the name of Tribal Development, we have spent a lot of money during the last several plans, but when accounting was made at the end of the last period of safeguards to the tribal in the constitution, it was found that actual benefits trickling down to the tribal have not been consistent with the promise we have made. Expenditure has not resulted in the benefit that should have accrued to this population. Unfortunately, the developmental programs for tribal areas did not yield the desired results...." It further observed that more than 75 per cent of total benefits have not reached the tribal and cautions that "we cannot have development at this rate" (1975: 98).

Evaluating the impact of animal husbandry, it records, "in this sector.... lot of money has been spent in the name of the tribal and the benefits never reached them" (p.100). The same document refers to a report that records, "Some responsible tribal bodies have refused to accept larger programs in tribal areas for fear of exploitation." Such an observation by the tribal does no credit to those who plan, execute or talk of tribal development. The organizational structure has failed to ensure the benefits of the programs to the target groups. The process only widened the psychological gap between the tribal and the non-tribal, government included. Such promises that all their problems would be solved by the end of 1989 (GOI,1977: 1-2), are frowned upon. In spite of all the strategies and efforts of these years, 85 per cent of the tribal families remain below the poverty line, compared to the national average of about 38 per cent (quoted from the Performance Appraisal documented by the Seventh Plan Working Group in Ray Burman, 1995: 67).

The results of the Tribal Sub-plan (TSP) strategy developed during the 5th plan are not in proportion with the expectations and the investments so far (Report of the Working Group for the Scheduled Tribes in the 8th Plan). Reports of Committees and Commissions appointed by the Government from time to time outline a dismal picture on the achievements of various programs (Roy Burman 1995: 14-16).

Efforts to develop the Primitive Tribal Groups in Orissa began with the establishment of the Bondo Development Agency in 1976. It covers 32 villages and a population of 4.431 persons (1991 position). A report prepared by the Scheduled Caste and the Scheduled Tribes Research and Training Institute, Orissa (1996: 167) records: "assessment of the progress and evaluation of different developmental programs in the area has depicted that the desired goals have not been achieved to an appreciable extent. What this "appreciable extent" is can be understood from the data from the same report (pp.138-140). There are 8 primary schools on record. All are supposed to be 2-teacher schools. In two schools, the teacher strength is as per sanction. In two others, only one teacher each is posted, four others go without teachers (Table No. IV 9.1 p. 138). Six schools do not have building. Two have incomplete structures (table unnumbered p. 130). In another report published by the same institute in 1984 records, "prior to the operation of the Bondo Development Agency, there were eight single teacher primary schools in eight Bondo villages....run by the Education Department.... All the lower Primary schools exist only in paper and the teachers appointed have rarely visited these schools" (p.125). The present report observes, "It appears that after publication of the above government report no follow-up action was taken. The information remained confined to the book only. No impact was generated due to lack of pursuant action against teacher absenteeism" (p.140). This observer is a retired Director of Elementary Education of the Government of Orissa whose duty was to take pursuant action during his active tenure of service. This is development in the Education Sector with the Micro Project operating for 20 years.

V
Understanding Development

Initiative to development and change has come to be regarded as an urgent and pressing national responsibility. A large number of governmental and non-governmental agencies are involved in this endeavour. It is deliberately pursued and consciously oriented towards quick results to be in tune with the large national policies.

Though development is popularly regarded as an economic process, equal emphasis is also placed on the qualitative aspects of human development. It is looked upon as an organized and institutionalized activity with the aim of satisfying the basic needs as well as to psychologically orient the target population to adopt new skills, attitudes and life styles; so that they build up the inner strength to appropriately orient their social and cultural infrastructures to stand the pressure of the changing situations and accrue benefits from the developmental inputs to lift themselves to a higher level of life. Judged from this angle, development is a multi dimensional process to progressively improve the social, cultural, economic and human conditions of the people, all vital sectors, necessary for a balanced growth of the society (Schneider, 1975).

The developmental strategy should also include ways and means to utilize latent, unused and underused human resources, skills and knowledge and to motivate the individual to produce more and better. It should also include tangible efforts to bring effective freedom to unify the people for the greater task of nation building.

Effective development is, therefore, a comprehensive, balanced or integrated activity. It is obviously a dynamic process, which signifies goal-oriented, guided and gradual change for something considered to be less desirable to something thought to be desirable or more desirable (Sparkman, 1961).

There is no single cause for economic underdevelopment and cultural stagnation. Many forces - economic, social, political, religious, historical and cultural - are at work. At certain points of time they may be mutually reinforcing and at certain other points, they may be mutually contradictory. There is no single science, which can provide all data or the conceptual apparatus necessary to identify, analyse and understand the problems of a people who are at different levels of technological, economic and cultural development.

The anthropologists, however, do have special skills to offer. They can provide adequate data to identify the cultural forces to steer the development wagon to avoid head on collision with the resistant spots of community life and culture. Their skill can be used to bring in people to associate effectively with the developmental programs, who are otherwise passive and indifferent onlookers or even active resistants (Mandelbaum, 1978).

A goal oriented development should be ultra realistic. It should be able to fix up achievable targets and be formulated on the basis of adequate and reliable data. It is needless to say that for the formulation of the developmental strategy, a clear methodology of approach, not only in delimiting or defining the beneficiaries of the program, but also a clear knowledge of their socio cultural base and their physical environment, is required. Accordingly tribal development should be viewed as a program emphasizing certain achievable targets, a process emphasizing upon what happens to people not only economically and socially but also psychologically, and institutionalization of the newly discovered skills and procedures leading to social change without completely breaking away from the past.

A strategy for development must be able to identify vantage starting points and facilitating environment for action at the micro level. Plans conceived in terms of the tribe as a whole may not be useful when the tribe has a huge population such that sections there of live in widely different environmental conditions. Therefore schemes for development should be conceived and developed within the socio cultural norms of the community, based upon the micro level parameters. Such a formulation shall lead to the discovery of priorities of each community or group. It may be necessary to place education on the top of priorities of a community whereas some one else may require health care measures to begin with. Contemporary researchers on Human Resources Development assert, "Human resource is the only resource whose upper limits are not known to the person himself or herself"(Chaudhury, 1996). Thus human potential is limitless. To harness this potential, a clear understanding of the strength and weakness of each community need to be assessed. Each community has its moral and value bases, which are, as Sol Tax puts it, "Unarguable absolutes". People come to them of their own wills, of their own initiatives, over their individual path, the endless ways of their own cultures, traditions and experiences. When Elwin (1958) advised to "approach the tribesman with the mind of the Tribesman" or when Jawaharlal Nehru suggested that the tribal people should be allowed to develop along the lines of their own genius" (1958), they were probably thinking in the same lines as Sol Tax did.

The approach inevitably requires an adequate assessment of the needs of the target population and a thorough understanding of its cultural base. Non - understanding of the cultural background of the target population has, in past, led to the failure of many well-meaning programs. For example, the scheme of building colonies to provide houses with farmland to tribal groups to wean them away from nomadic habitats, completely failed.

The Commissioner for Scheduled Caste and Scheduled Tribes attributed this failure to the divergence of the colony way of life from the cherished cultural values of the communities involved (GOI, 1961).

Therefore development inputs should follow efforts to ensure active participation of the people (women included) in their own development where optimum use of locally available resources-human as well as material, shall be made. Such models, to be functional, should ensure cultural as well as geophysical sustainability, be based upon locally available resources (material, human as well as epistemological). Thus the term strategy should not be treated as a mere administrative jargon but be related to the organizational values of the community, environment and the community's resources.

REFERENCES

Chaudhury, S.S. 1996. "HRD: A Blend of Organizational Softs and Hards," *The Stateman*, April 19,1996, Calcutta.

Chaudhury. Bhagirathi. 1996. "Tribes and Development," *Orissa Today, An Annual Survey*, Sun Times, Bhubaneswar.

Elwin, V. 1963. A New Deal for Tribal India. Government of India, Ministry of Tribal Affairs, New Delhi.

Government of India. 1961. Report of the Scheduled Areas and Scheduled Tribes Commission (Chairman U.N. Dhebar)

____. 1969. Report of the Study tour of the Tribal Development Programme (Committee on Plan Project, Chairman-P. Shilu Ao.)

____. 1975. Tribal Development in the Fifth Plan, Some basic Policy Papers, Volume II, Ministry of Home Affairs, New Delhi.

____. 1977. "Approach to Tribal Development in the Sixth Plan: A Preliminary Perspective," Occasional papers on Tribal Development, Ministry of Home Affairs, New Delhi.

____. 1990. National Conference on Problems of Scheduled Tribes (31 March 1990), Ministry of Welfare, Tribal Development, Government of India.

Government of Orissa. 1996. Development Handbook for the Bondo. SC & ST Research and Training Institute, Bhubaneswar.

Holmberg, Allen R. 1968. "Among the Siriano Nomads of Long Bow," (pp.136-141) in Mortan H. Fried (ed.), *Readings in Anthropology.* Vol. II (22nd Edn.).

Mandelbaum, David, G.1978. "The Potentials of Anthropology," (pp.24-41) in D.C. Simkin, Sol Tax. W. J. Morrison (eds.), *Anthropology for the Future.* Research Report No. 4, Department of Anthropology, University of Illinois, Albama, USA)

Nehru, Jawaharlal. 1958. Foreword *in Philosophy for NEFA* (2nd Edn.) by V. Elwin, Shillong.

Roy Burman, B.K. 1995. "Tribal Situations and Approach to Tribal Problems in India: A Preliminary Appraisal," Discussion Paper, Rajiv Gandhi Institute for Contemporary Studies, New Delhi.

Schneider, Harold K. 1975. "Economic Development and Anthropology," *Annual Review of Anthropology,* 99: 271-292.

Sparkamn, John. J. 1961. "Economic, Social and Political Implications of Community Development," Community Development Review, 6: 1-10.

Swain, Saraswati. 1986. "Food Practices and Nutritional Status among Tribal of India" paper presented in the national seminar Genetic and Socio Cultural Dimensions of Tribal Health, organized by the National Institute of Family Health on March 15, 1986 in New Delhi.

Tax, Sol. 1959. "Action Anthropology," *Journal of Social Research,* III.

Vaid, N. K. 1996. *Tribal Development.* (Vaid's Anthropological Series, Vol. I) New Delhi: Ashtam Prakashan.

SIX

BREAKING THE BOUNDS OF LIMITED DEPENDENCE

KUMKUM BHATTACHARYA

In these fast changing "instant" times that things at all endure, that there are things that we want should endure and there are those for whose endurance we put in our efforts. Things that last bring with them a sense of stability, of being in equipoise and being predictable, a pleasant comfortable feeling. This comfortable feeling is disturbed by the tensions aroused by the often-contrary forces of endurance and change, one apparently backward and the latter seemingly forward. Some social systems possess the resilience of combating both change and endurance, others possess the capacity for absorbing change and reducing tensions and there are others not so well-equipped to smoothen the process of change, for which they may have perfectly valid reasons. Then there are others that aggressively confront and adopt change without seeming to suffer the backlog of antiquity. Apart from these social capacities, it is the perceptions of these capacities of one social group by another, the expectations that are harboured about each other, the stereotypes that shape mutual attitudes[1] and prejudices[2] and the understandings in varying degrees of the difference in pace in dealing with change that play an important role in combat capacities. All forms of social categories and collectivity assume significance in shaping our expectations and opinions about others, about ourselves and about us in relation to others and vice-versa. This is a familiar idea, almost passe and we no longer question its veracity. However, we overlook its dynamic nature over time and situation and believing wholly that any change in any society can be induced, accelerated and evolved following universal patterns. When it comes to the specificity of change desired or aspired in a particular society that is perceived as lacking in something(s) it is then that we realize the futility of mere acceptance of the above truth. A probing into the deeper layers of interpersonal/inter-group interactions becomes necessary in order for our efforts to bear fruit in the form of change/development/enhancement, whatever one may choose to term it.

Development is another of many terms that mean various things to different people, yet there is by and large, consensus about some of its broad markers that enjoy acceptance by default, of being adhered to by the majority/minority that dominates. That the concept of development is shaped by our membership in social categories and collectivities is often ignored in the by and large areas of consensus. Development in itself, is treated in a sacrosanct manner by the dominating classes, as if they (or should I say we) are specially endowed to deal with this necessary good (!) for the lofty goal of "betterment" of sections of the human specie and all things related. The word by itself is a goader of activities, capable of motivating and arousing excitement, especially of the agents rather than the targets of development. Considering the number of personnel it sustains and the number of bodies it institutes and decides the direction of government policies, it is certainly worth its salt. The positive aspects of development are indispensable, however, a blanket policy for all sections of the population seems not to be paying dividend, and mere consensus is not enough.

Development as a process offers scope for loosening of the bindings of tradition to take on modernity,[3] as well as makes the fine judgement between what to retain and to jettison, provided the target population makes the assessment of its own unique situation. Each community/population/individual is ever changing according to the perceived demands of time, some slow, some faster than others are. This pace can only be measured on a large time scale, whereas on a smaller time scale, like the ones that we are used to deal with in keeping with our predilections for predicting and projecting, we end up only with trends in development, not the outcomes and these trends do not always stand the test of time or may be skewed in uncertain directions. I make these statements basing my observations on our enthusiastic and often diachronic support of "harsh" and rather sudden development measures having little patience for results obtained slowly. Let me cite the example of agriculture; not many years ago it was technology that was pushed at the cost of indigenous technology/knowledge because there was urgent need for it, but today we are mourning the loss of this knowledge that has not only become extinct but also discontinuous. As a result there is hardly any link between tradition and modernity.[4]

It is in this kind of scenario that people find themselves poised and this paper deals with a tribal community, the Santals, the travails of their living in this day and age with the mechanisms by which they deal with them – how they adjust and how perceptions of themselves and their neighbours' affect the adjustment process and how they view their own aspirations, expectations and needs. This paper attempts to show how personality being socialized in a plural environment containing all the forces mentioned above (and many more), gives shape to a dynamic identity,[5] often revealed in their strategies of adjustment, on place of strategies employed traditionally.

India offers a unique situation in which tribals seem more exposed to forces of modernity for reasons ranging from plurality of habitat to the near impossibility of any longer being isolated demographically. It is not categorically known as yet whether these forces disturb their tradition and if there is conflict of values between the two. How comfortable they are with change, how much of the change they have been able to absorb and assimilate are the questions that are being raised here. I also seek to find if there is accord between their and our understanding of the issues concerned. I admit all this concern costs in time taken away from development; nevertheless, it is becoming increasingly evident that something needs to be done to clear the impasse if we seek lasting change, or else we shall continue to mistake the wood for the trees.

The kinds of writing that are available on the tribes indicate two major trends – one ethnographic and two, writings that could be clustered under categories: Development and Tribes; Tribal Situation; Education and Tribes; Health and Tribes; Socio-economic Condition of Tribes, etc. The writings, to a great extent sidetrack and ignore the actual felt needs, aspirations and expectations of the tribes in the relentless pursuit of standards that are believed to be universal and generally applicable. Very few writings belong to the genre where attempts are made to highlight the strengths of tribal societies or cultures or those aspects of their social organization that even people of non-tribal societies value and include in their view of an ideal social order and moral character.[6] For anyone writing on the Santals, it is mandatory to refer to Archer's lyrical work, "Hill of Flutes…" as an authentic representation of the profoundly beautiful songs and poetry of the Santals. It is unfortunate that the interest stops there; worse, it fuels the romanticism that clouds us from touching their lives, their beings in a real manner, preferring safe distance to contact. May be we are apprehensive that our flimsy exotic ideas will not stand the test of reality.

The Dynamics of Santal Identity vis-à-vis Common Perceptions

In this paper I seek to present the ground realities of the nature of Santal identity vis-à-vis common perceptions. What are these common perceptions? Let me take up first the perceptions of those who are in day-to-day contact[7] with them. For this it will help to identify the sectors in which these contacts take place. In a rural setting[8], with its labour intensive agriculture, the Santals work as day-labourers, often working for one landowner on a regular basis, some engage themselves seasonally or some are migrant labour. The other sectors in which the Santals are employed are the mills for rice, sugar, and brick kilns, building sites, road laying and the forestry department. In other words the Santals are a part of the work force. Interviews of a cross-section of the employers reveal that they generally commend their capacity for hard manual labour, relative problem-free service, regularity in attendance, neat dress, clean habits and general ignorance of service rules. These opinions undergo a change when Santal festivals come round. They are then seen as stubborn, capricious, unreasonable, irregular, demanding, exhibiting drunken bravado and sudden display of cunning about terms of service. The single piece of behaviour that irritates each of the interviewed is their obduracy. When asked about the reason for absence, the standard reply over and over again is "I didn't come" with no elaboration or variation putting all present and future conversation on hold! Visiting a Santal village is normally a pleasant experience – liquor is served, girls and women do not shirk conversation and the children do not crowd around visitors and the villagers try their best to show hospitality without impinging on personal space or inclination. However, during the days of their festivity, it is advised to the visitors that it would be prudent to keep away and people are warned against visiting or approaching these people. An exaggerated picture of drunken debauchery and orgiastic revelry seizes the imagination and the prevalent opinion is that all restraint and sexual inhibitions are thrown to the winds. The visitor cannot predict the kind of reception that will be accorded; there is no guarantee that the deference that is owing to one's position of superiority will be shown.

"Even our good intentions go awry. Drinking makes them lose all perspective and proportion, in fact their behaviour borders on rudeness. During this time it is quite dangerous to be too familiar with them and it is difficult to maintain distance or preserve one's honour. It is better to avoid all contact with them during the days of their festival, safer to indulge them and turn a blind eye."

Amorality among the Santals is another reservation that is commonly held against them. Santal women are easy prey for their employers. Provision of little luxuries is enough to entice them. Under the influence of liquor married women too turn flirtatious. Such views lead to the opinion that Santal women enter readily into prostitution because of the social leniency towards sexual behaviour. Incidences of extra-marital relationships, abandonment of husband, child or wife, living together without going through the solemnity of marriage, opportunities for pre-marital sex, social sanction for divorce and so on are reported and focussed on to bolster arguments in favour of Santal amorality.

Those who are not direct employers of the Santals, but see them from a distance and compare them with groups that occupy similar economic condition, tend to view them as backward, underdeveloped, primitive, poverty-stricken, immoral and severely handicapped in the face of modern pressures; often despairing of any possibility of effective change through developmental means. Socially the Santals are accorded a low status, lower than the Muslims and the low caste Hindus. Religion of the Santals is perceived as primitive and non-Aryan in nature. Educationally the Santals are lagging behind, having large numbers of dropouts and absentees, being casual towards the demands of education and unprepared for its rigorous. Health management is achieved through magico-religious practices and witch hunting is still in existence. Economically the Santals are perceived as unable to transcend the subsistence level of survival.

The Resourceful Social Order

In a related paper,[9] I have discussed the identity of the Santals at two levels-one, primordial and two, interest group identity. To elaborate and move beyond that premise, I am attempting to show that in the cross pressures of people's perceptions of the Santals and their own strivings to redefine themselves in the perspective of changed times, they are being compelled to break out of their traditional world of limited dependencies. In the process of breaking out, the conflict between tradition and modernity is getting sharpened to a greater or lesser extent, expressed in the manifestation of identity crisis. Increased membership in plural societies, increased universalization of needs, demographic pressure and access to most forms of communication, efforts on the part of the government for affirmative action and positive discrimination, are some of the reasons for opting out of tradition or to redefine themselves.

Analyzing the facilities of the Santal social and cultural milieu, it will be noticed that there are inherent strengths that could be put to use in the attempt at successful or less anxious adjustments; provided we alter our outlook and they feel the need to enter into meaningful dialogue with the process of change.

Santal society is non-inhibitive, homogenous and egalitarian.[10] It can be proud of a religion that does not foster fundamentalism or create divisions in society.[11] Their socialization process is sensitive to the needs of children and youth.[12] Their society accommodates various forms of union of man and woman [13] and values community life without trespassing into personal privacy.[14] Women enjoy more equal rights in society.[15]

Observing their behaviour, even a gross overview will reveals that they do not exploit nature to the extent that we, with all our concern, do; however, the Santals earn more than their share of blame for deforestation. They recognize nature as being bounteous and the source of their sustenance. They are poor but they do not exhibit the despair and abjectness of poverty. Instead they could be considered akin to the originally affluent people,[16] not beset with the limits of necessity or propriety, as the middle classes are wont to, with their measured help, hospitality and lavishness! The Santals are peace loving, it is not often that they display aggression towards each other or others. Apart from the Santal uprising in 1855, and the Kharwar movement in the 1870s and the demand for separate statehood in more contemporary times (Jharkhand movement), there is not much evidence of aggression as a common reaction to situations among the Santals.[17]

At the local level, there are not many significant reports of violence or aggression; the incidences of witch-hunting or revolt against missionary practitioners are isolated and sporadic events. There is no report of Santals desecrating temples/mosques/churches. In fact they are enthusiastic about festivals and ceremonies of all religious groups, they have adopted some of the Hindu gods and goddesses to worship in their own fashion (Shiva, Kali and Saraswati). They regularly attend all religious/non-religious fairs and mela.

The interaction pattern of the Santals is one of withdrawal with dignity. They do not shy away when approached, but do not go out of their way to initiate interaction, rather they maintain a stoicism of mien. They are accustomed to their neighbours and of living in the same areas/villages with the Hindus and the Muslims, though they occupy/inhabit the fringe areas, maintaining both geographical and social distance.[18]

Their capacity for hard manual labour has kept them from swelling the ranks of the unemployed, a boon for the government. Their capacity to generate a sense of joy or fun (*raska* in Santali) is rejuvenating that releases the sometimes-crippling effects of frustration and conflicts. Their cycle of festivals provides them with cathartic mechanisms; channeling energy through accepted social ways of drinking, singing and dancing. The distinct worlds of the children, adolescents and adults are accommodated in their pattern of culture. They are community minded, yet do not interfere in each other's physical or social space, cooperative rather than competitive and do not clamour for attention.

Breaking Out

The Santals who are more in contact with the dominant sections tend to show different patterns in their reactions and mechanisms of adjustment than the Santals who are living in relative isolation or in Santal dominated areas. The Santals, who are the universe of this paper, belong to the former category. The Santals of the Santal Parganas, a district in Bihar from where some of the data has been collected, have a different experience of the cross pressures. The Santals of Birbhum are bilingual, they speak Santali and Bengali. The Santals of the Santal Parganas are also bilingual; they speak Hindi/Bengali and Santali. The difference between the two lies in the fact that the non-Santals of the Santal Parganas, who are in direct contact with the Santals either in commerce or as close neighbours, are often quite facile in Santali. It is not so in Birbhum, rather some of the Santali words have acquired derogatory connotations (*majhi* that has high value in the Santal society, is used to refer to them derogatorily whereas, they prefer the term *hor; bonga* that means spirits is used by the non-Santals to signify eccentricities). This may appear as a subtle distinction but what needs to be appreciated is the positive effect it has on the morale of the Santals. Certainly interactions among the latter (Bihar) are more at par, linguistically the Santals are not isolated and there is imparted a sense of importance of being counted on for something.

The common perceptions regarding the Santals are of the nature that they are naturally translated into attitudes of apathy on either side. Faced with the onslaught of negative attitudes coupled with their own direct experience of failure and ineptitude the Santals are left with no option but to be severely disadvantaged to actively counteract the dominant image of themselves. The dominant attitudes find reflection in the apathetic acceptance of their image as being true, leaving no scope for positive self-criticism or re-evaluating their strategies in the light of experiences. Changes in attitudes would provide space in which the Santals and non-Santals could step out of their bounds and arrive at a fresh view of shared positive assessment. As of now the assessment is grossly one-sided and loaded against the Santals.

During the annual exercise of enrolling students in my department for the undergraduate and postgraduate courses, I along with my colleagues face a dilemma. We look forward to an increase in the number of tribal applicants and the reservation policy of the Government of India seems a step in the right direction. However, when it comes to the actual formalities of admission we scrutinize their constitutionally marked identity from all possible angles, more so when we find that the applicant seems to be divested of "recognizable" markers. It then begins to dawn that the cleverer and the resourceful are capable of seizing the day. A niggling feeling comes to the surface – that whatever they gain for themselves will only be put to selfish ends, accomplishments will not filter to the others and will also not translate into action for the uplift of their poor and backward brethren. In the event when an educated and employed tribal makes effort to recruit his co-tribes, utilizing the benefits of position, the accusation is one of nepotism and fostering incompetence. Thus, an educated tribal with all the years spent in acquiring learning is expected to give all up for social service, and the tribal who is in a position to effect help and assistance to co-tribe, is expected to abstain from such active intervention. Further the person is expected to recognize the "evils" of the reservation policy!

Looking at the education that is offered in our system and the available employment facilities that seem heavily dependent on the kind of education acquired, becoming part of the mainstream is not easy. The Santals find it even more difficult and the government is yet to work out alternative channels to the mainstream or widen the base with diverse training and learning. There is enough evidence to show the ineptness of formal mainstream education in the light of Santal experience.[20]

The Santals lay stress on learning from primary sources, rather than from secondary ones, that as are available is esoteric and alien to the ambience of their culture. There is an intimate link between economic need and urge for education. The middle class takes to education like a duck to water because for them education is the only means of livelihood, they do not own land to fall back upon, do not value (for themselves) manual labour and do not have any generated surplus to sustain themselves. Thus employment directly linked to educational and professional training suits them and they are willing to invest time and money for it. Against this backdrop, the position of the Santals is indeed shaky

Discussion

This paper is one of a series of papers about the Santals and possesses a symbiotic link with the others. In the various papers referred to in the text I have tried to look at the Santals from different angles; plurality and Santal behaviour; socialization; religion; and Santal identity.[21] A fair number of years of work among these people is responsible for opening my vision and question my own perceptions regarding them. Like anybody else I, too own up to stereotyped notions, may be some have remained even today or some have been strengthened.

In tracing the genealogy of my way of looking at the Santals, I identify my encounter with the Christian Santals of the Santal Parganas as the watershed. I observed but could not comprehend the reasons at that time for, the relative success that the Christian missionaries had in bringing the Santals into the mainstream, whereas persistent government policies to uplift the Santals could not be described as reaching targets or as being successful. A lot was/is being "done" for them, but somehow the desired or projected changes were/are not being crystallized, reinforcing notions that the Santals are probably unable to reap the benefits of development. Questions are raised about the costs of development that was mentioned at the beginning of the paper. What was it that the missionaries did? If we pause to recall the diligence and single-mindedness of the early missionaries, their willingness to reside in uncharted terrain in the midst of these people, sharing the paucity of facilities and service and yet displaying their zeal in ways they thought right, we shall get our answer. They gained the necessary mileage by imparting to them a sense of dignity, of being considered important and interesting so that others could be concerned about their welfare. They achieved this by listening and recording their stories, tales, history, medicinal skills, customary laws, social organization, religious practices, vocabulary, cosmology and other cultural attributes like songs, dances and cycles of festivals.[22] All this helped in building bridges. The intimate knowledge that the missionaries gained about the Santals did not stop them from making efforts at proselytization. There could not be two more disparate religions, Christianity and religion of the Santals, on the contrary, for the Santals to reap the benefits that they offered it was necessary to "weed out" the undesirable elements from the Santals' way of life as perceived by the missionaries. It does not speak of a noble selfless motive on the part of the agents of change. And it is this that irks us, using the power of religion to bring about change/development and we are quick to point out the tragedy of lost heritage to material gain. Our cherished "ideals" of secularism, universalization of opportunities, democracy, heritage and tradition make all such developments suspect. Especially in the sphere of education, the hitherto dominant and easy access of the missionaries to these marginal people is being questioned.[23]

Education has always been and is a crucial factor in bringing about change, however, how it achieves its goal needs to be clarified. If education is considered as a means of making more organized adjustments to life situations, of being able to live a harmonious community life without aggressive competitiveness, then it must be said that the Santals are not making a bad job of it; certainly better than what most of us have made with the tensions of our ever increasing aspirations and competitiveness. On the other hand, when education is seen as a means to move in step with modernity, to attain pre-set standards to be considered educated, or to put to use formal education in employment, then undoubtedly, the Santals have a long way to go. For any success, the Santals need to feel the importance of education as urgent and develop confidence in their powers of precept, a confidence that can be bolstered by positive feedback from personal experience and others' perceptions and faith in self.

This holds true for all the sectors of the mainstream, to belong means to be counted for something. It is equally true that every individual, group or community has its own pace of becoming part of the mainstream that is dependent on efforts made for inclusion. These efforts should be on both sides, i.e. those who are in the mainstream and those who are not. Every social order, along with its range of cultural pattern possesses limiting tendencies that have to be breached. Among the requirements that are needed to be fulfilled in order to transcend the limited dependencies are: (a) a perceived continuity between tradition and modernity and to recognize the possible links between the two; (b) the urgent needs that have to be felt and created/ developed for bringing about change; and (c) confidence in one's abilities corroborated by the perceptions of those who exercise influence.

It is indeed remarkable that the Santals with an oral tradition have managed to survive, for such long periods of human history, within their world of limited dependencies, and have not felt as strongly, the urge to re-define themselves more contrastingly to their social history and go all out for reaping the fruits of development at least the kind that is offered to them. It is more of a contemporary problem, the pressures for change, for which, in some cases, the Santals express the tensions in behaviours that seem aberrant and thus reinforcing the stereotypes about them. They are yet to inculcate the ways and means to fulfill the urgent contemporary needs and to balance them with what they have been accustomed to, that of being marginalized and having to accept it.[24]

The Santals are breaking out of their limited dependencies in various ways. Apart from their scheduled status, they are more visible, more noticeable and becoming politically more active and potent. In fact, politics, the great leveller, provides an arena to go public with individual aspirations and ambitions as well as providing acceptable avenues of fulfilling individual goals pleading the cause of the "betterment" of greater numbers. In fact, it is this plea that gives individual political efforts legitimacy and helps in amassing support from one's own kind. Politics is a short cut to all that is striven for in development, however short-lived it may be.

However, our expectations from tribal leaders, as already mentioned, are unrealistic and bespeak of double standards. We expect that they will bypass their personal ambitions and aspirations to serve their downtrodden brethren. Why is it that despite the fact of having our share of the downtrodden and the have-nots, we are happy to perform social service rhetorically?

A certain section of the Santals are actively working on their script and pressing for education in their language and script.[25] They are showing enterprise in recording their songs for commercial release, staging plays with travelling theatre groups and producing full-length feature films. Their dances and songs are becoming media friendly and accessible to public. In the process though, their dances are becoming the pastime of the gentry/elite/ *bhadralok* who are in search of romanticism or alternative forms or models.

The Santals' means of livelihood have undergone a lot of change. They have moved into modern industries that are labour intensive like coalmines, factories, tea gardens, and railways as skilled and unskilled workers, swelling the ranks of modern work force.[26] Coalmines and the tea gardens enjoy traditional popularity among the Santals. Education and employment have given rise to a middle class [27] with its own aspirations and ambitions, forming an interest-group identity. In the individual areas, the ways of life and the adjustment patterns of the Santals indicate their search for a great tradition.[28]

This leads to a "loyalty" towards indigenous culture and attempts are made to preserve its "pristine, virginal" nature to be used as a means of negotiating with the dominant cultures. The importance of the symbols of the dominant cultures is reflected in the institutionalization of the hitherto unfocussed symbols of their tradition like language, script, literature, religion and the performing arts (there are many more), to establish the credentials of distinction in an increasingly plural milieu.

Coming back to the micro level, the locus of my respondents, Birbhum,

West Bengal is away from such "mainstream" Santal efforts at rank enhancement. Christianity is not that widespread, the Christian Santals found here are not part of the first lot to be converted by overseas missionaries. The Christian Santals here are the outcome of individual options. The Santals here do not have many avenues of economic upliftment, this being underdeveloped industrially. Politically too, this area is in the backwaters; the Santals here have not been included in the demand for Jharkhand, in fact they are encapsulated in the dominant political force of West Bengal in which they do not always have distinct voices with special needs. Here rank concession [29] works more socially than otherwise. The dominant view is one of looking down upon the Santals that they have come to accept and ignore, as only they can, with dignity and least apparent disturbance. Their perceptions of non-Santals as alien or *diku* (the Santali word for alien) probably help them to maintain distance. Their history bears evidence of their perceptions of the alien/*diku* as justified; we cannot claim any such excuse for harbouring similar feelings of alienation from them. We have to recognize that the Santals are in a process of transition, they too are confronting the forces of change, and that the negative attitudes and prejudices of others compound their condition. The situation becomes even more complex as the Santals facing the pressures of change perforce have to jump a few of the intervening steps, expressing variously the tensions that are reflected in behaviour that may be socially aberrant or alienated from their culture and society. Living as members of plural societies, there is no possibility for the Santals to be unaffected by pressures of this day and age.

Acknowledgements

A version of this paper was read in the XIVth International Congress of Anthropological and Ethnological Sciences held in Virginia, USA, in July 1999. I am grateful to Professor Baidyanath Saraswati, Dr. R.K. Bhattacharya and Dr. Jeanne Openshaw for their comments and suggestions on the paper.

NOTES

1. Attitudes—an enduring system of positive or negative evaluations, emotional feelings and pro or con action tendencies with respect to a social object. Krech, Crutchfield and Ballachey. 1962. *Individual in Society.* N.Y., USA: McGraw Hill.

2. Prejudice—an unfavourable attitude towards an object that tends to be highly stereotyped, emotionally charged and not easily changed by contrary information *ibid.*
3. Modernity- as opposed to tradition, indicating change in a specific direction with the object of accommodating the changes over time. Obviously modernity is differentially perceived and internalized. "It is ...normative shifts and rationalizations of the life-world and its cosmology which have defined the notion of modernity", Singh, Y. 1998. "A Life-World of Disenchantment..." *Sociological Bulletin*, 47 (2): 155. "A dichotomy between tradition and modernity is untenable. What we witness in real life is an interactive or adaptive relationship between the two" *ibid.*: 165.
4. Bhattacharya, K., "Traditional Wisdom and Expertise in Agro Technology Generation and Use–Some Concepts" unpublished paper presented in the Indian Social Science Congress held in 1993, abstract available in the proceedings of the Congress.
5. Bhattacharya, K and Bhattacharya, R. K. 1995. "Santal Identity in Transition", in K.K.Chakraborty (ed.) *Tribal Identity in India: Extinction or Adaptation.* Bhopal, Indira Gandhi Rashtriya Manav Sangrahalay. In this paper we have talked about two types of identity–primordial and interest identity, to distinguish between one brought about through socialization within a community and the latter shaped by the cross pressures and currents of being a member of a plural society; in both cases identity is seen as an adjustment mechanism. See also Brass, Paul R. 1991. *Ethnicity and Nationalism: Theory and Comparison.* New Delhi: Sage Publications.
6. There is a distinction between character and personality. Personality has no value loading and character is the value-loaded manifestation of personality. Hilgard, Atkinson and Atkinson. 1975. *Introduction to Psychology,* New Delhi: Oxford and IBH. There is a tendency to use the word character when thinking about the tribes or others who do not belong to our ilk. There is also a hint of the issue of "morals" in that thinking.
7. "Contact" is preferred over "interaction" as the latter assumes a kind of exchange between persons who share something in common. There is very little in common between the Santals and the non-Santals.
8. The bulk of this data is from Santals of a few villages in Birbhum, a district in West Bengal, and a few villages in Santal Parganas, a district in Bihar.
9. Reference as in note 5: pp: 59.
10. *Ibid.*: 60. Also, Somers, George E. 1977. *The Dynamics of Santal Tradition in a Peasant Society,* New Delhi: Abhinav.
11. Bhattacharya, K. 1995. "Religion of the Santals," in R.K. Bhattacharya and Ashok Ghosh (eds.) *Sociology in the Rubric of Social Science. R.K.Mukherjee Felicitation Volume,* pp. 257, Calcutta: Anthropological Survey of India, Government of India.
12. Bhattacharya, K. 1999, "Socialization in a Santal Village," *Journal of Comparative Cultures,* No. 4, August 1999, pp: 13-41, Faculty of Comparative Cultures, Sapporo University, Japan. I was invited to deliver this talk in the Universities of Sapporo and Ritsumeikan University, Japan in February 1999.

Also a paper "Growing up in a Santal Village," jointly with R.K. Bhattacharya in Georg Pfeffer and D.K. Behera (eds.) *Contemporary Society: Tribal Societies,* Volume 1, pp. 303, New Delhi, Concept.

13. Archer, W.G. 1974. *A Hill of Flutes, Life, Love and Poetry in Tribal India, A Portrait of the Santals,* London: George Allen and Unwin Ltd.
14. Bhattacharya, K. 1991. "Aspects of Polyethnic Behaviour" in Baidyanath Saraswati (ed.) *Tribal Thought and Culture, Essays in Felicitation of Surajit C. Sinha.* pp. 204, New Delhi: Concept.
15. See reference in note 5, pp 60.
16. Sahlins, Marshall D. 1974. *Stone Age Economics*, pp. 2, 37, London: Tavistok. I have used the term to show the difference in perceptions of want and poverty by the Santals and other comparable (economically) groups. Like their world, their needs are "finite and few and technical means unchanging but on the whole adequate," and "goods do not have to be within control, they are to be believed accessible."
17. There is some historical evidence to suggest that collective expression of aggression against an individual(s) called *bitlaha* used to be in operation in the past and the process of making such a decision elaborate. However, a declaration of such revolt has become rare and difficult to effect given the restrictions of the state enforcement provisions.
18. See reference in note 14.
19. See reference in note 12.
20. Baski Boro. 1994. "An experienced Santal's thoughts on education," in *Sreyashi* (annual vernacular journal edited by Sm. Amita Sen and Sm. Debashree Ghosh, Santiniketan, West Bengal).
21. See reference in notes 14,12,11 &5.
22. Boding, P.O. 1925-27. *Santal Folk Tales*, 3 Volumes. Oslo, H. Aschelong & Co. 1925,1927 &1940 (3 Parts), *Studies in Santal Medicine and Connected Folklore.* Calcutta: Asiatic Society of Bengal.
    1942. *Traditions and the Institutions of the Santals.* Oslo: Oslo University Ethnographic Museum Bulletin.
    Culshaw, W.J. 1949. *Tribal Heritage.* London: Lutterworth Press.
    Culshaw, W.J. and Archer, W.G. 1945. "The Santal Rebellion," *Man in India,* Vol.XXV.
23. Mishra, Lakshmidhar. 1995. "Physical and Pedagogic Infrastructure," in Bhupinder Singh and Neeti Mahanti (eds.) *Tribal Education in India.* New Delhi: Inter-India Publications.
24. "Most of India's tribal people live below the poverty line...indigenous people who are integrated into a national society face discrimination, exploitation in housing, education and in matters having to do with language and religion. Those remaining in their traditional territories face disruption of their cultures and forced displacement as their lands and natural resources are claimed for national development," Singh, Bhupinder and Mahanti, Neeti (eds.) 1995. "Who are the World's Indigenous Peoples?" in *Tribal Education in India,* pp:105-106, New Delhi: Inter-India Publications,
25. Jena Smruti R. 1999. "The Problem of Script in Mother Tongue Education:

A Case of Santali," in the proceedings of the National Seminar of Research and Innovations on Home and Language Issues, Central Institute of Indian Languages, Mysore.

26. Ghosh, Subodh. 1995. *Bharater Adibasi* (The Tribes of India), 3rd Edition, pp. 78, Calcutta: National Book Agency.
27. *bid:* pp: 78-79.
28. Orans, Martin, 1965, *The Santals in search of a Great Tradition.* USA: Wayne State University Press. There may be dispute over the choice of terms describing traditions as great/little. However, the distinction is appropriate when two traditions, one with a long and coded history based on texts and a social order divided into organically linked subdivisions; and the other with a history of oral transmission and a homogenous social order, are compared/understood in perspective to each other. Modern thinking may make us desist from using such categories that may be negatively construed but there is much that can be explained by these categories within certain parameters.
29. *Ibid:* pp: 123-125, " 'Rank concession' means the acceptance of social inferiority... to accept inferior status is to accept the attributes of rank in a superior society."

SECTION III

CHANGING CULTURAL PATTERNS AND SOCIAL NETWORKS

SEVEN

FOREST SMELLS AND SPIDER WEBS: Ritualized Dream Interpretation and Power of Memory among Andaman Islanders

VISHVAJIT PANDYA

Introduction

In 1983 when I first started my field work among the Ongees of Little Andaman Island in the Bay of Bengal I carried with me some small soft stuffed toys in form of pigs and turtles. They were intended as gifts that I had procured for Ongee children. Within the small circular campsite made up of about nine sleeping platforms and thatched roof for each family I distributed my gifts among children. Ongee children grow up seeing the pigs and turtle as animals that are hunted and consumed, so the gifts were easily accepted but not as "warm cuddly toys to sleep with" within the campsite. They were tucked away as things under the thatched roof. However Ongee parents were astounded. They wanted to know why would children of outside world want to sleep with animals with exaggerated facial features. I had no explanation to offer them. Personally I had a childhood of just nice stories being read while I remained calm and quite and said my prayers. Parents made sure that I heard plots that were morally good, resolved conflict and had no bloody violent war - as was in many Indian mythological plots. The idea of how to fall asleep is important cultural construct since the emphasis is on one should wake up after good sleep with a memory of good dreams. However sleep is always a problem if you know that next morning is your birthday or Christmas day. In many children's childhood events of the morning make the sleep of the previous night a commemorated memory.

Like the stuffed toys intrigued Ongees, I too was immensely surprized that at the end of the day going to sleep within Ongee campsite was not at all a quite moment. Ongees before falling asleep would talk aloud all they did in the day and what they had dreamed about the previous night. Over a period I realized that all Ongees tried to reach to a consensus that they had identical dreams and days experience, a memory interpreted and derived to go to sleep with, much like all the children with some narrative, or a stuffed animal to go to sleep with making the event of going to sleep a ritual.

Today most Ongees have a very different life style. Life in circular campgrounds within the forests has been replaced by living, in private quarters, arranged in rows. In the last ten years Ongees have shifted steadily from relying on hunting and gathering to becoming workers at coconut plantation and residing in a designated settlement area. Within the context of changes the basic Ongee notion of going to sleep *(umuka)*, of waking up and of discussing dreams *enay-te-gebey*[1] ("meanings-made"), has remained a unchanged concern. What really has changed for the Ongees is the way of sleeping and dreaming. It is this very Ongee explanation that I propose to utilize in understanding what dreams are about within the Ongee world-view.

Dreamer reciting a dream for the analyst to interpret sets up a process that locates the dreamer between conscious and unconscious.[2] Ongees too listen to each other dreams and interpret it for centring each "self's" action within society. This process of listening to each others dreams is identical to what Crapanzano (1992: 32) regards as ethnographer's symbolic understanding, through transference and counter transference, which articulates a discursive context that includes the symbolicity of the centred and centring images of the "informants" (ibid.). In Ongee practice of collective listening of dreams, each individual is centred and dreams are textulized for constructing what could be regarded as Ongee dialogical self (Clifford, 1988: 38-54). This makes dream discussions, among Ongees a cultural context in which, our psychoanalysis and our ethnography become a "fused horizon" (Gadamar, 1975). These fused horizons of Ongee's own ethnography and their own psychoanalysis has continued over the period in which the culture has experienced range of changes that have impact on sleeping, dreaming and talking about it among the Ongees. This makes dream and its very image among the Ongees an independent but adequate meta-language that communicates their psychoanalysis and ethnography as a communication process for themselves.[3] Within the Ongee culture it self the dream is a meta language that makes ethnography and psychoanalysis reflexive and mutually translatable (Marcus and Cushman, 1982; Kracke and Herdt, 1987) as their own commentaries on experience and reality, contrasting and reflecting on behaviour organized around concepts of the person, memory, and power. Analysis of the Ongee dream discussions and the image or metaphor of dream is an attempt to establish a frame of analysis from which Ongees derive "a realist reflexive ethnography" as well as treat dreams as their "psychodynamic text."[4]

Forest Camp Sites: The Place for Dreams and Talks

Since 1983 when I first visited Ongees of Little Andaman Island, many changes among the Ongees are apparent. In the past most of the community would set up sleeping platforms and leantos in the forest during the pig hunting season (May to September).[5] Within the forest camp grounds as the night set in Ongees retired on the sleeping platforms of each respective family under a leanto, often facing the fire in the centre of the camp ground, talking to each other across the camp grounds. One by one individuals either emerge as trying to convince that they did see a particular dream or as the sing song declines in it's intensity individuals one by one would fall asleep.

Fig. 7.1: Forest Camp Grounds. The arrows indicate movement patterns in relation to place to meet before sleeping and direction to move after waking up.

A session of discussions and singing known as *tonki ti megegatebeh* (meanings for morning), mostly cuts across the genders and age divisions. Dream discussions *tonki ti megegatebeh* are highly stylized with words being dramatically stretched out. Often it starts with what was done during the day such as who went looking for betel nuts because they had dreamed about it in particular part of the forest and how little was found or; who took whose dogs for hunting pigs and was the pig fat enough, like the smell of cooked pig fat in the dream or; which part of the forest seems to have more and heavy honey combs or; which part of the creek has no crabs left in it and how wrong the dream was.[6] These just stating aspirations, as we would express in phrase like "I have a dream!," but combined with it are desires

Fig.7.1

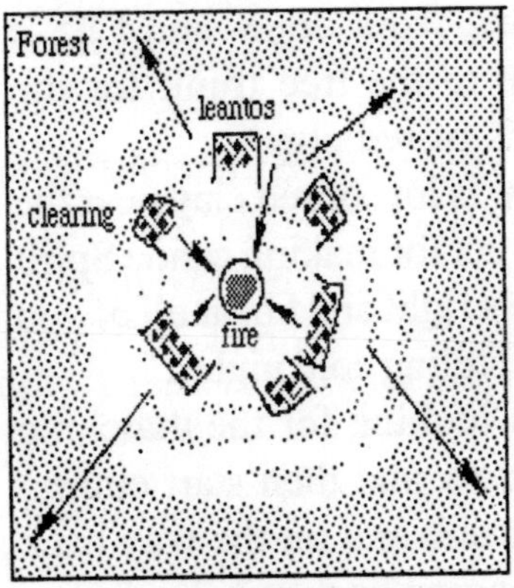

CAMP GROUND

of spirit communicator indicating what should be done or what is going to happen. Often what spirit communicator[7] narrated as their dreams was a response to series of needs and wants expressed by camp mates as "my dream." Two common themes emerge within the Ongee dream discussions. First where to find what in which part of the island in relation to time and season. Secondly, did the dream of the previous night actualise on the following day? Generally this discussion or exchange of information about what activities were undertaken in the day, successfully or unsuccessfully develops into all the camp mates discussing what they would like to do on the following days. Here is a typical example of what I heard within a forest campsite of about nine shelter surrounding a campfire in the centre of campground in late August evening of 1984.

Shelter 1(man) — "I better find a small tree as the one I see in the dreams to cut down to make a new canoe for my nephew."

Shelter 4, 5 and 6 (women) — "We have been dreaming rains and the thatch is leaking we need to get some new thatching made!"

Shelter 3 — "We are running low on the supply of warm red clay we need to get some, I have smelled the rains in my dreams and felt shivering cold, but I have not seen where we are going to get red clay!"

Shelter 7 (Torale) — "I have had dreams of down pour -we must get the thatching work done- and I have seen that close to the tree trunk for the canoe is a stock of red clay!"

Shelter 1(man) — "Yes! Yes! there is lots of red clay near the tree we need to get for making canoe Spirit communicator is right and I hear all of you seeing rain and feeling cold nights."

Shelter 2 and 8 — "We should go looking for the thatching material tomorrow and then start cutting down the tree trunk and on the way back we can start bringing back red clay lumps we have been smelling the rain on the hot ground we will need the thatching and the warming red clay."

All dreams are heard and during the day the activities undertaken, are based on the dream discussed on previous night. This makes the practice in daytime and structure of night dream mutually reflexive in making meanings. Individuals recite what they have been dreaming of or not dreaming of, often indexed by olifactorial references to places, events and activities. Sometimes what is seen and smelled in the dream on being collectively interpreted coincides with the intent of days activities is glossed as *eneyemaga-tegebe* dream success. In case of failure the discussions on dreams *nakeboi-ke-tegebe* continue before going to sleep to arrive at a consensus on what changes are being dreamed and what changes are actually experienced by the individuals in the forest (cf. Carey, 1976: 200-1; Dubois, 1961: 45-6, 294-340 and Schebesta, 1926: 146).

The dreams talked among Ongees often deploys olifactorial indexes,[8] smells that vary in intensity, escape, can be traced but are not visible. Smell is contained making the container of or source of smell an issue to be interpreted, contested and negotiated. Much like the image seen in the individual dream that has to be collectively visualized by interpreting the dreams within the camp. For example some individuals may report that they have been all dreaming about the smell of ripe jackfruit, smell of roasted seeds of the fruit. Together they form a group say A, who at daybreak will team up to go and look for the jackfruits in the forest. Those who do not join group A, form group B, and insist that they did not dream of any wet forest floor smell or decaying jack fruits indexing that in their dream they have not experienced the change into the ripe jack fruit season. So the dream is a work of making smells that index places and coordinate activities of day to day life. Once the majority of the camp mates can interpret the individual dreams as indicative of the change to ripe jackfruit season they all collectively go seeking and gathering the jack fruits.

Often the camp mates wait till the whole group starts smelling the damp forest floor and decomposing overripe jack fruits littered under the tree, in their collectively discussed dreams. Ongee dream work and interpretation is about construction of meanings through translation. Translating smell from dreams into actual act of looking for the smell image compiled by the group's interpretation and then matching the sense of smell and vision within the space. Thereby creating the forest as an ethnographic space where multiple sensory landscapes are made meaningful (cf. Stoller, 1989: Introduction). Much like the Surrealists who utilised the dreams as a discourse based in vision that generated literature and collage out of dreams that were foundations of "Automatic writing" (See Breton, 1978). Individuals whose dreams are different from others, go as individuals looking for what the dream presents them with. If they frequently succeed in gaining what they see and smell in the dream they become influential individuals known as *Torale, one* who communicates with spirits during dreams and makes meanings before others can. *Torale is regarded* as a

> "Weaver of dream like a very large spiders web from which nothing escapes, it is a web that is unlike other webs, spread across the horizon and so is the torale able to see, smell, move and say more."

As Ongees fall asleep they talk about what they did not find (actuality/reality/negative) in the time experienced and what they would like to gain (ideal/approximation/positive) in the time that has yet to be experienced. Both, gains and losses, connected by the process of searching or looking for, an act that underlies the fundamental lifestyle of the traditional Ongee hunters and gatherers.[9] Often the individuals whose dream do not fit in with the most common interpretation of dream either remain quite or try to relate with the others dream talk or may decide to pursue all alone the activity they interpret out of their dream.[10] This makes individual Ongee dreams' interpreted by the narrator, another individuals in campsite further interpret the dreamers interpretation as they listen to the dreams.

This interpretation of the interpreted dream by the collective is called *Gilemamamey ibukibe*, end of forgetting. For Ongees to end the possibility of things being forgotten is a way of saying what should be remembered. *Gilemamamey ibukibe* is regarded as something important that has to be remembered. What is to be remembered is the outcome of a collective interpretation, since it conditions collective practice and existence.[11] Often during the day when all that was dreamt and deciphered was accomplished the camp mates would say that "It was a good day of gains! Tonight we will have *gigabawe* (singing sessions, literally to cause attraction and attachment)." For Ongees this sort of singing was not just a "joint social activity" (Radcliffe-Brown, 1964: 248-52) but above all asserting the faith in capacity to collectively interpret dreams and connect the success of interpretation to the memory of previous successful events as outcome of collective dream interpretations. Subject of the songs are often events of various sorts from the past such as great hunts, historical encounters are regarded as successful remembrance of all. Such events become reference points for the songs sung in the night within the camp. Individuals sing one line indicating the reference point to an specific event and other camp mates join in the chorus to repeat the line and then some other individual will add another line by singing in a pitch that is different from that of the chorus. So line by line the memory of events are added to the songs and the low-pitched repetition of the chorus line keeps going on. The song comes to an end if no one adds to the lines as individual or chorus just refuses to repeat the individual line. A way of saying "we do not remember that aspect of the event!"

As the sun sets down on a forest campsite, the interpreted dreams are interpreted by the collective as something to be remembered for the next day. Much like the events from past through singing are remembered. So end of a "good day" is a construct of collective dream interpretation of smell and place interconnected and remembering past events connected within in the form of song lines. However the Ongees do not regard the two different forms of discourse, narrating the dreams for interpretation and collective act to sing events remembered, as separate. For them it is all one idea that has to be remembered and be reminded of as a process of connecting dreams, smells, places and past events of success. Many Ongees regard this remembering and connecting as a complete "Spiders web" (*dane korale*).[12] A term for the dream and image of individuals and forest camp site, constructed by interpretation of smells, images and past actions. Something that is built by narrating dreams and singing. Connecting the dream for the next day and memory of the past. Ongees explained that

> "to talk about the dreams and sing about the past makes a good spiders web that connects all the open space to catch its' food - it is a weave with all the lines are woven to let the spider know what is caught where —We in remembering and dreaming make a web for all individuals to gain."

Fig. 7.2: *Dane Korale:* A perfect and complete home of Spider. Image of a proper, perfect and positive dream.

Fig. 7.2

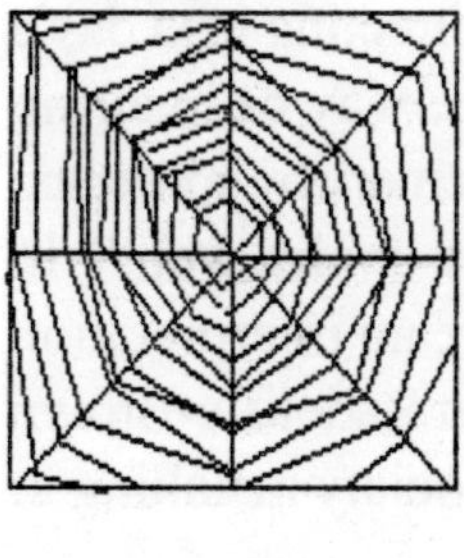

This interpretation of an interpreted dream by the collective for the Ongees is the termination of forgetting and installation of memory. As a result, often before camp-mates fall asleep, closing consensus statement on what would be done at daybreak is declared. It is something that has to be remembered as a product of collective interpretation, since it will condition collective practice. This practice not only brings forth individual dreams and personal interpretation's, but also remembrance from the past of great hunting events or historical encounters. For Ongees going to sleep is not a quiet moment but a time of intense verbal reenactment of various memories that are recited and sung. Dream work and real work are interpreted; meaning is made meaningful.

Ongee Process and Form of Dream

Ongees believe that each individual living body is made up of two distinct parts. *Mateeah* the external body that is visible, and concrete. It responds to the time and conditions around. The second part is, *enteeah* body internal that is not visible and abstract but conducts the activities and feelings of the external body. *Enteeah* for the Ongees is a form of the body that is detachable and goes out of the *mateeah* when an individual is asleep and collects all the smell left behind by the individual bodies (cf. Radcliffe-Brown, 1966: 167). The state of dream is the process of body internal moving around all over the island and collecting the smells scattered by the individual in the duration of being awake. This process of "smell fragments or bits" being collected is *dane korale*, a spider making web, dreaming. Dream as seen by the individual is images and smells transferred by the body internal while individual is asleep by consolidation of the scattered "smell bits" left around by the body external. While smell being collected images of the place are transferred to the individuals in state of sleep. Since all individuals share the forest campsite and activities it becomes possible to connect the smells and places from dream and to construct interpretation of a Dream. "A large spider web made by lots of small one connected together."

Fig. 7.3: *Dane korale*: A spiders large home as imagined by the Ongees by sleeping in the forest camp.

Fig. 7.3

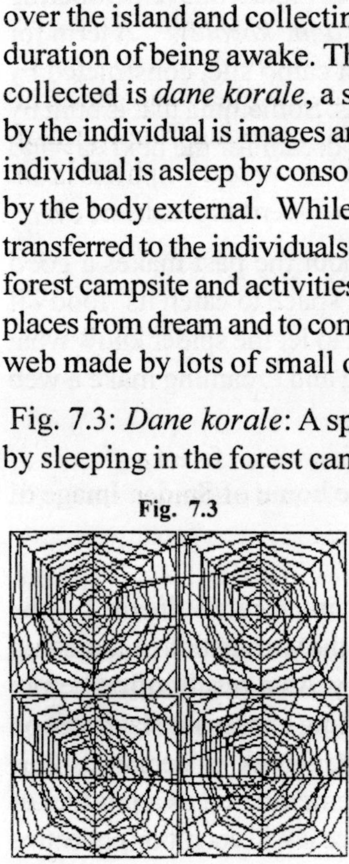

This makes possible the duration of interpreting the dreams a way to coordinate most individuals and construct memory for directing next day's function. This is an Ongee way of insuring success and accumulating memory by upholding the desire to make a "large spider web." In the success of collective dream interpretation is the collective gain of what Radcliffe-Brown regarded as Andamanese society installing in the individual a sense of dependence, a system of sentiments regulating the individual to conform with the society (Radcliffe-Brown, 1966: 232-35).[13]

The importance of the dream shared and talked about in fact conditions the rule of not waking up the sleeping person (Radcliffe-Brown, 1966: 167). Ongees always wait for the individuals to finish *umuka* sleep so that the individual's body internal has completed making the spiders' web.[14] To let a person finish dreaming or sleep in and not wake up insures the return of the body internal and also facilitate the dream or his spiders web to interconnect with the other Ongees dreams/ spider web. Ongees say that, by not waking up somebody asleep

> "We make sure that the person remains with us as living being all his smell scattered through out the day must be put back to make body strong like the web of spider. To wake up a person in the sleep would break the web! On waking up person will not know what to do and what others are planning!"

The idea of letting the "web be complete" and all people interpreting the recited/interpreted dream is Ongee way of "centring" the self and multiple self into one society. What for Freud was the image of "mushroom and navel" for Ongees is a spiders' web.[15] For us different dream types make different forms of anxiety and symptoms of "abnormality" emerging from world of conscious and unconscious. For the Ongees the power and emphasis is on dreams being interpreted to make things as normal,[16] centring each and every individual into a society. It marks completeness of society and individuals in it not separating the world smelled and seen while sleeping but unifying it with the world that can be smelled, seen and acted upon while being awake.

Sleeping and Dreams within Context of Settlement

Around 1990 most of the Ongees who use to shift between forest and coastal camps settled down in Island Administration managed settlement areas of Dugong creek and South Bay on Little Andaman Island. Occasionally Ongees go out hunting but mostly depend on rations being distributed through Andaman Island Administration (See Awaradi, 1990: 195-221). Much of the payments in kind are made for the labour provided by the community of about 96 Ongees as they work on the coconut plantation. In fact Ongees living in the settlement makes it feasible to organize the labour force to work at the coconut plantation on day to day basis. The establishment of settlements also has brought with it aspects like posting of a social worker, who is in charge of managing all the payments implementation of "developmental policy" and providing rations along with overseeing health department personnel posted at the settlement, an electrician to oversee the power generation, a plantation overseer and a school teacher. It has become a shrinking forest in which Ongees are allotted living quarters in the settlement and are surrounded by increasing number of outsiders. Much of the forest has been cleared in the neighbourhood of the Ongee reserve forest and small agricultural communities have settled down. All this presents the Ongees with a different image; an image of market, things made outside, and above all it has introduced the notion of money as a means of acquiring all that the "outsiders" have. It is a situation of two world-views colliding. One of Ongee as a hunter and gatherer in the forest, something that embodies the past. Second being and the world view, based on present political economy of manufactured commodities, work and wages that provide money in hands of Ongees.[17] It has now become more practical for the Ongees to live on the settlement and stay close to the quarters of the authorities, the ration store and the plantation.

Fig 7.4: Settlement Grounds. The arrows indicate movement patterns in relation to place to meet before sleeping and direction to move after waking up.

Fig. 7.4

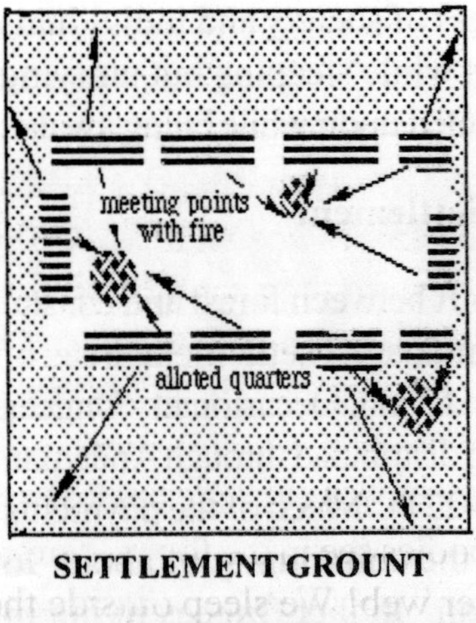

SETTLEMENT GROUNT

Within the settlement the rectangular space is organised in rows of individual family sleeping quarters. Each structure raised about five feet high on stilts is an enclosed wooden room and tin roof. Life in circular camp grounds, with sleeping platform covered only on the top and back side, has been replaced by living in private quarters arranged in rows. However some families continue to live outside the "settlement area" or, for a duration move out and live in the traditional campgrounds within the forest, especially for ritual ceremonies or at the insistence of the *torale*, spirit communicator. Most Ongees residing in the settlement, in small groups collect around fire set out side the house to hold session of discussions (*tonki ti megegatebeh*) and then retire to their allocated quarters for sleeping. This practice of holding discussion has continued from the days when most Ongees stayed outside the settlement area and rarely used the houses provided to them. What has transformed is that Ongees now do not fall asleep while discussing but after discussion have to get up and go to sleep within the enclosed house.

Most Ongees who have now become habituated and dependent on the life within the settlement regard that dreams are seldom same and subject to interpretation. With in the walls, enclosed space illuminated by electricity, sleeping and dreaming in settlement is different. With changing times and space the dream or the "spider's web" itself has changed. Factors responsible for these changes in "spider's web" are many like the enclosed house that restricts the movement of body internal, as well as talking across the space from sleeping platforms as was the case in forest camps. But the most important explanation lies in the fact that the social worker and overseer who maintains the coconut plantation at the settlement are regarded as frequent breaker, (*gatuwey-negeey*) of the spiders web, since they go around at 8.00 in the morning trying to wake up Ongee to report to work. The fact that a minimum payment is assured to Ongees by government policy but not able to get them to work was often seen by the plantation in charge as dealing with "Governments paid, lazy, good for nothing, son in laws!" So from Ongee perspective the ethnographic reality is based within the altered way in which they have to go to sleep and the dramatically different ways in which they have to get up in the morning. It may be true that things, and money is available by being in the settlement but the life in the settlement has restricted the moving in and out of body internal due to sleeping quarters and morning wake up calls. As a young couple living outside the settlement with his mothers brother known for being a spirit communicator said,

> "People in the settlement have broken incomplete spider's web there sleep broken by the *Babulee.*[18] They fail to see what the body internal wants to show them in the forest, so they continue to live in the settlement - sometime they come to sleep with us specially on occasions when they want to remember what it is to be able to make the web! Individuals who always stay in the settlement have lost the power to get up! on their own and make a large spider web based on what the different internal bodies see in the forest- people in the settlement have no large spider web! We sleep outside the settlement so that we can dream and continue to remember and make memories."

According to the uncle, who lives with his young nephew and his wife, the people residing in the settlement do not gather as a whole group to really listen to the dream work. They meet for a short duration before going to sleep, they fail to convey to each other any meanings and the gatherings are small and multiple.

> "After talk they go to respective quarters for sleep, they can never weave together a large web… and then they work only on the plantation and are waken up! So the body smell is never really scattered over the parts of forest, consequently the web is never complete. It is not a complete web but small broken webs. Ongees of settlement hence tend to keep forgetting. Even if they go to the forest they gain nothing because they smell little in the dreams and that limits what could be talked about."

I was reminded by the Ongee making their own ethnographic observations that, the individuals in the settlement had designated latrines in a row and store from where they could collect rations. This was a case of smells all mixed up due to proximity of built structures within the settlement area. This had implication on the dreaming and forming of "webs."

> "There (Ongees in settlement) smell fragments are so mixed up in a small area that the web was not wide enough to locate things like pigs and crabs, fruits and turtle. Like the broken web from gaps of which food for spiders escape the people of the settlement were really never able to remember and gained nothing from the forest."

Fig. 7.5: *Gatuwey Dane korale*: Imperfect Spiders web. Image of improper, incomplete and negative dream

Fig. 7.5

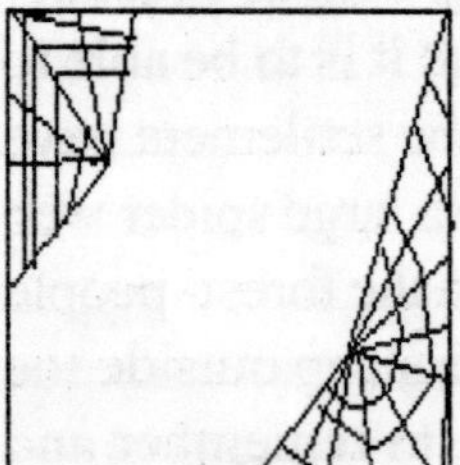

Where one sleeps for Ongees constitutes power of the person to articulate the society's idea of a spiders web in which psychoanalytical as well as ethnographic discourse is embedded. It precisely this that makes Ongee dreams not only a change between body internal and body external, smell seen and seeing the smell but also about power of change. As result the spirit communicator (*torale*) or *Oko Jumu* (Radcliffe Brown, 1966: 177-78) are regarded as having power and influence as they dream, since their body internal flies upwards while other body internal just move in the forest. This distinctive quality of spirit communicator sleep provides him with a vision of all the "possible spiders web that could be made." A view that includes both forest and settlement. A dream that may start as an individual's daydream but becomes vision dream for all.

In 1993 when I asked the Ongees, living in settlement but known to me since days of forest camps why they could not succeed in hunting any more? I was expecting to hear the failure being explained in terms of forest being lost to growing number of outsiders. But the Ongees explained the decline in hunting practice due to lack of a proper sleeping place[19] that would generate dreams about hunting space.

> "To do good forest work like hunt we need to discuss dreams of forest. We do not dream forests anymore! We are forgetting to work in the forest because we are reminded to get up and work in the plantation!. . . We now dream only coconut plantation. We do not have any *tonki ti megegatebeh* just few small *meeting-ey*."[20]

Individuals gather at places near or below the quarters built on stilts, and then they went back to their respective sleeping areas where the walls restricted the body internal to bring back all the smells scattered in the limited areas. The settlement is a different place to sleep that does not support holding of *tonki ti megegatebeh* (a session of dream discussions and singing). For Ongees the "group therapy" like talk about the dreams before going to sleep was not powerful enough. Generally in the late evenings within the settlement area of Dugong Creek either there are no talks held before sleeping or two or three fires are set up in different locations and individuals keep moving from one to the other sessions. Much like the authorities and outsiders having *meeting-ey* among themselves. It was never a "complete and perfect spiders web." Since they could not fall asleep talking they had to get up and leave the gathering once they got sleepy. In this process Ongees feel that they never remember any thing and the "web remained always small and incomplete." Things could escape from it, much like the forgetting or not being successful at hunt.

> "For us sleeping and dreaming has changed. We dream different since we live differently in different space and experiences are different, unlike the spirit communicator and people outside the settlement our bodies both internal and external does not see or smell much and

so we remember less and what is not seen or smelled can not be said before going to sleep."[21]

Fig. 7.6: *Dane Korale*: A spiders large home as imagined by the Ongees sleeping within the settlement

Fig. 7.6

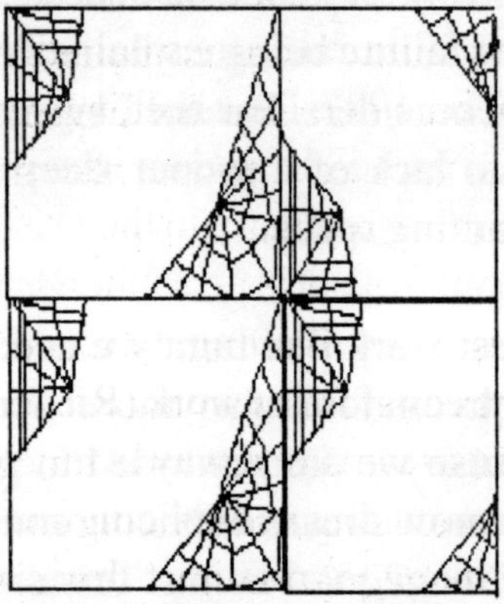

Conclusion: Some Implications and Considerations

For Ongees dreams are not entirely subjective, private and illusionary but aspects of real and community life. Ongees are concerned with meaning of what the image is symbolising within the dream as well as what reality may be attributed to the dream. Power is in capacity to bring the two meanings together and produce a memory before falling asleep. The ritualised context where text like dreams are interpreted, individuals' dream and sense of self within the intertextuality of the dreams presented get located within the collective. As dreams are recited and heard along with the singing it bring together both the "unacknowledged memory" and "acknowledged collective forgetting" (cf. Battaglia, 1993). Forgetting and remembering in form of narrating the dreams, discussing dreams to make a meaning, followed by singing songs commemorating events of past is Ongee culture's acknowledgement of shared purposeful activities that articulates relations of power and work for individual person within forest or settlement. However issue of memory and lack of it is not a problematic but is something that is resolved in Ongee explanation of change in the structure of sleep and context in which dream work is talked.

Through dreams Ongees talk about self and other in idioms, something fundamental to Anthropology and the anthropologised Ongees. However

Ongees do not insulate ideas of person and self in their description of dream experience. Dream telling and interpreting is culturally constructed within the society and changing times unfolding the cultures logic that different places generate different ways to sleep and dream. Dreams are different not because of individuals but because of the places and smells that individuals are subject to. Therefore when dreams are told, inferences are and can be made not only about the way particular person construe themselves but also about social traditions, customs, cultural values beliefs and change (Dombeck, 1991; Tedlock, 1987; Kracke, 1987; Domhoff, 1985). This is Ongee cultures' own hermenutic approach to the self and an interpretation of one's person hood; a process that takes place regularly in the late evening among Ongees. One's self and an interpretation of one's personhood is constantly reinterpreted by the dreams recited in the late evening, to create new interpretations of self, reintroduced into ones own framework (Ricuer, 1992: 17). The Ongee interpretation of different dreams in a way is much like our ethnographic practice much dependent on cutting and splicing abutting context to context, (See Radcliffe-Brown, 1966: 235) relating "them" to "us." This process of connecting context to context is also the conscious process the dream interpretation is all about the Ongees in forest camps or in the settlement. The very image of spiders' web, embodiment of all that can be interconnected, is an Ongee culture's explanatory and referential frame for what dream is. Dreams as they are presented and interpreted among the Ongees makes it possible to connect, smell to place, site to sight, body internal to body external and past within the forest camp to present and future in the settlement.

It could be argued that Ongee notion of self is produced by a dialectic between referential aspects and reflexive aspects of self a constant activity that regularly engages one to localised understanding of person, history, and memories within the forest and within the settlement. The context of dream being discussed among Ongees fosters lack of a singular interpretation and an opacity of historical changes, such as forest camps to settlements. However Ongee interpretation and discussion of multiple dreams among themselves does not generates conflict. For Ongees different dreams and interpretations exist because of degrees of change in their political economy; that is change from hunting and gathering in forest to working in plantation both are real and interconnected. This interconnectedness creates a continuity or a shift between different sleeping contexts and not a strong clear division.[22] In fact the change in situation prevents dreaming and this makes the dreams in settlement overcome the conflict or resolve the tension of what is remembered, and that which is forgotten. In other words Ongees in the process of sleeping in settlement design and discuss dreams that are conducive and interpretable for continued existence in the settlement. As a result often at the sessions held within the settlement individuals would ask the spirit communicator,

> "Have you been dreaming of the helicopter landing down with government guests? When would that be? We can smell all the new gifts they would bring for us! We will all dance for the visitors and be so tired that for few days we will stay away from smell and sweat of the coconut plantation!"

Since dreaming in settlement is different the past life of being in the forest is not potential dream image that individuals have to process as memory any more. Absence of the perfect web like dreams of the Ongees in the settlement in fact generates no memories to be organised via discussions or singing, no smell fragments lost in forest have to be consolidated by the body internal. Forgetting the ways of the forest and remembering the settlement only has becomes the concern of dream interpretation sessions.[23] In recognition of the dreams in settlement that are conditioned by the political economy and power relations of production, Ongees see a generation of "no memory" emerging; *Inachekamey!* something forgotten. All this for Ongees is a process of creating "a productive plantation worker" and dependent consumer of non-forest commodities. As a result, young Ongee children now regard the morning wake up call of the plantation in charge as just a regular feature like the morning bird's call. "When *babulee* comes to wake up we get to put on the clothes given by the *babulee*, it is time to go to social worker's house and get work and food for the day."

Sleeping and dreaming in settlement for Ongees is not unsettling in relation to the context of forest. They just mark the change from the ones experienced and generated in the forest. It is not a matter of this meaning or that meaning but an issue of making public and social the mutually separate meanings of dreams to coexist, through the process of remembered memory and forgotten memory. From Ongee perspective; it is not a critique of change in itself, but is about the consequences of change, in which Ongee dreams not only change, but also communicate about change.[24] Things that one dreams about change because for Ongees change itself is a dream. So the Ongees of Little Andaman always say that the, "*Dane korale* (spider's web, dream) is constantly changing because the spider keeps weaving it again and again."

NOTES

1. In Ongee language *Gategebe* is the root word for "meaning," adding prefix *tehy* makes the word *tegebeh* literally implying make meaning.
2. See Freud on case of wolf man (1959: *The Dynamics of Transference,* pp. 312-322).
3. In my approach I therefore want to differentiate the Andamanese material on which psychoanalytical interpretations are based (See Kracke, 1978: 137) from the use of ethnography to construct indigenous interpretations in relation to parallel process of understanding ethnographic reality and psychoanalytical questioning (Obeysekere, 1981).
4. Anthropologists concern with "self" is an important issue identifying self as a cultural construct expressed through symbols, images and metaphors that are socially shared and publicly communicated (Geertz, 1974; Marriott, 1976, 1980; Levy, 1973; Rosaldo, 1983). Indigenous theories of self have been outlined to formulate "ethnopsychology" but the focus has been on explaining inconsistent concepts of world and self modified in course of social interaction. Focus has been on the content of referential meanings of the informants' accounts about themselves and their culturally organised world. My concern is with the process by which Ongees themselves in the late evening interact as individuals draw upon congruent smell-images from dreams as well as resolve inconsistencies in the dream and society observable in daily interaction. Ongee culture in a way provides the vocabulary and image to the individuals for presenting themselves that becomes the basis for interpreting self.
5. During season of turtle hunting (October to April) Ongees shift campsite to coastal area.
6. See Pandya (1992) for how dream discussion within the campsite parallels the game of hide and seek played between Ongee adults and children.
7. *Torale*, Ongee spirit communicator (Pandya, 1993: 150-63) is identical to Radcliffe-Brown (1966: 177-78) outlining the position of *Oko-Jumu* as being an individual with power over others obtained by privileged dreams in which spirits are in direct communication. In his dreams he can inflict sickness as well as cure (cf. Man, 1883: 28-29).
8. For the central principle of smell within Andamanese culture and how it indexes ideas about time see Radcliffe-Brown's discussion on names (1966: 118-119) and how the seasons are actually constituted as the "calender of smells" (1966: 311-12). Note how the names and seasons both are issues dealing with change. The importance of smell and the value it has specifically within Ongee culture has been analysed as means to articulate safety and gain (See Pandya, 1993: Ch. 4).
9. As a consequence the Ongees distinguish between two major group identities as turtle Hunters, those who can see well and Pig hunters those who can hear well. All marriages must be negotiated between the two groups (See Pandya, 1993: 21-23).
10. In case the individual succeeds in his or her individual pursuit the dream and

act is shared before going to sleep and the individuals try to report on following days if they have been dreaming of similar images and cooperate with the activity that a lone individual had started.

11. Within the Ongee culture the "end of forgetting" and "interpreted meanings to be remembered" play an important role in the initiation ritual of the boys. After series of pig hunts lead by the initiate over 15 to 20 days and nights of initiators singing to the initiate the end of initiation (*Tanageru*) is marked by letting the novice sleep in an isolated sleeping platform and on waking up the camp mates recite all the aspects that the novice should not forget. This collective recitation that marks the end of initiation ceremony is also called *Gilemamamey ibukibe* (See Pandya, 1993: 239-46, and 261-80).
12. In course of field work, in order to understand references to image like spiders web Ongees while moving through the forest would frequently point out to me the webs and say- "See this is a good dream" or point out to an imperfect web and state "No good! nothing is connected things can escape from this web." Much was gained by the Ongees always eager to show the actual image and the idea it represented and in fact this is a way in which many Ongee children are socialised (See Pandya, 1992).
13. I regard this process of dream interpretation as Ongee psychoanalysis as well as they doing their own ethnography, paralleling to what method Radcliffe Brown derived (1966: 235) by stating that when same or similar custom is practised on different occasions "meaning of a custom is discovered by ascertaining what that common element is"(ibid.). This method of ethnographic analysis is what Ongees are doing by listening to each other's dream interpretation to come to a common understanding that effects next days' activity. Consequently Radcliffe-Brown regarded the Andamanese "savage" capable of rationalising under "ethnologist attacking with questions, as "seeks to rationalise his behaviour; being impelled to certain actions by mental dispositions of whose origin and real nature he is unaware" (ibid.).
14. The image of the spiders web and actual variations as they can be seen in nature were often pointed out to me and referred to as place by which no one has moved by, I have used the pointed out images as a way to depict the metaphoric use of Ongees and my ethnographic depiction. In a way this is following what Lacan (1977) regards as the metaphor of mirror for articulating properties and function of the self.
15. On Freud's idea of centring see *The interpretation of Dreams* (1954: 525, 428) where the images of navel, of a mushroom growing, of fertility and reproduction metaphorise the female sexual organ in interpretation.
16. Perhaps the Ongees before going to sleep, practice what we now days call as a group therapy for individuals who congregate and acknowledge the problem collectively as in the case of violent individuals or substance abusers. This makes the self comprized of whole spectrum of nuances and meanings, implicit and explicit notions of power correlating Ongee ethos, social structure and institutions (Fogelson, 1977: 193). The issue of power as expressed through dreams and memory are "not simplistic causal relations" but "correlation between"(ibid.) culturally constituted explanations and

mechanisms in response to the belief about the process of sleep and dream and effects or reflections of institutional and social structural changes (cf. Levi-Strauss, 1963).

17. Often the two worldviews collide for Ongee individuals. They fail to realise why they are given limited wages for the plantation work, but if they give to outsiders something collected from the forest they get immediately large amount of money. Plantation labour provides money (wages) only at the end of the month, this is seen as an anomaly by the Ongees. It is also a problem for the social worker who frequently has to open the ration store in a day and give food supply according to individuals demand. Ongees refuse to take and keep supplies for say a week. With the clash of two world views accounting and responsibility in relation to time, work and money is constantly questioned and asserted between Ongees and the outsiders managing the plantation and settlement on behalf of the Administration.

18. A term derived from *Babu*, Hindustani for administrative authority who goes around waking the "late risers" to report to work at coconut plantation.

19. See Dumont's account (1972: Ch. 5) of Panare Indians' outlines the cultural importance of the space constructed as a place to sleep in, with range of meanings.

20. In fact the irregular scattered gatherings held between the rows of Ongees quarters is referred to by the term "*meeting-ey*" (derived from English term meeting) acquired from the presence of the increasing number of administrative staff in the settlement who visit each other at the home for official business or just for a cup of tea and are heard saying "we are having a 'meeting'!" Interestingly enough in 1983 my long interview sessions were regarded by Ongees as, "talk and write work" but in recent times they frequently use the same encounter as "*meeting-ey*"

21. In a letter to Lowie dated 6th May 1938 (Stocking, 1976: 6) Radcliffe-Brown wrote "I do not think that any anthropologist had at that date ever done what I did, namely collect and record the dreams of a number of individuals with the aim of determining variability of type. I gave a paper at Cambridge before I went to the Andamans on the study of individual variability in communities of different type, and presented a sketch of my results in 1909. This particular part of my work was not relevant to the subject of my book and so was included." Although the letter was a defense of Andaman Islanders, the ethnography produced by work done in 1908-09, Radcliffe-Browns' account first published in 1922 (1963) and the letter to Lowie makes the point that Andamanese culture recognised the issue of Individual and individual variation of dreams- the variations were not only elicited by Radcliffe-Brown as an ethnographer but must be a concern of discussion as among the Ongees I have studied.

22. This notion in the shifts of dreams is also supported by the variations in the discussed dreams within the forest camps and coastal camps, which in past used to be set up, in accordance of seasonal changes.

23. In relatively recent field work among the Ongees I was informed that spirit communicators now contact body internal of the different *babulees* and

often can sense the day plantation work will not be undertaken as they have smelled *babulees* sick body.

24. Often when Ongees do not want to say some thing or should not say, like names of dead relatives they say "I forgot! I had not learnt to sleep."

REFERENCES

Awaradi, S.A. 1990. *Master Plan (1991-2021)*. Port Blair: Andaman Nicobar Administration.

Battaglia, D. 1993. "At Play in the Fields and Borders of the Imaginary: Malanesian Transformations of Forgetting," *Cultural Anthropology,* 8 (4): 430-42.

Breton, A. 1978. *What is Surrealism, Selected Writings*. New York: Monad Press.

Carey, I. 1976. *Orang Asli: The Aboriginal Tribes of Peninsular Malaysia*. Kuala Lumpur: Oxford University Press.

Clifford, J. 1988. *The Predicament of Culture*. Cambridge: Harvard University Press.

Crapanzano, V. 1992. *Hermes' Dilemma and Hamlet's Desire*. Cambridge: Harvard University Press.

Dombeck, M. 1991. *Dreams and Professional Personhood: The Context of Dream Telling and Dream Interpretation among the American Psychotherapists.* Albany: State University of New York.

Domhoff, G W. 1985. *The Mystique of Dreams: A Search for Utopia through Senoi Dream Theory*. Berkeley: University of California Press.

Dubois, C. 1961. *The People of Alor*. New York: Harper and Brothers.

Dumont, J. 1972. *Under the Rainbow*. Austin: Texas University Press.

Fogelson, R. 1977. "Cherokee Notions of Power," (pp. 185-94) in Fogelson and Adams (eds.), *The Anthropology of Power*. New York: Academic Press.

Freud, S. 1954. *The interpretation of Dreams*. London: George Allen and Unwin

_____. 1959. *Collected Papers*. Vol. 2. New York: Basic Books.

Gadamer, H. 1975. *Truth and Method*. New York: Seabury.

Geertz, C. 1974. "From the Native's Point of View" On the Nature of Anthropological Understanding," *Bulletin of the American Academy of Arts and Sciences*, 28 (1): 26-45.

Kracke, W. 1978. *Force and Persuasion*. Chicago: University of Chicago Press.

_____. 1987. "Encounters with other Cultures: Psychological and Epistemological Aspects," *Ethos*, 15 (1): 58-81.

Kracke, W. and G. Herdt. 1982. "Introduction: Interpretation in Psychoanalytical Anthropology," *Ethos*, 15 (1): 3-7.

Lacan, J. 1977. *Ecrits: A Selection*. New York: Norton.

Levi-Strauss, C. 1963. *Structural Anthropology*. New York: Basic Books.

Levy, R. 1973. *Tahitians: Mind and Experience in the Society Islands*. Chicago: University of Chicago Press.

Man, E. H. 1833. *The Aboriginal Inhabitants of Andaman Islands*. London: Royal Anthropological Institute.

Marcus, G. and D. Cushman. 1982. "Ethnography as a Text," *Annual Review of Anthropology*, 11: 25-69.

Marriot, McKim. 1976. "Hindu Transactions: Diversity without Dualism," (pp. 109-42) in B. Kapferer (ed.), *Transactions and Meanings*, London: Tavistock.

_____. 1980. "The Open Hindu Person and Interpersonal Fluidity," paper presented at the Meeting of Association for Asian Studies, Washington D.C.

Obeyesekere, G. 1981. *Medusa's Hair*. Chicago: University Chicago Press.

Pandya, V. 1992. "Gukwelonone: The Game of Hiding Fathers and Seeking Sons," (pp263-279) in B. Hewlett (ed.), *The Father-Child Relationship: Developmental, Symbolic, and Evolutionary Perspectives*. New York: Walter de Gruyter.

_____. 1993. *Above the Forest*. New Delhi: Oxford University Press.

Radcliffe-Brown, A R. 1966. *The Andaman Islanders*. New York: Free Press.

Ricoeur, P. 1992. *Oneself as Another*. Chicago: University of Chicago Press.

Rosaldo, M. 1983. "The Shame of Headhunters and the Autonomy of Self," *Ethos*, 11: 128-34.

Schebesta, P. 1926. *Among the Forest Dwarfs of Malaya*. London: Hutchinson and Co.

Stocking, G. 1976. "Radcliffe-Brown, Lowie, and The History of Ethnological Theory," *History of Anthropology Newsletter*, 3

Stoller, P. 1989. *The Taste of Ethnographic Things*. Philadelphia: University of Pennsylvania Press.

Tedlock, B. (ed.) 1987. *Dreaming: The Anthropology and Psychology of the Imaginal*. Cambridge: Cambridge University Press.

Wallace, A and R. Fogelson. 1965. "The identity Struggle," (pp. 365-406) in Boszormenyi-Nagy and Farmo (eds.), *Intensive Family Therapy*. New York: Harper and Row.

EIGHT

KADO BIKRI: Informal Process of Land Transfer among the Kutia Kandhas

ARIMA MISHRA

The paper focuses on exploring the process of informal yet institutionalised means of transfer of land and analyzing the resultant economic decline among the Kutia Kandhas[1] in Lanjigarh block in the district of Kalahandi. The informal practice of mortgaging of land is known as *Kado Bikri* among the Kutia Kandhas. *Kado* refers to the land at a particular stage in the agricultural cycle - when the land is ploughed and ready to be sown. The poignancy of the transaction in *Kado Bikri* needs to be understood in the context of the range of connotations - economic, social as well as religious land meaning earth entails among the Kandha community. The evidence on *Kado Bikri* is drawn from a six-month (between 1996-97) fieldwork in village Irkuli in Lanjigarh Block.

The problem of land alienation among tribal communities has been a focal concern among social anthropologists. The problem is not new but dates back to the early British rule in India. Anthropologists are however more concerned and vocal about the incidence of the same in the post-independence context in the light of the facts that elaborate legal provisions exist restricting the transfer of land from the tribal to the non-tribal. Despite the wide acknowledgement and treatment of the problem, the existing studies have a tendency towards focusing the analysis of land transfer based on the evidence on "sale" of land by the tribal to the non-tribal. Even where other means, i.e. mortgage have been acknowledged, the details of the process of loss of the land are missing. The focus on sale as a means of loss of land has twisted the whole issue treating it as a problem of failure of implementation of the legislation. In this context, the paper seeks to argue, *firstly*, that land transactions are not always transparent and because they are often not, the issue is not always of implementation failure but more fundamental than that is the inability of the official records to reflect and capture the process of transfer of land. I do not wish to imply that analysis of formal land sale transactions for an understanding of land alienation is not important but simply that it is insufficient.

Secondly, it does not suffice to know how does the informal transaction on land take place but it is important to unveil the ways and means of sustenance and legitimization of these transactions. In this regard, the notion of trust in credit transactions becomes crucial. *Thirdly* and which in fact follows from the second is the fact that land transactions are not simple one to one transaction. The complexity is derived from the fact that these transactions can be examined in relation to a network of credit transactions often laying bare the nexus between land, cultivation and credit transactions where land is an asset that is pledged for security to avail of credit. *Fourthly*, the analysis of credit transactions needs to be linked to the phenomenon of time if only to be able to unearth the process of economic decline. In this regard credit transactions need not be one-time phenomena. The time element is used in two contexts. The first is the analysis of the impact of a particular transaction on the household over a period of time. Here the generation method may help. The second, I am interested in the analysis of different units of time and their significance in the analysis of land and credit transactions. The different units of time are: (a) agricultural calendar and the credit practices which bear meaning within this calendar (b) borrowing seasons Vs. lending seasons (c) social calendar (transactions that respond to different contingencies such as marriage, etc.)

An analysis of such kind, the paper seeks to argue, would reflect better on the process of economic decline accompanying the gradual loss of rights over land among the tribal communities.

The paper would proceed through three sections. The first offers a profile of the village and the communities. The second discusses the evidence on the practice of *Kado Bikri*. The third sums up the analysis and discusses relevant questions.

I
Village Irkuli: A Profile

Irkuli is in the Biswanathpur Panchayat of Lanjigrah Block. The block has an area of 40193.76 square km and is flanked by Rayagada and Phulbani districts and located in the south east of Bhawanipatna, the district headquarters. As per the 1991 census, the block has a population of 60974. The tribal constitutes the major portion of the population. Among the tribal, the Kutia Kandha constitutes 45 per cent followed by Dongria Kandha (mostly settled on hilltops), Sabar and Gond. Among the non-tribal, the Harijans and the Sundhis constitute the majority.

Irkuli is a small village with an area of 80.13 square km. It is situated in the northern direction, around 3-4 km from Biswanathpur, the headquarters of Lanjigarh Block and hardly a km away from Ambodala road in the neighbouring Rayagada District. The village is surrounded by the Hatisal reserve forest. The village comprises twenty-four households. The Kutia Kandhas primarily inhabits the village. Kutia Kandha is a sub-group of the Kandhas, the others being the Dongria and Desia.[2] It has often been said that the Desia Kandhas are more or less Hinduized. They are also referred to as advanced agriculturists (Patnaik and Patnaik, 1982). Dongria Kandhas are relatively concentrated in Gunpur and other areas of Rayagada district. They are found in minority in Lanjigarh block. In this block, they stick to living on the hill tops and come down to the plain only during weekly *hat* (market) and the famous festival of *Bali yatra.*[3] The Dongrias are distinct with their curly hair but more importantly with the elaborate fixing of combs on their hair (a fixed number differentiating boys from girls). It is said that the Dongrias display superiority in their dealings with other inhabitants because of their claim to have been related to the Nimgiri Raja (Watts, 1970). The Kutias also claim superiority for their relative exposure to the outside world. Marriage between these two sections is not allowed. The Kutia Kandhas are usually dark, tall and they also have curly hair. For the Kutia females, the ornaments include primarily the *phasa* (nose rings) and *hugla* worn round the neck.

The language spoken by the Kutias is Kui, which unlike Oriya, does not have a written script. Their familiarity with the Oriya language is through the interaction with the Oriyas, that is the reason why the elders could converse freely with me in Oriya, the younger ones in village Irkuli could not understand the language.

Beliefs in Earth Goddess and the Notion of "Outsider"

Ethnographic literature on Kutia Kandhas is relatively few. The Kutias remain popular for their infamous Meria (human sacrifice)[4] which has been replaced by *Podh Puja* (sacrifice of a buffalo). While the Kutia Kandhas are supposedly the original inhabitants of this area, almost all the villages have some "outsiders," as they refer them to, either Harijans or Sundhis. The notion of a single tribe village hence is missing. The outsider communities form a minority in terms of numbers but are very dominant and no aspect of tribal life at the present time can be understood without placing it in the context of the transactions between the tribal and others.

It is important to understand the range of connotations associated with the term of reference of "outsider" to tap fully the historical aspects of the relationship between the tribal and the non-tribal in this area and its contemporary significance in the light of the present discussion on land transaction. The outsider has a meaning of a nomad who does not have a permanent place to live and hence lack a spatial identity. This is a derogatory term which reflects the relationship between the Kandhas and the Harijans even beginning from the early British rule when the process of immigration of outsiders to the area began. The meaning can only be understood in terms of the Kandhas' association and identity with land meaning "earth."

The Kandhas have a specific relationship with the Earth Goddess who is also referred to as *Dharni Mata* (Mother Earth). Several Kandha myths exist on the relationship between the two. However as per the most popular myth (Kapuntali-Niranthali)[5], the Kandhas are supposedly the first human beings on earth and it is the Goddess who helped the Kandhas create earth to make it feasible for them to live. The sacrifices (previously human being and later buffaloes) offered to the Earth Goddess thus symbolize the fertility of the soil and hence harvest. The Earth Goddess is symbolized through a stone, a pillar or even a tree. Every village has a sacred space either in the beginning or at the end of the village for worshipping the Goddess.

The relationship between the Kandhas and the Earth Goddess is reflected in their religious vis-à-vis social festivals, i.e. *Dharni* or *Podh Puja* (which is also known as pausa parba) and Bihan Parba. These are also agricultural rites. *Podh Puja* usually takes place during or after the harvesting season while Vihan Parba is celebrated before the sowing of seeds. *Podh Puja* is the single largest socio-religious-economic event among the Kandhas. *Podh Puja* refers to the ceremony of sacrificing a buffalo to the Goddess Earth. The sacrifice of buffalo and the blood sprinkled on the earth is believed to increase the fertility of the earth, which means better harvest. While the preparation begins even years before the actual ceremony, the ceremony lasts for two-three days. Even on the day when the buffalo is sacrificed, the dialogue with the Goddess Earth through the chanting of sacred words (which only the Jani, the priest is aware and has the right to do so) goes on for hours together. The gist of these words is that the buffalo is sacrificed in return for the request for plenty of food and general well being of the Kandha villagers. There are a number myths centering round the essence of the puja, but the fact is that the *Podh Puja* can be then outsider both physically and socio-culturally. The tribal consider the presence of the non-tribal communities as posing a threat. The economic dominance of the non-tribal communities is implicitly recognized as the tribal quietly experience the process of rapid economic decline through losing their land and other assets to these outsiders. Thus, the interaction between the Kutia Kandhas and the outsider communities has not resulted in either assimilation or complete rejection. While elements of rejection are evident in their term of reference as outsiders, the economic dominance of the outsiders is prominent resulting in an economic decline among the Kutiaś. It is not so much as assimilation or rejection[6] that is important but to ask and explain the decline both economic and physical of the tribal communities.

The Kutia houses are distinct with two rows of houses, each house with two doors in the east-west direction. The village comprises seventeen Kutia households. Fourteen of them are spread in one row and the rest three facing them, the road dividing the two rows. The proliferation of the households has taken place with the married sons setting up a separate household. The biological relationship reinforces the sociological one in the principal of residence. The princeple of kinship in the pattern of residence is evident, as the brothers tend to build their houses nearer to each other. The biological relationship reinforces the sociological in the principle of residence.

The rest seven households belong to the Sundhi community. Sundhis are traditionally a distiller caste (distilling country liqour). The Sundhis in Irkuli are known as Garjatias[7] those who originally belong to the south of India and were long settled in the Kondmals in Orissa which formed smaller Garjats, kingdoms. Even despite the prohibition, these Sundhis are engaged in making country liquor not for large scale sale but for their own consumption and for occasional sale to the Kandhas. The relationship between Sundhis and Kandhas has often been perceived as interesting, the liquor being the principal force binding the both. However, as the present analysis makes clear, the transactions are more complicated, as they seem to a layman.

The Sundhis immigrated to this village most probably during early forties. The exact course and reason of migration was provided by the Sundhi households. Sarathi Behera (father of ego Krishna Behera), belonged to a landlord family and had owned large amount land in village Ishalana in Lanjigarh block. But his was the only family in the village (this is perhaps in administrative category mist have been a "village enclave" which did not have any map nor curvey. These kinds of villages used to be frequent prior to the settlement). Because of the fear of tiger he left the village and came to Ishabari, another village consisting of forty sundhi families. However he could not own any land there. One of the Sundhi landholders of around twelve acres in Irkuli died, subsequently this land was given to Sarathi to pay *malgujari* (land-tax). The sons are cultivating the ancestral land in addition to the land from the Kandhas. *Kado Bikri* as the following analysis shows sums up the shift in the status of the Kandhas from owner of the soil to an uncertain *raeets* (land holders) and an accompanying emerging status of the Sundhis as relatively bigger landholders. Thus what follows is the discussion of a simultaneous process of economic decline of the Kandhas and economic incline of the Sundhis.

II
Kado Bikri

The brief reflection on the profile of the two communities in the village will help one understand the details of the credit transactions that take place between the Kutia Kandhas and Sundhis. This also helps one to comprehend the kutias' expressions as "It is the sundhis who are the *raeets* (landholders) of this village." "They never had land but buying it from us and cultivating." These remarks are important considering the historical aspects of land rights of both the Kandhas and the Sundhis. The fact that I limit my analysis of credit transactions to the Sundhi community that are the *sahukars* (moneylenders) for the tribal is justified from the following Table 8.1.

Table 8.1: Sources of credit, percentage and nature of transactions

Source	Percentage	Nature
Government	25-30	bullock, diesel, pumps, fishing land development
Relatives/kin	NIL	
Sahukars/mahajan	70-75	*Baka, udhar rina* etc.

As it is seen, major portion of the credit transactions take place with the *sahukars*, Needless to mention that the Sundhis and to some extent the Harijans (the scheduled castes) of nearby village Melughutu perform the role of the *sahukar*.

The following Table 8.2 indicates the nature of credit transaction and accompanying interest rates.

Table 8.2: Credit transaction and interest rates

Baka (hiring of bullocks)	Rs 300 or 180 kg of paddy for one agricultural season
Udhar (borrowing)	simple borrowing of rice or ragi for consumption this does not have interest as the period of the capital repayment is maximum a month
Rina (loaning)	When *udhar* is not being paid, it is charged with interest and becomes *rina.* This is also applied to borrowing money for wedding expenses or even seeds by 100 per cent interest. This also involves credit on mortgaing different assests
Kado Bikri	mortgaging of land

These are not exclusive practices but need to be examined in relation to one another. If only to facilitate the analysis, the credit transaction can be examined in relation to different months of a year. This would have an advantage of decoding the relationship between land, cultivation and credit transactions and further, the monthly availability or non-availability of credit and the compulsive mortgaging of assets. Here it should be mentioned that no credit transaction is indefinite, it is sustained and regulated by the debtor's ability to repay which is often known as the credit worthiness of the debtors (Mukherjee, 1971; Rangasami, 1974; Watts, 1983). The element of trust in the credit transactions which has often fascinated anthropologists, developmental economists alike, is important in this context but does not necessarily guarantee either low transaction cost or long-term sustenance of the transaction. Further, trust operates at different levels and to different extents. In this context, the relationship between *udhar* and *rina* in the credit transactions becomes important. While in the first, trust becomes a prerequisite to avail of credit, in the second, what matters in the long run is the ability of offer security. This is important to know if one seeks to understand under what circumstances land is being mortgaged and how and why is the transaction a binding one between the Kutias and the Sundhis.

The Kutia households cultivate both on *dongar* (hills) and *raiyati* (plain land on which they have occupancy rights) land. As far as the *dongar* is concerned, individual household cultivates around 36 decimal of forestland in one cultivating season. The forestland is called *patra.* The legal status of the *patra* land is not clear. But in some cases, they have been asked to pay tax for cultivating the same. The principal crops cultivated are paddy, *ragi*, *gurji, kultha, janha.* These crops are sown almost simultaneously between June-July/August. The crops on the *dongar* are sown in rotation thus it is *kultha* in one year and *gurji* in another. Paddy and *ragi, janha* are however constant and cultivated each year.

Around eighty per cent of the households stated that the output from their own fields sustains them for a period of 3-4 months during and after the harvest season. For the rest twenty per cent it goes only for 1-2 months. This includes the post-harvest costs particularly that of *baka* and in some cases the seeds. Some variation can also be explained in relation to the size of the family and the amount of land held. But there is no significant variation with regard to these two among the Kutia households.

The months have been rated differently according to the easy availability of procuring food, be it own harvest or easy availability of credit from the sahukars. Thus the best months of the year are usually *bhudo lanju* (september) and *diar* and *pusa lanju* (Nov-January). This is related to their cultivation pattern. *Bhudo lanju* has a slightly different significane. Firstly beacuse this comes after the *kada maas* (hunger months), i.e. roughly April-August. Secondly the harvesting of early paddy and *janha* (this is eaten as rice) from the *dongar* land does not demand any repayment of credit.

October and Feb-March are also relatively looked upon with ease as one can avail of *udhar*, simple borrowing of rice for consumption. *Udhar* is relatively easier in October because of the approaching harvest months. It will be difficult in March or there may be an interest of hundred per cent. As some of them stated "if we prostrate and beg at their feet[8], rice of the previous years will be given at double the interest rate." I may add here that the Kandhas never had a concept of hunger month. This is a later development. *Kada maas* referring to hunger month is not a *kui* term but an oriya one. What I wish to emphasize here is that an analysis of the hunger months in relation to the non-hunger months clearly reflects a process of economic decline among the Kutia Kandhas. Secondly, the process can only be understood in the context of an increasing attenuation of their rights on land, i.e. both hill plots as well as raiyati land. I am dealing with the latter in this paper.

The difficult or lean period range from April-August when the output from one's own harvest is exhausted and also credit for consumption from the *sahukars* is not available. Even during these six months, April-July are more difficult. The denial of credit by the *sahukars* is thus expressed *"panna baratsate igari piju batise bamu"* (Go back and come only when the rain comes, the *sahukars* tell the Kutias if they ask for credit) understood in the context of the specific relationship the Kandhas have with the Earth Goddess is not contested. The notion of their origin and identification with soil is sought to be reinforced through this puja. *Podh Puja* is necessarily a village level affair where two-three neighboring villages get together and host the puja alternatively.

Bihan Parba symbolizes the ceremony of offering seeds and then sacrifices to the Earth Goddess as well as the mountain deity. Unlike *Podh Puja,* this is a household affair. Some seeds are spread out on a bamboo plate, the hens, goat are made to eat those seeds. These then are sacrificed to the Goddess. Without this ceremony sowing is considered to be inauspicious. Sacrifices during these festivals are compulsory. "The blood shed of the sacrificed animals before the earth goddess is essential to guarantee the fertility of the earth and ensure a bountiful of harvest" (Watts, 1970: 44). The dance and music that accompany the festival particularly during *Podh Puja* serve to ward off unwanted spirits.

The range of beliefs associated with the Earth Goddess reinforce the Kandhas' claim to be the original inhabitants and owners of the land. The fact of the Kandhas being the traditional holders of land with rights and privileges is widely acknowledged in the colonial administrative reports as well as anthropological literature (Risley, 1891; Thurston, 1906; Ramsay, 1952; Bailey, 1957; Boal, 1982; Patnaik and Patnaik, 1982; Elwin, 1954. Ramsay refers to them as the *zamindars* or owners of the soil.

The reference "outsider" in this regard hence has a spatial notion of people falling outside the physical boundary of the Kandha Land. This is symbolic because the Harijans and the Sundhis are physically an integral part of the tribal villages at least in the present context. But the term of reference of outsider continues to dominate.

Implicit in the usage of the term "outsider" is a range of feelings towards the Harijan and Sundhis, who the Kandhas do interact very closely yet they try to retain their distinctiveness by considering one should mention that the non-availability of credit may imply denial of *udhar.* Credit can be availed of when assets are mortgaged. The assets that are usually mortgaged are jewelry and land. Due to the limited possession of jewelry, land is the widely mortgaged item. The practice of mortgaging of land is called *Kado Bikri*. Land is also mortgaged when *udhar* is not repaid and hence the Kandhas are forced to share the land as part of the interest. Credit with interest is called *rina* as different from *udhar*. Land is also mortgaged for catering to the wedding expenses.

Kado Bikri refers to the sale (*Bikri*) of land. *Kado* refers to the land at a particular stage of the agricultural cycle i.e when the land is ploughed and ready to be sown. It is quite surprising that while the Kandhas clearly say that *Kado Bikri* is a practice of mortgage, the Sundhis look upon it as sale. This is observed in the context of their answers to the questions "Have you bought any land? How much land do you possess apart from the ancestral share?" they refer to the land acquired under *Kado Bikri*. The notion of sale is perhaps related to the nature of the transaction, which makes the recovery of the land difficult for the Kutias.

It is difficult to know exactly the origin of this practice because of the dearth of published reports on the history of the land tenure in this area. While tribal land alienation was not foreign even to the 18th century[9], this kind of practice has not been mentioned anywhere. The survey and settlement Report 1955-56 of the Ex-Zamindari area mentions *Kado Ghina* but does not offer any details. It is also not clear how far can this be attributed to the scarcity of research study on the Kutia Kandhas particularly on land holding and related transactions. Whatever may be the timing of the origin of this practice, it can definitely be argued that the process has hastened during the last thirty-forty years. This may be related to the older men stating that their father's generation had a better and a comfortable life style characterized in terms of greater output of paddy, ragi, greater number of holding of assets i.e, bullocks, goats, hen, the lavishness of the *Jula* (bride price) system and the feast. And also the fact that the Sundhis with whom this transaction is mostly carried out, migrated to the village only in early fifties.

There is no fixed interest rate for the mortgage of land under *Kado Bikri*. While at one level, it is related to the quality and productivity of land, it is still uncertain and varies in individual cases. The land is usually mortgaged in return for some money or sometimes money as well as a pair of bullock (the transaction of borrowing bullocks is known as *"Baka"*). The money is lent for a certain number of years, the stipulated period within which the money with interest should be returned if the land is to be recovered. The interest is usually decided considering the desperation of the Kutias who are in a vulnerable position and the better bargaining power of the Sundhis. To my surprise, neither the interest rate nor the amount of land mortgaged for the principal amount of money tallied when I tried to collect information on individual households from both the Sundhis as well as the Kandha households concerned. For instance, one of the households supposedly had mortgaged one acre of land for an amount of Rs. 1000 for a period of 2 years. But it was denied by the Sundhis who claimed that the amount is Rs. 3000 for a period of 6 years. This is how a large amount of land has been claimed by the Sundhis.

Trust in *Kado Bikri*

The transactions in *Kado Bikri* are oral. There is no witness, material or non-material to the transaction. The oral nature of the transaction cannot be attributed to the illiteracy of the tribal. It is assumed that the transactions are based on trust on the *sahukars*, The tribals prefer the same saukar who "gives credit even when it is dark" (dark meaning any emergency). The element of trust here can not be understood in terms of the low transaction cost as it is clear in the given information on the exchange. Nor can it be analysed in terms of favouring either of the components of the dichotomy between inter-personalized trust (kin network) or trust on the system (Giddens, 1990).[10] Giddens (1990) discusses trust and risk in the context of his work on modernity. Modernity he argues is a distinct a mode of life, which sweeps away in an unprecedented fashion all the traditional types of social order. In the context of trust, he notes that in pre-modern culture trust is localised. He has identified four localized contexts, i.e. (a) kinship, (b) local community, (c) religious cosmology, and (d) tradition. All these four help in regularizing trust relationships. These sustain trust in the social relationships. The trust here is intrepersonalized. The risk in such kind of trust relationships emerges not from the framework of relationships but more from the physical environment i.e. natural hazards, etc. In contrast, in modern cultures, the trust is not localised but globalized, Trust rests in not any personal relationships but in the abstract systems. The trust here does not provide either the mutuality or intimacy. The expert systems refer to traditionalized bureaucracies, technologies, the different formal lending institutions in the modern societies characterize such kind of trust where the parties involved, trust the formalized codes, abstract principles which regulate the transaction. The risks in such kind of relationships emerges from as Giddens notes, investment markets, changes in the global division of labour and lack of expertise of the expert systems,

The trust in *Kado Bikri* conforms to neither of these. As we have already mentioned the transaction is oral and does not involve any fixed procedures leave aside rule of the transaction. It varies in different contexts with different individual households. Secondly, despite a binding relationship between both the communities, there is no kin relationship (even fictive) developed. Terms of reference between both these communities are personal names. Terms of addresses are vague. While the Sundhis address the Kutias in public by their names, I did not come across any Kutia doing the same even once in my presence.

The binding nature of the relationship is not centered around any inter-personalized trust but because it involves different kinds of interests for both the parties who want the transaction to continue for different reasons. The Kutias have no alternative but need the credit as in a way they are trapped in the whole system. To the Sundhis, the interest is more than obvious, as they cannot get a better way of acquiring land for cultivation. Some of them have taken to cultivation of cash crops on the land acquired by them from the Kutias.

The element of trust in *Kado Bikri* may come closer to Rober's (1994) analysis of credit practices as evolving local models to adapt to situation at hand. However his analysis of "Kaloba" in Kabwe, Zambia works on a different plane precisely because it involves cash exchange on a monthly basis (the principal amount with interest to be repaid at the payment day of every month). It does not involve any security. The pledging of land as a security where it is the principal means of livelihood has a different significance to the transactions as well as the parties involved.

Kaloba refers to a "business of short-term lending of money." Even while it is an informal practice, the procedure for interest and time of repayment are clear. The interest is 50 per cent and has to be paid back on the payment of salary day and if a customer fails to pay, an additional 50 per cent is charged to be repaid on the next payday. The similarity of *Kado Bikri* with this practice is limited only to the extent that it could be seen as a local model for adapting to the economic stress faced by the tribal The similarity ends here. The basic difference is that the *Kaloba* is a simple and single transaction involving the lending and accepting the repayment in cash. This is the basis of the relationship between the "skylocks," the Kaloba lenders and the borrowers. But *Kado Bikri* is interwoven in a network of credit transaction between the Sundhis and the Kutias and the trust is rooted here and the trust is a necessity. The trust while certainly helps in getting credit at the initial stage it does not guarantee low transaction cost as it is seen in the original exchange. In fact the transaction involves an element of coercion. The market rate of the same quantity of land is ten times higher than the rate on which it is mortgaged.

Kado Bikri is definitely an informal practice but seems to have been institutionalized. Perhaps one can refer to this as an informal or "alternative economic institution"[11] (Halperin, 1996) operating in parallel to the "mainstream economy."[12] However, the institutionalization of the practice does not mean any codification of procedure because as it will be shown, the interest rates and the period of mortgage are all erratic. This is also manifested in the different versions on the actual individual practice (both in terms of the money lent and the period of mortgage) by the Kandha and Sundhi households. It is routinized perhaps in the sense that it seems to have existed for a long time. The practice is still hush-hush and information is not be shared with outsiders including government officers. This is not simply because the practice is illegal but it is integrally linked to a series of other transactions where the debtors are trapped.

The element of trust in the practice is not related to the ability to repay (because there is a huge gap between the value of the amount borrowed and the value of the land mortgaged) but in the mutual interest of keeping the transactions going. The transaction is a continuing and a binding one in the sense that it is usually borrowed initially in return for some money and the amount of money does not conform to the quality of land. This is done to lend again some nominal amount only to be able to reclaim the land after some years. This binding nature of the transaction is reflected in the expression of the Kutias as "*mahajans* (moneylenders) are always *mahajans* and *rinis* (debtors) are *rinis.*" Roeber is right in stating that "Informal credit is systemic to the extent that it is routinised but does not mean that it is rationalized." Hence principle of trust in *Kado Bikri* should not deter one from examining the long-term impact it has on both the Kandha households as well as the Sundhi, particularly the former.

While it is very difficult to quantify the land transferred because of the hush-hush nature of the transaction, yet an attempt was made for the purpose. It is clear that all of seventeen households are involved in this practice and have lost land in the process, information on the same for all households could not be collected because of the constant fear of the moneylenders. The Kandhas were scared if I would release the information to the government officers or even let the Sundhis know that they have confided the information. I remember Badmunda Majhi who had lost majority of his good quality of land whispered "I have shared the information on Kado. I hope I will not be in trouble." I made him convince that it is strictly for academic purpose. He nodded with hesitation.

The available information on fifty per cent of the households is stated below which would give an idea about the tricky nature of the transaction and the amount of land transferred from the Kutias to the Sundhis.

Table 8.3: *Kado Bikri* and the process of land transfer

Household	Amount of Land* under mortgage	Original Exchange Transaction **
H1	2 acres (Att) and 36 decimal (Bahal)***	Approx Rs 800-1000 (6-7 years)
H2	2-1/2 and 22 decimal (Jalchar)	Rs 700 + 4000 + one pair of bullock
H3	3 acres (Bahal)	NA
H4 ****	36 decimal (Bahal)	Rs 2000
H5	35 decimal (Bahal) 1- 1/2 acres (Att)	Rs 800 for 4-5 years
H6	1/2 acre Bahal	Rs 200 each year for 5 years
H7	2 acres (ATT)	NA
H8	1 acre (Att) 35 decimal Bahal	Rs 500 for five years

* The local unit of measurement is "duli" which is measured in terms of the seed capacity of the land. The conversion method from duli in terms of acre stands as: one duli (att) with sowing capacity of 5 maan (approximately 15 kgs. of paddy) = around 17 decimal of land (1/6th of an acre)

** The exchange transaction was at the initial period of contract, which must have continued for some more years. As it is already mentioned, it is a binding transaction so the money is lent gradually and in different phases. So the households found it difficult to tell me what was the original and perhaps fixed number of years against which the money was lent and the land was given. This particular aspect of the transaction has enabled the Sundhi households to be able to reclaim the land. Hence wherever it is written NA, the transaction goes back to a number of years which the household in question could not recollect.

*** There are three types of land, i.e *Bahal* (the best quality low land), *Berna* (low land but not so fertile) and *Bhata* or *Att* (up land). The market value of the respective land varies in terms of the quality the highest for *Bahal*, followed by *Berna* and then *Att*. Perhaps I should mention that the market rate (sale) for one acre of land is approximately Rs 20,000-25,000.

**** This particular household seems to have been able to recover the land, which was given for a period of two years. One should add that this household is referred to as the 'better-off' one among the Kandhas. The land sale transaction shows that he has been able to buy one acre of land from his Kandha neighbour. This is the only formal sale transaction in the last five years.

While the aforesaid land mentioned has already been lost, the amount could be more as some of the female members of the households confided that usually half the amount of land held are under *Kado Bikri* for seventy eight per cent of the households. Hence my analysis does point to a trend towards land transfer than the actual and accurate land lost because of the difficulty in getting data on the same.

The absence of the reflection of the informal transfer in the Record of Rights is remarkable. In the last five years only one formal land sale transaction has taken place. The land has been transferred from one of the tribal households to another in the village itself. The following data on the amount of landholding as reflected in the record of rights almost denies any change in the landholding pattern through generations.

Table 8.4: Land holding of households as per Record of Rights (ROR) of 1968 and 1992

Household	ROR 1968	ROR 1992
H1, H2, H3 (Joint)	F 10.97	F 10.59
H4, H5, H6, H7 H8 (Joint)	F 6.05	6.96
H9, H10	11.72	11.33
H11 and sons (H12, H13, H14)	12.97	10.15
H15	7.94	8.13
H16	8.09	8.19
H17,18, 19 20, 21, 22 (SUNDHIS)	12.00	12.00

As it is clear, the Record of Rights suggests that there has hardly been any land transaction in terms of loss or gain between 1968 -1992 while the evidence on land transfer through *Kado Bikri* shows that around 30-40 per cent of the land has already been lost to the *Sundhi* households. Secondly the H. No. 17-23 households who are *Sundhis* while confided that they have acquired land of the Kutias through *Kado Bikri*, it is not reflected in the RoR. Thus as per the official Record of Rights, the Kutias continue to remain relatively bigger landholders while the Sundhis have marginal land. In this context, the Kutia households' remarks that "It is the Sundhis who are the raeets of our village" make no sense. The feeling of uncertainty and insecurity about their *raeet* status can only be understood once the process of gradual loss of rights over their land is unearthed.

Bailey's Economic Model and Analysis of Land Transfer

In the context of the aforesaid evidence on *Kado Bikri*, Baileys (1969) analysis on the economic model of descending spiral and his observations regarding the land market in Bisipara have limited analytical and empirical validity. A major question which concerned Bailey (1957) in his analysis of the integration of a near to subsistence economy with a capitalistic one is "why did land come into the market?" Why do peasants sell land? His concern is of course related to his study of the differential access to opportunities that market economy offers and its impact on the traditional caste structure. Bailey notes that the "combined action of inheritance and pattern of consumption enjoined at certain crises of life" (1969: 134) can explain the fact of land being marketed. In this context Bailey talks about the economic model, i.e. descending spiral. The model suggests that the sale of land by a peasant is directly related to his possession of other assets for meeting the contingencies in life. Hence it goes "Estate A will sell field to meet the cost of wedding but could buy an ox out of surplus income, B will lose a filed to replace plough cattle but the owner seldom needs to borrow paddy, C can borrow paddy because the lender thinks it will remain solvent, but the owner of an estate is selling fields to meet everyday needs. In the last case, the person's career as a land owner is close to an end."

Bailey further argues that the ability to recover land is further directly related to access to employment opportunities outside land. Since the opportunities are more diverse and the equal chances of the impact of inheritance on land holding have prevented major land concentration. He states "The opportunity of the small man to make money and the vulnerability of even the largest estate in the village to division at inheritance, combine to prevent the land drifting permanently into the hands of some few owners" (p.48). I have three difficulties with Bailey's economic model and his analysis of land transactions.

The first, I do agree that the sale of land is related to one's possession of other assets and secondly the equal chances of the division of land through inheritance. But the latter does not rule out the possibility of land concentration or increase in landholding through the process of land transfer. For instance as the evidence on *Kado Bikri* shows, both the Kandha and Sundhi households are equally affected by the rule of inheritance but the Sundhis have been able to add to their ancestral share at the expense of the Kandha households. As it has already been mentioned this addition is the amount of land transferred through *Kado Bikri*.

Secondly, Bailey is talking about a market where land is formally sold but the presence or absence of land concentration and land market transaction cannot be understood only through this formal transaction. What comes out clear from the analysis is that the reliance on formal land sale to understand land transactions would be highly inadequate. Hardly ten per cent of the transactions have taken place through this means in the village studied.

The third difficulty is that land market transactions are not necessarily a direct one to one transaction. It is complicated as the evidence shows because it is related to a series of transactions. To understand the role of land in *Kado Bikri* we had to explore the network of credit transactions particularly *udhar* and *rina* and the role of *Kado Bikri* in these. As it has been mentioned the ways of understanding the place of *Kado Bikri* is that when *udhar* (borrowing) is not repaid and automatically becomes a *rina*, land is the only asset to be pledged. Needless to mention that, this pledging of land is done through *Kado Bikri*.

The analysis on *Kado Bikri* makes explicit the process of economic decline among the Kutia Kandhas particularly with regard to the loss of land. Further, this decline is reflected not merely in the decline in the capacity to produce more food, and hence in the eating pattern, but in the marriage ceremonies, the system of bride price, the possession of assets other than land. What also needs to be stressed, the working of the transactions and its impact becomes clearer only when it is looked upon as a process. As it is clear, the loss of land has been gradual. The period of study of the transaction roughly covers the 60-90s. This processual notion is better reflected in a generational study of the households. We reproduce here the ethnography of one household who can be used as a linkage between three generations ever since they can trace the lineage of the village.

Household X

Landholding F = 12.97 (Bahal of 5.28)

Ego = 7.62 (Bahal of only 48 decimal)
Three acres sold to the harijans of nearby village and three acres lost to the Sundhis through *Kado*

S = Around 2 acres through informal division of land

Yield of paddy F = While they found it difficult to calculate the output of other products, the yield of paddy was explicit. It was roughly around 40 puti (roughly 2400 kgs)

Ego and sons = It hovers around 12-15 puti (720-1000 kgs).

Assets other than Land = F = Cattle = 20
Goats = 12
Hen = 10-12
Bullocks = 4 pair

Ego and sons= Goats 3 (one of these is hired under the transaction of what they call Adi Gsepe Manamu, we are trying the original goat. This means the goat will be hired and nurtured. The nuture acts as part of the interest. After a few years, the lender and borrower will share the goats reproduced from the Female Gaot)

Hens = 3-4
Bullocks = Three pairs (two hired under *Baka*)

Consumption of Food items F = The output could help sustain the whole year. Ragi was eaten neat. Consumption of meat and liquor was frequent

Ego and Son = The eating of rice is limited to the days of the weekly market or during the harvesting season. Eating of roots, *ragi pej* (Starch) and *Kandul pej* (kandul is a form of pulse), *janha, kursa* which are used as rice like items are frequent. While the father's generation used to eat some of these, it was out of choice. While in the Ego and son's generation it is more of constraint.

Marriage Custom and Ritual: E He stated proudly that his own marriage was lavish if only to reflect his father's economic status. The important part of the Kandha marriage is the system of *jula* or bride price. The bride price reflects the economic status of the both the bride and bridegroom families. Another interesting observation is that married women are valued higher and can demand higher bride price than unmarried or what they refer to as inexperienced ones.

The *jula* for the Ego's wife included 60 litres of *arki* (country liquor), fomented rice, six sarees, Rs 70 as cash, one goat, one buffalo, 5 kgs of rice and kosla. Around 120 persons had gone to the bride's village from the bridegroom side.

Sons = Referring to the last two sons, Ego hesitantly stated that the *jula* practice has to be relaxed to the extent that for the youngest son they did not offer any *jula* because the feast could not be matched accordingly. For the second youngest son, the *jula* included two goats, two hens, a couple of saris and a few bottle of liquor.

What comes out clear is the economic decline between generations and its reflection in a varied ways. Hence credit transactions are not static phenomena nor merely cyclical but reflect a gradual decline for some and incline for others as between the Kutias and the Sundhis.

III

Thus what I have tried to do in the aforesaid analysis is to explore the working of the informal credit transaction, i.e. *Kado Bikri* and its impact on the economic life of the Kutia households. The analysis makes clear the following: (a) It is important to unravel informal land transactions for the analysis of loss of land among the tribal communities. Focus on sale transactions may not offer sufficient reflection on the process of land alienation. This is the reason, information on tribal landholding based merely on official sources such as the Record of Rights, or R.I (Revenue Inspector) and V.L.Ws (Village Level Worker) may be misleading as has been attempted elsewhere (Mohanty *et al.*, 1993). (b) Even the analysis of land mortgage transactions need to be placed within the network of credit transactions within which it operates and hence makes sense. (c) The analysis of credit transactions like the *Kado Bikri* cannot be studied as an one time phenomenon under a given time and space. It is a continuing transaction and hence a temporal analysis facilitates a better understanding of the transactions and its long-term economic impact.

NOTES

1. This tribe has been referred to in a variety of ways, i.e. Kondhs, Khond, Kond, Kandha, etc. We stick to the reference "Kandha" as the way it is being pronounced among the Kandhas themselves as well as others in the study area.
2. There is one more sub-section which has little mention is the Penga Kandhas who are found in Kashipur block of Rayagada district. This section in Kashipur seems to be early practitioners of female infanticide. While the killing of infants has long been abolished and replaced by buffalo, the festival continues to carry the same name *Toki Mara Parba* (Festival of killing female infants).
3. Bali Yatra is a very popular festival among the Kandhas. It is celebrated in the month of September. Lanjigarh block is famous for the elaborate and

strict celebration of the festival, hence villagers not merely adjoining villages but also from neighbouring district of Koraput join in the celebration. It is a popular sight of villagers walking throughout the night to come to the festival. The festival serves to reassure the belief in the power of the Earth Goddess. This is s done through two symbolic acts by the *devtas* who are believed to be gods personified, i.e walking through fire, siting on a thorny bed made for the purpose. These are acts, which are believed to be impossible to attain by a normal human being. The festival has also come to symbolize a platform for the selection of partners as marriage by capture (where a Kandha boy elopes with a girl with or without the consent of the girl. The bride price is then fixed between the parents, when it is amicably solved and fixed, the marriage gets a social sanction) is the most popular form of marriage.

4. Human beings used to be sacrificed to the Earth Goddess in return for fertility of the soil, plenty of harvest and for over all prosperity. See for more details on this, Macpherson, 1865; Boal, 1982; Pathy, 1995; Patel 1995.
5. Elwin, 1954
6. See Nathan (1997) for an interesting discussion on the range of responses of and the impact on the tribal communities to the increasing pressure of integration of the tribal society to the non-tribal ones.
7. The other section among the Sundhis is known as *Dakhinias* (those who belong to the south). Dakhinias are mostly concentrated in the plain areas of the district.
8. This is more an expression than an actual practice.
9. See Deo, 1989
10. These two kinds of trust broadly characterize the traditional pre-capitalistic and capitalistic systems respectively. A rotating credit association as Geertz argues is "an intermediate institution, a product of a shift from traditional agrarian society to an increasingly fluid commercial one. It has the ability to use traditional relationships to fulfil non-traditional functions."
11. To the Government officers however the *Kado Bikri* would look like "anti economy" in the sense of deviating from the mainstream economic principles, i.e. deviating the rules and restriction on the transfer of land.
12. See Polanyi, 1957 on discussions on Mainstream economy. Polanyi defines mainstream economy as "the major, recognized and accounted for (by either qualitative or quantitative mechanisms) institutional arrangements (principles) organizing a given economic processes or set of processes." Related discussion on informal economy can be found in Halperin (1996) and Smith (1989).

REFERENCES

Bailey, F.G. 1957. *Caste and Economic Frontier.* Bombay: Mancester Press.

Bailey, F.G. 1969. "An Oriya Hill Village," in M.N. Srinivas (ed.) *India's Villages*. Bombay: Asia Publishing House.

Boal, Barbara. 1982. *Konds: Human Sacrifice and Religious Change.* Bhubaneswar: Modern Book Depot.

Deo, Fanindam.1997. "Withdrawl," in Dev Nathan (ed.), *From Tribe to Caste*. Shimla: Indian Institute for Advanced Study.

Giddens, A. 1990. *The Consequences of Modernity*. Stanford C.A.: Stanford University Press.

Government of Orissa.1977. *Draft Final Report of the Ex-Zamindary, Lanjigarh, District Kalahandi*. Cuttack: Board of Revenue Orissa.

Halperin, Rhoda H. 1996. "Rethinking the Informal Economy: Implications for Regional Analysis," in by R. Issac (ed.), *Research in Economic Anthropology*. JAI Press.

Macpherson, W (ed.) 1865. *Memorials of Service in India from the Correspondence of the Late Major S.C. Macpherson*. London: John Murray.

Mohanty, K.K. et al. 1993. "Pattern of Land Holding among Major Tribes of the Tribal Sub-Plan in Orissa (Based on the Universal bench-Mark Survey 1978-80)," *Adivasi*, XXXIII: 2: 1-11.

Mukherjee, Ramakrishna. 1971. *Six Villages of Bengal*. Bombay: Popular Prakashan.

Nathan, Dev. 1997. *From Tribe to Caste*. Shimla: Indian Institute for Advanced Study.

Patnaik, N. and P.S. Das Patnaik. 1982. *The Kondh of Orissa*. Bhubaneswar: THRTI.

Pathy, Jaganath. 1995. "Colonial Ethonography of the Kandha: White Men's Burden or Poltical Expediency," *Economic and Political Weekly*, January 28, 220- 228.

Padel, Felix. 1995. *The Sacrifice of Human Being: British Rule and Konds of Orissa.* Delhi: Oxford University Press.

Polayni, Karl. 1957. "The Economy as an Instituted Process," in Karl Polyani, C.Arsenberg and Harry Pearson (eds.), *Trade and Market in Early Empire: Economies in History and Theory*. New York: Free Press.

Ramsay-Cobden, L.E.B. 1960. *Bengal District Gazetters: Feudatory States of Orissa.* Howrah: Glasgow Printing Co. Ltd.

Rangasami, Amrita. 1974. "Contractor's Opera," *Economic and Political Weekly*, IX: 5.

Risley, H.H. 1891. *Tribes and Castes of Bengal*. Calcutta : Bengal Secretariat Press.

Roeber, Carter A. 1994. "Money-lending, Trust and the Culture of Commerce in Kabwe, Zambia," in Barry I. Issac (ed.), *Research in Economic Anthropology*. JAI Press.

Smith, M.E. 1989. "The Informal Economy," in Stuart Plattner (ed.), *Economic Anthropology.* California: Stanford University Press.

Thurston, E. 1909 [1975]. *Castes and Tribes of Southern India.* Vol. III. Delhi: Cosmo Publications.

Watts, M. 1983. *Silent Violence: Food, Famine and Peasantry in Northern Nigeria.* Berkely: University of California Press.

Watts, N.A. 1970. *The Half-Clad Tribals of Eastern India*. New Delhi: Orient Longman.

NINE

GHARWA ART IN THE TRIBAL LIFE OF BASTAR

VIJOY S. SAHAY

Since time immemorial, with their age-old artistic skill in bell metal craftsmanship, the Gharwas-a little known community of the Bastar district in the state of Madhya Pradesh in India have given concrete shape to the abstract magico-religious beliefs and practices of the tribal world of Bastar. Though not a tribe, but the entire socio-economic and cultural interactions of the Gharwas take place with the tribes of Bastar. The main tribes that inhabit the region are Gond, Maria, Muria, Bhatra, Dhurwa, Halba, Dandanimaria, and Abujhmaria. Halbi dialect is the *lingua franca* of these tribesmen. According to 1991 census, the total tribal population of the district is 15,29,957, which constitutes 67.36 per cent of the total population. Of all the tribes, the Abujhmarias are least developed. They still wear scanty clothes, and except on ceremonial occasions, seldom come out of the protected forest area.

The Gharwas are, in fact, an offshoot of Ghasia - a scheduled caste, who were traditionally grass-cutters and looking after the horses of the erstwhile ruling royal family of Bastar state. A section of them, sometime in the past, learnt the *lost-wax process* of bell metal craftsmanship, and thereby, emerged as an artisan group claiming higher position in social hierarchy. Very little studies have been done, hitherto, on this otherwise anthropologically significant community. Only scanty references about them can be found in the works of Hiralal and Russell (1916), Grigson (1938), Elwin (1951) and Meera Mukherjee (1978). Hiralal and Russell, and Verrier Elwin have suggested that the Gharwas and the Ghasias are one and the same. Meera Mukherjee has mainly dealt with the Gharwa art. Herself being an exquisite bell metal craftswoman, Ms. Mukherjee has minutely discussed the details of *lost-wax process* employed by the Gharwa artists in her book *Metal Craftsmen of India.*

According to an estimate, the total population of Gharwas is around five thousand. The number of Gharwa families is estimated to be around fifteen hundred, out of which five hundred families are supposed to be engaged in their traditional occupation of bell metal craftsmanship.[1] Such a small population of the Gharwas is scattered randomly in entire Bastar. Their maximum concentration is in Kondagaon. However, single and isolated Gharwa families can also be found in the interiors of the districts, which supply artifacts to the tribesmen of several villages, such as the family of Kejuram of Kotgaon near Narainpur. The clients of Kejuram are mostly Muria tribesmen, who come from as far as fifty kilometers to ask for the images of the deities. The names of the villages where the cluster of Gharwa families are found are as follows: Jagdalpur, Kondagaon, Chilkuti, Erakot, Karanpur, Albai, Temra, Khurkhosa, Nagarnar, Dahikonga, Geedam, Narainpur, Parchanpal, Bastar and Nangur. In Jagdalpur town, the Gharwa families are settled in three localities, viz. Gangamundapara, Gharwapara and Bailabazar.

Tribal Religion of Bastar

The tribal religion of Bastar revolves round the concepts of *matas* and *devas*. Be it a poor harvest or an epidemic; loss of human lives or that of cattle, increase of unnatural deaths and adultery in the village or prolonged sickness of an individual, the tribes of Bastar continually propitiate a number of deities in the forms of different *matas* or *devas*. Only offering of sacrifice to the deities can pacify the wrath of malevolent spirits. Illness and epidemic can be prevented by offering sacrifice to a *mata* in the forest or at the *deviguri* (abode of a *mata*). Different types of illness require propitiation of different categories of *matas*. Offering sacrifice to *pardesin mata* in one's house is harbinger of fortune; the *rao deva* protects the village from intrusion by any evil spirit; numerous other *devas* also work as scare devils. Regular propitiation of *devas* frightens the evil spirits and drives them away from the village. A *sirha* (witch doctor/shaman) can only tell which of the *matas or devas* is to be propitiated at a particular hour of crisis.

Such is the extent of fear and superstition, together with magico-religious beliefs and practices in which the tribes of Bastar have lived in so far. Even during the time of peace and harmony, the *matas* and *devas* of the spirit world of Bastar tribes are worshipped and propitiated regularly by the villagers. Offerings and sacrifices are made at the individual level as well as village level. However, at both the levels of propitiation, the presence of a *sirha* is considered necessary.

The images of the deities that exist in abstract in the mind of the tribesmen in general and *sirha* in particular are, artistically, given concrete shape by the Gharwa artisans in the form of bell metal images. For an outsider, it is quite difficult to minutely distinguish between a *pardesin mata* and a *telgin mata* or a *kankalin mata*, as the ornamentally designed images are so subtly made. Similar is the case with the images of different *devas*. It is only the *sirha* and the "more experienced and knowledgeable" tribesmen who know the perfect disposition of a *mata or deva.*

In case of any physical or natural crisis, a tribesman consults a *sirha*, who, in turn, invokes the spirit under his "command or possession." At such times, *sirha* is supposed to be possessed by the spirit, and under hallucinatory condition, announces the name of the deity to be propitiated. Thereafter, the tribesman approaches the Gharwa artist for the image of the deity required to be propitiated by the *sirha.* When a tribesman goes to the house of the Gharwa, he necessarily carries with him some amount of rice and *salfi* (local intoxicant). Respectfully, he offers them to the Gharwa and asks for making the image of the "prescribed" deity. The Gharwa, in turn, accepts the gifts gracefully and assigns a date to his client for the delivery of the image.

On any of the auspicious days of the week, the Gharwa starts making the image. While making image of a *mata*, he observes fast everyday, as long as he works on it. For the sake of maintaining ritual sanctity, he takes bath early morning, maintains silence as long as he works, and abstains even from tobacco chewing. After completing his work of the day, he prepares rice offered to him by his client. This meal is called *upasikhana.* When the image is ready, either the tribesman comes to the house of the Gharwa to receive it, or sometimes, Gharwa himself takes the image to the house of his client. In any case, at the time of delivery of the image, he receives considerable amount of *gifts* in kind and cash. Sometimes, he is also rewarded with cattle and other livestock.

Besides making the images of tribal deities, the Gharwas also make tribal ornaments and some other articles of daily use such as lamps, bell metal pots of different shapes and sizes, *tori,* etc. Important among them is *tori,* a trumpet-like musical instrument used in *ghotul* (tribal youth dormitory in Bastar). In order to summon the unmarried boys and girls to assemble in the evening for staying night over, the *tori* is blown amidst drumbeats. Verrier

Elwin (1947) has given detailed account of *ghotul* of Bastar in his book *Muria and their Ghotul.*

The Concepts of *Mata* and *Deva*

The *matas* and *devas* of Bastar tribes are the "anthropomorphic forms" of female and male deities, respectively. The *matas* are more feared because they are not only protectors as the *devas*, but also healers. In times of illness or any other physical crisis, a *sirha* mostly prescribes the propitiation of a *mata*. The tribesmen also believe that the wrath of a *mata* would bring chaos in the life of an individual, or a family, or village as a whole. While the abode of a *mata* is called *deviguri*, that of a *deva* is called *devasthan*. The influence of a *mata* is so powerful that besides the tribesmen, even some of the non-tribes, including the Gharwas, keep the image of any of the *matas* in their houses as *kuldevi* (deity of the clan or lineage).

The *mata* cult, among the tribesmen is, no doubt, indigenous in origin, but the forms of images appear to be influenced by the goddess cult of the Hindu tradition. *Danteswari devi* has been the patron deity of the erstwhile ruling family of Bastar state. Her influence in Bastar is so ubiquitous that it has, today, become a household deity. It appears that the images of *danteswari devi* installed by the rajas of Bastar at different temples must have, initially, influenced the Gharwa artists while making the images of *matas*. Therefore, in spite of variations, a structural uniformity exists among the various images of *matas*.

The long list of the *matas* propitiated on different occasions by the tribes of Bastar is as follows:

> *hinglajin mata, pardesin mata, telgin mata, banjarin mata, dokra mata, kankalin mata, gilgil mata, jalani mata, mauli mata, jhitkimitku, kunwarimasan mata, dulardai mata, gondpatin mata, tilakdai mata, rewagadi mata, chaurasin mata, lohra mata, sitla mata, burhibawri mata, kesha mata, mahamai khambha, gondin mata, pendrawedin mata, kalanki mata, madin mata, devgosin mata, pikribundin mata, jhumri mata, darasbundin mata, gangadai mata, jharanbundin mata, gumdakarin mata, railakodin mata, karnakotin mata, ghatmundin mata, karitelgin mata, waman mata, bishramsargin mata, mensaijarin mata, bahamanikadin mata, awrabundin mata, purladai mata, barahdawani mata, telinsati*

mata, fodaiburhi mata, kesharpalin mata, siramia mata, sargidogri mata, khandakankalin mata, gopagosin mata, satbahin mata, kodaibundin mata, kasin mata and *luhadokri mata*.

The *deva* cult is also indigenous, but the images suggest later influence. For example, all the *devas* are found riding a horse, sometimes wearing western dresses and brandishing a sword. One of the images of *rao deva,* while riding a horse, was found with a double barrel gun in its hand. This suggests the fear of firearms that the tribesmen must have encountered at the time of the advent of the Englishmen in this region during the late eighteenth and early nineteenth century.

The names of the *devas* are as follows:

rao deva, khodia deva, neha deva, baramania deva, kantarao deva, jatiarao deva, khonpat deva, madia deva, khaderao deva, durmuria deva, bhillarao deva, hudkirao deva, jhitkurao deva, gond deva, thakur deva, themarao deva, pondgarrao deva, shikatrao deva, khuksirao deva, ghoda deva, bhudarao deva, jangra deva, pat deva, bagh deva, chikhalraj deva, dondbula deva, barha deva, bhimabhimul deva, thade deva, mauli deva, rajarao deva, tondarrao deva, bhairam deva, dumarao deva, ningibhima deva, khutibhima deva, ulat deva, jhula deva, dola deva, harmaraj deva, dokra deva, kunwar deva, bankunwar deva, sian deva, dalar deva, sonkunwar deva, chaurasi deva, chaukbhairav deva, pilabhairav deva, ghodadai deva, ghodia deva, aag deva, dheribula deva, dalbula deva, beha deva, baramanim deva, billasava deva, charkirao deva, jhitkurao deva, duma deva, gond deva, ratungsirao deva, chikhalrao deva, barharao deva and *hamarao deva.*

Gharwa Art and Lost-Wax Process

Gharwa art is popularly known as *dhokra* art. In countryside areas of the Hindi speaking states, *dhokra* means "old." Old couples are often referred to as *dhokra-dhokri,* a synonym of *burha-burhi*. The nomenclature of the art itself suggests its antiquity. The technique of *dhokra* art is known as lost-wax process. In French, it is called *cire perdue* technique. This process is so ancient that the bronze images discovered from the sites of Indus Valley are believed to have been made by the lost-wax process. The eminent archaeologist George F. Dales , who has done extensive work on the archaeology of South and South East Asia, in his discussion on metal analysis of Harappan archaeology observes:

> "The Harappan had a working knowledge of a number of manufacturing and forming techniques, including work hardening, softening by annealing, smelting, sinking, raising, running on, *cire perdue* casting and open mold casting"(1986: 129).

About the antiquity of *cire perdue* technique, Meera Mukherjee writes:

> "... the technique followed by the folk artisans differs in basic details from the technique of classical image craft, while it bears close kinship with the primitive *cire perdue* technique of similar artisans in countries bordering the Mediterranean, and in the Americas" (1978: 41).

She further observes:

> "No clue has yet been found either to establish an indigenous origin of the technique or to help trace its import into India along a possible route. No explanation is forthcoming again as to why these artisans are clustered in and around the forests of Central India" (ibid.).

This ancient technique of bell metal craftsmanship still survives in some of the remote parts of Madhya Pradesh, Bihar, Orissa and Andhra Pradesh, and significantly, the artisans practising lost-wax process in India invariably live in and around the tribal habitat.

The implements that are used in lost-wax process by the Gharwas of Bastar are *pichki, pharni, jhara, matani, chhaini* (chisel), *hathora* (hammer), *tangia* (axe), *churi* (knife), *chimta* (tong), *ghaila* (crucible), *chipna* (stand for wax wire), *raimal* (sand paper), *suja* (awl), *narja* (scale) and *dhoukni* (blower).

First of all, a clay core of the desired image or the object is made. Great care is taken in the preparation of the clay that repeatedly undergoes mixing and processing. A rough clay model of the image is made. When the model is ready, it is dried before waxing. Pure *beeswax* is procured from the market, and after several rounds of processing, the wax is forced into *pichki* in such a way that skeins of wax wire of a uniform diameter comes out through *pharni*. Thereafter, the wire winding on the clay core begins. This is, qualitatively, the most artistic aspect of the Gharwa art. First, the whole of the clay core is wound by wax wire, and then it is decorated with minute designs.

When the decoration work on the image is complete, covering of wax is done again with clay. At the bottom of covering, a channel is left for the molten metal to flow into the mould. Thereafter, a crucible is made on which the scraps of bell metal and brass are put and placed appropriately near the channel. It is then sealed with clay.

Firing is done on a small furnace upon which the ensemble of the mould is placed in such a way that the crucible is at the bottom. Temperature is maintained by constantly blowing the fire with *dhoukni*. After two or three hours, when it is ascertained that the metal has completely molten and the wax has burnt and evaporated, the mould is seized with the help of a tong and inverted. Thus, the molten metal runs through the channel and occupies the void created by the burnt wax. After half an hour or so, when it cools down, the mould is broken and the image is found ready.

As the demand of Gharwa art has increased today, therefore, slight difference in technique and use of some implements can be found between the urban and the rural Gharwas. For example, whereas the rural Gharwas use the traditional *dhoukni* for blowing the fire in furnace, in Kondagaon and Jagdalpur, the Gharwas use modern machines for this purpose. However, despite such differences, the basic characteristics of lost-wax process remain identical.

Dynamics of Gharwa Art

During the last three decades, the Gharwa art has undergone swift change. Earlier, the Gharwas made the images of tribal deities, ornaments and other articles mostly on demand by the tribesmen. But after the universal recognition of Gharwa art, its demand changed overnight. Earlier, the *sirha*, after offering sacrifice to the deities left the images in the forest itself, now the images have been beautifying the drawing rooms of the rich elite and art lovers of the cities world over. Several emporia have been set up today in Jagdalpur which are supplying the Gharwa items to Delhi, Mumbai, Calcutta, Chennai, Hyderabad and other cities of India and abroad.

It all began in 1966. Mr. Arun Guha, an amateur wood craftsman, came to Jagdalpur in the *Dandakaranya* project that year. His artistic mind was struck to see the expertise of the Gharwa artists in lost-wax process. He learnt the technique himself and married a woman of Gharwa community, who herself was a *dhokra* artist. Credit goes to Mr. Guha for enhancing the popularity of *dhokra* art of Bastar. On the occasion of Asia 72, Mr. Guha displayed his items of *dhokra* art in New Delhi.

The difference between Guha's images and those made by the traditional Gharwa artists was that whereas the images of elephants and horses made by Gharwas appeared static, such as, straight and perpendicular legs of a horse or an elephant, those made by Guha showed "movement" such as, a galloping horse or an elephant with raised trunk. It should be noted that all the *devas* and many of the *matas* of Bastar are found riding a horse or an elephant. Thus, Guha was not only instrumental in bringing popularity to *dhokra* art, but he also influenced its style.

In a taped interview at the *Dancing Cactus*, Guha once told this author, "Earlier, there were three schools of Gharwa art, viz. the Erakot School, the Keshkal Valley School and the Jagdalpur School. When the township developed at Jagdalpur, the Gharwas from different parts of Bastar came and settled here. This resulted into the amalgamation of all the three schools."

The articles displayed in Asia 72 were soon recognized by the lovers of such folk art and were bought at high price. Along with Mr. Guha, a number of Gharwa artists, including the most celebrated Jaidev Baghel of Kondagaon, received President's Awards. All this triggered the journey of Gharwa art from the *jungle* of Bastar to the "concrete jungles" of world metropolises. Guha also established an emporium named the *Dancing Cactus*. He died in 1995.

Today, Gharwa art of Bastar has international demand. Many Gharwa artists have travelled abroad and demonstrated their skill. Mr. Jaidev Baghel has received certificates and awards of merit from Australia, Moscow, Germany, England, Holland and many other countries. He recently sold one of the images to a foreigner at a price of Rs.75,000. Mr. Mangal Nag has procured an order of several lacs of rupees from a firm for making coat hangers for an American group of hotels. At the center of the triangular coat hangers, a Maria dancer is shown with his drum. Today, every Gharwa artist enthusiastically shows the certificates and awards that he has received from different organizations. The demand of Gharwa artifacts is so high that in every house of Gharwas in Kondagaon, one finds "brokers" from the metropolitan cities booking orders of their choice.

In Kondagaon, production of Gharwa art has assumed the form of a "small-scale industry." Whereas it is true that the demand of Gharwa art has increased, and its artists have received national and international recognition, it is equally true that in this "march from art to industry," the quality of the products has considerably decreased. Such unprecedented and unguarded proliferation of this ancient art brought with itself counterproductive results.

The decline in the quality of Gharwa art began, as and when the government began to buy its products. Instead of evaluating the price upon the quality of artistic designs and craftsmanship, the artifacts were purchased on the basis of their weight. As a result, the Gharwas began to mix heavier metals for increasing the weights of their products in order to enhance their income. Moreover, as the demand was earlier not very high, the craftsmen spent much of their time and skill in decorating and finishing their products. Now the artists neither pay that attention to the quality of metal, nor to the quality of designs.

Simultaneously, some other factors were also at work for the decline in the quality of the Gharwa art. Whereas the demand of the Gharwa artifacts had "increased" in the cities in India and abroad, it had considerably "decreased" among the tribesmen of Bastar. The reasons were apparent. Medical facilities had increased in the otherwise forested and inaccessible areas; there was impact of education all around; roads were built and various other means of communication had developed as never before. Instead of running to witch doctors, the tribesmen began to rush to the hospitals and health centers at the time of any physical crisis. The articles of daily use and ornaments, which the tribesmen earlier procured from the Gharwas, were now available in local markets and rural shops, which were manufactured in factories. All these factors, obviously, changed the very originality of Gharwa art.

Conclusion

Whether the Gharwa art will completely lose its identity and assume altogether a new form? Whether the tribesmen would still ask a Gharwa artist to make images of any of the *matas* or *devas*? Whether the tribes-women would still wear ornaments made by the Gharwas? Whether the *tori* would still be blown in the *ghotul* in order to summon the young and unmarried boys and girls to assemble in the evening for night stay? Or, whether the unprecedented demand of the Gharwa artifacts by the city dwellers would persist forever? These are the questions need to be answered today by anthropologists.

As the exposure of Gharwa art at the national and international level is a phenomenon of only a few decades, it is too early to find answers to the above. Nevertheless, one can reasonably envisage the shape of the things to come.

No doubt, as long as the Bastar tribesmen continue to consult a *sirha* and propitiate the *matas* and *devas*, the originality of Gharwa art would also continue to exist. Today, two sections of Gharwa artists have emerged. One, who produces the items of demand by the city dwellers, the other, makes the items demanded by the forest dwellers. Kejuram of Kotgaon lives alone with his second wife among the Muria tribesmen. He has acquired a lot of land and cattle by making images of *matas* and *devas* for the Murias. In no case he wants to live with his children, who have settled in Kondagaon, and are engaged in making items of *order* from the cities. There appears to be a schism between two generations. However, Ram Singh, son of Kejuram, admits that though he makes the items of demand in bulk, but he is not as skilled an artist as his father. Qualitatively, his father makes superb images.

It is true that developmental works would continue in Bastar as in any other tribal and rural areas of the country. And, with the increasing pace of development the tribal and rural people would renounce many of their age-old superstitions and magico-religious beliefs and practices. The tribesmen are gradually getting exposed to the modern technologies and innovations. This has directly affected the tribal "worldview." With the increasing dependence upon technology, their dependence upon spirit world is correspondingly decreasing. It is very natural a phenomenon. As a result, Gharwa art has also reached its turning point.

However, it is not important whether the tribesmen continue to consult a *sirha* for the sake of Gharwa art or not. It is more important to ensure that the originality of Gharwa art is saved from extinction. And for this, the tribesmen need not be deprived of the fruits of development. They need not follow any of the superstitions and magico-religious beliefs and practices. It only requires a proper monitoring and management of Gharwa art by the administration.

The Gharwas are, today, at the crossroads of identity crisis. As Gharwas, they are identified by administration as Kasers, an OBC group; therefore, they admit their children in schools with Ghasia as surname. Whenever a Gharwa has to contest an election from a reserved seat, even for local bodies, he procures a certificate of Ghasia from administration. As Bastar is a tribal district, therefore, in order to avail more constitutional privileges and safeguards, the emerging leadership of educated and more conscious members of the community, today, has been attempting to "alter" altogether the "history" of the community itself. Now, in frustration, they have started claiming their tribal origin from Abujhmar, which is far from truth. Moreover, considering the demand of Gharwa artifacts, *Parchanpal Shilpgram* of Bastar has been imparting training in *lost-wax process* to non-Gharwas also. If it continued for long, this ancient technique of image making may slip from the hands of this community, causing more unemployment and frustration to its members.

Therefore, it is high time that the government pays attention to the critical situation and saves this ancient art from further decline, and also the artists from socio-economic and political turmoil. The following measures need immediate attention:

- Gharwa artifacts should be purchased not on the basis of their weight, but artistic skill, designs and craftsmanship.
- The community should be enlisted as scheduled caste.
- Easy loans and raw materials should be provided to them through co-operatives.
- The middlemen should be prevented from meddling in the affairs of sale and purchase of Gharwa art products.
- The co-operatives should function under the strict surveillance of a monitoring committee, constituted by the government, to ensure that the artists get maximum benefits of their products.

NOTE

1. Neither the Census of India, nor the District Administration at Jagdalpur, has any record of Gharwa population. The accounts referred to in the text is quoted from the records of *Parchanpal Shilpgram Emporium* of Bastar, an NGO engaged in promoting art and craft of Bastar by imparting training to tribal and rural youth in handicraft.

REFERENCES

Dales, George F. 1986. "Some Fresh Approaches to Old Problems in Harappan Archaeology," (pp.117-136) in Jerome Jacobson (ed.), *Studies in the Archaeology of India and Pakistan*. New Delhi: Oxford and IBH Publishing Company.

Elwin, Verrier. 1947. *Muria and their Ghotuls*. London: Geoffrey Camberlege, O.U.P.

_____. 1951. *The Tribal Art of Middle India*. Bombay: Oxford University Press.

Grigson, W.V. 1938. *The Maria Gonds of Bastar*. London: Oxford University Press.

Hiralal & Russell. 1916. *Tribes and Castes of the Central Provinces of India, Vol. I-IV*. London: MacMillan & Co.

Mukherjee, Meera. 1978. *Metalcraftsman of India*. Calcutta: Anthropological Survey of India.

TEN

IMPACT OF CHANGING ECONOMY ON THE LIFE OF MUNDA WOMEN OF A FRINGE VILLAGE OF SAMBALPUR CITY

SNIGDHA HOTA, NIBEDITA NATH, NANDINI BISWAL and DEEPAK KUMAR BEHERA

Change is a universal cultural phenomenon and the processes of change over a period of time constitute the dynamics of culture. Cultural change is studied over a baseline of human behaviour as of given time and nature (Herskovites, 1974: 446). The difference between social and culture change is largely theoretical, for these two are so closely interwoven that distinction is difficult (Behera, 1996: 8).

Social change consists of constellation of various processes of change in social structure in terms of place, time and context. The component units of social structure are "persons" (Behera, 1996: 8). If we consider human beings as units of social structure, the change at the individual level changes the structure of a society. Human beings are connected by a complex network of actually existing relations (Radcliffe-Brown, 1952: 190). When individuals undergo change the "actual social structure" changes, but the "general social structure" remains stable.

The individual behaviour is governed by the normative pattern of a society. However, the norms are not uniform for every individual. The status of an individual in a society is one of the determinants of the norms that s/he has to follow. Gender is one of the bases of social stratification and status determination. The normative system of the society allocates each gender its set of roles. These roles determine the position of the two genders with respect to each other, which also undergoes change with change in culture and society.

Social change brings changes in the construction of gender, which in turn shapes the actual social structure. Even today highest value is attached to the ever compromising, silent, invisible and sacrificing woman. The tribal communities are always different from the non-tribal. As culture is dynamic, the tribal have faced and are facing changes. Nevertheless the tribes have retained the principal elements of their ways of life, these are modified to a lesser extent (Vidyarthy and Roy, 1977: 454). Today, tribal communities are no longer isolated groups living in deep forest or in hilly areas. The line of distinction is gradually becoming blurred. Improved communication facilities have created conducive environment for change to take place. Taking in to consideration these factors a study has been conducted among the Munda women in a fringe village of Sambalpur city.

Review of Literature

The term "sex" has a biological connotation whereas "gender" is a cultural construct. Gender means how men and women are socially and culturally constituted and how such constructions have ideological meaning delineating relation of power (Anandhi and Roychoudhury, 1994: 3). The concept of gender is relative to the value system of the concerned community. Like social structure the concept of gender is also an abstract one. It constitutes all the ideal typical attributes that the community expects from a female. It is one of the bases of role allocation and role performance in every society.

The tribal women are thought to have a better social position than their non-tribal counterparts. In recent times the processes of economic change and acculturation seem to have altered the situation. The changing economy has brought tribal communities close to the caste societies. This has influenced the tribal to imbibe the tradition of subjugation and underestimation of women. There are many facts, which indicate inferior status for tribal female. They do not have property rights except in matrilineal societies. The tribal girl-child is forced to stay at home to look after her younger siblings. She generally does not get nutritional food and proper health care (Dashora, 1995: 208). A study among 300 hundred women of Santal Pargana shows that the extent of modernity so far as health care is concerned is very low (Rajyalakshmi, 1991: 23-38). The acceptance of family planning methods is found to be low in tribal population than that of the non-tribal due to high economic value attached to the children (Reddy and Mahadevan, 1986: 45-48). In a changing economy the status of tribal women is overshadowed by men's dominance (Deepkumar and Ramchandriah, 1986).

Objectives

Against this backdrop, the paper tries to portray a picture of Munda women living in a fringe village of Sambalpur city. It tries to analyze the impact of a changing economy on the life of Munda women. The changing economy has brought about some noticeable changes in the social structure of the community. The rapid growth of *bidi* industries, transfer of agricultural land from Munda to the non-tribal and the increasing contacts of the Munda with the non-tribal in the economic sphere have changed the gender relations in the community. The paper makes an attempt to examine the adverse impact of the economic changes in the life of Munda women. It also analyses various coping strategies adopted by Munda women in a changing economy.

Methodology

The study was carried out in village Malipali, which is inhabited mostly by the Munda. The present study is diachronic by nature and takes in to account the impact of changes on the life of the Munda women in the recent past. The impact assessment was made through a comparative study of the past and present situations. The changing economy started influencing the Munda community around 1970. The rapid growth of *bidi* industries, transfer of agricultural land from Munda to the non-tribal and the increasing contacts of the Munda with the non-tribal in the economic sphere all gathered their momentum around 1970. Therefore, the said year has been taken as the cut point for making a comparative analysis (before-after) on the life of Munda women. An ethnographic reconstruction (situation before the cut point) was made with the help of elderly women of the community who could provide us with inerrant data about the role of Munda women in their traditional economy. While elderly women were interviewed in groups for the collection of benchmark data, many younger married women were contacted for the collection of information about the present changing situation. Data were collected through observation, interview and group discussion methods.

The Munda

Orissa is a highly tribal populated state with as many as 62 Scheduled Tribes (Behera, 1997: 14). The Munda are believed to have originated from a

Kolarian stock. The term "Munda" is employed by Kols for the headmen of the village and came into general use as an alternate name of the tribe. They are specified as Scheduled Tribe in the states of Bihar, Madhya Pradesh, Orissa, Tripura and West Bengal. The Munda is one of the major tribes of Orissa having a population of 2.2 lakhs. They are known to have migrated from Chhotnagpur region to Orissa. The main concentration of Munda population is found in Sundergarh and Sambalpur with a population of 1,49,418 and 60,608 respectively (1991 Census).

The Munda have their own dialect called mundari. In mundari dialect, the term "Munda" means prestige and wealth. They believe in Singbonga as their supreme deity. Besides this they also worship other ancestral spirits (Verma, 1995: 33).

The Munda of Malipali have two sub-divisions, namely, Mahali and the Kaliha. These two sub-groups are endogamous. The Kaliha Munda are considered to be superior to the other group. The different clans found among the Munda of the village are: Hara (tortoise), Aind (a fish), Barla (leaf), Chhatra (an umbrella like structure made out of bamboo stripes), Naga (a snake). A good number of the Munda of Malipali are converted Christians.

The Village

The study village Malipali is situated 1.5km away from the Sambalpur city. Located besides the state highway between Sambalpur and Rourkela, the village is well connected with the outer world. This tribal dominated village has a population of 805 of which as many as 586 are from the Munda community. The other ethnic groups that live in this village are Khadia (108), Sahar (39), Ganda (19), Keuta (18), Oraon (10), Khandayat (5) and Kamara (20). The village has a primary school and a health center within a radius of 1km. The Munda of the Malipali live mostly in *kachha* houses and are members of nuclear family.

The village economy is primarily based on agriculture and *bidi* industry. Though the lands around the village are irrigated type, yet mostly non-tribal people of village Sankarma own those. Of the 105 Munda households, only 56 have some land. The landless Munda mostly work as agricultural labourers and *bidi* workers. Malipali being an irrigated area provides some wage earning opportunities to the Munda during major part of a year. Women are engaged in most of the agricultural operations either in their own land or on land owned by the non-tribal. As *bidi*-making activities that take place in a family, women and girl children shoulder up major part of the responsibilities.

Construction of Gender in Munda Community

Munda is a patriarchal tribe. Patriarchy can be defined as system of social structures and practices in which men dominate, oppress and exploit women (Walby, 1990: 20). In a patriarchal society generally more value is attached to a male child. Though the Munda are reluctant to accept the fact, gender disparities exist in their contemporay cultural practices. This is evident from the fact that majority of the parents interviewed preferred to have a male child.

The over all literacy of the community is low. Female literacy is much lower than the male literacy. The elderly women are mostly illiterate. The situation is bit different for the younger generation. All parents send their children to the school for primary education. However, the female children are dropped out when they are about to enter the secondary level in the school. This is the time when they are supposed to assist their mother in various household chores including taking care of the younger siblings. They also participate actively in the *bidi*-making work. The parents have lesser expectation from the male children in this regard. The girls are more overburdened with household works than their male counterparts. Therefore, learning from school remains a secondary activity for the girls. The girls do not find also such education life-oriented and therefore do not feel like spending long seven hours in the school premises with its overformal environment.

The age at marriage of the Munda women of our sample village is very low. In fact, that has hampered the development of the girl-child. The life cycle rituals also show differentiation between the two genders. The initiation ceremony of *kanphuda* is performed for a girl at the age of four to five year and for a boy it is performed around twelve years of age.

A married woman is considered to be a full-fledged member of her in-law's family only when she conceives her first child. A ritual called *anchrel* is performed after the third month of her pregnancy. In this the pregnant woman cuts a piece of turmeric in presence of her parents and in-laws.

Factors Influencing Change

Social change is an inevitable process. However, social change cannot be explained in terms of a single factor. There are various factors, which determine the rate and direction of change. The factors of social change may be demographic, biological, geographical, technological, economic and political.

Christianity has been an important factor of cultural change among the tribal (Vidyarthy and Roy, 1977: 458). According to an estimate the tribal Christians comprise about one sixth of the total Christian population in India. For about one fourth of the Munda have been converted to Christianity (Vidyarthy and Roy, 1977: 459). Under the modern processes of change urbanization and industrialization have literary brought about revolutionary changes in some parts of tribal India (Vidyarthy and Roy, 1977: 412). Along with the growth of urban population the areas of town is rapidly increasing. The implementation of various types of welfare and community development schemes meant for the tribal areas has brought about certain economic and social changes in tribal India (Vidyarthy and Roy, 1977: 461). As mentioned earlier, the village is located besides a state highway. Around 1970, a number of *bidi* industries were established in this region. This brought about remarkable changes in the occupation pattern and economy of the Munda community in general and Munda women in particular. The increasing contacts with the neighbouring Hindu community in a changing economy motivated them to adopt some Hindu traditions. Vidyarthy and Roy (1977: 454) reported that there are several points of contact between the Hindus and the tribal communities living within an urban area. The Munda of Malipali come in contact with the caste population of the adjacent village Sankarma almost on a regular basis. The contact between the Munda and the non-tribal increased manifold, when the only road connecting Sankarma to the highway was constructed through Malipali. Further the land gradually got transferred from the tribal Munda to the non-tribal people of the village Sankarma. When the Munda became landless they started supplying agricultural labour force to the caste Hindus of this village. Thus a patron-client relationship emerged between the people of both the villages. The people of Sankarma are economically better off than the people of Malipali because they posses more land and have more permanent engagement in the formal sector. The transformation of economy and influence of neighbouring communities have brought about far reaching changes in the social structure of the Munda community.

The Girl-child in the Changing Scenario

Crippled by traditional and oppressive thinking, the girl-child has been relegated to a place of seclusion from social presence (Seth, 1995: 105). This was not true for a tribal girl-child of Malipali before 1970. However, in recent time one can observe a paradigm shift in the life of the tribal girl-child from a free flowing carefree life in to a life of continuous restrictions. These restrictions increase with age. This is unlike their past tradition where " young boys and girls had considerable freedom of movement. They could meet each other in weekly markets, fairs and festivals" (Choudhury, 1997: 75). This conditioning of the Munda girl-child is also a product of the need of the community. That need in turn is a product of economic change. The women of the community contribute substantially to the household economy. This keeps them out of their home mainly in agricultural seasons. So their daughters have to stay back at home to look after the younger siblings and to perform other household chores. It is not unusual for tribal women to work outside to earn. But the duration of stay has now increased because the lands are now irrigated and instead of one crop the land now produces double crops. This has unusually stretched the agricultural season.

The influence of the norms of the neighbouring communities can be marked in some spheres of the Munda girl-child's life. The Munda community is known for their lively dances. Dancing of young girls during the festivals was never seen as an offence. However, the parents now prevent their daughters from participating in dance. They consider it derogatory for the young girls to dance evaluating that in terms of caste Hindu tradition. Though married women participate in dances, young girls are not encouraged to do so.

Changes in the Institution of Marriage

A whole range of change is also marked in the institution of marriage. The Munda of this village, as mentioned eavlied, are divided into two sub groups, namely Mahali and Kaliha. Each group is ideally endogamous. However now marriages between members belonging to these two groups have become a common pattern. In the past matrimonial alliance between these two groups was considered to be a breach of mores. The two families involved in such intermarriage were socially boycotted by the community. However in recent time the punishment has become lighter. Both the families get excommunicated only for a shorter period. They get re-assimilated into their respective groups by offering a sacrifice in the form a hen and a goat to the village deity and entertaining the elderly people of their respective sub-groups with *kusna* (rice bear). Then the girl gets accepted by her in-laws and also as a member of her husband's sub group. The increasing degree of interaction in the economic sphere has led to frequent cases of inter-marriage between the two sub-groups.

In the past, inter-religious marriage between a Christian and a non-Christian Munda was something unthinkable. However, the marriage of boys and girls belonging to the two religious groups is not uncommon in recent time. Rather it is happening at a more regular interval. In that case, the girl shall have to take baptism before her marriage. Some times her parents go through the same process in order to gain acceptance. The Munda community treats the inter-group and the inter-religious marriage almost in the same way. Social institutions cannot remain totally unaffected from the outside influence. Gender specificity and gender insensibility have entered into the institution of Munda marriage. The practice of dowry, an integral part of Hindu marriage, has entered into their social system. However bride price continues to operate as a traditional practice at a minimal level. The marriage traditions of Munda are undergoing gradual changes coming in contact with the so-called civilized traditions (Mitra, 1997: 106). It is significant to note here that the amount paid in cash and kind by the bride's parents in the form of dowry far exceeds the bride price. This changing practice has adversely impacted the young girls as they are now seen as burden to the family instead of resource. It is an age when the birth of a girl in the Munda community is seen as curse, as skyrocketing dowry has eroded all the pleasures of their traditional marriage. As reported by Choudhury (1977: 75) "unlike Hindus, the Munda concept of marriage rests on terms of near equality between husband and wife." The changing economic situation especially after 1970 has also affected the relation. It has turned in to a hierarchical one, the wife givers being always inferior to wife takers.

The forms of marriage have also undergone certain changes. Among the Munda a young woman could elope with a person of her choice and this union was socially accepted when the bride price was settled (Choudhury, 1978:14). But now the Munda of Malipali have started seeing elopement as a social evil. The parents want their daughters to give in marriage only through negotiation process. Parents who got married by elopement are now critical about the same form of marriage. This changing attitude of the parents is a clear reflection of the influence of neighbouring caste Hindu on the Munda community. These changes can be viewed as a process of sanskritization because the neighbouring communities are perceived as higher in the local hierarchy by the Munda. They try to imitate some of the their practices to move higher in the social ladder.

Munda Women in a Changing Economy

As mentioned earlier the Munda women play a vital role in their economy. The flourishing *bidi* industries of the region have brought about radical changes in the life of the Munda women. In search of cheap labour these industries have targeted tribal families of our sample village. Living in an irrigated village with no or little land, the economy of the Munda has been in a state of continuous want. Therefore, the Munda families now work for the *bidi* industries under compulsive situation. Working as *bidi* workers requires long hours of sitting at a stretch and the job is monotonous. So the male persuade the females to do the job. Women's engagement as *bidi* workers on the one hand has increased their workload manifolds. The mechanization of agriculture on the other hand has lessened the work burden of the Munda male who normally supply the labour force to the non-tribal landowners. Ploughing, the most important agricultural operation done by the Munda male as part of their wage-earning activities, is now performed with the help of tractors. The other agricultural operations, viz. weeding, replanting, harvesting, etc. are considered as female's jobs. Those labour-intensive works are left behind by the men to be performed by their female folk. This shows that the changing situation has reduced the workload of men at the expenses of increasing pressure of work on the female. Ideally the male members of the community should have taken up the *bidi*-making job, as mechanization has taken away their job in the agricultural field. However, the male members avoid doing this job and prefer to spend their free time more in merry making activities like gambling and drinking.

Besides putting additional pressure on women, the *bidi* industries have triggered off many other negative social consequences. *Bidi* indutry is a highly unorganized sector. It always employs causal labour to keep the investment at the minimal level. Though making *bidi* is a skilled job the industry does not have to train its manpower. The young girls start learning the skill from their mothers at a very tender age. The employers want the work to be done at home in order to avoid unnecessary labour problems. Therefore, they are not under any special obligation to provide working space for the *bidi*-making operation. The workers are paid in terms of the number of *bidis* they produce rather than the number of hours they spent for doing the job. The poor women and girls find no other way than stretching their working hours at home, even sometime beyond their physical limits, for earning more wages. They are paid thirty-six rupees per 1000 *bidis*. A woman or grown up girl-child on an average makes roughly 2000 *bidis* in a week. But they are generally not paid for the total number of *bidis* they make. The *munsi* (the one who collects the *bidis* from the workers) rejects some of those as being defective. The Munda women accept the extra-burden without any protest, as it is not expected from them to voice their views against injustice. The law also cannot help them, as they are not the permanent workers of the industry.

The *bidi* industry also employs large numbers of female child labourers. As mentioned earlier the girls learn the job by the time they reach six to seven years of age. As soon as the young girls get acquainted with it, they are introduced to family labour process. As there is a surplus labour in this sector, the workers are paid low wages. The female workers of the village are paid at so low rate that they enlist the help of their female children. Similar observation was made by Burra (1981: 19) in her study of female *bidi*-workers of Nizamuddin.

Bidi-making involves a number of health-hazardous. In fact *bidi* rolling leads the women and girl children to two types of occupational diseases. One is caused by the injurious effect of inhaling tobacco fume and the other is the result of long hours of continuous job. Diseases like tuberculosis,. asthma, allergy belong to the former while backache, body ache, stomach ache, gas trouble, piles and rheumatic complains belong to the second category (Mohandas, 1980: 152; Behera, 1997: 813).

Women's Participation in Religious Activities

Contact with non-tribal has been proved instrumental in changing the religious beliefs of the non-converted Munda. In certain cases this contacts have given a fresh lease of life to a tribal group by providing it with better tool of adoption (Hasnain, 1996: 92). Hinduization is a wide spread phenomenon in tribal India and our sample community is not an exception to the process. In this process, the Munda have moved away substantially from their earlier traditions and rituals. They have borrowed some new elements from the Hindu-fold and made those integral part of their religion. The Munda of Malipali are found to observe several Hindu rituals, viz. Nuakhai, Phagunpuni, Diwali, Bhaijuntia, Puajuntia, along with their own rituals. They have adopted these rituals in their system with some minor modifications. The Munda religion is centered round ancestral worship. Women are prohibited from participating in many rituals. They strongly believe that any offering made by a female will not reach the ancestors.

The major Hindu rituals that the Munda women of Malipali have adopted are Laxmipuja, Bhaijuntia and Puajuntia. In all these three rituals within the

Hindu fold, worship is done by the females. The Munda women have adopted *Laxmipuja* as it is and they also worship the same goddess Laxmi in this puja like the Hindus. Howvever in the other two rituals, one would find some interesting modifications. Instead of worshipping goddess Durga in Bhaijuntia and god Dutibahana in Puajuntia, the Munda now worship god Karma (a tribal deity) during these festivals. The women of Munda community are not allowed to worship Karma. This is done by only the male members of the society.

It is significant to note that as many as 12.1 per cent of the Munda families of the village are Christians. The converted Christians of the community still adhere to some of their pre-conversion practices. They not only participate in their traditional rituals but also continue to keep matrimonial alliances with the non-converted Munda. The women have certainly gained equality in religious practices from the change. Unlike their non-converted counterparts, the converted Munda women are somewhat better treated within the fold of religious practices.

People have begun to loose faith in their *bonga*. Like elsewhere in India as reported by Vidyarthy and Roy (1997: 456), a Brahmin is sometime invited by the Munda of this village for marriage ceremonies and death rites. All these changes have taken place due to their increasing contacts with the non-tribal and acceptance of some non-tribal communities as their reference groups.

Women's Health Care in a Changing Situation

One of the determinants of the quality of life is health. The women of this community have not experienced any major change in this area. The male folk of this community do not give enough attention towards female health. Many times they are taken to the hospital at a late stage. It is not the physical distance from the health services but the attitudinal distance that is responsible for their poor health condition. Another crucial area for female is the reproductive health. The age at marriage of the female of this community is unusually low, i.e. thirteen to fifteen years. This accounts for prolonged reproductive life. "A women married early is likely to conceive early and gets trapped in the vicious circle of conception-motherhood-nursing motherhood" (Raman, 1999: 82). The acceptance of family planning methods is found to be the low among the Munda women. The caste-Hindu are more in favour of family planning as compared to Munda population due to high economic value attached by them to children. Similar observations were also made by Reddy and Mahadevan (1986: 45-48) elsewhere.

The delivery takes place at home. A Munda woman is rarely taken to a hospital during her pregnancy. The traditional midwife called *kuser* assists during delivery. Therefore even today the community continues to view women only as potential mothers. Women are not treated here as independent being having control over their lives.

Women's Participation in a Changing Political Sphere

The Munda had their traditional village panchayat. The head of the panchayat was called *pahan*. The office of the *pahan* was hereditary (Verma, 1995: 34). The Munda of Malipali also have their traditional village panchayat. It does not have any fixed structure. The constituents are some elderly males of the community. But there is no *pahan* in it. There is no restriction on the number of people involved in decision-making process. One of the reasons of this coexistence and survival of the traditional panchayat along with the elected self-government is that the people have an understanding of the traditional political system and have faith in it. The modern day legislatures are too complicated for them to understand.

The Munda women are kept away from the traditional political process as well as from modern political institutions. However the male members participate in modern political process like campaigning for different political parties in recent time. The women folk still remain away from politics. Their participation in the political sphere is mostly limited to voting during election. Even the decision on whom to vote is taken by their husband/father/brothers. The political awareness of women is limited to the village panchayat. Even those who are elected representatives of their gram panchayat, never take any decision independently. They normally act as per the contra dictory suggestions/decisions of their respective husbands/fathers. They are unable to tell the name of the MLA or MP or PM or President.

The Girl-Child's Education

Female illiteracy is high among the Munda. Female education has suffered due to problem ranging from financial to cultural. The entry of the girls into the labour market at very tender age is one of the reasons for their dropping out from the school. The parents force the girl children to leave school and start making *bidi* back by home. They start contributing to the meger income of their family when they are six to seven years of age. Earning money at a tender age means a few more rupee to spend. This also tempts the girl to join the labour force. Working in *bidi* industry has shorten their childhood.

It is in the adult's interest that the female children are engaged in this economic activity.

The unfavourable condition in the school is also a dissuading factor for the girls to continue their education. They also don't find the course curriculum interesting. The parents and teachers also show an apathetic attitude towards their educational progress.

Despite the recognition of importance of women education in all the five year plans not much has been done in action (Sunder Raj, 1999: 411). As a result the scenario of female education in this community continues to be gloomy. The village has only one primary school. Even the girls who somehow rather complete their primary education are not allowed to go for further study.

Participation in Decision-Making

To evaluate the position of woman in the society it is important to know her participation in the decision-making process. It is a general view that men's economic contribution is responsible for his upper hand in decision-making process. Munda is a patriarchal tribe. Patriarchy ascribes its male members an important position in the decision-making process. But the role of a tribal women is different from her non-tribal counterparts.

The Munda women of Malipali contribute substantially to the economy. Along with the household work she works in the agricultural field and also earns by *bidi* making. In spite of all her contribution she is marginalized in the process. The male (heads-of-the-households) are the sole decision-makers in the most important items of decision-making. Children's education, purchase of household articles, casting vote are the areas where man dominates. Santhi (1999: 142) reported that, "tribal women are an inseparable asset to the tribal economy and hence whatever they earn belongs to them". However, that was not found to be true in case of the Munda women of Malipali.

Here we must take in to account the two processes of cultural change, i.e. "cultural drift" and "historical accidents." Cultural drift is the working out of those sequences that seem logically to follow from the way in which a culture is organized, the interest of those persons who make up the society and the ends they seek in terms of the values and goals sanctioned by their culture. Historic accident is a phrase applied to those sequences of events in the life of a people, unforeseen and from the inner logic of the culture, unpredictable, that give new directions to the changes that mark the course of their history, so that sequence that might otherwise have been expected to occur are altered (Herkovites, 1974: 452). Some of the changes experienced by the Munda can be explained in terms of "cultural drift" and some others are the resultants of "historical accident." The radical changes brought about in the economy by the *bidi*-industries can be seen as a "historical accident". A whole range of changes is experienced by the Munda community in the sphere of religion, marriage, health, etc. due to the influence of neighbouring communities. It can be seen as a case of "cultural drift." It might have been possible that the economy of the community would have taken the same course. But the influence of *bidi*-industries has changed the course of change. As a result education has suffered a severe set back. The designed change is not achieved.

In addition to their traditional role, women under study are also engaged in paid jobs. But the patriarchal ideologies have even refused to recognize the economic contribution of women as valuable one. The rise of Munda women's participation in the unorganized sector is more due to economic compulsion rather than any change in work ethos. It has not, however altered the patriarchal mode of thinking (Rustagi, 1997: 166). The traditions play its parts in depriving the Munda women from real control over their earnings. Being conformist to the patriarchal ideologies they surrender their earning to the head-of-household (who is always a male member) or spend it in fulfilling household needs. A Munda female invests her childhood for her parents and rest of her life for her husband or in-laws. She grows into womanhood without a right to individual expression of desire (Seth, 1995: 108). Hence to envisage them as an economically independent entity in the society would be a chimera of the fact.

The economy of the community has undergone radical changes. But the gender equation of the social order has either remained same or gone against the women. The stabilizing elements of social structure (the normative system and the sanction system) try to maintain the order. Whenever there is a scope for women to elevate her position in the social order, the social structure reorients it to preserve the existing status quo. She always finds herself against the gradient.

REFERENCES

Anandhi, S. and A. Roy Choudhury. 1994. "Patriarchy and Gender Relations: An Overview," *Social Action,* 44 (2): 1-14

Behera, D.K. 1996. "The Invisible Little Big Workforce: Plight of the Female Working Child in India," Eugeen Verhellen (ed.), *Monitoring Children's Rights.* The Netherlands: Kluwer Law International,

Behera, D.K. and N. Nanda. 1997. "Gender Inequalities in a Tribal Context: Some Reflections from Orissa," (pp.149-162) in Georg Pfeffer and Deepak kumar Behera (eds.), *Contemporary Society Tribal Studies,* Vol.1. New Delhi: Concept Publishing Company.

Behera, B.K. 1996. *Tribal, Culture, Modernisation.* New Delhi: Khama Publishers.

Behera, K.S. 1997. "The Role of Tribes in the History and Culture of Orissa" in Santosh Kumar Sethi and Susmita Pani (eds.), *Tribal Culture of Orissa,* UGC Publication.

Burra, N. 1981. "Beedi Workers of Nizamabad," *Economic and Political Weekly,* 8 August.

____. 1978. *Tribal Women in India.* Calcutta: Indian Anthropological Society Publications.

Choudhury, N.C. 1997. *Munda Social Structure.* Calcutta: Firma KLM plt.

Dashora, R. 1995. "Status of Tribal Girl Child," *Social Change,* 25 (2&3): 207-216.

Deepkumar, V.S and T. Ramchandriah. 1986. "The Role of Women in the Economy of a Nomadic Tribe: Narikaravo of South-Eastern India" in proceedings of *National Conference of Tribal Women and Development: Problem and Perspectives.* Udaipur.

Hasnain, N. 1996. *Tribal India.* Delhi: Palaka Prakashan.

Herkovites. M. J. 1974. *Cultural Anthropology.* New Delhi: Oxford Publishing Company.

Mitra, Santosh Kumar. 1997. "The Marriage Traditions of the Juangs of Keonjhar-A Study", in Santosh Kumar Sethi and Susmita Pani (eds.), *Tribal Culture of Orissa,* UGC Publication.

Mohandas, Das. 1980. "Beedi Workers in Kerala: Conditions of Life and Work", *Economic and Political Weekly,* XV (36)

Sethi and Susmita Pani (eds.). 1997. *Tribal Culture of Orissa.* New Delhi: UGC Publication.

Radcliffe-Brown, A.R. 1952. *Structure and Function in Primitive Society.* London: Cambridge.

Raman, P. 1999. "Early Marriage and Reproductive Health Status of Women," (pp.76-87) in R. Indira and D.K. Behera (eds.), *Gender and Society in India.* Vol II. New Delhi: Manak Publications.

Rajyalaxmi, C. 1991. "Health Modernity in Tribal and Non-tribal Women in Santhal Pargana," *Social Change,* 21 (1): 23-38.

Reddy, M.M. and K. Mahadevan. 1986. "Values Attached to Male and Female Children," *Social Change,* 16 (1): 45-48

Rustagi, P. 1997. "Women Empowerment in Unorganized Sector: Some Issues," *Social Action,* 47 (2): 166-180.

Sahoo, Akhil Kumar. 1997. "Cultural Forces vs Developmental Forces," in Santosh Kumar Sethi and Susmita Pani (eds.), *Tribal Culture of Orissa*. New Delhi: UGC Publication.

Seth, P. 1995. "Girl Child and Social Change," *Social Change*, 25 (2-3): 107-155.

Shanthi, 1999. "Women in Tribal Societies: An Overview," in R. Indira and D.K. Behera (eds.), *Gender and Society in India.* Vol. II. New Delhi: Manak Publications.

Sunder Raj, D. 1990. "Whither Women's Education?" *Social Action,* 49 (4): 401-402.

Vidyarthy, L.P. and B.K. Rai. 1977. *The Tribal Culture of India*. Delhi: Concept Publishing Company.

Verma, J. 1989. "Women Education—A Media of Social Change," *Social Change*, 19 (2): 18-23.

Verma, R.C. 1995. *Indian Tribes Through Ages*. New Dehli: Publication Division, Ministry of Information and Broadcasting, Govt. of India.

Walby, S. 1990. *Theorizing Patriarchy.* London: Backwell.

ELEVEN

TRIBE, CASTE AND KINSHIP IN ORISSA

N.K. BEHURA

Introduction

Orissa is situated between 17° 49′ N to 22° 3′ N latitude and from 81° 29′ to 87° 29′ E longitude on the eastern coast of India. It is bounded by the states of West Bengal on the north-east, Bihar on the north, Madhya Pradesh on the west Andhra Pradesh on the south and by the Bay of Bengal on the east. Orissa had a hoary past and glorious history although it came into existence on April l, 1936.

The history of Orissa dates back to antiquity its famous ancient names being Kelinga, Odradesha, Koshal and Utkal. The history of Kalinga goes back to Pre-Christian era. It entered into the period of recorded history during the age of imperial Nandas of Magadha. Chandragupta Maurya overthrow the Nanda dynasty and brought Kalinga under his control. The third Maurya emperor invaded Kalinga around 261 B.C. and conquered it. After 1st century B.C. Kalinga was ruled over by the imperial Guptas and Kusanas. From the beginning of 6th century it was ruled by the Sailodbhavas (600-736 A.A.), the Somevamais (885-1100 A.D.) and Chalukyas (1559-1568 A.D.). Mukundadeva was the last Hindu king of Kalinga. After him the kingdom ceased to be independent. Bengal Newab, Moghul emperors and Maratha rulers gradually established their hegemony over Kalinga till the advent of the British. The British occupied Orissa in 1803, and before that the state was under the administration of the Maratha Rulers for about 40 years. Under the British administration, Orissa remained as a part of Bengal prosidenty along with Bihar till 1912. Bihar and Orissa remained as a composite provinco till April l, 1936 and thereafter Orissa became a separate province of India.

The People of Orissa

Orissa occupies an important position not only in the history and geography of India, but also in its cultural milieu and racial composition. Orissa is a land of diverse cultures and varied population. As per 1991 census, Orissa has a total population of 31,659, 736 out of which 27,424,753 (86.6 per cent) live in 51,639 rural,villages, and 4,234,963 (13.4 per cent) reside in urban areas. The total number of male population is 16,064,146 (50.73 per cent) and female population comprises 15,595,590 (49.26 per cent). Population density per sq. km. is 203 in the state.

Orissa has a sizable tribal population. There are 62 such communities belonging to three language families, namely Indo-Aryan, Austro-Asiatic (Mundari) and Dravidian. The total tribal population of the state is 7,032,214 (22.22 % of the total population) as per 1991 census. The number of male population is 3,512,891 (49.95 %) and female population is 3,519,323 (50.05 %). About 6,670,506 persons (94.8 %) reside in rural areas and only 361,708 persons (5.2 %) live in urban areas.

In Orissa, there are 93 Scheduled Castes, and according to 1991 census the total Scheduled Caste population comprises 5,129,314 persons (16.20 % of the total population). The total number of Scheduled Caste male constitutes 2,596,464 (50.62%) and the female population comprises 2,532,850 (49.37 %). From the foregoing presentation, it is evident that the sex ratio in the state of Orissa among three major categories of population is quite favourable as there is no significant variation.

Literacy is a prelude to the development of human resources, and therefore, it is an index of the quality of people. After five decades of Indian Independence the rate of general literacy of Orissa (as per 1991 Census) is 49.09 per cent as against the national literacy of 52.19 per cent. Male literacy in the state is 63.09 and female literacy is 34.68. The percentage of literacy among the Scheduled Tribe population is 18.10 (1991 Census), with male literacy and female literacy being 27.93 and 8.29 per cent respectively. Literacy position among the Scheduled Caste population of the state is slightly better. The literacy percentage among them is 30.19, with male and female literacy being 43.03 and 17.03 respectively. Thus in the literacy front Scheduled Tribes are the weakest. Scheduled tribes, Scheduled Castes and caste Hindu communities of Orissa constitute a composite socio-cultural universe. There are cultural, linguistic and racial affinities between them.

"In ancient days, Orissa was known to be an unclean, uncivilized region where the non-Aryan Savara tribesmen predominated. Though the generic term 'Savara' was applied to all the tribal folk of Orissa in ancient India, it may sefely be surmised that some other tribes besides the Savara tribe of Orissa were also present in the ramote past" (Mahapatra, 1977: 19). The racial picture of Orissa by and large conforms to proto-Australoid type with dark-brown skin colour, long head and broad nose. One of course comes across of sporadic occurrence of Mongoloid and Mediterranian racial elments, specifically among certain categories of Brahmans and Khatriyas, who might have come to Orissa at a later period of time. It is appropriate here to refer to the work of Mishra and Samal who write that the "post Samundragupta invasion witnessed the process of Sanskritization which radically changed the tribal culture of Orissa" (1997: XXVIII).

The Tribal Social System

In accordance with the provisions of the Article 342 (1) of the Constitution of India, the president of India notifies a community as Scheduled Tribc on the recommendation of the concerned State Government and the Central Government for being eligible to enjoy constitutional sefeguards and protective discrimination. There arc a total of 427 Scheduled Tribes in India, out of which 62 are in Orissa. About 45 per cent of the total area in Orissa is declared as Schadulcd Area, excepting the coastal belt rest of the districts of the state are either partially or fully declared as Scheduled Area. Out of a total of 314 Community Development Blocks, 118 are Tribal Blocks, which are included under Integrated Tribal Devolopment Agencies (ITDAs).

Tribal communities are designated by various native or indigenous appellations, such asp *Janjati* (folk castes), *adivasi* (original inhabitants), *vanyajati* (forest castos), *adimjati* (primitive castes), *girijan* (forest castes) and *anusuchit janjati* (Scheduled Tribes), The last nomenclature is a constitutional one. Nihar Ranjan Ray, in his quest for the meaning of the term "tribe" in Indian context, suggests that the sanskrit term *Jana* used to be referred to those simple and techno-economically backward communities in ancient times. He further says that the term *Jana* is derived from the root word *jan*, which means to be born give birth to, and hence has a biological meaning (1972: 9). Ray also opines that the term *Jana* in ancient times referred to the autochthonous people like the Savaras, Kullutas, Bhillalas,

Khasas, Kinnaurs, Asura and a countless number of others who are today known as "tribes", christened by the British whose policy was to segregate these communities from rest others. In 1874 the colonial government introduced the concept "tribe" with a concealed political motive. In 1901 census these communities were enumerated as "tribes" to retain their ethno-cultural identities, and in 1931 Census enumeration this nomenclature was retained. The Government of India Act of 1919 and 1935, scheduled the tribal communities in order to keep them as a separate block of citizens. Although the simply homogeneous and relatively vulnerable communities were designated as Scheduled Tribes, no substantial measure was initiated for their welfare.

Most of the tribal communities inhabited hilly, forest and inaccessible areas of the country. The territories they occupied came to be known as *Janapada* in ancient literature. These areas were referred to as *atavikarajyo* (forest torritory), *mahakantara* (greatly inaccessible region) and *pratyantodosa* (frontier rogions) in old records (Ray, 1972, 11). Thus in Indian context, the tribe refers to as indigenous *jana* or native simple communities, are designated as *anusuchit Janjati* or Scheduled Tribes in modern India. Out of the total of 427 Scheduled Tribes, 76 relatively vulnerable ones have been categorized by Government of India as Primitive Tribal Groups for special treatment.

Scholars have classified tribal communities of the country on the basis of their economy. In the exercise they have taken into consideration the main or major econcmic activity of a tribe. The economy of tribal communities, by and large, is undifferentiated, which means that a tribal community under compelling circumstances, does not depend on a single economic activity instead it relies on some other allied economic activities which their environment permits to take up. For instance, whose major economic activity is either settled agriculture or shifting cultivation, the same community simultaneously also takes up animal husbandry, hunting of games and gathering of various forest produces. As per this parameter tribal communities have been classified as (i) settled agriculturists, (ii) shifting cultivators, (iii) pastoralists, (iv) simple artisans, (v) nomadic performing artists, (vi) hunter-gatherers, and (vii) industrial-urban workers.

They partly depend on hunting-gathering activities because a majority of them inhabit the placid forest environments. From primeval times they have been depending on forests as a perennial source of necessities of life. Thus their economy, life-style and ideology cannot be thought of without forest. From birth to death their life revolves round the forest. They are so much part of the forest that they adopt natural species of plants/animals/birds as their totems, and foster ritualistic attitude towards them. A totem symblizes collective sentiments, solidarity and culture of the group that has adopted it. Tribals regard forest both as a natural as wall as supernatural entity.

Tribal economy is overwhelmingly subsistence oriented; circulation of goods is largely based on barter. There is no scope for accumulation of capital. It is less monetized and less market-oriented. Natural resources are owned and regulated collectively by the community. Individual ownership is gradually developing. There is less specialization at occupation. Economic competition is still low and subdued.

As regards the social structure the largest reference group is the ethnic community - the tribe or sub-tribe which constitutes a single ethno-cultural group occupying a more or less contiguous territory. A tribe or subtribe is segmented into patrilineal totemic clans. Their social structure is homogeneous, non-hierarcic, segmentary kin-based and relatively closed. Social solidarity, cohesion and egalitarianism comprise the hallmark of tribal social structure.

Those tribal communities are relatively more isolated in their active contact with the larger culture community of the "Great Tradition" of India, compared to the traditional Hindu peasant communities. However, the tribal societies have been in touch with the peasant communities through the network of weekly market and administrative agencies where they are involved in economic and administrative transactions. These tribal or little communities of India are not completely shut off from contact, both directly and indirectly, with the large or great culture community of India. By implication, more or less, this great community is the caste community. The caste community fosters and perpetuates both "Little Tradition" and "Great Tradition."

The social groups that perpetuate "Little Traditions" in relation to an indigenous civilization are labelled as "peasant communities," as distinguished from the isolated nearly self-sufficient "tribal or folk-societies," which Redfield has conceived as an ideal type (1953). In contradiction to the "folk societies," the "peasant communities" are frequently in interaction with urban and centres of culture through complex networks. Therefore, the study of caste is useful to have a comprehensive knowledge of Indian society and civilization as the Hindu social system is a major part of it, and has influenced it in more ways than not.

The Caste System in Orissa

In order to comprehend society in Orissa, one has to delve into its socio-political history, while keeping in view its folk predominent demographic scenario and encysting geo-physical conditions. One can safely conjecture that during ancient and early medieval periods society in Orissa was folk-orionted. Majihima-Nikaya, an important Buddhist literally source, mentions that the Utkal Janapada had been inhabited by Vassa and Bhanni, two tribes, who are *ahetuyadi* (indiscrote), *akriyivadi* (indolent), and *nathakavadi* (animists) (cf. Mishra and Samal, 1997: XXVIII). During the period following the rise of the Imperial Guptas in Magedha, Kalinga too witnessed a process of sanskritization, which radically changed the tribal culture of the Kalings region (Mishra and Samal, 1997: XXVIII). During this time the Imperial Eastern Gangas ruled over Kalinga (from 498 A.D. to 1434 A.D.). Anantvarman Chodagangadeva succeeded Rajaraja-1 in 1078 A.D. to the throne of Kalinga. It is logically surmized that during his reign Oriya script evolved. Rath attests that during the eleventh century A.D. a standing tradition of Oriya language and literature had been established (1997: 531).

Orissa, though has been an integral part of Indian civilization from prehistoric times, yet it provides a complex and peculiar situation. In modern times, Orissa comprised many chiefdoms, which were often integrated into a larger kingdom, and subsequently got disintegrated. "Again, there was some consolidation of the chiefdoms under another large kingdom in a cyclical process of flux" (Mahapatra, 1997: 706). Major chunks of population of those erstwhile chiefdoms are various tribal communities, who belong to either of the three language families, namely, Indo-Aryan, Austro-Asiatic and Dravidian.

Mohapatra outlines Orissa as a cultural region in the following manner: "The centralized state, the feudatory states owing allegiance to the state of Kalinga, tribes, predominanting the population in many of the feudatory states, prevalence of quasi-feudalism in the polity, several religious sects in the Hindu religion, the village characterized by interdependent castes or jati and patron-client relationships, and the central king's court, royal priests, estates and services paralleling those of the state deity, Lord Jagannatha, besides a large number of monasteries and temples, small towns and markets comprised the major features of society in Orissa" (1997: 706).

In Orissa, a major part of the population, apart from the Scheduled Castes and Scheduled Tribes, belongs to the fourth Varna of Shudra order, who are *Ekaja* (once born). Castes or Jati belonging to the *Dwija* (twice born) Varna, namely, Brahman, Kshatriya and Vaishyas are few and their total population is much less. Brahman and Kshatriya population in the state of Orissa may not be more than seven to eight per cent. Vaishyas are all immigrants to this region since the colonial times. There are no Vaishyas in

Orissa whose mother tongue is Oriya. There are documentary evidence to prove that Brahman had been brought to Orissa, both from southern and northern India by kings to perform rituals and religious rites. In Orissa the population of Shudra Varna, as a block, outnumber the population of Brahman, Kshatriya and Vaishya Varnas or the Scheduled Castes and Scheduled Tribes. As a number of clean and a variety of ritually unclean Jati categories or castes arc included in this order, the population of Shudras would be around fifty per cent. Among the Shudras the percentage of Karan (writer) caste population is not significant. It is believed that in the historic past Karans had come from the neighbouring states, both from the north and the south to assist the local administration. Among the clean Shudra castes, *Khandait* (quasi militia), Mahanayak, Chasa, Paika, Oda, Kalinji, Kolta and Kurmi are basically farming castes and occupy, more or less, equivalent position in the local social order; although in the past they did not intermarry. Among those castes, the Khandait and Mahanayak claim Kshatriya status because of their martial tradition. Shudra Varna includes all the artisan, vocational and ritual service castes and among them all the Gauda (milkman) caste is numerically prepondrent.

In Orissa peasantization of tribal and their integration with the Hindu social order is an old social process. After Integration they remain as a category of peasants or take up different caste-based avocations. Before the enforcement of the Constitution, advanced tribal communities resented the appellation "tribe," which they considered derogatory, but afterwards they steadfastly stuck to the nomenclature because of the protective entitlements which it brought along with. However, the processes of retribalization and depeasantization have not taken place in Orissa. After assuming caste status and avocations members of some of the erstwhile tribes continue to retain their original tribal ethnic identity, for instance, caste nomonciaturos as Kandha Kumbhar, Kandha Kamar, Bathudi Kumbhar, Bathudi Kamar, Bathudi Dhoba, Bhunya Chana, etc. testify this fact.

In religious as well as secular literature, Orissa has been referred to either as Kalinga or Odiadesha or Utkal or Koshala, and as a centre of heterodox faith, for which, in Brahmanical scriptures Kalinga or Odiadesha was branded as a land of uncivilized people. Kalinga was a conglomeration of chiefdoms with a centralized feudal lord. The ruling chief or king was the preserver of the social order as wall as a powerful catalytic agent for change. He could bestow the status of a Shudra caste on a community hitherto outside the fold of caste system or elevate the status of a caste in the social order. Likewise he could also take away the existing status of a caste (Hutton, 1946 : 49).

Thus the king was the authority to accord approval to the relative interactional position which a caste group claims or has been assigned. The process of caste formation in the Orissa region went on for centuries, commencing from mid-sixth century. Historians are of the opinion that the post-Samundregupta invasion period is significant because it witnessed the process of sanskritization which radically changed the tribal culture of Orissa. In ancient literatures, Orissa has been referred to as a land of uncivilized people. The implication of this statement is that the style of life of the majority of the inhabitants is not Sanskritic or textual.

Kinship

It is a structured system of relationships common to all human societies, in which individuals are bound to one another by complex interlocking and ramifying ties. Particular kinship bonds, isolated from others, may and often do serve to unite individuals into social groups such as nuclear family or lineage, but kinship systems as wholes are not, and do not produce social aggregates. When one looks at the kinship system of the tribes and caste communities of Orissa one finds certain similarities and some differences between them, because the tribal societies and caste communities have been interacting with each other for centuries. There are significant elements of continuity between tribal and caste communities. They have almost identical structural features as social units, with belief in a common descents rules of exogamy and endogamy and segmented into minimal and maximal lineages. Both have a tempered classificatory kinship terminological system whose maximum limit of application is set by the maximal lineage, relative age and generation kinship facts, such as, lineality, collatorality, gender, bifurcate merging and bifurcate collaterality are equally important in both the cases. The village is the most important territorial unit for the tribes as well as for the caste communities.

A tribal social structure is "elementary" by nature. Individuals are grouped according to kin group or clan. The largest significant reference group is the tribe or a segment of it, the "sub-tribe," which is endogamous. Such a social unit is segmented into a number of homogenous exogamous totomic clans, excepting the Saora, amongst whom totemic clans are not found, but such units are called Birinda, which are maximal lineages. Clans symbolize territorial cohesion and strong corporate identity. Each clan is segmented into lineages which serve as strong corporate groups.

In kinship system there is clearcut categorization of consanguines, and affines. In terminology, emphasis is laid on differences in generation, differences between lineality and collaterality, differences between affines and consanguines, differences of sex, differences of age, differences in the sex of a relative standing between the speaker and the kinsman to whom the term is applied, recognition of reciprocity (Gr Fa. Gr So) and polarity (cousins/ *samandhi)*. Mode of use of kinship terms includes both terms and address and reference: linguistic structure of the terms includes elementary terms, descriptive terms (elfa. olmo) and derivative terms (Gr Fa, Gr Mo) and their range of application includes denotative terms (it may denote one kin as Fa, Mo, and sometimes applies to several kins as Br., Si).

In caste social structure reference group expands beyond the village or caste/subcaste to the linguistic region or may even cover the Hindu social universe. A caste is usually segmented into exogamous units, called gotra, which are in some cases totemic and in some others non-totemic. The kinship system is "tempered classificatory" as the maximal lineage sets the limit to the application of kinship terms. But the caste kinship system is "complex" unlike the tribal system, because in this case individuals are not very precisely categorized as consanguines (real and potontial) and affines (real and potential). In caste social system marriage field is complex and marriages are determined by the size of primary groups/secondary groups to which prospective mates belong, social class, social fluidity and social background. Status of a person's caste is determined by socio-cultural values relating to purity and pollution and commensal position. Specific rank of a caste within a region is determined by a combination of factors, such as, relative economic position with reference to landholding, relative political dominance, relative numerical strength and symbolic validation in ritual habits in relation to the Great Tradition or scriptural Hinduism.

Marriage

Marriage is the threshold of group formation. It is correlated with the principles of descent and residence. It establishes legal parents and legitimizes children, and it also establishes sexual rights and regulated inheritance of property. It helps to replenish human population in socially accepted manner. It also provides security and balanced upbringing of children. Both among the tribes and caste groups marriage involves a number of kinship statuses within the group formed by the marital unions between it and other similar groups within the kinship system at large.

Among the tribes, Scheduled Castes and caste Hindus most marriage are monogamous. However, among the tribes, Scheduled Castes and lower caste Hindus there are cases of polygynous unions, but in most of the cases, such unions are concubinage. Polygynous marriages are both sororal and nonsororal.

Marriage opitomises transactions between two parties - the bride and bridegrooms and certain designsted kins of each. The totality of marital rights and marriage prestations constitute a single fund of value apart from the set of rights in bride's sexual and procreative capacities and domestic services. Bride price or dowry and marital rights move in opposite directions and remain on opposite sides. Among the tribes and Scheduled Castes as well as among the low caste Hindus payment of stipulated bride price is a must, which ought to be refunded by the parents of a married woman if she deserts her husband. In case a man divorces his wife, then he forfeits the bride-price.

Ancillary values which influence marriage relationship are spouse's political power, social status, social geography and command over rescurcos. Most marriages are performed between adults, yet among tribes, Scheduled Castes and low caste Hindus child-marriage is practised. Among the caste groups as well as among the tribal communities there is a correlation between status and affinity. Persons always aim at maintaining their social status in marriage relationships. Though Tribal communities are egalitarian, yet there are status differences. Among the caste groups most of the marriages are isogmous and few marriages are hypergamous and hypogamous.

Descent and Residence

Decent among all is counted in the male line and thus it is patrilineal. Residence after marriage among the tribes is patrivicinal and among others it is patrilocal. Among the tribal communities a young man builds a separate house in proximity of his parents' house before marriage. He gets the cooperation of his parents' and brothers in this endeavour. Among the Scheduled Castes sometimes a youngman is required to construct a house for himself if there in paucity of accommodation in his natal home.

Mode of Acquisition of Bride and Marriage Booth

There are several modes of bride acquisition namely, negotiations, rendering service, capture, purchase, intrusion, exchanges, adoption, wife-inheritance (junior levirate) and elopement. Negotiated marriage is considered most prestigious. Among the tribes, negotiation, service, purchase, intrusion, exchange and capture are the various modes through which brides are acquired. The most common mode of bride acquisition. among the tribes is "capture." In this case payment of bride price is deferred. Among the Scheduled Castes, costes negotiation, purchase, elopement, intrusion and exchange are the different ways of bride aquisition, and among the low caste Hindus similar methods are adopted. Among the higher castes only negotiated marriage is preferred. Among the tribes, Scheduled Castes and Caste Hindus of South Orissa, cross-cousin marriages are performed with preference for matrilateral cross-cousins. Some cases of cross-cousin marriages have also been noted from southern Orissa districts. Under secondary preferential marriage rules sorrorate, junior levirate and concubinage are performed among the Scheduled Castes and low caste Hindus. When there is marriage by service, purchase, intrusion, exchange capture or adoption, the marriage is solomnized at the house of the groom. Only in respect of marriage through negotiation the booth is at the natal home of the bride.

Family

Family is both a social group and social institution, where persons are united by the ties of marriage, blood or adoption constituting a single household, interacting and communicating with each other in their respective social roles as husband and wife, mother and father, son and daughter, brother and sister, and creating and maintaining a common culture. Among the tribes of Orissa nuclear families are found predominatly. Extended familiest, both horizontal and vertical, are also found, but in less number.

Nuclear family is the basic social unit among all. In some cases those are compounded into composite ones like molecules in an atom, such as, polygynous, patriarchal, extended families and Hindu joint families. Family among all is characterized by common residence, economic cooperation, reproduction and enculturation. There is some functional importance of mother's brother not withstanding the custom of cross-cousin marriage.

Kin Categories

Kin category means grouping of kins on the basis of shared kinship criteria such as consanguinity, affinity, bifurcation, collatorality, generation, sex and relative age. Categorization contributes to the ordering and smooth functioning of a society. In Orissa all societies make a clearcut distinction between consanguines and affines. Among all those tribal communities and caste groups who do not practise preferential cross-cousin marriages, affinity disappears with remoteness of time and space, whereas among all those who practise it affinity is reinforced. Among the tribal communities distinction between consanguines and affines is very clear for their territorial affiliation and small size. Distribution of clan (birinda is case of the Saora) territories is very precise and clearcut. Clans/birinds are unilineal descent groups, which fullfil important functions. A clan consists of a number of maximal and minimal lineages. As all societies are patrilineal in Orissa only patriliniages are found. A lineage is a consanguineal kingroup produced by the rule of patrilineal descent. Affines of a male ego are not included in his patrilineage. Patrilineages in most cases constitute residential kin groups. Among the caste groups gotra is the mythical descent group which, is exegamous. It is not a close-knit functional group like lineage or kutumba-bhai group.

There are lot of commonalities in the kinship structure of tribes and castes, particularly the castes of lower Hindu order in Orissa. The commonality renders a folk-oriented image to the culture of Orissa.

Conclusion

One finds a lot of interpenetration of socio-cultural phenomena between the tribal socio-culture universe and the caste society of Orissa, although the relatively simple tribal societies have come under greater influence of the socio-politically predominant caste society. There are significant elements of continuity between non-Hindu tribal and Hindu peasant socio-cultural systems. "Caste" and "tribe" in Orissa have almost identical structural features as social units, with a belief in common descent, rules of exogamy and endogamy. In both cases the mythical descent groups (clan/gotre) are segmented into close-knit functional lineages. Principles of classification and grouping of kins are the same and the limit of tempered classificatory kinship terminology is the maximal lineage. There exists polytheism in both the social systems, and the pantheon includes manes, village tutelaries, high, low and departmental deities. There is always a corporate socio-cultural reference to religion. In other words religious ceremonies reinforce and reenact social solidarity. Certain rituals are always directed towards the pragmatic consideration of fertility of women and crops. The natural universe is believed to be charged with supernatural power, and sickness as well as suffering are attributed to supernatural causes. Collectivism and village solidarity are positively valued and are given priority of consideration over individual interests and goals.

Tribal communities and caste societies constitute a total sociocultural universe and represent different stages in the scale of social evolution. The present day party politics is notionally atomising them. The thesis which is being floated here is that most of the caste categories of the Shudra varna in Orissa have possibly emerged out of the tribal universe during the historic past.

REFERENCES

Behura, N.K.1993. *Tribes, their Development and Quality of Life. Calcutta:* ISCA.

Bohamman, P. 1963. *Social Anthropology.* Newyork: Hott, Rinchart & Winston.

Das M. N. 1977. "Ancient and Medieval Empire and Kings," in Souvenir of Indian History Congress: Bhubaneswar (P.G. Dept. of History)

Dutta, N. K. 1969. *Origin and Growth of Caste in Inda.* Vol. I. Calcutta: K.L. Mukhopadhyay.

Ghurye, G. S. 1979. *Caste and Race in India. Bombay:* Popular Prakashan.

Hutton, J. H. 1949. *Caste in India—Its Nature Function and Origin.* London: Oxford University Press.

Kapadia, K.M. 1966. *Marriage and Family in India.* London: Oxford University Press.

Karve, I. 1965. *Kinship Organisation in India.* Bombay: Asia Publishing.

Kulke, H. 1986. "Royal Policy and the Structure of Mediaval Hindu Kingdoms." A eschmonn, H. Kulku and G.C. Tropathy (eds.) *The Cult of Jagannath*, Delhi: Monohar.

Mahapatra, L. K. 1997. "Society in Orissa," P.K. Mishra & J.K. Samal (eds.), *History and Culture of Orissa.* Vol. II New Delhi: Kaveri Books.

Murdock, G. P. 1949. *Social Structure,* New York: Free Press.

Mishra P. K. & J. K. Samal 1997. "Introduction," *History and Culture of Orissa.* Vol. I New Delhi: Kaveri Books.

Rath, B. 1997. "Development of Oriya Literature," in *History and Culture of Orissa.* Vol. II. New Delhi: Kaveri Books.

Redfield, R. 1953. *Primitive World and its Transformation.* Chicago: University of Chicago Press.

Roy, Niharanjan, 1972. "Introductory Address," in K.S. Singh (ed.), *Tribal Situations in India.* Simla: Indian Institute of Advanced Study.

TWELVE

A BACKGROUND OF THE NAGA MOVEMENT

R. VASHUM

The Naga movement has been one of the most persistent and most active revolutionary movements in the Indian sub-continent and South-East Asia *inter alia* which is still a rallying factor to reckon with for the rise and resurgence of insurgency movements in the North-East India. The movement covers the frontiers of North-Eastern India and North-Western Myanmar (erstwhile Burma) comprising of about 1,00,000 sq. km. In India, the Nagas are concentrated mainly in Nagaland (state); 4 districts of Manipur, namely, Tamenglong, Senapati, Ukhrul and Chandel (constituting about 70 per cent of the total territory of Manipur state); Changlang and Tirap districts in Arunachal Pradesh; and the South-Eastern frontiers of Assam, especially, along the North Cachar Hills district. In Myanmar, the Nagas are located in Sagaing sub-division and the Kachin state.

The Naga national movement is a struggle, which is essentially ethnic and political in nature. In other words, the struggle of the Nagas is for establishing an independent (ethnic) nation-state for the several ethnically related tribal groups, which had come together and recognized themselves as "Nagas" or "Naga."[1] Thanks to the British colonialists for popularising the generic term "Naga," especially since the early 19th century for their (British) colonial administrative and ethnographic conveniences. The British who conquered the Nagas (about 1/3rd of the Naga territory) and brought under their regular administration had directly or indirectly created a feeling of isolation and separateness of the Nagas from the Indians and the Myanmarese, and gifted the Nagas a sense of unity among the various Naga tribes.

The unity among the Nagas fostered by the British, the Nagas pride of being a Naga, and their desire for freedom among other forces, particularly, the Nagas' experience during the World War I are mainly attributable for the rise of Naga nationalism, sometime, in early 20th century, which also marked the beginning of the Naga national movement for independence. The Naga national movement had been shaped by many factors—the traditional Naga way of life (Nagas ethos), Nagas contact with the Ahoms and the British, World Wars I & II, forces of modernisation, etc. This paper intends to give a background discussion of the inception of the Naga national movement.

The Naga national movement is a complex one with many factors contributing to its formation and developments. The movement can be said as the outcome of the various accumulative forces of the socio-cultural, ethnic, historical, political, religious, and geographical factors which are inextricably inter-linked with each other to give rise to what we know today as "Naga nationalism" and "Naga national movement." One could fail to understand the real picture of "Naga nationalism" and "Naga national movement" without knowing the historical background and ethos of the Nagas. Therefore, at the outset, it would be worth mentioning some of the past account of the Naga society in relation to other communities before getting into the actual and main facets of the Naga national movement for self-determination (sovereignty).

Village State

The Nagas have been inhabiting in their homelands for centuries in solitude in their own right. They lived in villages which are generally located on hill-tops which probably helped them to have a commanding view over the surrounding areas for strategic and scenic purposes and avoid wild animals and mosquitoes. Naga villages present typical systems of government of monarchy and republic and every village was independent of each other. For instance, among the Konyaks (lower), Semas, Maos, Tangkhuls, Zeliangrongs, etc. there is prevalence of monarchical systems although they vary from each other in some form or the other. Of these, the kings of Konyaks, Semas and the Maos were said to have considerable power compared to those of other tribes. Among the lower Konyaks and the Maos, some sort of confederation is found where the Great kings act as the titular head over some other villages.

The Angs (the kings) of Konyaks would have "under them villages varying from 4 to 21 paying tributes to the Great Ang. Each village had one Ang but above them stood the Great Ang who, of course, had no power whatever to interfere with the affairs of other *Anghs* under him"(Shimray, 1985: 56). The Mao king of 18 villages would receive tributes from other villages in the form of paddy and legs of animals killed. In each of these monarchical village state, kingship is hereditary. In the days of yore, the "king enjoyed free labour, and contributions from the subjects in the form of paddy; but he was not an autocrat. In practice, the councillors ran the administration. The function of the chief was more or less ritual" (ibid.).

Among the Aos, Lothas, Sangtams, etc. republican type of government was prevalent. Among the Aos, *Tatars* (Councillors) were the representatives of the people; one could become the chief in Ao villages by way of one's merit and influence. It is not hereditary but chosen by the villagers. In Lotha tribe, the chief of the village is chosen of one who was considered the greatest warrior and performer of "Feast of Merit." This system was based on the principle - the wisest and the strongest rule the village state (or republic). This was also true in the case of the upper Konyaks who unlike the lower Konyaks (monarchical) were republican. This is one peculiar instance in Naga society where two systems of government are practiced in one tribe having the same culture.

Although republican in nature to some extent, the case of the Angami Nagas was of "extreme" democracy as Elwin (1961) and others had termed it. The Angami tribe had a nominal head of the village known as *Kemevo*. Its functions were both religious and administrative. In religious matter, he could issue formal order. On the other hand, he had no power to issue formal order in secular matter; the decision of the public of any public meeting (which could be called by any influential person of the village) was final and binding. The Angamis considered their village fellows as equals. This was, perhaps, one of the main reasons for not having council even as they gave no importance to the nominal chieftainship.

In short, the administrative systems in Naga villages differed widely, as Elwin had summed it:

> "Naga society presents a varied pattern of near- dictatorship and extreme democracy. There is a system of hereditary chieftainship among the Semas and Changs. The Konyaks have very powerful chiefs or Angs who are regarded as sacred and whose word is law: before the greatest of them no commoner may stand upright. The Aos, however, have bodies of elders who represent the main family groups in the village and the Angamis, Lhotas, Rengmas and others

are so democratic that Hutton remarks that in the scase of the Angamis it is difficult to comprehend how, in view of their peculiar independence of character, their villages held together at all before the coming of the British Government" (1961: 6-7).

It may also be added that in a patrilineal and patriarchal Naga society, be it monarchical or republican, the administration in the village was carried on by the village council or in rare case like those of the Angami villages the village public took over the administration. In general, a Naga village was said to be self- sufficient, and by and large maintained its sovereignty with the principle of socialism and democracy. Any interference, tresspassing or encroachment by members of other village(s) in its territorial jurisdiction usually provokes inter village war where head hunting could be followed justifiably. In other words, inter-village geo-political relations were strictly observed. This long tradition of the Nagas with relative self-sufficiency, freedom, isolation, passion for independence, and their sovereignty over their respective homelands could have made them psychologically conscious of what they were/are/should with deep rootedness so that as we shall find in the following discussions, they are averse to any outside interference or encroachment in their territories.

Nagas and the Ahoms

The Ahoms are said to be one of the first outsiders to come into contact with the Nagas (it is not known exactly who were those Naga villages and tribes who encountered with the Ahoms) sometime in 1228 A.D. when the former entered Assam through the Naga Hills(in the Patkai Range) from Myanmar. The Ahoms are also mongoloids but speak Siamese-Chinese speech. Sukapha was the first prince of the Ahom kingdom in Assam (cf. Gait, 1963; Alemchiba, 1970).

The Ahoms "first contact with the Nagas was violent. The Nagas resisted the advance of the Ahoms into Assam through their land and there was fierce fighting in many places" (Ramunny, 1993: 5). It is said that Sukapha treated the Nagas with in the words of Gait (1963: 79) "ghastly barbarity" causing "many of them to be killed and roasted, and compelled their relatives to eat their flesh" (ibid.: 78-9). Once they settled down in Assam, the Ahoms and the Nagas developed a new attitudes towards each other (NSF, 1995: 3); and it appears that here were periods of enmity as well as friendship-the Ahoms never considered the Nagas as conquered subjects (Horam, 1975: 6) in their long association for nearly 600 years, viz. from 1228 to 1819 A.D.

(cf. Alemchiba, 1970: 29). But according to Elwin (1961), the "Ahom king regarded the Nagas as their subjects and took taxes from them in the form of slaves, elephant tusks, spears, hand-woven cloth and cotton" (p.18).

Whatever may be the nature of the relationship of the Ahoms and the Nagas, it was only a section of few Naga tribes and villages who came into contact with the Ahoms for centuries together, while the rest of the numerous Naga tribal sections were not touched, and so continued to live in their respective age-old village states.

Nagas and the British

The Naga relation with the British (1832-1947) had been of mixed results for the Nagas. On one hand, the Nagas were gifted with uniting the various Naga tribes and subsequently inducing consciousness of their identity and rights, and leading them towards modernization and broader worldview. On the other hand, the Nagas lost their sovereignty and most of their cultures in the process of modernization even as they (Nagas) were divided geo-politically and placed under two nation-states - India and Myanmar.

In the initial stage of the British contact with the Nagas, it was not the intention of the British to conquer Naga country. It was rather necessitated for the British to conquer the Nagas because of two main reasons: (i) the British had to pass through the Naga Hills on their way to Assam which was their main target for commerce; (ii) the Nagas had subsequently caused enough troubles by way of raids, etc. for the British subjects (viz. plain peoples of Assam bordering the Nagas), and that it was obligatory for the British to intervene in the matter, in which process they started conquering the Naga territories.

The Anglo-Naga relations may be broadly divided into four periods: *Period of Exploration* (1832-1838) during which period the British had to face stiff resistance from the Nagas, especially, the Angami Nagas. The British suffered immense loss in the course of exploring ways and means to furnish safe communication between Manipur and Assam. The Nagas suffered great loss during the British military expeditions (*Period of Expeditions*: 1839-1850) to the Naga Hills. It was followed by the *Period of Non-interference*. The British somehow subjugated the Naga resistance (*Period of Control*) since 1866, which culminated with the British departure from the Indian sub-continent in 1947.

During the British rule in the Naga Hills,[2] the policy adopted was, according to Mackenzie (1979: 55), not of "coercion" and "contemptuous devastation," "but a firm" and kindly policy of "defense and conciliation." In fact, there were enough autonomies and protections given to the hill peoples including the Nagas. The implementation of the Inner Line Regulation of 1873 was one such instance.

It may also be worth mentioning that the "Naga tribes were, by a Regulation of 1880, 'Excluded' from coming under such laws as may be complex or in any way unsuitable to them. The Nagas have traditional laws to guide their conduct and village courts to deal with crimes both civil and criminal. These were effective enough and the British Government did not seek to make changes. The Governor-General of India could, as laid down in the Government of India Act of 1919, proclaim any part of India to be a 'backward area.' This word being strongly objected to, it was decided to call such territories 'Excluded Areas.' Remembering the special requirements of such areas and recognizing the need of protecting the people of such areas from possible economic exploitation, they were excluded from general constitutional arrangements" (Horam, 1975: 15). It was in April 1, 1937, that the "Naga Hill districts along with the North-East Frontier Tract, the Lushai and North Cachar Hills were declared 'Excluded Areas' of the province of Assam" (ibid.).

Rise of Naga Nationalism

Naga polity[3] was in essence, to set in some sort of sequence, developed from village (villageism) to village confederation (village confederationism in few cases like those of the Konyaks and the Maos) to tribe (tribalism) and to collective tribal association (Nagaism), where the appearance of the last concept "Nagaism" manifests emergence of "Naga nationalism," in the modern sense of the term. In other words, Nagaism originated from the village after their prolonged tradition of respective sovereign village states. The concept of larger than the villag states which we call today "tribe" was also prevalent among the villages through kinship bond, political or otherwise, although it was not well organised. It appears that some tribes like the Angamis, Zemis, Rengmas, etc. had developed some sense of solidarity as hillmen as against the more advanced plain people even in the days of the Ahoms. When the British passed through these Naga areas, fierce encounter took place, although it was separately fought. In this sense, Naga nationalism was seen for the first time in an incipient form when the Naga tribes resisted the entry of the more superiorly well-equipped Britishers in the lands of the Nagas in 1832. Nevertheless, in the real sense of the term, the consciousness of the Nagas for nationhood, their identity and rights could be traced during and after the World War I.

Although, the First World War had no much direct impact on the Nagas, the war made them indirectly feel more conscious about their identity and their existence itself. During the First World War, the British government recruited about two thousand Nagas and sent them to France as Labour Corps. In the words of Yonuo (1984: xii-xiii), the "journey across seas and countries awakened the spunk of the Naga nationalism like other parts of India and they began to develop the concept of a Naga nation which had not dreamt of before." Accordingly, in 1918, an association called the "Naga Club" was formed with the joint efforts of government officials, villages' headmen, including those Nagas who returned from France *inter alia*. This Club which was the first of its kind and its members drawn from various Naga tribes was social and political in nature.

In 1929, the Naga Club submitted a historical Memorandum to the Simon Commission (the Commission was set up by the British Government in 1927 to study administrative working system in India and recommend improvements) in Kohima, wherein the Nagas demanded for excluding from the proposed "Reformed Scheme" of India, and to leave them alone like they were before. The Nagas preferred to be under the direct administration of the British government so that their rights are protected and guarded against all encroachments from the non-Nagas. Despite the plea of the Nagas, the Naga Hill Districts were merely clubbed as an "Excluded Area" in 1937, which was just at par with various other "Excluded Areas" throughout the rest of India.

There was also another development in the Naga Hills as early as the mid-1920s and onwards, apart from the activities of the Naga Club. One Mr.Jadonang Kabui, who was enlisted as British soldier in Mesopotamia in the First World War, started a religio-political movement in 1925 for overthrowing the British rule in the Naga country. He also developed a cult called "Haraka" (Haraka, "pure" in Zeliangrong language) which is a type of animism. By 1930, Jadonang's movement which revolved round the "Haraka" and which could be considered as a kind of national liberation movement, spread all over the Naga inhabited areas. But he was soon to be arrested by the British authorities in 1931 and hanged to dead in the same year causing much effect to the downfall of the movement. However, after Jadonang's death, his 16 year-old cousin sister Miss Gaidinliu succeeded as the spiritual and political leader. As ill luck befall, Gaidinliu was also arrested in 1932; and by 1934 the movement founded by Jadonang stifled.

In late 1930s and early 1940s, there had also been some developments as to the shaping of the future of the Nagas. When Burma became independent from the British, it was felt imminent for the withdrawal of the British rule from India. In 1941 Sir Robert Reid, then former Deputy Commissioner of the Naga Hills, and Governor of Assam, realising the ethnic and cultural differences between the Naga tribes and the rest of British India and Burma, recommended a scheme to carve out a trust territory called Crown Colony comprising the "Naga Hills, North-East Frontier areas in upper Assam and the hill areas in upper Burma" (Ao, 1993: 276; cf. Vashum, 2000).

In his confidential report, Sir Reid stated, "we have no right to allow this great body of non-Indian animists and Christians to be drawn into the struggle between Hindus and Muslim, which is now and will be in the future, with ever increasing intensity, the dominating feature of politics in India proper.... They cannot be left to Indian political leaders with neither knowledge, interest nor feeling for the areas. In any case, if my main premise of separation from India is accepted, their intervention could scarsely arise.... Personally, I am in favour of Dr.Hutton's idea of a North- East province vaguely embracing all the Hill fringes from Lushai (or Lakher) land on the south right round to the Balipara Frontier tract on the north, embracing on the way the Chittagong Hill Tracts of Bengal and the Nagas and Chins of Burma and perhaps the Shan states too. I could put this under a Chief Commissioner and he, in turn, could, I imagine, have to be divorced (as in Burma) from the control of the government of India (presumably a federal body by them) and put perhaps under some appropriate department at Whitehall" (quoted by NSF, 1995: 5-6).

Meanwhile, Sir Reginald Coupland, a constitutional expert, reviewed Sir Robert Reid's proposal known as *Coupland Plan.* The Coupland Plan envisaged that the Government of India and Burma might have a treaty with the British and each should take a share of responsibility for the areas as "Trust Territory." This idea was effectively criticized by a later Governor of Assam, Sir Andrew Clow, in 1945 and the Nagas themselves equally opposed it, though on their grounds, for they had no affection of any kind of colonialism and they proved as strong as any Congressmen in insisting that "the British must go" (Elwin, 1961: 51-2). Had the Nagas then lent the slightest support or encouragement to the scheme, the "Trust Territory" might have been established (Alemchiba, 1970: 166).

The World War II, generally known as the "Japanese war" by the Nagas, was a great experience for the Nagas. It is said that bitter war took place in the Naga Hills. Nagas were said to have participated in both the warring forces. Kohima was one place that experienced great "horror" during the war, so also in many other Naga areas. The event and impact of the massive war in Ukhrul area (then sub-division of Manipur State) which is often under reported, may be briefly discussed here. The Ukhrul sub-division is said to have experiences the bloodiest war, particularly, at Shangshak and Ukhrul. It is said that about 427 and 412 Japanese armies were said to have died in these two areas respectively. The Allied Force is also reported to have lost many lives in the war. Shishak (1996) a native and World War II veteran recorded that in Ukhrul sub-division (viz. the Tangkhul Naga country), ten British and one Japanese warplanes (jet fighters) were shot down. He mentions that many Naga civilians were shot dead by both the forces for one reason or another.

The local people were caught in a critical situation as far as their loyalties and securities were concerned. The locales had to go to the forests and hide with much fear and anxiety. They were just helpless. The villagers could not attend to their daily chores of activities nor can they go to fields. Fear psychoses were the rule no matter what. All this happened just in a span of just over five months (viz. March to July, 1944; this is also the duration of the Japanese stay in the area). During the war the Tangkhul Nagas were very backward. "There was only one Middle English School at Ukhrul proper, only one graduate and two matriculates"(Shishak, 1996: 10).

Later the Japanese had to retreat towards Burma from the Naga Hills after loosing holds in the Naga Hills. One main reason for the Japanese' defeat was believed to be mainly because of their failure in mustering the support of the Nagapeople, by and large, for the simple fact that (1) they were late comers, new to the place and situation, unusual experience in the rugged hilly terrain, and were considered strangers by the Nagas; (2) their rival (the British) on the other hand, had already established their hold in the Naga Hills and had influenced them in many ways; (3) language barrier. Apart from this, the Japanese were said to have lost their command in the Naga Hills because of bad communication which had often cut their supply of ration, logistics and other paraphernalia from Burma.

In order to unite the Nagas and for repairing the damage done during the Second World War, Mr. C. R. Pawsey, then Deputy Commissioner of the Naga Hills launched an organization in April, 1945, called the "Naga Hills District Tribal Council." But on February, 1946, in its Wokha session, the Council rechristened as "Naga National Council" (NNC) with Mr. Mayang Nokcha, as its president. The aim of the organisation was to "foster the welfare and social aspiration of the Nagas and it received official patronage as a unifying and moderating influence. Its original political objective was to achieve local autonomy for the hills within the Province of Assam and to train the people for self- government. It encouraged the Tribal Councils already set up by individual tribes and started others to administer their own local affairs and consider possible reforms" (Elwin, 1961: 51). At first, NNC did not speak of separation from British India as we shall find it in the following discussion; but later, things were not the same anymore, say from early 1947.

The Naga National Council made initial political aim expressed on 19 June, 1946, when they submitted a Four Point Memorandum to the visiting British Cabinet Mission who came to prepare the ground for granting independence to India. The four points are:

1. This Naga National Council stands for solidarity of Naga tribes including those in the unadministered areas;
2. This Council strongly protests against the grouping of Assam with Bengal;
3. The Naga Hills should be constitutionally included in autonomous Assam, in a free India, with local autonomy and due safeguard for the interest of the Nagas; and
4. The Naga tribes should have a separate electorate.

On August 1, 1946, Pandit Jawaharlal Nehru as president of the Indian National Congress in a letter to Mr. T. Shakrie, Secretary of the Naga National Council communicated about the future of the Naga Hills, which read as follow:

" It is obvious that the Naga territory in Eastern Assam is much too small to stand by itself politically or economically. It lies between two huge countries, India and China, and part of it consists of rather backward people who require considerable help. When India is independent, as it is bound to be soon, it will not be possible for the British Government to hold on the Naga territory or any part of it. They would b isolated there between India and China. Inevitably, therefore, this Naga territory must form part of India and of Assam with which it has developed such close associations."

"I am glad that the Naga National Council stand for the solidarity of all the Naga tribes including those who live in the so-called unadministered teritory. I agree entirely with your decision that the Naga Hills should constitutionally be included in an autonomous Assam in a free India with local autonomy and due safeguards for the interests of the Nagas."

"As for separate electorates for the Nagas, I am not clear in my mind as to how this will work. Generally, speaking, we are against separate electorates as this limit and injure the small group by keeping it separated from the rest of the nation. But if the Naga territory is given a measure of autonomy, some arrangement will have to be made for their proper representation."

"I see no reason whatever, why an extraneous juducial system should be enforced upon the Naga Hills. They should have perfect freedom to continue their village panchayats, tribal courts, etc., according to their wishes. Indeed, it is our wish that the judicial system of India should be revised, giving a great deal of power to village panchayats."

"About the unadministered territory which still contains, according to you, a number of head-hunters, I cannot definitely say how soon and in what manner it should be brought into the province. This is to be devised in consultation with the people concerned. Naturally, some special provisions will have to be made to develop these people." (See Vashum, 2000).

But the view of Jawaharlal Nehru on the future of the Naga Hills was not acceptable to the NNC. Accordingly, on February 20, 1947, the NNC sent a Memorandum to Lord Mountbatten, then the Viceroy of India for setting up an "Interim Government" for the Nagas for a period of ten years, at the end of which the Naga people will be left to choose any form of government as to their wish. The terms of the Memorandum are as follows:

1. The Interim Government of the Naga people will rule over all the people of Nagaland, having full powers in respect of Legislation, Executive and Judiciary.
2. Nagaland belongs to the Naga people and will be inalienable.
3. The Interim Government of the Naga people will have full powers in the matter of raising revenue and expenditure, an annual subvention to cover the deficit being given by the guardian power.
4. For defence and aiding civil power in case of emergency, a for considered necessary by the Naga National Council will be maintained in Nagaland by the guardian power (see Ao, 1993: 278).

The NNC's meeting with the member of the Sub-Committee of the Advisory Committee on the Aboriginal tribes on May 20, 1947, when the latter visited Kohima to assess the desires of the Naga people as to the status of the future governance, resulted in a dead-lock. The NNC apprised the Committee of the terms of the Interim Government for the Nagas as they (Nagas) desired so; but the Committee would not accommodate the proposed terms of the Nagas and so did fail to recommend it to the Constituent Assembly.

This event was immediately followed by the agreement, also called *"Hydari agreement"* reached between the Government of India (represented by Sir Akbar Hydari, then Governor of Assam) and the Nagas (represented by the Naga National Council) in their meeting held at Kohima from June 27 to 29, 1947. The preamble of the agreement reads that "The right of the Nagas to develop themselves according to their freely expressed wishes is recognised." But the agreement became one of the main points of contention for the future relationships between the Government of India and the NNC. Of all the nine points of the agreement, point nine bearing the sub-title "period of agreement" was the most controversial one. It says that "The Governor of Assam as the agent of the Government of Indian Union will have a special responsibility for a period of ten years to ensure the due observance of this agreement; at the end of this period the Naga National Council will be asked whether they require the above agreement to be extended for a further period, or a new agreement regarding the future of the Naga people arrived at."

The NNC understood this point nine as "The Governor of Assam as the agent of the Government of the Indian Union will have a special responsibility for a period of ten years to ensure the due observance of this agreement, at the end of this period the Nagas will be free to decide their own future" (as quoted in Ramunny, 1993: 26). Whereas the Government of India, spelled out by the Governor of Assam, interpreted the point nine as "At the end of this period the NNC will be free to decide what arrangements should be made for the future administration of the Naga country. It being clearly understood that such arrangement would not contemplate union with Pakistan or Burma but would maintain union with India" (ibid.).

However, in his writing, Phizo admitted that point nine of the Hydari agreement "was not a clear promise of self- determination. But it was an acceptable start to a majority of the Naga National Council, and both sides formally agreed to the document." (Quoted in Nibedon, 1983: 31). Phizo also recorded that, "that same very evening Sir Akbar Hydari warned several Naga delegates that if the Naga Hills District in fact refused to join the Indian Union, India would use force against them" (ibid.).

Meanwhile, at least two groups in the NNC did crop up the moderates constituting the majority and the radicals led by Mr. A. Z. Phizo who did not accept the Hydari agreement as they thought that the terms of the agreement were short of self-determination of the Nagas. Therefore, a delegation consisting of six members of the minority group including Phizo went to Delhi in July, 1947 to propose their view, that the Nagas be left outside the Indian Union when the British withdrew from British India.

In an interview with Mahatma Gandhi at the Bhangi Colony, in New Delhi on 19 July, 1947, the Naga delegation is said to have told the Mahatma, that they were resolved to declare their own independence a day before India did so, on August 14,1947, and asked him for his help. At this, according to Phizo, Mahatma Gandhi told the Naga delegation: "Nagas have every right to be independent. We did not want to live under the British and they are now leaving us. I want you to feel that India is yours. I feel that the Naga hills are mine just as much as they are yours. But if you say that they are mine, the matter must stop there. I believe in the brotherhood of man, but I do not believe in force or forced unions. If you do not wish to join the Union of India, nobody will force you to do that. When the Naga delegates pointed out that Sir Akbar Hydari was threatening to do exactly that, Gandhi exclaimed; "Sir Akbar is wrong! I will ask them to shoot me first before one Naga is shot" (see Nibedon, 1983: 33).

The Naga National Council, in fact, was not unanimous on the issue of Naga Independence- before, during, and even after the declaration of Naga Independence. The situation was then, as Elwin (1961: 51) quoted a Naga leader as saying, "While one group of Nagas favoured immediate independence, some moderates favoured the continuance of governmental relations with India in some modified form until they were sufficiently schooled in the art of running a modern State. There was a third minority which wanted to bring Nagaland into the position of a Mandatory State under the British Government for a specified period of time."

The Naga National Council did move quickly with their extreme line of action, and declared Naga National Independence on August 14, 1947. The Declaration was signed by nine members of NNC. According to Mildred Archer, the NNC on 14 August, 1947, had "drafted telegram to the press declaring the independence of the Naga Hills. Twelve copies were made and addressed to the leading newspapers. But before they were despatched the Postmaster referred them to Pawsey [then Deputy Commissioner of the Naga Hills]. He decided that they would only make trouble; so he ordered them to be withheld. Nothing therefore reached, the press- not a word appeared announcing their tremendous step" (quoted by Ao, 1993: 281).

In Kohima and Mokokchung School students enthusiastically took part in the Naga National Independence Ceremony. After flag hoisting in their respective headquarters processions were held shouting slogans "Long Live Naga Nation;" we declared "Naga Independence" (Ao, 1993: 280). However, British India did not recognize the unilateral declaration of the Naga National Independence. Then came, the Indian National Independence, which declared the following day, the 15th August, 1947; but it was boycotted by the Nagas.

It is interesting to know that in the Naga Hills there were "only two British officials in the administration, two other senior administrators had almost always been hillmen, with at least one of those Naga. The bulk of the administration was left to the *Dobashis*, appointed in the villages initially as interpreters but also responsible for settlement of disputes, and Gaonburas, headmen. The highly democratic structure of Naga village life made close administration superfluous, and the British had been concerned more with protecting the Nagas areas from exploitation than with development" (ibid.).

It will be suffice to say that the Nagas encountered enough bitter experiences in the past few centuries which directly or indirectly contributed to the learning and developing of modern nationalism and/or Naga nationalism. Till 1947, the Nagas' traditional way of life was not much affected by the British administration, except that, the Nagas were, in main, gifted with a new religion- Christianity, and modern education through roman script which also meant a great turn of their attitude towards a new and wider outlook, including thereby more consciousness of their existence which perhaps was the main causal factor for arousing Naga nationalism and/or Nagaism.

With great passion and enthusiasm, the Nagas declared independence on August 14,1947. But the Naga declaration of independence was not recognised by India and Burma. This was/is the crux of the problem. From 1947 onwards, we find that, there was one Naga, A.Z. Phizo, who stands out among all, in as far as the shaping of the Naga nation and the course of the struggle in the early decades in the history of the Naga national movement is concerned. And of course, there were/are some Naga nationalists who had created history of the Naga movement for self-determination even during and after the death of A.Z. Phizo; but they come later.

NOTES

1. "Naga" and "Nagas" are used in singular and plural forms respectively.
2. Naga Hills referred to here and elsewhere unless specified connote only some section of the Naga inhabited areas, and it is not the whole Naga territory or country or Naga Hills as used by the Nagas themselves.
3. Family is the atom of Naga polity. Families form lineages to constitute clans (usually scattered in two or more villages) which are represented in the village as main constituents in every policy and decision making. Villages form tribe or tribal hohos ("hoho" is the Naga term for "council"), and tribal hohos form the highest socio-political body, the "Naga hoho" whose

jurisdiction extends to all the Nagas. These bodies are crucial in Naga way of life in general and the Naga national movement in particular because of the authority binding (at least ideally) for its members.

REFERENCES

Alemchiba, M. 1970. *A Brief Historical Account of Nagaland.* Nagaland: Naga Institute of Culture, Kohima.

Ao, Tanjenyuba. 1993. *British Occupation of Naga Country.* Mokokchung (Nagaland): Naga Literature Society.

Elwin, Verrier. 1961. *Nagaland.* Shillong: Research Deptt., Advisor's Secretariat.

Gait, E.A. 1963 (1905). *History of Assam.* Calcutta: Thacker Spink & Co. Institute.

Horam, M. 1975. *Naga Polity.* Delhi: B.R. Publishing Corporation.

Mackenzie, Alexander. 1979 (1884). *The North-East Frontier of Assam.* (Original title, *History of the Relations of the Government with the Hill Tribes of the North-East Frontier of Bengal).* Delhi: Mittal Publications.

Maxwell, Neville. 1982. *India, the Nagas and the North-East.* London: The Minority Rights Group.

Nibedon, Nirmal. 1983. *Nagaland: The Night of the Guerrillas.* New Delhi: Lancers Publishers.

NSF (Naga Students' Federation). 1995. *The Naga Problem: An Account.* New Delhi: NSF.

Shakespeare, L.W. 1980 (1929). *History of the Assam Rifles.* Gauhati: Spectrum Publications.

Shimray R.R. 1985. *Origin and Culture of Nagas.* New Delhi: Samsok Publications.

Shishak, Yangmaso A. 1996. *II World War in Manipur 1944.* Ukhrul, Manipur: Personal Publication.

Vashum, R. 2000. *Nagas' Right to Self-Determination: Anthropological-Historical Perspective.* New Delhi: Mittal Publications.

SECTION IV

HEALTH ISSUES

THIRTEEN

BELIEFS AND PRACTICES RELATED TO PARTURITION AMONG KONDA REDDI TRIBES OF ANDHRA PRADESH

SUNITA BHARATI REDDY

Reproductive health refers to a state in which people can reproduce and regulate their fertility, women go through pregnancy and childbirth safely, the outcome of pregnancy is successful in terms of maternal and infant survival and well-being, and couples are able to have sexual relations free from fear of pregnancy and disease. Reproductive health behavior includes behavior related to marriage, family planning practices, breast-feeding, childcare etc. Unless the reproductive health behavior of the communities is not clearly documented and ethnographic studies conducted, it is difficult to carry out need based health care system.

About 67.76 million (7.95%) persons have been enumerated in the country (excluding Jammu And Kashmir) as members of the Scheduled Tribes (1991 census). Literacy among the tribal is very low i.e. 25.9 per cent and especially among tribal females (14.5%). For the tribal the forest represented a totality. It is the source of food, shelter, economic activity, social and religious customs and personal identity. The tribal was both the conservator and the natural protector of the forests. Deforestations have altered their identity. With the new developmental activities, around them and without properly rehabilitating them, the tribal are in the transition stage.

Tribal people's concept of health is more functional than biomedical. A person is considered healthy unless she/he feels incapable of doing normal work assigned to that age/sex in that culture. The cause of illness is also attributed to specific acts of commission or omission, "spirits," or in some cases physical factors in the environment. Healing can take place through herbal preparation or an act of atonement, or advised by a shamanic medium. There is an immense need for sympathetic sociological and anthropological research towards improving the quality of life of tribal people. For raising the level of health for these people, based on emic perspective, a multi-sectoral, holistic effort must be implemented.

Maternal child health (MCH) care is an important aspect of health seeking behavior, which is largely neglected among the tribal population groups. The planners have to take into consideration the lifestyle, belief, cultural milieu, social organization and the channels of communication of the tribal people before introducing developmental activities. The MCH services are almost non-existent and the childhood mortality is comparatively high. Comprehensive area specific health related studies are limited; most of the available studies are isolated, fragmentary and did not cover the various dimensions of health affecting the status of tribal women. Thus there is a need for proper understanding of their problems specific to time and place so that relevant development programmes could be identified, planned and implemented. It is necessary to take a holistic view of all the cultural dimensions of the health of a community.

Further, there are many urgent issues affecting the health status of tribal women. Detailed information are needed on maternal malnutrition, nutritional anemia, nutritional status of pregnant women and their nature of workload, the distribution of food within the family and its effect on the nutritional status of women, the complications of pregnancy and of childbirth, primitive practices for parturition, maternal mortality, birth weight of children, infant and childhood mortality and their sex differentials, nature of maternal and child health care practices, attitude towards family planning etc.

Status of Tribal Women

The Dhebar Commission Report (1961) mention that the tribal women is not drudged or a beast of burden, she is found to be exercising a relatively free and firm hand in all aspects related to her social life unlike in non-tribal societies. The tribal women in general and in comparison with caste based communities, enjoy more freedom in various walks of life. Traditional and customary tribal norms are comparatively more liberal to women. But the status of tribal women has gone from bad to worse as a result of the impact of social change, which has affected the social structure of tribal society. (Chauhan, 1990)

The forest based tribal economy in most part of the world is women-centered. Food was obtained by shifting cultivation and from minor forest produces (MFP) like flowers and fruits collected from the forest. Extraction from herbs roots and animals were used for medicines. All these efforts incurred an excessive workload on women. Because of the extensive felling of the trees by vested interests, the distances between the villages and the forest areas had increased forcing the tribal women to walk longer distances in search of minor forest produce and firewood. Given this additional workload even women in advanced stages of pregnancy were required to work in the agricultural fields or walk great distances to collect fuel and minor forest produce. The over strain on tribal women however was not adequately compensated due to the non-availability of forest produce and decrease in food grain production. As a result of deforestation, additional distance and less fertile soil, the availability of food for the tribal families was reduced. This has left serious implications particularly for the women who are responsible for the provision and distribution of food, in cases of shortage; they even deprive themselves of food in order to feed others.

In rural and tribal India, girls are usually married just after puberty and are exposed to an early motherhood and family burden. Most of these women hardly have any knowledge of their anatomy and child bearing. The elderly women of the family carry them into the world of motherhood. As children are much desired in our societies a women is faced with early obligations of motherhood. There is also pressure from the elders to prove the fertility, as barrenness is considered a big curse. Moreover, desire for a son forces women to become pregnant again and again. Successive pregnancies accompanied with low calorie of food intake and inaccessibility, unawareness and under utilization of medical facilities lead to high maternal mortality rate. 'Maternal depletion' is thus the result of early mating, continuous cycles of pregnancy and lactation. The inadequate diet and uninterrupted overwork lead to cumulative disorders such as anemia, general malnutrition, premature aging and early death.

Nutritional anemia is an acute problem for women in India and more so in tribal belt. Tribal women have heavy workload and anemia has a profound effect on their psychological and physical health. Anemia lowers her resistance to fatigue, affects working capacity under conditions of stress and increases susceptibility to other diseases. Maternal malnutrition, which is quite common among the tribal women, is also a serious health problem; especially for those having many pregnancies too closely spaced. It affects the reproductive performance and the birth, which is crucial to infant's chances of survival and to its subsequent growth and development.

Maternal mortality was reported to be high among various tribal groups but no exact data could be collected. Studies on maternal and child health care practices are largely neglected in various tribal groups. Expectant mothers to a large extent were not inoculated against tetanus. Studies have shown that crude birth practices are found in many tribal groups like Kutia Kondhs, Kharias, Gonds, Santhals, etc. The main causes of maternal mortality are considered to be unhygienic and primitive practices of parturition, puerperal infection, anaemia, haemorrahage, obstructed labour and sometimes-ruptured uterus.

Konda Reddi Profile

This paper attempts to presents an ethnographic account of one of the primitive tribal groups (PTG) of Andhra Pradesh. The 12 PTGs of Andhra Pradesh are: Bodo-Gadaba; Bondo Poroja; Chenchu; Dongria Khond; Gutob Gadaba; Khond Poroja; Kolam; Konda Reddi; Konda Savaras; Khond; Parengi Poroja; Thoti.

The Konda Reddis are an important and one of the largest Primitive Tribal Groups in India. They are mainly concentrated in the districts of East Godavari, West Godavari and Khamman of Andhra Pradesh. The habitat of the Konda Reddi, the Andhra Pradesh is located in between 12°38′ and 19°55′ Northern latitude and 76°15′ and 84°45′ Eastern longitude in South-East India. They extend from Sileruu River in the north to the Sabari River in west, and in plains of coastal Andhra Pradesh in east. In south it straddles the Godavari River. They are also concentrated in Meredmilli and Addateegala of East Godavari district. They are inhabited in hilly tracts, of over altitude from 1500 ft. 2500 ft. Based on their geographic settlements, they are divided into three district zones- hill settlements, river side settlements and settlements of lower track and plains

The villages are surrounded by undulating terrain, thick deciduous forest, rivers, streams and hillocks. They are still depended on slash and burn method of cultivation *(podu)* and gathering - hunting economy. The podu cultivation is still at the pre-agricultural level of technology and the hill slopes are unfertile. By this cultivation they produce insufficient crops like jana, samma, redgram and few items of vegetables. In additional to podu cultivation they depend on subsistence bamboo cutting (for which cash is given to them by the Forest Department) and works as day laborers. Moreover, they are depending on forest based economy which not only provide their food (i.e. fuels, seeds, flowers, leaves, roots, tubers, honey) but also materials to build huts and other purposeful articles, fuels for cooking as well as lighting and warmth (like, timber, bamboo), fodder for cattle, herbal medicines, rope, grass, lac, gum, soap-nut, tamarind. Agriculture is mostly rain fed. In hot dry summers, agricultural activity is in minimum. People mostly gather forest produce in this period. Jowar is grown both as Kharif and Rabi crops. Forest is the heart of their traditional life and culture. These tribal people are isolated from the outside world due to lack of communication and inadequacy of modern transport and educational facilities.

Their total population was 54,685 (1981 Census). The Konda Reddis are known as Pandava Reddi, it literally means "Hill Headman" but since they inhabit mountain and so is the Hill Reddis or Konda Reddis. Poverty is rampant. They generally wear very little clothes; even the moderate winters are too severe to protect them from chill.

Konda Reddis speak Telugu language. They use honorific terms like Nanagaru, Ammagaru etc. to the kinship terms. This indicates that people had a high position in the past. Locally it is believed that there was a fight between Kakatiyas and enemies. Defeated by the enemies, army officer of Kakatiya ran with his followers and their families to hills and settled there for years. The isolation from mainstream indicates no acculturation for a long period. Thus they retained their distinct culture without any change. Haimendorf (1945) too suggested that they are the descendants of Chandravamsha Rajas. There is no literature available regarding their origin. Even Konda Reddi people themselves feel superior to other tribes around. They do not consider themselves as "tribals." They say they are "Reddi Varu." Higher the settlements on the hills, superior are they in hierarchy among Konda Reddis.

There are very few studies on Konda Reddis. British Anthropologists, Haimendorf (1945) did an in-depth ethnographic study of Konda Reddis long ago. Only recently some of the scholars like, Duary (1995), Raju (1995), Chaudhury (1991) did study but only on specific issues like religion, ethnomedicine, material culture respectively.

Materials and Methods

The fieldwork was conducted in two Konda Reddi hamlets, namely "Yerrguntapaka" and "Tulsipaka" in Chintoor Mandal. Primary data was collected through observations, informal interviews, and case studies and by administering schedules to the key informants like pregnant women, lactating women, women having one or more children, old women and medicine-men.

As the topic was childbirth and child rearing practices, it needed a good rapport with young mothers, children, pregnant women and old women. Before making any attempt to obtain data on the specific topic, they were engaged for a long time in enquiring about their welfare, health problems etc. Further, informal meetings and deliberations helped in winning over their confidence. Focused group discussions helped in gaining lot of information and also to cross check the data. First aid kit was carried which helped in breaking the initial barriers and the researcher was approached by tribal for the treatment of simple ailments. This also helped in sustaining their confidence. The equipment like camera, weighing machine, tape recorder helped to gain their attention. In this paper an ethnographic account on beliefs and practices related to menstruation, marriage, pregnancy, childbirth, child rearing and ethno-medicine and utilization of modern health care facilities are reported.

Profile of the Villages

The two villages selected for the studies are located about 16 kms away from Chintoor Mandal headquarter which is 65 kms from Bhadrachalam in Khammam district of Andhra Pradesh. Tulsipaka village is on the main road to Rajahmundry, a town. Whereas, Yerraguntapaka village is in the interior, on the hill slopes cut off by a stream. The distance between these two Konda Reddi settlements is 4.5 kms. These villages are connected by a gravel road.

The huts in these villages are haphazardly built having two sections/ rooms. The front section has two doors. The second section is kitchen-cum-living room. Attics are common here. Each household has a backyard. The huts are built on basement made of mud. The walls of the huts are made up of split bamboos covered with slant-thatched roof. The doors are small and made of the split bamboos.

Hygiene

It was observed that the premises inside and also outside their huts were kept unclean. There were places with an open drainage system and animal fecal pollution. There were no compost pits. Cattle and dogs were let free to roam inside the house. As a whole, surroundings were unhygienic and untidy. Huts were lowly thatched and the hearth being inside produced lot of smoke, which was inhaled by the dwellers inside. It was quite harmful to both young children and adults. There were no bathrooms, women and children use to go to stream for bathing. There were no toilets either. People attended their natural calls either in the forests around or usually near the stream. Personally too people were observed to be unhygienic. Their habit of spitting frequently wherever they sit spread diseases like T.B. However, infants were given more attention, giving bath twice a day. But children were not observed to take bath frequently. At the most they went to stream, played in water, rather than took bath and came off. They did not use any soap or any other cleansing agent. Children mostly remain naked, playing, eating in the unclean premises. The source of water used for bathing was also used during natural calls and washing the clothes usually in running stream. The water used for drinking and cooking purpose also came from the same source. This multipurpose utilization of the water resources was responsible for many contagious diseases.

Further, it is known that tribal live in a physical environment, which is full of accidents and traumas. Fall from trees or a hill, violent fights, encounters with wild animals, burns while sleeping near the fire on a cold night are common causes. Small babies with severe burns in these two villages too were found.

Marriage

The Konda Reddi strictly follows tribal endogamy. Generally, monogamy is a rule, though one case of polygyny is also recorded. Sororate is followed but the cases of levirate is, however, not acceptable. Their divorce and remarriage is permissible. They have no ceremony in divorce or separation cases. Due to their burning poverty they want to live in small and nuclear type of families. The common marriage forms among the Konda Reddi's are marriage by exchange, by capture or elopement.

One interesting feature is that a girl is sent to her in-laws place before attaining puberty. Boy and girl starts living together before celebration of their marriage, give birth to children and start rearing them. When the couple accumulates money, give feast to the whole village and some cattle, to bride's kin group and thus marriage is performed. Thus a boy and a girl start a very early married life. Thus, among Konda Reddi's, a boy is married around the age of 14-15 years and girl is married at the age of 9-10 years.

The age difference is not much between husband and wife. But wife's death due to successive pregnancy and maternal depletion leads to remarriage mostly with sister of his wife, which can be otherwise called 'serial monogamy'. This leads to a wide gap of age difference between husband and wife. One case is that of, Patel (45yrs), Kannapa Reddi of Yerraguntapaka village whose first wife died during her ninth pregnancy, now married a girl of 15 years. It was observed that every women aging from 18 to 35 years is carrying an infant or a child of 2 or 3 years. Old women above 50 years are rare in these two villages.

Konda Reddi's prefer to bear equal number of boys and girls. Boys continue the name (patrilineal) and help in the old age. Girl child too is preferred, for she is a helping hand to her mother in sharing the households' responsibilities and bringing her younger brother and sisters. Due to marriage by exchange, they can get bride for their sons if daughters are given to other village. Further, bride price payment, make women an economic asset in this tribe and not a financial burden.

Food Habits

The staple food of the Konda Reddis is Jowar and rice. In the morning they eat Jawa (gruel made up of Jowar) and in the night they take rice. This gruel is taken with tamarind soup or red gram dal or other vegetable curries like beans and bottle gourd. Roots are also favored to make curries. They also consume rice very frequently besides sajja and grunte rice. Rarely, these people eat meat of the fowl, goats, pigs and wild animals, largely due to poverty. Many times they have access to food but they do not consume it because of their beliefs e.g. during pregnancy when a women should eat more, some of them eat less so that the size of the child remains small which decrease the pains during pregnancy.

Though there are no food taboos during pregnancy, but after delivery, the women is not supposed to eat rice for 15 days, pulses for one month, tubers and non-vegetarian diets for two months, thus denying whatever limited nutritious foods available for consumptions, aggravating their already poor health status. It is believed that if she eats non vegetarian before two months, the whole body will swell and she will die. They believe that fish which lives in water if eaten will fill water in the body of the female and ultimately lead to death. Konda Reddi woman do not consume any special diet during her pregnancy or lactation. As observed, pregnant woman rarely consume eggs, milk, meat, or other protein rich foods. Their food also lacks fats, which are energy sources during pregnancy and childbirth. Most of their foods like tubers, rice sorghum consist of carbohydrates. The Konda Reddi people do not eat beans till they celebrate the chikudu pandaga (beans festival), by then the beans dry up limiting the nutritive value. Most of the women are found to be anemic. For each pregnancy a woman loses 500-

600 ml of blood. It is hard to recover the lost blood and general health unless she takes calorific foods and there is good spacing of childbirths.

The diet pattern indicates the undernourishment and malnutrition these people are suffering from. Weights of infant to adult women were recorded to assess the general health of children and women. All were markedly underweight when compared with the standards for their age. The same was the case with pregnant women. A 20 years old woman with 6-month pregnancy was found to be 46 kg, 15 kg less than the recommended weight. Without exception, all were underweight.

Menstruation

As the diet is low in calorific value, girls usually menstruate late, around the age of 14 years. The first menstruation or menarchy is locally termed as Lavasaralu or Amsaralu. Monthly periods are called *Batiki poyindi.* When the girl first menstruates, she is kept in a small hut (built especially for her) outside the village mostly on the slope of the hills for seven days. She has to stay in the hut alone for seven days and nights. The mother or mother-in-law takes food for her. No man is allowed to see the girl for these seven days. Similarly, it is repeated for two more months for five and three days respectively. After the 3rd month, the girl puts the hut on fire. After coming home, she is given bath and allowed into the house. After that, every month when she menstruates, she is not allowed into the kitchen to cook food. She has to sit in one corner in the courtyard and sleep in a corner at nights. Women during these days cannot enter through the main entrance. She has to use the second door, which usually opens into the courtyard. Other female relative or husband or her grown up daughter cooks food. Husband is not supposed to touch her these days. She is not allowed to go for any ceremonies and even to fields. After 5 days she can resume her work. No ceremony is conducted for puberty. This shows that there is a lot of emphasis on purity and pollution rites in this tribe.

Care During Pregnancy

Pregnancy is considered as a natural state among the Konda Reddis and not a state of illness requiring medical attention. Women among Konda Reddis work till she gets labour pains. She does not take any rest. However, she may stop going to hillside, to cut the bamboos in the advanced months. But she does all the household chores, make baskets and even go to fields (podu) to cut jowar and collect pulses, apart from taking care of children. There is no ceremony related to pregnancy. There are neither food taboos nor consume any special diet during pregnancy. She eats twice a day with jowar as staple food, mixed with chilly powder and salt. Rarely did she eat vegetables like chikkudu (beans) and alsandalu (soyabeans).

Though immunization is feared for children, pregnant mothers are willing to take ante-tetanus injection believing that it will ease delivery. The local ANM could convince them that tetanus injection will help them in easy delivery. Very few women go to PHC/government hospitals for antenatal care. Given below is a case in point:

> Lakshmamma from Tulsipaka village, which is well connected with the road went to the private doctor, for she does not believe in government hospital and PHC, during her 3rd month of pregnancy she was given iron tablets for she was found anemic and she had to pay fifty rupees, which is quite a big amount for the poor people to afford.

Delivery

Locally, delivery is called nillu adadam. Delivery takes place at husbands home. In Yeraguntapaka village old women or local dai and other neighboring women and rarely husband assist in delivery. Delivery takes place in the courtyard, women has to run to the courtyard if she gets labour pain through the second door which is specially meant for these periods and during menstruation. A small hut is built in the courtyard, if the labour pains continue for a long time; they call *vydyudu* (medicine-man), who gives herbal medicines to apply on stomach and forehead. Following is the case study about the use of folk medicine and the fear of maternal death among the Konda Reddi women.

> Lakshmi is 22 years old and has two children, Pandamma 4 years, Chinna Reddi one and a half years old. During her first delivery she suffered severe labour pain for hours. For her second delivery too, she suffered for 2-3 days of labour pain. Her father, who is a medicine man, vydyudu, gave paste of roots to apply on stomach and to keep a bark called tadu cettu (Grewia tiliae folia) on the head and eat little bark. However, she feels that childbirth is very painful and would not like to bear any more children. But on the other hand, the old lady, Bajaramma told that she had 10 children, out of them only three

> are surviving and rest all died. She prefers to have more children, as many of them die and she is left with few. Unlike Bajramma, laxmi and Bumamma told that they do not want more (having 2 or 3 children respectively) children, as they had difficult deliveries and suffered with labour pains for 2 - 3 days. They all fear death (maternal death) during delivery.

Position of Delivery

Women among these tribes deliver in a squatting position. They say that delivery in sleeping position is very difficult as *pindam* (head of the infant) falls aside and it is difficult to come out where as in squatting position pindam comes out first making delivery easy. The involvement of husband in delivery is given in the following case study:

> Interviewing Bullemma's husband revealed that during his wife's delivery she had intensive labour pain (twarga niladaledu) and that the position of the head of the infant was wrong (pindam tirigindi). He showed the scholar a small knife and said that he himself turned the pindam by pressing it over the stomach of his wife.

Umbilical Cord

Assisting women or sometimes mother herself, cut umbilical cord of her infant, either with the sickle, or sharp edge of an arrow, wood or stone. They apply medicine made of *poga-aaku.* After burning it the ash is called *buggi*, which is applied to the chord for healing. They tie a knot otherwise they believe that blood will come out. Shedding of the umbilical chord is called boddu-puvva-do:lindi. The umbilical cord is buried in the ground where the infant is given bath regularly.

Postnatal Care

Soon after delivery both infant and mother are given bath with hot water. It is said that hot water induces growth where as cold water bath may lead to fever or even death of the infant. The first feed given to the baby is mother's milk only. When asked, what will happen if they do not give colostrum, they said the child will die and karma chutukuntundi. If mother does not lactate, other lactating women in the kin group feeds infant. For example in the case of Yerrap Reddi, when his wife delivered she could not lactate. Then two close kinwomen fed the baby with their milk

Breastfeeding is done on demand. It is believed that eating Papaya induces lactation. Women eat Papaya during pregnancy, which help them to acquire vitamins and minerals. Women do not take any nipple care. Supplementary feeding starts after one or one and half years which is quite late. They give jawa gruel made up of jowar twice a day as supplementary food. While weaning they do not give any special food to babies, whereas the infants should be given supplementary nutrition atleast four times a day, continuing with breast milk or other milk; thus leading to malnutrition and under nutrition among children. The general health of the children showed that they were very weak, thin and fragile. No ritual is performed before introducing supplementary feed.

Weaning is quite late. Breastfeeding lasts at least for two years. Early weaning happens only if the women become pregnant again. As in the case of Chellamma, who is six months pregnant now stopped breast feeding her daughter who is one and half year old. No other reasons are attributed to weaning except for the pregnancy. This is evident in Sommamma's case, a 30 year-old widow, who still fed her 4-year-old son.

Birth Interval

People were unaware about the temporary family planning methods and contraception. Though they were aware of vasectomy and tubectomy operations but there was not even a single case of such operation. They believed that after tubectomy operation, women became physically weak and could not do hard labour and climb the hills, so they were not in favour of family planning. Men, however felt that family planning was their wives' business. When ANM talked about family planning they hurled abuses and even drove her off from the village. Moreover, the temporary family planning methods like pills were not suitable for them. The pills have to be taken regularly, which makes difficult to remember. Men too were unaware of the contraceptives for their use. Women generally felt shy to tell about their gynecological problems.

There were no deliberate attempts to prevent subsequent pregnancy, except for folk medicines. To stop the births, bark of batta:pu cettu and kanne:ru cettu was made into a paste and drunk by both husband and wife. It was reported that Rasayana (fluids) passed through urine and stopped pregnancy.

The natural methods for birth intervals among the Konda Reddi tribes were the prolonged lactation amenorrhea. Another factor was lesser frequency of co-habitation during the harvesting season as men stayed away in the podu fields, day and night looking after the crop.

Reintegration of Mother into Society

The social re-integration of the women after childbirth, "rite of passage" has lot of significance in this tribe. This ceremony is locally termed as *kundalu muttuko:vadam* (i.e. touching of earthen pots), marks the end of her period of potential pollution and is the final cleansing act before her re-integration into the society. The woman's period of impurity varies from society to society. Traditionally, neither the women nor the child should come out of the confinement of the room during this period. Among Konda Reddis after delivery, a woman is given complete rest for three months. Usually household chores are taken care by husband or young daughter. Thus a girl hardly of six years is able to cook and take care of the infants. Mothers only job is to take care of herself and the baby, she is not supposed to cook food and even touch utensils. Women stay in the corner of a house and use only the second door. She does not use the main entrance. This is practiced because they believe that using the main entrance and kitchen will lead to impurity.

Infant Care

Mostly mother, grandmother (rarely), elder brother or elder sister takes care of infant. In the morning, mother gives bath to the infant with hot water. If available the body is massaged with oil before giving bath, no soap is used. Infant is put in a sleeping position on the thighs; neck is always supported during bath. To wash infants mouth mother put water in the infant's mouth and suck it out through her mouth. Infant though is given bath twice a day, is mostly kept naked. Even the children till the age of 10 years wear minimum clothing.

During the day, if mother goes for podu cultivation for a long time, she carries the infant along with her. There she puts the baby in a temporary cradle made up of cloth tied to two poles and mother breastfeeds whenever the baby cries. The baby is left at home under the supervision of elder brother or sister, when mother goes out for a brief period. During nights, mother sings lullaby for the infants. Not only mothers, elder brother and sisters of hardly five years as in the case of Rami Reddy, five Years, sung lullaby melodiously for his younger sister Chinnamma, four months old.

People attributed the cause of infant mortality to Spirits and Gods will. Still births are attributed to spirits saying: de:varu ti:ne:sindi (meaning spirits have eaten). A spirit which resides in hills called kondal dabal da:lni is blamed for child's sickness. Intrusion of this spirit is believed to cause severe pain and wound, which did not heal, which ultimately lead to death of infant.

Immunization

People generally fear immunization. They feel that when the child is not ill, why they should be given any injection. ANM reported that she immunized the children forcefully, when the parents were out in the daytime, and only brother and sister were at home. Her records showed that 90 per cent of children were given complete immunization as such there were no cases of polio, T.B, measles, diphtheria in these two villages as reported by ANM. She had to face lot of problems; she had to hear lot of abuses also.

Cultural Definition of Body and Fertility

The phenomenon of conception, pregnancy and delivery are understood rarely in a biological sense. Even in industrial societies with a long history of universal schooling people still understand their bodies in terms of folk or lay model rather than the scientific biological model. Throughout the world, health behavior of people is informed by folk or lay definitions of the body form and its functions. In some societies the contribution of a man in the formation of a child is also not recognized. They attribute the childbirth to some spirit ancestor or God and that the man just helps in making the passage. Among, Konda Reddis the role of man and woman in the formation of child is fully understood. They are aware of the fact that without cohabitation, childbirth is not possible it is said "kalasi kapuram unte pillalu puttutharu" i.e. cohabitation will lead to childbirth.

The formation of foetus inside the female body is located in the intestine. It is believed that though female has one stomach but she has two intestines, "pilla pegu" and "annam pegu," i.e. child intestine and food intestine. The "pilla pegu" is said to be responsible for the child formation. It is said that the barren woman lacks this intestine and so she can't produce children. Thus, they were unaware of the intricacies of conception, womb, foetal growth, uterus etc. They believe that the menstrual blood called "muttu" is converted into the child, which is stopped during pregnancy. However, the menstrual blood is considered impure, and that is the reason why during menstruation and after delivery woman is confined to a single room.

A woman without children is considered both personally unfulfilled and ritually in auspicious. Among Konda Reddis too, woman with more children has edge over others. Most of the women, when interviewed, expressed to have at least ten children. A woman, who can bear children, has all the exclusive rights of a wife. There is an exceptional case of polygamy. The reason is that first wife was unable to produce children. Rami Reddi of age forty-five had no children from his first wife Buchhamma, so he married again, now having five children. This exceptional case clearly indicates the importance of being fertile.

It is interesting to note that infertility is primarily considered to be the deficiency of the woman. Beyond this, barrenness may be attributed to some supernatural agency, but seldom is the potency of the husband questioned. This leads to the indifferent attitudes and also ill treatment towards a barren woman. This is clearly seen from the practice that for stopping births, both husband and wife are given medicine whereas for impotency only the women is treated with herbal medicine and is labeled barren if unable to bear children.

Ritual

A plant called "Veru Boda" having an underground root, which is sweet, is kept on a big leaf. The woman has to pray to Goddess saying:

"Devi naku pilla putali
Naku ee chettu avashodhamu kavalenu"

meaning "O Goddess, I should bear children and I need this medicine. Then she wipes the leaf and eats the root from this tree"

In case of spontaneous abortion or barrenness, these kinds of rituals are performed by the women to appease the Gods/ Goddesses and pray to bless her with children.

Beliefs in Spirits and Gods

People believe in spirits. They even celebrate a festival called saalu pandaga to appease spirits so that they won't harm them. Infant mortalities are mostly attributed to spirits called kondal dabal da:ini. When asked why infants die, they said "Died for punayam." They have strong belief in the medicine man called vejju or a shaman. Konda Reddis pray "amma thalli" and also "inti devudu" for the well being of mother, children and for the welfare of their family. Rituals by the shaman are quite common to propitiate the Gods and Spirits for the well-being and for conceiving.

A woman who was a teenager had a still birth before. In order to have a safe pregnancy this time, a Shaman, who was a 'Koya' man, was called. He performed a ritual, sacrificed a hen, broke a coconut and declared that something had gone wrong during the previous pregnancy, the local people fear this Shaman. They believe that he do magic on anybody and can do harm. He was reported to be an aggressive man he had attacked few people when they interfered in his business.

Gangamma deity who protects the villagers from the dreadful diseases like cholera, malaria, small pox, chicken pox etc is worshipped. The festival is held in the month of February and village headman selects a date. Head of the village, pedda kapu, worships the goddess and sacrifices goats, hens and offers the boiled rice. The sacrifice is done with the uttering of mantras. Before the sun set the function ends. No woman participates at the time of worship.

Health Problems among Infants and Children

Women suffer many infections during deliveries, as blood is a good medium for infections. There are greater chances of puerperal and urine infections after delivery. If the infection is not treated within a week, maternal death occurs. During pregnancy or after delivery, if women suffer from edema in which water is filled in the body tissues and face and legs are swollen. Locally, they believed it is caused because of eating non-vegetarian food. Hemorrhage, obstructed labour and also ruptured uterus are prevalent cause of illness.

Among Konda Reddis due to inaccessibility of health care system and lack of transport facilities, continuous labour pain for 2-3 days lead to a stillbirth, some times it had also resulted into maternal mortality. Through interviews it was known that most of the woman had first and second deliveries of stillbirths or infant deaths due to lack of proper obstetric care. It can also be attributed to the early marriage and early pregnancies. Women in their teens were not physically matured or mentally prepared for the motherhood, which lead to both maternal and infant mortalities.

Konda Reddi women rarely went to hospitals for treating gynecological problems. They do not go to doctor for pre natal or postnatal care. Childbirth takes place at home. Even if they suffered severe labour pain, they called vaidyudu but never visited doctor. The reason was that they felt embarrassed and feared the injections. Further they also felt shy to talk to outside men.

Konda Reddi women also face problems regarding transport. It became difficult for a pregnant woman to walk to the distantly situated hospitals.

In Konda Reddi villages, babies are exposed to soaking rain, chilling breeze and have inadequate clothing and housing with improper ventilation. These all contributed to respiratory disorders. Malnourished children were more likely to suffer from pneumonia, whooping cough or measles compared to healthy children. Malnutrition was not responsible for direct deaths but in combination or as a result of multiple infections, which lead to infant mortality.

Ethnomedicine

Among Konda Reddis too after diagnosing the disease or any health problem, treatment is started. The type and the causation of the disease, establish the type of treatment. Treatment for some diseases involves elaborate rituals. Ritual is done in the presence of the patient and close kin groups and *vaidyudu,* a *muggu* (symbolic design) is made with different colours. Rice, coconut, egg and chicken are often used for rituals, hen is sacrificed in the process, vaidyudu keeps chanting some hymns which usually involve the praising of various Gods, in personification of diseases and later requesting them to pacify. Young women and mothers totally rely on the indigenous medical system.

According to a study (Duary, 1995) Konda Reddis in Bison Hill in particular are believed and considered to be efficient medicine-men. The folk medicines are prepared by the witch doctors of both the areas for sterilizing a woman forever, without any surgical measure as also without any harmful side-effect. Though, the author do not claim to have discovered any particular folk medicine, but the intensive study of the indigenous medicine strongly suggests that a proper scientific investigations should be carried out in the pharmacopoeia of Bison Hill area. It is observed that the number of witch doctors or traditional medicine man is gradually decreasing but people's belief on their traditional folk medicines is as strong even today as it happened to be in olden days.

Primary Health Centre (PHC)

Primary health center was opened at Tulsipaka in 1991. It was an office of panchayat, converted into a hospital. There was no electricity, no furniture and no beds in the PHC at the time of study (1992). There were medicines which were outdated and of expiry dates as revealed by the doctor himself.

Under the jurisdiction of one doctor there were six PHCs, this forced the doctors to visit PHC very irregularly. Most of the time PHC was locked for no other health worker was present. This made the people indifferent towards PHC hospital. One patient even stated that the medicines of PHC were poisonous as she suffered badly after consuming them.

Family Planning and Immunization took 60 to 80 per cent of the time and attention of all primary health care workers including medical officers. Family planning was being promoted using all the influences of State power at the cost of primary health care, which was already very rudimentary in this tribal area.

It was reported that PHCs and Sub-centers were chronically without doctor(s) or health workers. The distances between the villages were vast and the roads non-existent. Thus, the Primary Health Care seemed to be absurd at the level of planning, non-operative at the level of implementation, and whatever rudiments of care existed served goals of family planning or Immunization Programme rather than those of the tribals.

Since tribal communities are different from the general population in disease patterns as well as in other determinants of health care. The primary health care for tribal areas must be conceived and planned anew. The priority problems must be decided based on the disease pattern of the concerned tribal population. Problems like accidents, burns, Sickle Cell Disease, malaria, T.B., leprosy, sexually transmitted diseases, and endemic goiter should be given priority. The workers must be selected from the tribal themselves and then train them.

Government Hospitals

Government hospitals seemed to be alien to tribal people, as they did not feel at ease. For this reason, mobile units and medical facilities in shandies were organized. Mobile unit with one doctor, one nurse usually visited different villages in weekly markets to serve the people of near by villages.

It is assumed that in the weekly markets tribal coming to buy commodities can approach the doctor easily with medicines displayed. But the interview with the doctor revealed that it is a poor planning on the part of government and officials, as the doctor in the shandy is poorly equipped without a room for medical checkup. He cited an example that if a patient comes with a complaint of "piles" then without examination he cannot judge the severity of the problem and give medication.

Private Practitioners

Konda Reddi people were ready to spend any amount of money to consult these private practitioners than availing free medical facilities at PHC and government hospitals. This was because they claimed that the diseases were cured very fast when they took the medications given by the private practitioners. Though again, the poverty restricts them to avail these facilities too.

Conclusion

The beliefs and practices of Konda Reddis show that there are some practices which are harmful. Therefore they need to be discouraged. They are:

- Pressing the stomach of pregnant women with knife to change the foetus position and cutting the umbilical cord with bamboo, sickle, arrow, stone etc.
- Late introduction of supplementary food to the infants.
- The practice of cleaning the infant's mouth by sucking water by the mother is an unhygienic practice.
- Practices of sleeping near the embers.
- Fear of immunization, for children should be eliminated and food taboos after delivery should be discouraged.

However, there are few healthy practices, which should be encouraged; these are:

- Breastfeeding immediately after birth and demand feeding for one or more years until the mother gets pregnant indirectly helps in spacing the children.
- Absenteeism during harvesting seasons to some extent helps in spacing.
- The practice of giving bath twice with hot water to the infant is a good practice and should be encouraged.

Suggestions

1. Since the overall cleanliness and hygiene is lacking, there is a need to make them aware of the importance of hygiene. Above all, on the part of the government it is very much needed that the basic

necessities, like, safe drinking water, sanitation, roads, transport facilities and nutrition and health education are made available.

2. Lakhs of traditional practitioners who are practicing alternative system of medicine did not get the due respect and recognition, even though it is the oldest, historically tested, is getting obliterate gradually due to the growing pressures of population, deforestation, and various developmental activities, so it is high time to preserve the indigenous knowledge scientifically through proper research and promote the techniques of their traditional knowledge among the mass population in general and tribal in particular.
3. India is a vast country with one billion population some of the states are bigger than few of the countries. A centralized health care system with standardized training will not serve the purpose, there is an urgent need to decentralize the health care system and need to localize the training, organization and management of health care services. Here a health worker working in the slum gets the same training and manual as that of a worker, working amongst the tribal in a forest based area. Therefore, indigenous systems of health care and indigenous practitioners will have to be incorporated in health care planning. Anthropological studies are essential for enhancing our understanding of the health problems of the tribal and to help them to plan their own health care.
4. Some of the value systems like that of the patient care or sympathy for the kinsmen need be encouraged and made use of in relevant situation. Since health-seeking behaviour affects the utilization of health care services in the community, an attempt to understand the utilization process would enable the administrators to provide relevant medical care services, which hopefully would lead to their better and proper utilization.
5. Certain anomalies existed in the Dai training programmes. The training concentrated more on how to cut the umbilical cord and how to deliver the child safely but the aspect of malnutrition, anemia, high incidence of premature babies and low birth weight were not considered. Though the dai's "unsafe practices" was highlighted as the main reason for the high rate of neo-natal mortality and maternal mortality, their professional experience and relationship with the community remained unappreciated by the health planners.
6. Women's groups working with dais and village women from many districts through out India are expressing a need to upgrade their skills

and education in health. They have designed a health literacy program that is focused on making good health care available to women through the education and empowerment of village health care workers. They use herbal remedies, training in self-help care, and the education of dais and birth attendants. To create a model of health care that serves the personal, varied and unique needs of women. Indian feminist non-government organization (NGO) called Jagori, is conducting residential trainings for village *dais* (midwives). Canadian midwife Diane Smith is conducting these training programmes for the past two years in Indian villages. They honour the process of birth as natural and instinctual, relying on the "forces of nature" and the use of practical, non-intervening skills to facilitate this passage.

7. The birth process is examined with the use of charts, life size models, body language, body mapping and role-playing. Mapping the journey of birth through water, tissue bone and body is done in a tactile and demonstrative way. Pictocin injections during labour, unnecessary fundal pressure, encouraging premature pushing, limiting a woman to certain birthing positions and improper management of the delivery of the placenta are all focal points of discussion. When their training concludes, the women receive a birth kit and certificate of participation. Follow up sessions are planned and scheduled. (Diane Smith, 1998) These kind of training should be conducted in the tribal areas too and help the local dais or midwife to upgrade their skills, encourage their own skills which are appropriate and scientific and making them adopt newer techniques to follow, at the same time judging the severity of the case and referring them to the nearest functional hospitals at proper time.
8. Infections during childbirth are a major cause of maternal deaths. These can be prevented if the five cleans in view of childbirth and delivery practices are adhered to and disseminate their knowledge to the dais. These are clean delivery surface, clean hands (of birth attendant), clean cord tie, clean blade, clean cord stump (without anything applied on it), as proposed by White ribbon alliance group.
9. Thus, when we communicate with tribal in the matter of health and nutrition, we must remember certain unique features of this group, which are, their cultural level, their socioeconomic structure, food availability and use, health status/health problems, health culture, a low level of literacy, geographic isolation/remoteness, lack of development infrastructure, barriers of language, and lack of

(or untouched by) newer media. (Almas Ali, 1989)

10. According to Salil Basu (1994) health care delivery should be designed for each specific tribal group in such a way to cater to their specific needs and problems by ensuring their personal involvement. The strategies like; formulation of realistic development health plans based on needs as felt by tribal women of the specific tribal groups and need for promoting nutritional and health education among tribal women. Further, it is proposed that tribal women/ girls should be properly trained as *"dais/ nurses."* Specific precautions need to be observed at the time of conducting deliveries at home, aseptic conditions need to be followed for cutting the naval cord. Primitive practices of parturition are to be discarded and necessary health education should be imparted by tribal nurses. Finally, maintenance of personal hygiene in connection with childbirth, abortion or menstruation should be properly explained by tribal nurses or dais in order to prevent the infections of the female genital tract.
11. It is proposed that the local people themselves should develop a proper health care center involving the local resources and knowledge as in case of the below given two examples—

In 1990, the Gudalur Adivasi Hospital came into being, now 30-bedded institution owned and run by the Adivasi Munnetra Sangam. The staff is entirely adivasi and their own philosophy and culture provides the foundation for its management. Another, Vivekananda Girijana Kalyana Kendra (VGKK), was rejuvenated by the tribal as a result of their own efforts and by making maximal use of their traditional social infrastructure, as well as existing government services (the participation of the tribal). Dais are already well integrated in to the community health programme of VGKK. Workshops are held regularly to have dais share their knowledge with each other and with the Kendra medical staff, as well as to have the Kendra staff share modern obstetric information with the dais. The dais are now an improved source of information on pre and post natal care for pregnant and lactating women; they have improved their methods of birthing and they are comfortably identifying and referring problem cases to the Kendra Hospital. The dais have shared "an interesting and novel way of handling deliveries among tribal women". (Jim Bramson, 1989)

Recommendations

Finally, summary of few recommendations are put forth like:

- Good health and good societv go together. This is possible only when supportive services such as nutrition, environment and education reach a higher level
- First improve upon information, education, and communications facilities and then strengthen demand-generation activities.
- Policy makers should make and modify the health programmes that should be based on the analysis of general health, sanitation condition, personal hygiene, diet and other social and cultural behaviors.
- Strengthen and improve the quality of family welfare service delivery, including establishment of first-referral units.
- Strengthen program management and implementation capacity.
- Preserve the indigenous knowledge scientifically through proper research and promote the techniques of their traditional knowledge.
- Training the dais, respecting their skills and knowledge. Further, training programs in preservation of fruits and vegetables by preparing jams, squash, pickle, cake preparation, dosa preparation, scientific methods of cooking etc should be conducted.
- Provide funds for innovative schemes like training programmes, community participation in forming their own health systems to improve service delivery.

REFERENCES

Ali, Almas. 1989. "Communicating with Tribals on Health and Nutrition," *Health for Millions*. New Delhi: VHAI.

Basu, Salil. 1994. *Tribal Health in India.* (ed.). New Delhi: Manak Publishers.

Chaudhury, S. 1991. "Continuity and Change in Material Culture of the Konda Reddi," *Vanyajati*, October 1991.

Chauhan, Abha.1990. *Tribal Women and Social Change in India*. Etawah: A. C. Brothers.

Diane, Smith. 1998. "Working With The Traditional Indian Village Dai," *Midwifery Today-International Midwife.* Winter 1998.

Duary, Nabakumar. 1995. "Religious Life of a Forest Dwelling Tribe in Andhra Pradesh: A Case Study on the Konda Reddis of Bison Hill," *Vanyajati,*. XLIII (4): 14-17.

Haimendorf, Furer C.V. 1945. *The Reddis of Bison Hills: A Study in Acculturation.* London: Macmillan.

Jim, Bramson. 1989. VGKK: Healthcare in the Hills of Mysore. *Health for Millions.* New Delhi: VHAI.

Raju, S. M. 1995. "Unreported Medicinal Uses of Some Plants from East Godavari District of Andhra Pradesh," *Vanyajati,*

Report. 2000. *The White Ribbon Alliance for Safe Motherhood/India.* (March, 2000).

FOURTEEN

WAY OF LIFE AMONG THE SAHARIYA OF RAJASTHAN

VEENA BHASIN

In hunting and gathering societies, land is the subject of labour, while for the settled agriculturist land is an instrument of labour. In all productive systems, the decisive factor is man's labour. A seasonal labour is a way of life among the rural poor of India in agriculturally backward areas by migrating to relatively developed areas. Seasonal employment during the peak seasons of sowing and harvesting has been a way of life for some of the tribals. Till the mid-seventies, mostly the tribals from Bihar used to migrate seasonally to work as agricultural labourers. Now more and more tribals are opting for labour. This article presents the case of the Sahariyas.

Out of the total 27.5 million people, there are 4.2 million Scheduled Tribes in Rajasthan. Majority of tribals in Rajasthan are concentrated in the southern region and distributed between three main groups, the Bhils, the Minas and the Girasia. The Bhil and Mina are well-known, whereas Girasia, Sahariya, Kathodi and Damor are little known outside southern Rajasthan.

The study presents the techno-economic adaptations among Sahariyas of Rajasthan who have been designated as Scheduled Tribe and recognized as a Primitive Tribal Group (PTG), which identified them in the state administration documents as a socially disadvantaged community. They inhabit marginally productive areas of the Baran district and have little access to services and resources. People belonging to marginal societies are feeling the pressures of dwindling resources and a burgeoning population. Sahariyas, are particularly vulnerable to these pressures since their life-styles are intrinsically linked to the surrounding ecosystem. Traditionally, a tribe of food gatherers, hunting, fishing, gathering and collecting the Sahariya made a living selling the forest produce they collected. That is now a part of the past as are the once wildlife rich forests, which have seen a steady depletion of animal and plant life due to indiscriminate hunting and cutting. Restriction on hunting and cutting of trees led to starvation, and that lack of natural resources has created a practice of labour. This paper describes and analyzes the strategies adapted by Sahariyas to cope with necessities of living.

For the development of Sahariyas, an elaborate plan has been drawn up in the form of Sahariya Development Project and is executed under the chairmanship of Additional District Magistrate and the planning branch of the district. Through various schemes they have been provided land and subsidies for other resources, yet they resort to seeking agricultural labour with locally dominant castes; to forest labour; and to any labour activity that comes their way. These Sahariya families migrate three-four times in a year, as their labour is required at sowing as well as harvesting time of Kharif and Rabi crops. During this entire period their children do not get the benefit of free education, secondly these families fail to get benefit from any long duration government sponsored schemes available at their place of residence.

The People and Area

Medieval history of Rajasthan does not mention Sahariya. Few accounts are available from the history of British time. Col. James Tod (1978) made certain observation about the group of people who were nature lover inhabiting Shahbad and Kishanganj of erstwhile Kota State and Morena, Gwalior, Shivpuri and Guna of central India. Few studies carried among Sahariya after Independence describe them as the poorest of the poor who are at the lowest end of the development scale (Mann and Mann, 1989; Doshi and Vyas, 1992; Ghatak, 1998). In 1965, a monograph about the Sahariyas of village Sanwara was brought out by Gupta, which provides their ethnographic account.

The Sahariya of Kota state and central India inhabited in dense forests and hills. The Sahariya of Morena, Gwalior, Shivpuri and Guna were reported to be notorious dacoits. The ravines of Chambal have been their hideouts. It is mentioned by historians that the Sahariya in reality did not indulge in dacoity, they served the dacoit gangs as transporters and provided their services when asked for.

During the British period, the Sahariya had subsistence economy all through the tracts of Rajasthan, Madhya Pradesh and Gujarat. They were hunters and gatherers practicing slash and burn cultivation. Their isolation in hills and forests separated them from neighbouring caste societies in their culture and religion. Sahariya were inhabiting in nucleated villages in the thick forest and hills in the Jungles of Mewar. From there they have been said to migrate to Kota in the 16th century. It seems that having lived in isolation, the Sahariyas ways of life had not been recorded till the colonial period. Till then they depended on forests for their needs. Other things of daily use were bartered for forest produce with the *Bohare* (shopkeeper or money-lenders) who used to visit forests from time to time. As their material requirements were fulfilled in these isolated tracts, they remained cut off from the main civilization. So it can be assumed that even before the coming of the British, they had contact with outside world. Merchants and moneylenders were doing trade in many villages, advancing loans and acquiring agriculture and forest produce. However, contacts with market economy were few and of limited nature, consisting mainly of barter of some items of agriculture or forest produce for supplies of few necessities, such as salt and iron, which they were incapable of producing with the resources of their own environment.

It has been reported that the erstwhile ruler of Kota state, Raja Jaswant Singh invited some Jat and Sikh cultivators for the development of the area and offered them land at nominal prices in the Sahariya region. They cleared large tracts of forests and acquired large portions of fertile land with irrigation sources, pushing Sahariyas deep in to the forest. In this process Sahariya lost their land.

Sahariyas were not able to withstand outside pressure because of their simple nature and low literacy. As Sahariya's economy is household and is for self-consumption, therefore they live in relatively closed, self-contained society, and even if engaged in trade or barter with other people, they are not economically integrated into wider social units. In contrast peasants society forms a wider economic, social and political units (Stavenlogen, 1975: 65; Wolf, 1966: 11). The extreme poverty of most of the Sahariya was caused by their subjugation to moneylender or *Bohare*. The essential difference between the Sahariya village and the villages of the caste peasants was that in Sahariya village money lender's capital relinquished a surplus without bringing about any profound change in the village while in the peasant villages the money lender's capital operated from within the village. Caste villages were settlements in which Clan or *gotra* organization maintained control over the land. They brought labourers, tenants, artisans and priests to serve them. A caste village thus a deliberate creation which incorporated various segments of a society within the hierarchical principles of caste ideology. The capital, like every thing else in the village, was used to serve people. The caste village was far more a complex entity in terms of the operation of capital than the tribal village.

In the Sahariya region, among the locally dominant castes, there is a fusion of economic and social powers, which lead to political power as well. Often the disputes between the Sahariya are settled by the locally dominant caste patrons, though Sahariya have their tribal Panchayat which has jurisdiction not only over the villages of Rajasthan but also over the villages located in Madhya Pradesh. The patron-client solidarity existing between the Sahariya and the other castes has not weakened their respective caste loyalties. In case of any mental, sudden or prolonged illness, the other caste people believe that they have been bewitched by Sahariya women either knowing nefarious magic or endowed with evil power.

With the arrival of settled agriculturalists the Sahariyas dependence on forests increased. Even after their arrival in the area, the Sahariyas for quite sometimes, continued their traditional economic activities. It has been reported that the erstwhile state of Kota recognized shifting cultivation and the Sahariya had to pay twenty-five *paisa* per *bigha* as revenue. However, shifting cultivation gradually declined, but Sahariya dependence on forest continued. Though strict laws restrict the use of forest resources, till now Sahariya indulge in burning of forests to appears deities after a wish has been fulfilled and in doing so they collect gum (which oozes out of trees) which is bartered for grain.

Majority of Sahariya inhabit Shahbad and Kishanganj tehsils of Baran district.[1] The large portion of Shahbad tehsil is surrounded by hills and forest. More than half of the area of Shahbad and Kishanganj comes under the forest. Agriculture is practised on one fourth of the remaining area. More than half the population of 127 villages of these tehsils was inhabited by Sahariya. In 1956, out of 82,000 (population of the area), 27,000 were Sahariya, 33 per cent of the total population. According to the census of 1961, out of the total tribal population of the state of Rajasthan (23,09,447), only one per cent (23,299) were Sahariya. According to the census of 1981, they constitute 41,427 person forming 0.99 per cent to the total population of the state. A majority of them, i.e. 99.2 per cent are concentrated in the Kishanganj and Shahbad tehsils of the Baran district, widely known as Hadoti (Hadavati), the land of the Hadas. The Hadas are a major branch of the Great Chauhan of the *Agnikula* (Fire Dynasty).

Traditionally Sahariya were forest dwellers and inhabited west of Aravalli range. They were hunters and gatherers. Large-scale deforestation and subsequent desertification gradually shifted them to eastern side of the Aravallis. Sahariya have known to have migrated in the recorded history to the areas in which they are now found. Apart from south-eastern plateau of Rajasthan, they inhabit the north-western region of Madhya Pradesh. In Madhya Pradesh, the Sahariya inhabit area covering the slope of the Vindhyachal range in the west, plains of Malwa in the south and the basin of river Chambal along the state boundaries (north south) of Madhya Pradesh and Rajasthan. In the princely state of Rajasthan, masses in general and the Sahariya in particular suffered from long great disabilities. Even after Independence in 1947 the consequential integration of the princely states in the region and the guarantee of equality gave them little protection. Sahariya are most backward and poorest of the Scheduled Tribes of Rajasthan. They were bought and sold like chattels till half a century ago.

Baran is situated in the south-eastern plateau of Rajasthan, a region widely known as *Hadoti* which is an expanse of fertile plan having rich black cotton soil. Physiographically, the Sahariya area in the Baran district may be divided into two parts–*upreti* (uplands) or high land villages stretching from Kalwada village in the west to Shahbad proper and *taleti* (lowland) low level settlements starting from Shahbad to Kasba. *upreti* is mainly falling in Kishanganj tehsil, and is largely plain and fertile with irrigation sources. The Sahariya concentration in *upreti* is thin. *Taleti* is mainly formed of hills and forests, forming large part of Shahbad Tehsil.

The climate of the area is very similar to that of the Indo-Gangetic plain with hot dry summers and delightfully cold winters. *Hadoti* receives an average of 35 inches (87.5 cm) of rainfall, which keeps it cool, and gentle breeze ward off the shifting humidity. During the monsoon months the Sahariya area is cut off from the rest of the district as small rivulets and *nallahs* overflow and forest roads are blocked at various places. There is surface water collection with little percolation. As a result of the slope, the rainwater usually gets drained into the river. The important rivers of the area are Chambal, Banganga, Banas, Kali-Sindh, Pawan and Parvati.

The climate on the whole is dry. In areas where there are no irrigation facilities and other constraints like infertile soil and the fall in the water table restricts cultivation in summer months. The vegetation of the area is of dry and deciduous variety, partly due to the nature of the soil and partly due to the climate of the area. The land of the forested area is hard and shallow. The forest is of mixed type; predominant trees, shrubs and grasses available therein are the following:

Mahua (*Basia latifia*), achar (*Buchanania latifolia*), salar (*Boswellia serrata*), gurjan (*Lannea coromandelica*), tendu (*Diospyros melano- xylon*), kher (*Acacia catechu*), dhokra (*Anogeissus Latifolia*), bahera (*Terminalia bellerica*), anwala (*cassia auriculata*), harsingar (*Nyctanthes arboritristis*), jamun (*Eugenia jambolana*), bor (*Zizyphus jujuba*), salaria (*Terminalia tomentosa*), chhola (*Butea morosperma*), peepal (*Ficus religiosa*), sen-senta (*Schima norvosum*), gharnia. Forest produce: *katha, chiranji, mooslt*, wax, honey, gum, lac, wood, mahua fruit and flowers, herbs, fruits, *anwala, bahera*.

The Sahariya culture has evolved, adapted and survived within the forest clad hilly terrain they inhabit, venturing and wandering amongst the forests with bow and arrows. These tropical deciduous forests provide them with sport, meat, liquor, food shelter and medicines.

The Sahariyas do not live in complete isolation. They usually live in multi-caste villages, where they inhabit a portion called *Saharana*, which literally mean a place where Sahariyas live. In multi-caste villages there is spatial segregation based purity and pollution. In Rajasthan, in the highly stratified villages, the lower and untouchable castes have their hamlets outside the village. The Sahariyas are also clustered in their hamlets, which are away from the main revenue village. For example, Mahrawta, one of the villages studied, is a multi-caste village having three settlements. One is the main settlement inhabited by Brahmins, Nagad, Dhakad, Kachhi, Kushwaha, Nathyogi, Kumbar and some scheduled castes. The second settlement situated at one and a half-kilometre is inhabited by Gujjars called Gujjar Basti. The third settlement Saharana, situated at about two kilometer from the main village and two and a half kilometre from the Pucca road is inhabited by Sahariyas. Saharana is connected to the main village by a *Kachcha* path.

Sahariya can be easily distinguished from the neighbouring caste population groups. They look undernourished, the children are thin with a protruding belly indicating protein deficiency. Report on Sahariya Development Plan (1979) states that they are malnourished and underfed. Being poorer of the poor they depend upon wild seeds, herbs and tubers (including *gowari, chayin* and *bujair*). Some of these are said to be intoxicating. These eatables if not properly handled for their final product, they cause ulcers and throat inflammation on consumption. If they do not have tobacco, they smoke chillam of mahua. If there is not enough flour for the bread they mix mahua with channa (gram) for making dough. At times they make Chappati of Tendu fruit, which is considered to be hot, *garam phal*. The poor health and physical disability is linked with poverty. Their isolation refers to both physical inaccessibility as well as lack of access to information and services. The loss of their assets (land as well as forest) and the detrimental effects of rising costs on the living conditions highlight their vulnerability and powerlessness. Their unhygienic living condition makes them more susceptible to diseases. Most adults as well as children suffer from eczema and scabies. The menfolk and children are seen in the scantiest of clothing. Men wear a loincloth and the most of the children till the age of nine roam about naked. Young boys and girls wear small under-wears. Girls before marriage wear small skirts tucked in at the back to resemble a loincloth.

The relationship of Sahariyas with locally dominant castes are like any other typical Indian village governed by the principles of purity and pollution, restrictions on commensality and matrimony are followed likewise. They visit the village when necessary and their other relations are like landowner and tenants/labourers. With artisan castes they do not have Jajmani relation but have to pay either in cash or kind. They have Jajmani relations with Gwala for pastoral duties. The dependence of Sahariya on some castes like the *Baniya* and *Kalal* is of mercantile nature. The exchange is monetised as well as non-monetized. They buy ornaments and eatables in these transactions. These merchants are regular visitors to the Saharana. In some Saharanas, the Baniya owns a shop close to the Saharana or a Kalal runs a shop containing, gur, pann, biri and several other household goods.

Ecological and Economic Profile of the Study Area

The data have been collected from four villages of Kishanganj and eleven villages of Shahbad. The placement of Sahariya habitations offer different economic opportunities. Sahariya inhabiting these areas are either part of the multi-caste villages or exclusive Sahariya villages.
The villages which form the part of this study can be grouped:

(i) Villages in the proximity of forest – Saharana Mahua Kheri of Agar Village, Saharana Matia Khera of Maheshpura village, Barara and Birman village;
(ii) Villages away from the forest, situated in the neighbourhood of main road, canal or rivers - Mehrawta, Unee and Kushiyara; and
(iii) Model villages where Sahariya have been rehabilitated by the state government – Khushalpura, Shubhghara, Shahpur and Gordhanpura.
The Sahariya inhabiting villages in the proximity of forest depend mainly on collection and gathering of forest produce, viz. resin (cheer),

honey, gum (gond), tendu leaves, mahua flowers, various roots and tubers and medicinal plants used in Ayurvedic medicine. The collecting season begins around March and finishes by July. Hunting both for sport and food is prohibited, while fishing is practised by Sahariya. Monsoon hinders the collecting activity as the roads get blocked by the seasonal rivulets, making difficult for the theckedar to visit the area. Many Sahariya own agricultural land in the forest, which they received at the time of settlement but have no permanent source of irrigation. The shortage of water restricts the land use. To compensate for the deficient in their economy, Sahariya opt for labour work.

The villages in the proximity of forest are characterized by scanty agriculture. Earlier the Sahariya used the forested area for cultivation but after the declaration of the protected forest, ploughing of forestland was prohibited. As a result most of the Sahariya became landless, leaving a few whose fields were outside the protected forest area. Thus the landless Sahariya, to supplement their meagre income from the forest produce, began working as labourers. As local agricultural labour work was not available they started working as forest labourers or going out of the area. There were many contractors from all over the Kota district who used to contact them on a regular basis. These contractors used to transport them or paid their passage, but remuneration for their labour was much less than standard rates. However, over the years, Sahariya became aware about importance and value of their labour and have started looking for work on their own and have started working for better remuneration. Saharana Mahua Kheria and Matia Khera are situated away from the National Highway and State Highway, connected by a kachcha path of eight to fifteen kilometres respectively. There is no regular bus service. The seasonal migration in this region is still arranged by contractors.

Villages away from the forest in the neighbourhood of road/rivers/canal are better off, taking full advantage of agrarian economy. Saharanas of these villages are poor and remain socio-economically backward, though they are being offered more economic opportunities in multi-caste villages than in exclusive Sahariya villages. The Sahariya of these villages instead of being dependent on forest produce are relatively more dependent on land owning and mercantile castes. They work as farm hand and agricultural labourers for land owning castes. They mainly take up the work of a hali, which requires working for an annual cycle in the fields of the owner. Generally men take up this work, though there are few exceptions. Few Sahariya own land and cattle. Few Sahariya cultivate their own land, because of poor quality of land and lack of irrigational resources. Under the milk scheme cream is bought from the villages. Very few Sahariya families have benefited from this scheme, as the milk yield of their cattle is low.

The model villages – Khushalpura, Shubhghara, Shahpur and Gordhanpura constructed by the state government for rehabilitating Sahariya lack the characteristics of Saharana. Khushalpur and Shubhghara are situated on a pucca link road at a distance of five and ten kilometres, respectively from the state highway No. 17, while Shahpura is half a kilometer from SH No. 17 connected by a *kachcha* path. The village Gordhanpur was originally constructed for the Bengali refugees after partition. They did not live there for long because of acute water shortage. They eventually shifted to nearby villages (already inhabited) of Parania, Gatti, etc. Thereafter, the Sahariya from Bhanwargarh/Kishanganj areas were given land (who were landless) and houses in Gordhapura. The land is of inferior quality and shortage of water makes the agriculture a non-profitable proposition. The pump sets provided do not work because of the low underground water level. Their economy is based on labour work. Little agriculture which they practice fulfils their household requirements of the food grains but is not reliable. They collect minor forest produce but it does not add substantially to their economy, as the open forest area is less and their activities are restricted in the Reserved Forest area.

A typical Saharana is a cluster of settlements of 40 to 50 households. There is hardly any space between the huts. In the middle of the Saharana under a Neem tree is a hut, which resembles a sitting place. Sahariya call this "Bangala." Saharana are devoid of all modern amenities like electricity, educational institutions, medical facilities and ways and means of communication. These Saharana are remote and out of the way. All the houses are kachcha. There are hand pumps and unprotected wells for water supply. Some of the pumps are non-functional.

The staple diet of Sahariyas is wheat. Other cereals consumed by them are jowar and bajra. Pulses most commonly used are urad, chana, tuar, moong and dried peas. Potato, onions, tomato, brinnjal, bhindi, tinda are the common vegetables eaten by them. Mustard oil is used for cooking but generally the vegetables are boiled in water with spices like chillies, ginger, garlic, coriander, turmeric and zeera (cumin seeds). Sahariyas are considered malnourished due to inadequacy of diet and also due to lack of awareness of proper diet.

Forest, land and human labour are the principal economic resources of the Sahariyas. The Sahariyas undertake various economic activities ranging from food gathering and collecting to cultivation and labour. These economic activities are combined depending on the time and space. The Sahariyas undertake cultivation but the collection of forest produce is their main source of livelihood in some areas. In the agricultural season, those who own land and have source to irrigate, cultivate their fields. Those who do not own land or do not have permanent irrigation source, work on the land of other people either as Hali or on Batai system. The crops grown under rain fed conditions are and remain, highly sensitive to variation in rainfall. The other major sectors of the economy–gathering and collecting and wage labour–expand and contract in response to performance in the agricultural sector. Other local institutions in the area operate on the principle of a guaranteed subsistence for all, including patron-client and jajmani relationship. But it does not hold good for Sahariyas. Patronage relationships have given way to different types of relationships of labour and tenancy. For labourers, this meant that they are now free to work for one or more employees but are no longer entitled to wage advances or to slack season subsistence loans from their employees. For tenants, this has meant that they are now free to share crop land for one or more landlords and to sell their produce directly but are less likely to receive production or consumption loans from landlords. Breman (1985: 444) in a study of changing agrarian relations in south Gujarat, points out that "the breaking down of vertical dependence mechanism does not in itself lead to better existence for those being freed from them." The same point of view has been argued by Appadurai (1984) that the loosening of patron-client ties, together with other political and economic forces, has led to partial emancipation for the poor without entitlement to a guaranteed subsistence. Jodha (1988) reasoned while comparing quantitative approaches to the incidence of poverty in two villages of Rajasthan, poor people give up exploitation arrangements with patrons only when they become more independent.

Table 14.1: Land distribution among Sahariyas in the study area

Category	Percentage
Landless	20.5
1-4 bighas	28.5
5-9 bighas	25.5
10-14 bighas	13.5
15-19 bighas	8.0
20 bighas and above	4.0

The pattern of land distribution is such that only fifty per cent of the households can live on land and from among them fifty per cent can have surplus, provided they cultivate their field themselves. Rest 28 per cent household have to supplement their income by gathering/collecting and labour activities. Landless households have to depend largely on sources outside their land. It can be seen from the above table that only 20.5 per cent are landless, which is in marked contrast to the general belief that Sahariya are landless labourers.

Occupational Structure among Sahariyas

Main occupations among Sahariyas are unskilled labour, hunting, gathering, fishing, forest work, farm labour and farming. The caste Hindus of the villages in the region do not indulge in gathering forest produce, as it is considered the occupation of the Sahariya who are forest-dwellers.

Table 14.2: Occupational structure among Sahariya in the study area (in per cent)

Category	*Male*	*Female*	*Total*	*Husband*	*Wife*
Economically inactive	53.6	60.25	6.8	1.0	12.0
Labourers	37.4	38.0	37.7	70.0	83.5
Cultivators	6.2	0.6	3.5	5.5	1.5
Petty businessmen	0.4	—	0.2	0.5	—
Service	2.4	1.2	1.8	6.5	3.0

It can be seen from the table that 56.8 per cent of the population in the study area is economically inactive. The percentage of young (0-14) is 50.9 in the sample size, while 4.4 per cent are 60 years and above. The rest 44.8 per cent are between 15-59 years who are economically active and indulge in different activities. Generally, the persons who collect forest produce do forest labour also. Agricultural labour is for annual cycle. Few indulge in shop keeping, carpentry, tailoring, etc. As literacy rate (8.2) among Sahariya is low, in males (11.8) as well as females (4.2), only 1.8 per cent are in service, that too as class IV employee in the government schools and forest. Only one Sahariya in the study area is working in the tehsil office.

Coping with Necessities

The calendar of economic activities shows that Sahariyas practice "mixed economy" wherein they have combined gathering, collecting, subsidiary agriculture and labour activities. Their labour activities include – agriculture labour, forest labour and casual labour (Table 14.3).

Table 14.3: Calendar of economic activities

January-February (Magh)	February-March (Phagun)	March-April (Chait)
Labour work wherever available; watching for fields; fishing fishing	Labour work; watching the fields; collection of fire-wood and grass; collection of *Mahua*; hunting and crop in their own fields or work as harvesting	Collection of *Cheer, Gond, Mohua* flower *Tendu* fruits, wood for self consumption and selling in market; fishing; harvesting of Rabi labour in nearby villages
April-May (Baisakh)	**May-June (Jeth)**	**June-July (Aashash)**
Collection of Tendu Leves, fruits, honey, herbs. Cheer. collection of Gond and firewood: fishing; labour work in the forest and village	Collection of Cheer, Gond, Tendu leaves and firewood; fishing: preparation of fields for showing: house repairs. etc.	Ploughing and sowing of Kharif crop: agriculture labour, forest labour firewood, grass, edible leaves and roots.
July-August (Sawan)	**August-September (Bhade)**	**September-October (Kuwar)**
Weeding in their own fields who cultivate their lands: agriculture labour, collection of edible roots and leaves	Agriculture and causal labour	Harvesting of early variety of millet: agriculture. forest and causal labour
October-November (Kartik)	**November-December**	**December-January**
Harvesting of early karif crop: collection of firewood and self-consumption and selling, ploughing of fields and sowing of wheat, agricultlure and forest labour	Harvesting of Kharif crop: agriculture, forest and causal labour; collection of firewood	Labour and collection of firewood

Sahariya households routinely plan for seasonal variations and fluctuations. The uncertainties of weather and resources pose hardships for these people who face chronic vulnerability in terms of access to resources. Available resources include physical assets such as land; human assets such as time and skill; social assets such as family, kin and patronage relationships; and collective assets such as common property resources and public sector services.

These are several dimensions of household livelihood system among Sahariyas. Sahariya economy is characterized not only by multiple activities but also multiple factors and institution in which households are engaged. The non-market activities are central to household livelihood system. The Sahariya household mix their resources and activities across a given year according to seasonal fluctuations. Under abnormal weather conditions Sahariya's seasonal coping strategies and household responses involve intensification or modification of regular seasonal strategies. For countering risk and uncertainty Sahariyas engage in multiple activities. Sahariyas do not distinguish between primary and secondary occupation. A majority of them engage in wage labour for some part of the year, either all the year or seasonally. Sahariyas are generally engaged in routine subsistence activities – primarily the gathering, collecting activities. Individual household members engage in multiple activities either sequentially or simultaneously.

Common Property Resources (CPRs)

Common Property Resources (CPRs) are an important form of natural resource endowment and of collective subsistence for the poor Sahariyas. Access to and use of CPRs show a seasonal variation. Sahariyas benefits from common grazing land, water sources and other physical products of forest, which supplement their income and provide employment. Many forest products contribute to subsistence, fuel and fodder. Some products are bartered or locally marketed. The commercial products are not collected extensively.

Local trees and shrubs provide the largest number of physical products. They also represent assets, which can be "encashed" if the need arises. The privately owned trees can be sharecropped, mortgaged or sold when the owner needs cash. Chambers and Lonrghurst (1986) have popularized the concept of trees as "saving banks" and insurance for poor rural people.

The poor Sahariyas who are landless labourers, landless tenants and small landholding households fulfil their subsistence requirements of fuel and fodder from CPRs. Other Sahariyas who are medium, large and surplus landholding households collect just 50 per cent of their fuel and 25 per cent of their fodder requirements from free sources. However, these CPRs have been overused and thereby, degraded because of increasing human and cattle populations and the lack of proper management and regulation.

Gathering and Collecting Activities

Forest produce of the area are: *Katha* (catechu), *chironji, moosli,* wax, honey, gum (*cheer/gond*), lac, wood/coal, *mahua* flowers and fruits, herbs, fruits, *ananwala, behera,* roots and tubers. The forest activities of the Sahariya are confined to the manufacture of *katha*, extraction of coal and collection of gum (*cheer/gond*), honey, *moosli*, *chironji* and *tendu* levels. They also collect wild fruits, roots and tubers, which supplement their meagre economic resources. Utilization of forest produce is restricted and controlled by the State Forest Department which auctions the coupes according to its laws. Wood for house construction and fuel is allowed to be freely collected. They are also permitted to collect stones for use free of charge. For other forest produce like *moosli*, honey, *tendu* leaves etc. Sahariya have to pay nominal charges.

Collection of Gum: Khair and *dhankari* yield gum of a high quality. *Katha* (catechu) is made out of *kher* tree. Gum is an adhesive substance secreted by many plants. Out of these, some are edible like *cheer*, *gond* of *khair* trees, etc. The *cheer* season starts in the month of *Phagun/Chait/ Baisakh* (March-April) and lasts till June end. Some Sahariya even migrate to *Saal* forests and stay in temporary shelters to collect *cheer*, which is collected in a piece of bark on alternate days. In some cases it exudes naturally but in others the collectors have to make the incision. Both husbands and wives go together to the forest. Contractor (*theckedar*) comes and collect the *cheer*, which is bartered for various articles. The *cheer* is sold at four rupees a kilo and the bartered amount is fixed accordingly. One kilogram of *cheer* is sold for two kilograms of salt or one hundred gram of chilly or eight bundles of *bidi* or five hundred grams of *gur*. *Cheer* collection was not part of the traditional system but was introduced from outside.

An edible variety of *gond* (gum) is also collected from the Khair tree, which is expensive than *cheer*. The exchange rate of one kilogram of *Gond* is five kilograms of wheat or *Bajra*. The amount paid to Sahariya is one third of the price at which *cheer* and *gond* are sold in the market.

Collection of Achar: Achar is fruit of tree, which grows abundantly in the area. The plucking of the fruit starts in the month of April and May. The kernel of the *achar*, called *chironji* is as big as gram and is highly nutritive and delicious. From twenty kilograms of *achar*, about three kilograms of *chironji* can be obtained and a person can collect five kilograms of *achar* in three to four hours.

Collection of Honey: In the months of April, Sahariya collect honey from honey combs which are abundant in rock shelters and hanging from tall trees. They go in groups to collect honey with a container and a thick rope provided by the *theckedar*. The Sahariya approach the hives at night and thrust the iron bars into them to scare away the bees; then they place or hang containers under them. A kilo of honey is bartered for three to four kilograms of wheat or millet.

Collection of Tendu Leaves: In the last week of May, collection of *tendu* leaves starts which last till the end of June. The *tendu* leaves are collected from deep forest. Leaves are broken with both hands and are collected in a cloth. They are tied into small bundles of fifty leaves each. Two halves of twenty-five leaves each are tied together with the fibre (of bark) of *chhola* and *saint* trees in such a way that the ventral side faces the interior while the dorsal side is exposed. Leaves are collected in morning hours and then bundles are tied. A family unit is able to make three to four hundred bundles, which is collected by the *Theckedar* in the evenings at the rate of ten paisa per bundle.

Collection of Mahua Fruit: From its flower liquor and from seeds oil is extracted. The fruit of *mahua* is collected in the months of May and June. After the fruit is dried completely, its seeds are separated and crushed for oil. From one kilogram of seeds, only three hundred gram of ghee is extracted and a person can collect about five kilogram of fruit.

Fresh or dried flowers and fruits comprise the raw material of the local liquor called *mahuri* or *mahudi*. *Mahuri* is generally prepared for self-consumption. The marriage season generally overlaps with the flowering season of *mahua*. It solves their major problem – the prime expenditure in liquor.

During summer months Sahariya collect the roots of a creeper *satavar*, which is used in ayurvedic medicine. Both men and women collect the roots, the women peel off the bark with a sickle and the men cut them into small pieces. A Sahariya family collects one or two kilogram(s) of *satavar* in a day, which is sold at the rate of five rupees per kilo.

The other medicinal plants collected are flowers of *palash* tree, *aanwala*, *bahede* fruit, *silajeet*, *safed musli* and *qiloi* (*Amritarisht*). Sen-Senta and gaharania grasses are made into strings, cords and ropes used for various purposes.

Fishing: To supplement their diet, the Sahariya eat fish during the summer. It is a collective activity, wherein two methods are employed. A group of men go inside the water body and splash it with their hands. The fishes come up because of the disturbance created by the splash and are caught tightly between the palms and the second person pierces it with a big needle and a thin rope. Enough fish is caught in five-six hours for the whole Saharana.

In the second methods poisonous plant extract is mixed in the small puddles (less than five feet). Two or three men go inside the water with a *potali* carrying poison of two herbs, which is dipped into water several times covering the whole area. The Sahariya eat many species of fish and also small turtles. It takes about a hour to kill the fish with the poison. The Sahariya stand by the waterside and wait for the dead fish to come up. The fish thus collected are equally distributed among the people of Saharana.

Farming: The terrain inhabited by Sahariya, in general, is characterised by hills and forests. It is reported that only one-fourth area of the Shahbad and Kishanganj tehsils is cultivable. Nearly fifty per cent population is residing in forest. Sahariya, forming about 33 per cent of the population, in two tehsils, generally occupy forest or uncultivable land. There are 127 villages where Sahariya own land and their population is more than fifty per cent in these villages. Sahariya till their land with traditional implements and techniques.

The local agriculture calendar is divided into three seasons: the *Kharif* or monsoon season (June to October); the *Rabi* or winter season (November-March); and summer season (April-May). Cash crops of the area are mustard, coriander, gram and soyabeans. Pulses and soya beans are grown as *kharif* crop along with *jowar*, *bajra* and maize. While mustard, coriander and gram are grown with wheat as *Rabi* crop. Some varieties are early growing. For those who are engaged in agriculture, (either as farmers or labourers) there are periods of greater or lesser activity. The labourers find local employment largely at the beginning and the end of the monsoon season, and at the end of the winter season. Their wages fluctuate according to the season and the crop.

For Sahariyas, the monsoon season is a period of hard work and low food availability. The Sahariya who own land and cultivate it, grow crops which are grown under rain-fed conditions. They prefer not to grow winter crops when irrigation is necessary. A significant number of Sahariya are hired for monsoon sowing and harvesting, but labour season is slack during the intervening two months.

There is a difference of six months between monsoon harvest and the harvest of wheat and barley in winters and only a limited amount of sorghum (*bajra*) is grown in summer, the monsoon period is a time when there is a shortage of food for Sahariya. The Sahariya face these hardships because the households are unable to generate and store surplus. This is a period of considerable stress for Sahariya labourers. The monsoon harvest brings relief to farmers but limited and brief relief to labour households. Because few local farmers employ labour for planting winter crops. The month following the monsoon harvest is the time of peak migration by labourers and they do not return before the end of the winter season. The cultivators keep busy through out the winter season, planting winter crops in November-December, harvesting the longer monsoon crops in January-February and harvesting winter crops in March-April.

Labour: About 37.7 per cent Sahariya in the study area, claim wage labour as their primary occupation. Sahariya work as agricultural labour, forest labour and casual labour. The local labour market of Kishanganj and Shahbad tehsils is of moderate size providing employment to many Sahariyas. The majority of Sahariya are employed as casual labourers rather than as permanent or attached labourers. The agricultural labour is hired across the area in the 15 kilometres radius. Of the households engage in wage labour, many migrate for some part of the year in search of employment. The households engaged in labour report labour as a primary or secondary occupation or as local, migrant or attached labour. Demand for hired labour in and around the study villages is limited by several factors. Mechanical thrashing has virtually replaced manually thrashing of wheat and barley, thereby displacing Sahariya labour from those operations. Majorities of the farmers in the study region are from backward castes whose use of family labour, both male and female, in agriculture is not constrained by caste-based consideration. Agricultural migrant labour circulate through several villages and different employers and most migrants move and work as family units. Seasonal labour migration of Sahariya does not fit conventional concept about migration as few Sahariya migrate to urbanised or industrial areas. Not all labourers stay away for either the whole season or for only one season. The study data indicates that there are workers:

(i) Who migrate for a single agricultural season lasting three to five weeks;

(ii) Who migrate for entire winter season (five months) or the combined winter and summer season (eight months);

(iii) Who migrate on semi-permanent basis, as they return to engage in cultivation, local wage labour or some other activity; and

(iv) Who migrate to become *hali* for a year.

Duration of stay depends on large number of factors: whether the migrant group is composed of single workers or a completely family units/whether they are landless or they have seasonal work.

On average Sahariya work for 85 mandays of their work in a year. This means they stay at a place of their work from two to three months in four periods of time. People left behind in Saharana are old men and women, pregnant women and women with small children. When the whole Saharana (leaving aside aforesaid persons) migrate to work, it is called *palayan karana.*

The season for long term migration (five to eight months) is the dry season from Diwali (generally October-November) to Holi (generally in March). Traditionally, the big land lords used to keep Sahariyas as *hali, i.e.* whole time servants for farm work for Rs. 200 per year. The *halis* were converted into slaves or bonded labour, because of their habit of taking advance loan. "Some 30-40 years ago a Sahariya could be easily hired for a day on half a kilogram of *jowar* and his wife for a pitcher of *chhachh.*" Sahariyas suffered for long great disabilities. Even after independence, the consequential integration of princely states in the region got them little protection from suppressing social demands and grinding economic exploitation. However, the traditional *hali* system has suffered a set back due to developmental activities of the State. Now-a-days a *hali* gets a fixed sum of money ranging from Rs. 700 to 2000 at the time of contract. The contract is made for an annual cycle. A *hali* may take money during the tenure, whenever the need arises instead of taking it in the beginning. A *hali* is provided with a set of clothes and porridge to eat during his term. But money is cut from his earnings for the same. Usually a *hali* ends up getting less money and at times no money at all.

In this system, Sahariya labour is exploited by land owning castes. Though they are hired for agricultural labour but they are forced to do pastoral duties, as well as, other domestic chores. Even after working so hard they do not receive their due payments. As a result in some cases the *hali* run away breaking their contract and have to abandon their Saharana for fear of being caught. When a *hali* disappears without finishing his contract, the landlord takes away his animals, if he has any, and other household goods. In case the absconder *hali* is caught, he receives a thorough beating and is brought back to work again or asked to return money with interest.

Sahariyas also work as forest labourers for coal and *katha* (catechu) extraction. *Katha* (catechu) extraction coupes are organized by the Forest Development in the month of March. A number of families shift to forest for a stay of six to eight weeks. They stay in the forest in the temporary shelters. Previously, *katha* extraction was organized by Bohra contractors who were cutting forest indiscriminately and unscientifically on the one hand and exploiting Sahariya labour on the other hand. Bohra contractors paid them *ek pyalidana* (*pyali* full of grain = 0.25 gm) in return of 1 *topla* full of *katha* (7 gm) until the forest department took over. The present rate of *katha* ranges approximately from Rs. 70 to 100 per kg. Those who join charcoal and *katha* coupe in the interior forests leave behind someone to take care of the crop, if they have land and are cultivating themselves. At present the State Trading Corporation of Forest Department is organising operation of fuel, bamboo and timber wood collection, charcoal making, *katha* extraction and collection of *tendu* leaves and Sahariyas are employed as labourers on daily wages. The number of timber and charcoal coupes is much larger, spread over the districts of Udaipur, Banswara and Chittorgarh, attracting many tribals, including Sahariya. In these coupe: fuel wood is collected as such; charcoal is prepared and timber wood is collected.

Once agricultural and forest season is over, Sahariya opt for any type of casual labour work which is available in the vicinity. They work as labourers at flour mills, they drive wheel carts, which carry grass bundles from forest to railway station, they work as road labourers, construction workers or as domestic help. The local labour market in Kishanganj and Shahbad tehsils is of moderate size, providing primary employment to the approximately one fourth households and secondary employment to another one fourth. The majority of Sahariyas are employed as casual rather than as permanent or attached labourers. The casual labourers are employed as either daily or contract employment. Under the daily wage system labourers are offered a specified wage for a fixed period of time. Under the contract system, they are offered a specified lump sum payment for performing a specific task. Within these broad frameworks, labourers are recruited and paid under different arrangement. The key variables are either they are recruited individually or in-group or are paid in cash or kind.

Daily wage labourers are recruited individually. There is a common understanding of the wage rate in the area and as well as how many hours is meant "daily" or day's work at any particular time in a year, even though wages vary by task and crop both across and within season.

Under the contract system, labourers are generally recruited as a team (*toli*). Each *toli* designates a leader, from among its members, who is the contact person for employers who scouts for labour, negotiates the contract and collect and distribute payments. Most labourers prefer the contract system as they can generally negotiate higher wages for the same operation than on the daily wage basis. Often the contract system works to the advantage of employer who avoids paying the minimum wage.

Share-Cropping: Sahariya, both landed and landless, try to overcome economic constraints relating to their specific asset-base by entering into tenancy. Although the market for buying and selling cultivable land is rather inactive in Sahariya area, the tenancy market is active and consists of share tenancy. The share cropping tenancy in this region appears to be flexible institution. Share tenancy allows households to make better use of their specific asset base across the different agricultural seasons. For example, Sahariya household which own land but have no pumps may choose to cultivate their land in monsoon season, share-crop out their land in winter and migrate to return in time for preparing their land for the next monsoon season. Similarly, landless households can opt to sharecrop in land in winter or summer if they own pump sets, or in monsoon if they own bullocks.

A variety of sharecropping patterns are prevalent in the region. Variation in these patterns has more to do with how input costs are shared than with how output or crops are shared. The most common type of contract is *adhera*, which entitles each party to half the crop. Under it, the land owner and tenant pool assets and share inputs costs in what is perceived by both parties to be roughly equal proportion.

The *batai* is another form of tenancy where Sahariyas hire land for cultivation. Depending on the number of assets provided by the owner, the *batai* percentage is arranged. If the owners provide irrigation, manure, seeds, plough and bullocks, the tenant get one fourth of the produce. If the bullock and manure belong to the tenant, then he may get fifty per cent of the total crop. In case the tenant and owner share the seeds, manure, bullock equally, then the tenant may receive two-thirds of the crop-production. There are other variations under this basic contract where owner provides land and irrigation; tenant provides all inputs and labour; owner provides land and share irrigation and input costs, tenant provides labour and shares irrigation and major costs.

As already mentioned, only a few Sahariya cultivate their own land, rest work as tenants or labourers in the fields of locally dominant castes. Even those who own land, do not prefer to cultivate themselves, because they lack managerial skills and technical know-how. Lack of irrigation, improved agricultural implements and machinery, improved seeds etc. does nct make agriculture a profitable proposition for Sahariya. Sahariya follows an other form of tenancy–*munapha* where they rent out land to other castes who bear the cost of production and share the crop accordingly. It entitles the tenant to a two-thirds share and the owner to one-third. Under this contract, Sahariya generally provide only land and the tenant provides inputs irrigation and labour. Generally, the quality of Sahariya's land is poor, Sahariya get only three fourth of the crop. In some instances Sahariya provide land and a pump set, the tenant provides the diesel oil, inputs and labour, the owner receives one third of the crop. Pump sets, bullocks and labour, not just land, are important factors in the tenancy contracts.

Not many Sahariya engage in more than occupation. Most Sahariya households have to synchronise the constraints of several occupations. Households which have access to non-irrigated land (either as owners or tenants) often migrate for wage employment during winter, when cultivation requires irrigation. Many households attempt to synchronize migrant wage labour with local wage labour, migrating during periods of low local demand for labour. Sahariya mixes different occupations in such a way that these do not overlap but complement one another. Depending on the relative flexibility of their livelihood system, individual household adjusts by seeking employment whenever it becomes available and necessary, combine cultivation/gathering. Labour households seek local employment whenever it becomes available, combine cultivation or other activities in slack seasons, and migrate if necessary.

Women play an important role in their household economy. They work in most operations of all sectors of the local economy and for longer hours each day than men, in addition to the domestic and reproductive activities associated with household maintenance and gathering, collecting of free goods, especially fuel, fodder and water. Women build most of the storage containers, notably the large clay pots (*kothi*) for land owning classes for which they are paid in cash/kind. Sahariya women operate effectively in most economic and social institutions, participating in both local (forest as well as agriculture) and migrant labour activities.

The present position and conditions of the Sahariyas is not an accidental affair. It has evolved because of the operation of several forces in the past. However reconstruction of tribal history has often been a difficult task, because they lack written records of their activities. Unequal distribution of land and instruments of production, unequal distribution of income and the rate of exploitation of labour characterizes the difference between tribal and non-tribal communities that inhabit these villages. These iniquities are associated with the forces of money lending on the one hand, and political power, education, etc. on the other hand. The dominant castes have better access to the co-operative and bank credit and subsidies, while the Sahariyas tend to rely on non-institutional credit nexus.

In an agrarian economy where land distribution is unequal, the relation between the land owning and landless provide a more or less complete configuration of the agrarian structure. The land owner with large holdings will need to employ outside labour to cultivate his fields. Conversely among the landless and smaller landowners, the propensity to sell labour will be greater. There can be a number of permutations and combinations in terms of employment of the outside labour.

Owners of the same land size may cultivate their fields differently, some may use family labour, while some others hired in labour. The different behaviour of different households depends on a number of factors like composition of the households, their social status, cultural restrictions, ideology of work, scope for employment and wage structure in wider arena, monsoon and market value of agricultural product etc. At the same time, the smaller farmer or landless may sell their labour *in toto* in the local region, only under conditions of coercion within the immediate agrarian system and/or a near total absence of other avenues of living. It may be stated here that land size and labour relation may only broadly relate to each other, and the rate of exploitation of labour has autonomy of its own.

Under the state government scheme, Sahariya have been granted land on *patta*, which they are not allowed to sell. The quality of land being poor and lack of the irrigation facilities has resulted in abandoning fields by some Sahariya. Those who are able to acquire irrigation facilities or during monsoon, cultivate their land. The landless Sahariya and the ones whose land is rocky generally resort to working as agricultural labourers.

Through various developmental schemes, Sahariya are being continuously rehabilitated and given cultivable land, bringing them into the mainstream of society and to lessen their dependence on (i) forest produce, as forests are being increasingly threatened; and (ii) labour as they have been found as leaving enmasse to various tehsils of Baran and Kota districts.

There is encroachment of Sahariya land by outsiders or locally dominant caste. Because of their low political awareness, the Sahariya are exploited by others. Alienation of tribal land by non-tribal merchants and moneylenders is serious in this region which had a hierarchy of tribute collectors and were brought under *Zamindari* system before the early 19th century. Due to difficulty in collecting information on original clearers of land as well as neglect of inter-village migration and that of expansion of cultivable land, it is not possible to know the exact position. None the less intensity of alienation was a fact. Report on Sahariya Development Plan (1979) mention that among Sahariya 62-86 per cent are under an average debt of Rs. 998. As Sahariya remain under debt they mortgage their land or give on some kind of tenancy. Apart from having unproductive land with low water availability, the Sahariya also lack managerial skills and technical know-how. They do not own agricultural machinery, improved seeds, etc. If they cultivate their fields the returns are uneconomical. In addition to unprofitable agriculture, Sahariya also regularly experience drought and famine-related scarcity. Sahariya's primary concern is to prevent impoverishment from this type of scarcity. Organization, management and planning of Sahariya economy and coping strategies are always towards the goal of keeping alive and to stay out of debt. It depends on the nature and extent of scarcity, the membership and the sharing networks of individual household units in particular area and the extent to which community members had been affected by scarcity in last years. Each drought and related conditions make the Sahariya less able to cope with the following drought. Jodha (1975) observed, that in Rajasthan, drought hit farmer is more prone to functioning under adverse terms of trade with high purchase prices, low sale prices and high replacement prices. And a farmer has to protect the productive capacity of his resource base to keep out of the downword process of pauperisation, which otherwise would lead to irreversible loss of assets especially of livestock and land. Sahariya who have been facing such hardships for a long time are a deprived lot and their deprivation is not just a matter of poverty or lack of income, consumables and wealth but also one of vulnerability and exposure to vagaries of the nature and exploitation by neighbours and outsiders. It seems that Sahariya have been caught in "deprivation trap" and its five interrelated clusters of disadvantages, i.e. physical weakness, isolation, poverty, vulnerability and powerlessness (Chambers *et al.,* 1987: 10). According to Chambers, the cluster of disadvantage lead to social, spiritual and material deprivation.

The Sahariya inhabit the area of the district which may be included in the "poverty square" of India, measured according to four indicators – infant mortality, female literacy, number below poverty line and per capita net domestic product and is centered mainly in the states of Uttar Pradesh, Bihar, Orissa and Madhya Pradesh (Chambers *et al.,* 1987: 26). The literacy rate among Sahariya is 8.2, which is lower than literacy rate of Rajasthan (38.55) and India (52.21). The female literacy rate among Sahariya is still lower (4.2) as compared to Rajasthan's average of 20.44 and India female literacy rate of 39.29. Infant mortality rate among Sahariya of study area is 131.58

(Neonatal rate is 78.95 and post neonatal rate is 52.63) which is very high as compared to 85.0 in Rajasthan and 70.0 (1999) in India. Sahariya's economy mainly rests on gathering and collection of food, fodder and fuel wood from the uncultivated tracts and forest areas by some members of the household, while others go for wage labour to surrounding areas. The members who stay in the village make items like baskets, ropes, etc., which are sold in the market along with forest produce. The annual mean income among Sahariya is Rs. 13416.69 per household, with an average size of household as 5.2.

Diet survey carried out among Sahariya tribal children indicate that a large majority of children suffer from under-nutrition and specific syndromes. It is recognised that as a result of extreme poverty, intake of various essential constituents of food proteins, fats, carbohydrates, iron and vitamin are inadequate and are far below the nutritional standards or Recommended Dietary Allowances (RDA). The calorie intake or energy levels are also below the recommended level. Survey data indicates prevalence of deficiency of vitamins, calcium and iron. Vitamin B or Riboflavin deficiency is a major nutritional problem, due to inadequate intake of green leafy vegetables, fruits and milk. Some of the clinical manifestation of vitamin B deficiency among Sahariya in the study area are angular stomatitis (47%) and glossitis (soreness of tongue). Vitamin A deficiency diseases encountered are bitots spot (17.6%) and conjunctival xerasis (4.2%), spongy gums (28%) and bleeding gums (42%).

As already mentioned, only a few Sahariya cultivate their own fields, rest work as tenants or agricultural labourers in the fields of the locally dominant castes. Even those who own land, do not prefer to cultivate themselves. On the other hand if they rent out their land to others for cultivation on a profit sharing basis *manupha/pati* where the cost of the agricultural operation is the onus of the other person, they not only earn money but are free to utilize their own labour elsewhere. Labour earnings are highly priced to Sahariya since most of the family members (including children aged nine-ten years and above) individually participate in such activities. For Sahariyas, such (additional) yearly pursuits are considerably valued.

Initially only few landowning Sahariya families from each village were following the pattern of dual earning, but soon others followed the suit, after calculating the cost-benefit of the same. And since they are used to hardships, they do not really mind the constraints they face at the place of work, provided there is economic gain.

At times, someone from the family stays back and cultivates the fields while other go out for labour. Absence of ready cash and immediate economic gains promote labour work among Sahariyas. As this is being realised by neighbouring castes who encourage them to give their land on *manupha/pati*. For these locally dominant castes these land holdings are not uneconomical as they have resources, technology and manpower to make it operational. It was seen that sometimes Sahariyas work on their own land as labourers, thus earning as landlords as well as labourers. Besides, for many villagers, (other than S.Cs) casual labour is more often than not an extreme step and are not well accepted socially unless there is a dire need for money. The *Adam Jati Sewak Sangh* and other development agencies organised Sahariyas and other tribals into Forest Produce Co-operative Societies with the right of seeking contracts at concessional rates without bidding, and the amount of royalty was fixed by the forest in consultation with Co-operative Department. There are five co-operative societies working in this area since 1960. Sahariya are not happy with the working of co-operative societies as they are still not getting big money and they feel that the place of contractor has been taken by someone else.

For agricultural development tube wells, pump sets, hand pump installation subsidies through LAMPS (Large Agricultural Multipurpose Co-operative Societies), subsidy for purchase of agricultural implements at the rate of 50 per cent rent has been provided by agricultural department and the same has provided additional subsidy at the rate of 25 per cent and the rest 25 per cent of the cost has to be borne by Sahariya themselves.

There is an ongoing scheme of revolving fund for providing loans to Sahariyas for agricultural improvements. Sahariyas are so poor that they cannot become members of LAMPS or any other co-operative society, which deprive them of availing facilities provided by the co-operatives. Therefore a scheme of providing assistance of rupees one hundred to Sahariya for purchase of ten shares of rupees ten has been started in 1994-95.

In 1986-87 a scheme was introduced to install a group diesel pump set as it is not possible for an individual family to install costly pumpsets, a group of minimum five families, who do not have proper means of drawing water from wells, rivers or *nallahs*, are supplied with diesel pumpsets free of cost – provided there land is situated at one place or adjoining areas.

Another scheme of installing community agriculture tube wells for a group of 5-10 Sahariya cultivators having atleast five hectares of land adjoiningly is also being introduced for increasing agriculture production. Sahariya are also being provided with subsidy for purchase of plant protection equipments. Subsidy at the rate of 75 per cent is provided by the Agriculture Department under regular state plan but Sahariya are not able to bear even the rest of the cost. So the Sahariya Development Project is providing additional subsidy at the rate of 20 per cent and the rest 5 per cent of the cost has to be borne by Sahariya cultivators themselves.

However, despite the abundance of the plans for the overall development of Sahariyas, the pace of development appears to be rather slow, and not many have benefited from the elaborate schemes. These paucities mainly seem to be the result of lack of awareness, enterprise amongst Sahariyas, ever-dependence on aid, lack of post benefit follow-ups by the donor organizations, including government agencies. In addition, the post benefit operative costs as well as remaining amount of money to be invested in case of schemes, are considered unaffordable to Sahariyas, as their economic condition has not improved much.

It may also be mentioned that, despite various assistance to cultivators, as well as allocation of land (5-15 bighas) to Sahariyas, it was noticed that the Sahariyas migrate en masse to other part of the Baran district and adjoining districts to participate mainly in the labour force (mainly agricultural) during sowing and harvesting. Before migration they lease out their land to other cultivators, mainly non-Sahariyas and receives cash in advance. For the Sahariyas, whose method of cultivation is still traditional, and who are yet unable to reap benefits from various schemes meant for them, this ready cash is an additional income, apart from the one they receive through labour. They only see short term profits (according to their point of view, since they are rather poor) and fail to see the long-term ones, if they cultivate their own land and avail of various schemes after putting in certain investments.

It has however also been noticed that even after availing certain benefits from the Sahariya Development Schemes, the material have not been put to their proper use or left unused completely. In the village Shubhghara and Khushalpura, two model villages built by the government authorities, it was observed that PVC pipe and diesel pump sets are lying idle. On inquiry it was found that either the remaining length of the PVC pipe the cost of which is to be borne by the Sahariya are yet to be acquired or diesel to run the pump sets are unaffordable as it not available free of cost, or the wells from where the water is to be drawn are dry, due to drought like situation in the area.

It was observed in the village Hirapura that according to officials the whole village has been electrified, but the Saharana of the village was without electricity despite the presence of electricity poles. It was pointed out that the recurring cost of electricity surcharge as well as bulbs etc are unaffordable by the Sahariyas, although the village may will have been electrified under the scheme for them.

There is lack of knowledge and apathy among Sahariyas regarding the developmental schemes. In fact, many are even unaware that such elaborate plans exist. And, at times, only the local leaders, sarpanchs, ward punchs (Tribal) may reap benefits of the schemes, as they are relatively more aware and are in touch with the authorities. The ward punch of Saharana Matia Khera of village Mahespura has grown vegetables profitably after acquiring subsidised seeds from the Agricultural Department and drawing water from the well with the help of diesel pump set, PVC pipes etc.

It has also been alleged the non-tribals have also received benefits from the Sahariya Development projects, after taking thumbprints of the Sahariyas. Since, they are illiterate, they are not able to challenge the same, or even do not know about such misuse.

It can be stated that despite all efforts by government agencies for raising economic standards of the Sahariyas the situation remains the same. The Sahariyas are caught in a vicious circle. The government with aid and subsidies has not been able to achieve much; the co-operative societies have failed even to accomplish much, and the missionaries do not operate in this area. The starting of industries is not possible for entrepreneurs do not exist in this area. The Sahariya with their ignorance and poverty are caught in a deprivation trap.

Government should undertake a comprehensive industrial and agricultural survey of the area; and set up some big industries in public sector. Raw material can be secured from the adjoining hills and forests and the power required can be secured from Kota district. There is a feasibility of starting of a newspaper factory, a large sawmill, and a state agricultural farm where the Sahariya can take up regular jobs.

REFERENCES

Appadurai, Arnun. 1984. "How Moral is South Asia Economy? A Review Article," *Journal of Asian Studies,* 43 (3)

Breman, J. 1985. *Of Peasants, Migrants and Paupers; Rural Labour, Circulation and Capitalist Production in West India.* Delhi: Oxford University Press,

Chambers, R. and R. Longhurst. 1986. "Trees Seasons and the Poor," *IDS Bulletin,* 17 (3)

Chambers, R., N.C. Saxena and T. Shah. 1987. *To the Hands of the Poor: Water and Trees.* London: Intermediate Technology Publication.

Doshi, S. L. and N. N. Vyas. 1992. *The Sahariya in Tribal Rajasthan: Sunshine on the Aravali.* Udaipur: Himanshu Publications.

Chatak, N. K. 1998. "Sahariya," in K.S. Singh (ed.), *People of India: Rajasthan.* Mumbai: Popular Prakashan Pvt. Ltd.

Gupta, G. S. 1965. *Sanwara: Village Survey Monograph.* Census of India 1961. Vol. XIV, Part VI A.

Hardiman, David. 1985. *The Coming of the Devi: Adivasi Assertion in Western India.* Delhi: Oxford University Press.

Jodha, N.S. 1975. "Famine and Famine Policies: Some Empirical Evidence," *Economic and Political Weekly*, X (41).

——— 1988. "Poverty Debate in India: A Minority View," *Economic and Political Weekly*, XXIII (45, 46, 47).

Mann, R. S. and K. Mann. 1989. *The Life and Culture of Sahariya in Tribal Culture and Change.* Delhi: Mittal Publications.

Sahariya Development Plan 1979.

Stavenhagen, Rodolfo. 1975. *Social Change in Agrarian Societies.* New York: Anchor Press.

Tod, James. 1978. *Annals and Antiquities of Rajasthan.* Delhi: M. N. Publishers.

FIFTEEN

KAMARA WOMEN OF CENTRAL INDIA: An Analysis of Factors Affecting Fertility

S.S. GURU, BHARATI PANDA, MANTO PRADHAN and KANCHAN PADHI

Population explosion has become a major problem, especially in the third world countries where economic development is, only partially accomplished, while the population has been rapidly increasing, outstripping the supply of food, jobs, housing, health-care and other facilities. In this context, understanding of the various factors responsible for high rate of population growth are of great significance. It is common knowledge that in India the population growth is mainly due to decline in the mortality rate. However, the future growth of India's population shall largely be determined by the fertility/reproductive trends and not by the mortality trends. Therefore, the demographers these days emphasise the study of fertility.

Fertility is the actual reproductive performance, whether applied to an individual or a group (UN Multilingual Demographic Dictionary, 1958). Reproductive behaviour varies from region to region and from society to society. A number of biological as well as socio-cultural variables, viz. age at menarche, age at marriage, age at first live birth, education, income, family structure, value attached to children, etc. affect the reproductive performance/ life of an individual or a community.

The present paper seeks to highlight certain factors influencing the differential reproductive performance of the Kamar women of central tribal belt of India. The main objective is to examine the influence of certain important variables on the reproductive performance of Kamar women and to test a few hypotheses.

The Kamars, a community of nearly 13,500 persons, is a circumscribed tribe living in the fastnesses of hills and forests of South-eastern part of Raipur district of Madhya Pradesh. The area which forms the Kamar habitat is situated in two tahsils-Bindranwagarh and Dhamtari. Considered from the standpoint of development blocks and the sub-plan project, the Kamar habitat comes under the ITDP, Gariaband, comprising the blocks of Chhura, Gariaband, Mainpur and Nagri, the former three lying in Bindranwagarh tahsil and the latter one in Dhamtari tahsil. All the four blocks are contiguous and constitute a compact area. The Kamars are believed to be the autochthonous of the area. Perhaps the earliest written reference to the Kamars in modern times is available in the note by John Ball in his jungle Life in India. J.F. Hewitt (Report on the Land Revenue Settlement, 1869) states "The Kamars utterly refuse to cultivate and generally live in the remote forest habitats supporting themselves largely on forest collections and small games." Kamar's mode of life underwent a drastic change over which they had practically no control. Because of motorized transport their monopoly of transporting timbers via rivers ended. Also, an absolute ban was imposed on the age-old *dahya* and *beora* cultivation with the result that production of food grains became almost zero. Wild animals became scarce and the jungle became less and less bountiful in the supply of roots and tubers. Since no alternative land was allotted to them, bamboo work and labour for wages are the sustaining factors of the Kamar economy at present.

Data for the present study come from randomly selected 120 ever-married Kamar women living in different villages of Gariaband block during a month-long field work with the help of a pre-tested interview schedule.

Results and Discussion

Age at Menarche

Menarche is an important physiological event in the life of every female. The onset of menarche among the respondents is seen to vary from 11 to 16 years of age. It is revealed that majority of the respondents had their first menstruation between 12 and 13 years of age. After that there is a gradual decrease in the number of women attaining puberty with increase in age. The mean age at menarche is calculated to be 13.21 years with standard deviation 1.28 (Table 15.1).

Table 15.1: Age at menarche of Kamar women

Age at Menarche in years	Frequency	Per cent
11	06	05.00
12	37	30.83
13	31	25.83
14	23	19.17
15	18	15.00
16	05	04.17
Total	120	100.00

Mean±S.E. 13.21±0.12
S.D.±S.E. 1.28±0.08

Age at Marriage

Age at marriage of girls assumes greater significance as a biological-cum-socio-cultural determinant of fertility. Biologically age at marriage is related to fecundity and sociologically, the age at marriage is used to set a social time table for starting, spacing and stopping child bearing (Pillai, 1985). Studies all over the world reveal an inverse relationship between age at marriage and the length of child bearing span and the level of marital fertility.

Nearly one-third of the Kamar mothers had their marriage between 13 and 15 years of age. It is noticed that 16-18 age range of marriage is most common among the Kamars while one-fifth of them had married as per the legally approved age at marriage (Table 15.2).

Table 15.2: Age at marriage of Kamar women

Age at Menarche in years	No. of women	Per cent
13-15	39	32.50
16-18	57	47.50
19-21	24	20.00
Total	120	100.00

Study of association between age at marriage of women and the number of children born to them reveals an inverse relationship. Women who had married within 15 years of age experienced the highest incidence of childbirth followed by those attributable to the 16-18 years age range. A sharp decline in the number of childbirth is noticed among the women who were married off at the age between 19-21 years. Thus there is a steady reduction in the number of childbirth with increasing order of age at marriage. The differences noticed in the number of childbirth corresponding to different levels of age at marriage of women are found to be statistically significant (Table 15.3). The data suggest that raising the age at marriage would ensure low fertility.

Table 15.3: Age at marriage and number of children

Age at marriage in years	No. of Children			
	10-2	3-5	6+	Total
13-15	13-15	2 (5.13)	6 (15.38)	39 (100.00)
16-18	14 (24.56)	37 (64.91)	06 (10.53)	57 (100.00)
19-21	19 (79.16)	4 (16.67)	1 (4.17)	24 (100.00)
Total	35	47	38	120

Note: Parenthetical figures denote percentage $X^2 = 28.5721$ 1%

Age at First Live Birth

Every society attaches considerable importance to the birth of the first child of a lady. The age at first live birth of a woman has a great significance in fertility since it indicates her entire reproductive span. Majority of the respondents experienced their first live birth between 15-17 years of age followed by 30 per cent who had their first live birth between 18-20 years of age. The number of respondents who had their first live birth between 21-23 years of age account for 14.17 per cent (Table 15.4). It is further noticed that more number of children were born to a higher proportion of respondents who had their first live birth between 15-17 years of age. With increase in the age at first live birth the number of respondents having more number of children decreases. An overwhelming proportion of respondents, whose age at first live birth ranges between 21-23 years, had less number of children. The differences thus observed are significant (Table 15.5).

Table 15.4: Age at first live birth of Kamar women

Age at first live birth	No. of women	Per cent
15-17	67	55.83
18-20	36	30.00
21-23	17	14.17
Total	120	100.00

Table 15.5: Age at first live birth and number of children

Age at first live birth	No. of Children			
	1-2	3-5	6+	Total
15-17	9 (13.43)	26 (38.81)	32 (47.76)	67 (100.00)
18-20	14 (38.89)	17 (47.22)	5 (13.89)	36 (100.00)
21-23	12 (70.59)	4 (23.53)	1 (5.88)	17 (100.00)
Total	35	47	38	120

Note: Parenthetical figures denote percentage $X^2 = 31.2220$ 1 per cent.

Education of Women

Education in general, and female education in particular, works in various ways to influence woman's (mother's) attitudes and abilities to discharge the role of a health agent in the family and also in the acceptance of family planning (welfare) methods, thereby leading to low fertility. The position (status) of a woman in the society depends largely on her educational attainments, which ensure a greater social network, which may be helpful in the postponement of marriage and spacing of children. An educated woman regards the utilisation of modern health care facilities not is a boon but as a right (Caldwell, 1979). Education also helps a woman to break with tradition, which is a powerful cultural constraint among the tribals.

Table 15.6: Educational status of Kamar women

Level of education	No. of women	Per cent
Illiterate	53	44.17
U.P	31	25.83
M.E.	24	20.00
High School	12	10.00
Total	120	100.00

Table 15.7: Level of education and number of children

Level of education	No. of Children			
	1-2	3-5	6+	Total
Illiterate	5 (16.13)	17 (32.08)	31 (58.49)	53 (100.00)
U.P	7 (22.58)	18 (58.07)	6 (19.35)	31 (100.00)
M.E.	14 (53.33)	9 (37.50)	1 (4.17)	24 (100.00)
High School	9 (75.00)	3 (25.00)	— —	12 (100.00)
Total	35	47	38	120

Note: Parenthetical figures denote percentage.

The female illiteracy is at a very high level among the Kamars. Respondents who had five or less years of schooling account for 25.83 per cent. On the other hand only one-fifth of them were educated up to M.E. standard.

Respondents having high school education constitute only 10 per cent (Table 15.6). It is further noticed that illiterate respondents experienced higher of childbirth, whereas less number of children were born to women having higher standard of education. The differences observed in the incidence of childbirth for differential level of women's education are statistically highly significant indicating an inverse relationship between women's education and fertility (Table 15.7).

Structure of Family

The urge for sex and procreation and the strong desire to perpetuate the cultural traditions have every where provided the justification for the existence of the family system. "The family system is universally conditioned by the local cultural tradition" (Majumdar and Madan, 1980). Family among the Kamars is monogamous. Structurally some are nuclear and others composite. Nuclear family set-up is more common among the Kamars (56.67%) while 43.33 per cent of them live in composite families (Table 15.8).

Table 15.8: Structure of family

Structure of family	Frequency	Per cent
Nuclear	68	56.67
Composite	52	43.33
Total	120	100.00

The resistance to social change is more in a composite family than that of a nuclear family set-up where the spouses enjoy greater freedom in family decision making. It is also noticed that fertility is high in a composite family where the presence of many members enhances the scope of child rearing (Davis, 1955). The observed differences in the number of child birth corresponding to family structure is statistically significant thereby indicating that composite family system encourages high fertility (Table 15.9). The tendency to perpetuate the traditional way of life may be responsible for the high fertility. It was also reported by the health workers of the study area that it is easier on their part to motivate the couples living in nuclear families to adopt the family planning (welfare) methods.

Table 15.9: Structure of family and number of children

Structure of family	No. of Children			
	1-2	3-5	6+	Total
Nuclear	27 (39.70)	28 (41.18)	13 (19.12)	68 (100.00)
Composite	8 (15.34)	19 (36.54)	25 (48.08)	52 (100.00)
Total	35	47	38	120

Note: Parenthetical figures denote percentage X^2 = 13.9455 1 per cent.

Conclusion

We observed that the composite family structure, lack of education, marriage at an early age as well as the reluctance to accept family planning (welfare) methods jointly contribute to the high fertility among the respondents in the study area. We suggest that suitable steps should be taken to educate the women folk so as to motivate them to adopt family welfare methods. Further care should be taken to ensure the regular visit of the health workers to these areas for improving the situation.

Though the younger couples are largely amenable to adopt family welfare measures and protect their reproductive health, they are being discouraged by elderly members to do so in composite families. In order to make the health education more effective and functional the elder population particularly the women in the post reproductive age group need to be drawn in to the family welfare awareness building programme.

REFERENCES

Caldwell, J.C. 1979. "Education as Factor in Mortality Decline: An Examination of Nigenian Data," *Population Studies*, 33 (3): 45.

Hewitt, J.F.K. 1869. Report on the Land Revenue Settlement of the Raipore District, Chattisgarh Division.

John, Ball. 1916. *Jungle Life in India: the Journey and Journals of an Indian Geolcgist*. London: Thomas Dela Rue and Co.

Davis, Kingsley. 1955. "Institutional Patterns Favouring High Fertility in Underdeveloped Areas." *Eugenics Quarterly*, 2 (1): 62.

Majumdar, D.N. and T.N. Madan. 1980. *An Introduction to Social Anthropology*. Bombay: Asia Publishing House.

Pillai, V.K. 1985. "Predicating Age at First Marriage: A Review of Recent Models," *The Journal of Family Welfare*, 32 (1): 15.

United Nations. 1958. *Multilingual Demographic Dictionary*. New York.

SIXTEEN

SOCIO-CULTURAL AND ENVIRONMENTAL FACTORS OF HEALTH AMONG SAHARIA: A Primitive Tribe of Rajasthan

PRAMOD MISHRA and A.K. KAPOOR

Introduction

World Health Organisation (WHO) defined health as "a state of complete physical, mental and social well-being, and not merely the absence of disease and infirmity." This statement is extensively quoted, although WHO has developed its view considerably since then. This historic definition has also been heavily criticized, mainly on two grounds. One is that it is totally unrealistic and idealistic (how often does anyone truly feel in a state of complete well-being?). The other criticism is that it implies a static position, whereas life and living are anything but static. The idea that health means having the ability to adapt continually to constantly changing demands, expectations and stimuli can be seen to be separable.

Another criticism of the WHO definition is that it appears to assume that someone, somewhere, has the ability and right to define a state of health, whereas we have seen that people define their own state of health in a myriad of different ways. On the other hand, the definition can be defended on the grounds that it embraces the notion of positive health and acknowledges the central place of social and mental well-being.

There are different dimensions in the concept of health. These may be classified as follows:

Physical Health: This is, perhaps, the most obvious dimension of health, and is concerned with them mechanistic functioning of the body.

Mental Health: It means the ability to think clearly and coherently.

Emotional Health: This means the ability to recognize emotions such as fear, joy, grief and anger and to express such emotions appropriately. Optional or "affective" health also means coping with stress, tension, depression and anxiety.

Social Health: It means the ability to make and maintain relationships with other people.

Spiritual Health: This, for some people, is connected with religious beliefs and practices for other people. It is to do with personal creeds, principles of behaviour and ways of achieving peace of mind and being at peace with one self.

Societal Health: So far, we have considered at the level of the individual, but a person's health is inextricably related to everything surrounding that person. It is impossible to be healthy in a sick society, which does not provide the resources for basic physical and emotional needs.

The Holistic View: All aspects of health are interrelated and interdependent and thus we have to subscribe to the holistic view of health, which is of greater value.

The environment has a direct impact on the physical, mental and social well-being of those living in it. The environmental factors range from housing, water supply, psycho-social stress and family structure through social and economic support systems, to the organization of health and social welfare services in the community. In its modern concept, environment, includes not only the water, air and soil that form our environment but also the social and economic conditions under which people live. The key to man's health lies largely in its environment. Health and culture are very much connected with ecology. The traditional health care system and treatment are based on their deep observation and understanding of nature and environment.

Tribal groups of India inhabit widely varying ecological and geo-climatic conditions in different concentration throughout the country and are distinct biological categories with characteristic cultural and socio-economic background (Basu, 1986). The health of these tribal population groups is as such a function of the interaction between socio-cultural and socio-biological practices, the genetic attributes and the environmental conditions. The widely varying prevalent health practices, use of indigenous herbal drugs, taboos and superstitions are also responsible for determining the health behaviour and health status of the tribal groups.

Through the ages, the tribal groups have retained their individual social and cultural identity by rigorous practicing of different social customs. It is an established fact that socio-economic factors, socio-cultural variants like nutritional practices (food habits) inter-related with soci-biological norms such as mating-pattern, preferential marital alliances, age of marriage have tremendous impact on the fertility and mortality pattern. The impact of environment and genetic factors are further additive factors, which complicate the situation. Nevertheless, it is well understood that the tribal groups perpetuate the misconceptions, beliefs and taboos that emanate from their socio-religious system. Those also have an additive effect on fertility, mortality and morbidity.

From an overview of the distribution pattern of tribal groups, it becomes evidently clear that they inhabit hostile terrains. Invariably these areas are highly endemic zones for malarias and various infectious diseases. Non availability of safe drinking water, proper sanitation and hygiene, coupled with tratitional health practices, create conditions for higher mortality and morbidity rates.

In the present paper an attempt has been made to study the socio-cultural and environmental factors of health among Saharia which is a primitive tribe of Rajasthan.

The Saharias of Rajasthan

The Saharias are the only Primitve Tribal Group of Rajasthan and inhabit in the Shahabad and Kishanganj Tehsils of Baran District. According to 1991 census, the total population of Saharias in Baran District is 47,822. Saharia is an endogamous tribe divided into a number of clans; each clan is named after the ancestor or a place to which they originally belong.

Distribution

The Saharias of Rajasthan are concentrated in two tehsils of Shahbad and Kishanganj which also coincide with panchayat samitis. The Shahabad Tehsil can be divided into two distinct divisions: (1) Upreti or upland and (2) Taleti or lowland. The Upreti constitutes Kishangnj Tehsil and the western part of Shahabad Tehsil. The remaining part of Shahabad Tehsil comes under the classification of Taleti.

Hamlet Pattern

Saharias do not have disperse pattern of living as found among the Bhils of Southern Rajasthan. They do not have separate and scattered hamlets. However, the hamlets are slightly away from the main villages. Each village has a cluster of Saharia families in a separate hamlet known as "Saharana." In the Saharana no other caste people live. In the centre of each Saharana they construct "umbrella type" shelter house which is called panchayat bungalow where all Saharias sit together to discuss, gossip and settle their disputes. Shoes are not allowed in the panchayat bungalow. Women are also forbidden from entering the hall. It is believed that as married women come from other villages, secrecy cannot be expected from them.

Marriage

Saharias is an endogamous tribe but each clan in it is exogamous. They believe in totem and taboos and observe them during various rituals. Marriage alliance between the mates of same *gotra* is prohibited by virtue of their affiliation to a common totem. Widow marriage or remarriage called *nata* is permissible among the Saharias.

The family of Saharias is a nuclear family with the youngest son staying with the parents and the elder sons moving out with their families of procreation into separate homes.

Traditional Health Care System

The tribals in India believe that most of the diseases, especially epidemics, are caused by evil spirits. They also believe that any breach of taboo will anger the clan god and the culprit will be punished. In fact, the tribals associate the disease to sorcery, breach of taboo, object intrusion, spirit-intrusion and soul loss (Majumdar, 1958). To protect from the wrath of supernatural, the tribals worship benevolent and protective deities and spirits. In case of diseases supposed to have been caused by evil eye, sorcery or witchcraft, they seek the help of the traditional magician-cum-witch doctor in the community.

In the tribal society, the social and cultural activities revolve around gods and spirits. They have specific gods for each and every activity of life. Likewise, they have gods for health, disease and calamities. They worship these deities to protect them from evil spirits, diseases and epidemics. For example, the Saharias worship Tejaji, a deity related to snakes. Tejaji protect them from snakes and save their life in forests.

Like other tribes in India, the Saharias have also erected structures, though not as elaborate, conspicuous and posing as found among the non-tribal rural communities to house the images of various kinds of supernatural beings. Both at the individual as well as at the community level, the Saharias realise the responsibility of a safe placement of such images. Represented through various symbols and figures of various forms and material, they are kept at one or different places in and around the tribal settlements or in the near proximity of natural surroundings. Such religious places remain open to one and all irrespective of age, sex, etc. Man's interaction with such supernatural does not merely end in the preservation of symbols and images. Rather, it is seen that they are worshipped and appeased on specific occasions in the year. Offerings of various kinds, and sacrifices are made to them on specific occasions. The whole of community holds strong to keep up such values and traditions.

The Saharias believe that the supernatural if disturbed through any gesture or forgetfulness, could create condition that would prove damaging to the community health. The Saharias try to appease the supernatural by offering prayers, worshipping them regularly and also on specific occasions like religious festivals, marriage ceremonies, etc.

The socio-cultural tradition does play an important role in the context of health and treatment among the Saharias. The common beliefs, customs and practices connected to health and diseases have been found to be intimately related to the treatment of disease. When a person goes to a traditional medical practitioner he gets socio-psychological reinforcement which he cannot get from the modern medical practitioner. The social reinforcement based on the understanding of traditional beliefs and practices is often lacking and may be one of the reasons for making a modern medical practitioner unsuccessful in the tribal areas.

The Saharias have specific gods for their health and disease, for calamities and so on. All those deities have their own respective departments and areas of influence, effect and control as well as nature of action. Diseases caused by wrath of deities are listed in Table 16.1.

Table 16.1: Disease caused by wrath of deities/ghosts

Sl. No.	Class of Disease Causation	Disease Associated	
		Local Name	English Name
1.	Wrath of gods *(Devta)* or goddesses *(Devi)*		
	a. *Badi Mata*	*Badi Mata*	Small Pox
	b. *Sitla Mata*	*Sitla Mata*	Chicken-Pox
	c. *Amba Mata*	—	Safe Delivery
	d. *Tejaji*	—	Snake Bite
	e. *Hanuman, Jind, Thakur*	—	Fever
2.	Evil Spirits and ghosts a	*Bade Maharaj*	Typhoid
		of the dead	Chotte Maharaj
		Malaria	
		Dibbirog	Pneumonia
		Dhanushban	Tetanus
3.	Evil eye or *Nazar Lagna* or *Dakini Lagna*	*Dakini Lagna* or *Bhoot Lagna Upri Hawa*	Fits

Like other tribes in India, the Saharias also had, in the past, their own explanations of sickness, on the basis of which they developed their peculiar ways of curing diseases. Their system of medicine (traditional medical system) is still in practice to a considerable extent especially among those who live in interior areas. That disease which is caused by evil spirit can only be cured by spiritual powers, is the main idea behind their system of treatment. Therefore, for all chronic and acute ailments, they go to their witch doctor locally called *Janteyar.* All diseases like typhoid, tuberculosis, tetanus, pneumonia, measles, polio are believed to be caused by evil spirits and ghosts of the dead. They also believe in hierarchy of deities and have placed some deities in senior position. Typhoid is believed to be caused by a senior deity so it is called *Bade Maharaj*. Similarly, as they believe, tuberculosis or tetanus is caused by angry soul of forefathers.

For treatment of such diseases, the Saharias go to a witch doctor or *Janteyar*. A Janteyar represents a particular deity and he is believed to be the representative of that deity. When the deity appears through him, his body starts shivering rapidly and his contact with this world breaks for a short span of time. During such moments he tells about diseases, the cause of ailment and suggest remedies. For different diseases, he suggests different treatments. To a few patients, he gives "spiritual ash" purified by reciting *mantras* (hymns).

Restrictions on having certain foods are also imposed by *Janteyar.* For example, once the family members of a typhoid patient were told to burn an *agarbati* (incense stick) near the patient in the morning and evening and to avoid the consumption of liquor, meal and oil in vegetables. For some ailments, the Saharias resort to herbal medicine, which they prepare themselves with the help of various plants found in the forest.

The following case studies reflecting their traditional as well as modern health care system will help us to understand the various socio-cultural factors related to health.

Case study I

Kailash, aged 24 years is suffering from Upri Hawa. According to her husband, she was taken to *Janteyar* for treatment but she did not recover from illness. For the last 3 days she was screaming, shouting, singing. Now she is taken to Baran for treatment.

According to the Kailash's husband there are cases of *Bhoot Lagna* or *Hawa Lagna* in which the person starts singing, dancing, shouting. Then he/she is taken to *Janteyar* one day before *Poornamasi* or a day before *Amavasya* (of Chaudas). The *Jantayar* gives him/her the treatment. The *Jantayar* takes some maize grains in his hand chants some *mantra* and then goes in trance. His body starts shivering and then he tells the cause of the ailment. He tells the name of the deity, who is angry with the sick person and tells the person to make offering to that particular deity. Only then the sick person will be cured. The *Janteyar* is given ghee, coconut, sugar. The *Janteyar* doesn't take any money because if he takes money his power will be finished. The people in interior villages are more superstitious. They will leave the settled colony if 4-5 deaths occur in that Saharia settlement

Case study II

Kanwar Lal is residing in the village Chaurakhadi. When interviewed he told that he was having fever and initially he thought that there was no need of consulting a doctor because his condition was not serious. He consulted a *Janteyar* for treatment. But the condition started deteriorating and then he rushed to PHC at Shahabad and he said that he was given prescription on paper only and was not given any medicine from PHC. Then he stopped going to PHC at Shahabad and now he is going to Sipri in M.P. for getting treatment at a hospital. According to Kanwarlal at PHC the doctor gives prescription on paper only. The patients are not given any medicine and the villagers are not happy with the services available at PHC.

There are cases of mental illness also prevalent in the village. For mental illness a *Jantayar* is a consulted. He goes in trance. His body starts shivering rapidly and if the *devi* or *devta* comes to him then he explains the cause of illness and tells the patient to make offering to that particular deity. The deities which come to him are mainly *Thakur*, *Jind*, *Khains*, *Bheran*, *Kali* and *Bijasun Mata*. If the deity does not come to him then it means the patient will die after some time.

Case study III

Shravan, a resident of village Pathari told that when a child dies during breast feeding it is believed to be caused by a ghost known as *Kaccha*. The dead body of the child is kept in a place, digged and then covered with mud. For avoiding such death the *Janteyar* ties a black thread around neck and fore arm of the children. According to Shravan, a child named Raju died for the same reason 2 years back. He was then 1 year old.

Case Study IV

Man Singh a resident of Khusalpura village was having conjunctivitis. He followed the domestic treatment for this disease and found the treatment very effective. According to him the paste of leaves of *bamoor* tree was put on his eyes. He also puts the milk of goat as eye drops. This was done for about a week and then the conjunctivitis was cured.

Modern Medical System

In addition to the magico-religious method of treatment the Saharias also follow allopathic system of medicine. In the past the Saharias used to consult spiritual doctors for treatment of sickness. But now, with the advancement, faith in supernatural concept is on decline and the Saharias have faith in allopathic doctors also. But the Saharias who live in interior areas mainly practice ethnomedical system (traditional medical system).

But it was observed that in some villages different treatments (spiritual, herbal and allopathic) go side by side and people have equal faith in all the treatments. They don't give preference to any particular method of treatment.

According to a school teacher from Shahabad the Saharias are not able to purchase medicines due to poverty. Even if they could purchase they cannot continue them for a long period and this results in discontinuance of treatment after a short period. They also change doctors quite often during treatment. At an advanced stage of the disease many a times doctors also fail to treat it. Then the Saharias again have to resort to their traditional methods of treatment or continue to move from one doctor to another and spend a substantial amount of money on treatment. Continuity of sickness for a long time is not uncommon among the Saharia. The longer the period of sickness the higher is the expenses on treatment.

Case study V

Chaita, a resident of Mundiar has been suffering from Tuberculosis for the last 3 years. He went to PHC Shahabad for medical check up 3 years ago. But he did not follow the entire course. After one year his condition became critical and then he consulted a private doctor (Bengali) but there was no improvement in his condition. He said that there are no medicines at PHC. There is a TB camp at Shahabad on 23rd of every month. Intially he used to go to TB camp for 3 to 4 months but after that he stopped going to attend the TB camp. Then he went to Kelwara, a 16-beded hospital. The facilities are good at Kelwara. There is an X-ray machine also. He was admitted for 3 months and now he is perfectly all right. He said that medical facilities are not good at PHC Shahabad. There is an X-ray machine but it is not working and doctors also sometimes scold them and then they stop going to PHC. Then they consult private doctor for treatment but it requires money and they cannot afford to consult such doctor every time. Then they go to bigger hospitals at Baran or Kelwara. According to him the life of poor people is like hell. Nobody listens to them. Noone takes care of them. According to him when a person falls ill initially he consults a *Jantayer;* when the condition deteriorates then only he consults a western doctor.

Case study VI

Raghubir is residing in the village Faredua. He is suffering from night blindness (*ratondi*). Initially he consulted a *Janteyar* for treatment. But when there was no improvement in his condition then he went to Kota to get treatment in the big hospital. He said that in this process he has already spent a lot of money. He said that only when *Janteyar* fails to cure the disease then they consult private doctor or go to PHC. When the doctor at PHC fails to bring any improvement in the condition of the sick person then they go to Baran or Kota for treatment.

Case Study VII

Dharamjeet lives in the village Matiakhad. His wife is suffering from T.B. According to him there is no proper arrangement for treatment of villagers. If anyone has a trouble all of sudden, he is taken to Shahabad PHC in a bullockcart where many a times doctors refuse to see the patient. Then they are examined by the compounder who also asks for money and does not give medicines from the hospital. Dharamjeet also reported that Government doctors do not give proper treatment. Noone at the PHC pays attention to them. Only private doctors treat them properly.

Case Study VIII

According to Saku Bai though most of the Saharias have visited atleast once the Primary Health Centre, but they are not satisfied with the facilities available at the PHC. The doctor gives prescription on paper only and the patients were not given any medicines from PHC. Sometimes the doctors also refuse to see the patients and then the Saharias consult private doctors who pay attention on them. But they have to spend a lot of money in this process. The Saharias are not afraid of immunization. When PHC staff visit their colonies them they get their children immunized. All the children below 1 year were found immunized at the time of fieldwork.

Nutrition Pattern

A healthy diet has to supply enough energy, protein, vitamins, minerals and other essential nutrients to maintain the body and to support physical activity (Truswell, 1992). It must also supply sufficient energy for growth in children, for foetal growth in pregnant woman and for lactation in breastfeeding mothers. The commonest dietary problem among the Saharia is not having enough food of any kind, leading to protein energy malnutrition. This is still depressingly common in interior villages where the diet doesn't supply enough energy and it is still deficient in particular nutrients.

In the past, food habits of the Saharias were fully wild and primitive. Various forest products and flesh of different animals formed their food. They were carnivorous. Among the forest products, which the Saharias use in the form of food include mahua, chiranji, gum, honey and amwala.

The grains which Saharias used to consume in the past were of inferior quality from the point of view of nutrition. Now the Saharias eat jawar, bajra and wheat. But the consumption of cereals, pulses and vegetables is very less, mainly because of low production and the cost factors.

The Saharias are fond of liquor. They brew alcohol from the wild flowers and seeds of mahua. Both men and women consume mahua liquor and it is deeply ensconced in tribal life, be it ceremony of childbirth, marriage or festival.

Infant Feeding

Detailed interviews showed that the Saharias do not give any special diet to the children except the breast-feed. The solid food is given normally after one year or so in most cases. The implications of this observation are born out by the prevalent high rates of malnutrition (*subha bimari*) among the Saharia children.

Nutrition During Pregnancy

No special care is taken of a pregnant women among the Saharias. She takes the routine diet during the entire period of pregnancy. Milk is given only if the family has milching cattle. The pregnant women work in field also.

The Saharia women know that intake of milk, dalia, green leafy vegetables is good for the growth of foetus. But due to poverty they cannot afford to buy what they should eat during pregnancy.

Sanitation and Hygiene

Sanitation among the Saharias is very poor. The houses of Saharias are constructed with stones and mud. There are no window in these houses. The houses of Saharias are filled with darkness even during day time. When the meals are prepared the room fills with smoke and causes suffocation. Due to this, the Saharias are more likely to develop asthma and respiratory infections. This is particularly true for children. Crowded housing increases the transmission of infection between residents. Within the household compound, enclosure for the animals is made which leads to poor environmental sanitation. During the rainy season it becomes a breeding ground for mosquitoes leading to spread of malaria.

The sources of drinking water are wells, rivers and hand pumps. In some villages water which comes from the hand pumps is dirty. Many Infectious diseases such as cholera, typhoid and polio are carried in water. The principle source of these infections is the pollute water from village ponds, rivers, wells, etc. There was recent outbreak of infectious diarrhea among the children of Sandhri village. This was caused due to contaminated water.

Personal hygiene is also quite poor among the Saharias. Due to poverty and illiteracy the Saharias are unaware and ignorant about the fatality of such poor environmental sanitation.

Illiteracy

Majority of villagers are illiterate in spite of the fact that some villages have own primary schools. They are not quite capable of having access to health care, even if they are aware that the ailments are dangerous. They can do nothing and feel helpless. Unless the people are made literate they cannot realise the importance of health education.

Transport

Again if one assumes that people have necessary money and awareness for medical treatment, communication facilities are so poor that it is difficult to have access to medical treatment. Even the post and telegraph facilities are almost non-existant in the interior villages. In case any epidemic breaks out there would be massive peril before the news reaches the district administration.

Etiology of Disease

Our analysis indicates two aspects of the disease, i.e. symptoms and etiology. While the symptoms recognised are indigestion, continuous fever, cough and cold, all remaining conditions explain the etiology of diseases. Chart-I shows all these notions in the form of framework, which analytically gives us a broad-outline of various types of causes attributed here.

There are only two cases where the informants have indicated scientific explanations. These are mosquito-bite in case of malaria and the attack of germs in case of tuberculosis and small pox.

It was found that the Saharias do not believe in "one cause one-disease" type of thinking. Rather they believe in multi-causal explanation involving the interactions of several human and super-human factors, which also include numerous socio-economic and environmental factors. Table 16.2 shows the symptoms and etiology of disease recognised by the Saharias.

On the basis of our intensive and extensive fieldwork among Saharia tribe we found the following reasons responsible for their poor health status:

Chart 1: Showing concepts of "Etiology"

Concepts of Etiology

- Scientific concepts
  - External agents
    - — mosquitoes
    - — germs
- Conventional concepts
  - Natural
    - — food
    - — environmental conditions
    - — personal habits
    - — hardwork but inadequate diet
  - Supernatural
    - — wrong done to god
    - — angry soul of forefathers
    - — evil spirits

1. Unhygienic living conditions, delayed treatment and malnutrition affect their health badly. Even pregnant and lactating mothers and children are not provided with nutrition's diet.
2. Another factor responsible for high rate of sickness is heavy drinking habits among men, which adversely affect their health. This results in mal-nourishment, loss of body weight and decreased resistance to infections.
3. A large number of people in the tribal belt suffer from tuberculosis. This is due to malnutrition. The food taken by Saharias is neither nutritious nor does it meet the calorie, protein and vitamin requirements of the body. They eat inferior kinds of grain like jawar and bajra. Milk is consumed only occasionally.
4. There is no utilisation of maternity and child health (MCH) services. During pregnancy the Saharias do not consult a doctor in order to have MCH Services. They approach the doctor only in case of complication or abnormality.

Table 16.2: Symptoms and etiology of disease recognized by Saharias

Sl. No.	Disease	Causes Assigned (In Percentage)				Don't know
1.	Cholera	Taking rotten food (38.0)	Taking excess diet (22.0)	Indigestion (13.5)	Dirty living conditions (11.0)	(15.5)
2.	Malaria	Biting of Mosquitoes (71.0)	Dirty living continuous (19.0)			(10.0)
3.	Typhoid	Taking food during fever (70.0)	Continuous fever (10.0)	Irregularites done during fever (6.0)		(14.0)
4.	Small Pox	Excess heat in body (32.0)	Wrong done to some god (28.0)	Using hot material in food (19.0)	Attach of germs (11.0)	(10.0)
5.	Tuberculosis	Smoking (45.0)	Cold and cough (33.0)	Attach of germs (6.5)	Heavy work but inadequate diet (3.5)	(12.0)
6.	Fits	Wrath of deities (92.0)				(8.0)

Note : Figures in parenthesis indicate percentage frequencies based on 100 interviews.

5. Delivery conditions in interior villages are found to be extremely unhealthy. There is no local sweepress in some interior villages. When a delivery is conducted she is called from other villages and it takes 2 to 3 days. This also affects mother and child's health.
6. Superstition is also a factor responsible for poor health status of Saharia. When a person falls ill initially he resorts to magico-religious treatment and if the sickness continues only then he consults an allopathic doctor.
7. Poor economic condition is also responsible for low health status of Saharia. The Saharias eat inferior millets like Jawar or Bajra. Milk

is consumed only by those Saharias, who have milching cattle. Due to poor economic condition the Saharias are not able to buy milk and vegetables.

8. Unawareness of proper health care practices such as sanitation, hygiene, food and nutrition is also responsible for high morbidity rate among the Saharias. In some of the villages there are no drainage systems and sanitary arrangements.
9. Several diseases are caused due to lack of safe drinking water. In some villages hand-pumps are not working. Pond water is used for drinking as well as for washing and bathing. Drinking water at Shahabad is having more calcium content and is unsafe for drinking.
10. Due to lack of facilities like roads and transports it is not possible for health workers to reach the interior villages to perform their duties adequately. In rainy season it is not possible to approach villages in the interior. During that period the area is not approachable even by jeep because the tyres of jeep get trapped in the clayey and slushy soil and that is why the village becomes unapproachable.
11. It was also found that some doctors and ANM take their duties and responsibilities lightly. They consider their posting to these tribal villages as a punishment. Some young doctors were found preparing for post Graduate (MD/MS) entrance examinations. Corruption and exploitation of different nature are also rampant.
12. Lack of education is another factor responsible for poor health of Saharias. The uneducated people believe that more children means amore working hands and they do not adopt family planning measures. Only women were found adopting family planning measures. They also have strong faith in magico-religious treatment of curing illness.
13. The reason for poor health status of Saharias is not only inadequate and non-accessible health services. There is only one Primary Health Centre (PHC) at Shahabad.
14. Neither there is any chemist's shop in the interior villages nor any doctor or health personnel to take care of poor tribal.
15. There is no effort by the government to impart health education to the Saharias.

Unhygienic living conditions, delayed treatment, malnutrition and lack of safe drinking water affect the health of Saharias badly. Apart from improving the overall conditions of the Saharias the most important step which the government should take is to improve their economic condition and to impart health education to Saharias. The government's emphasis should be more on preventive medicines than curative, which is very expensive for the poor tribals.

Acknowledgements

The study has been supported by a research grant from ICSSR to Pramod Misra and from University of Delhi to A.K. Kapoor.

REFERENCES

Basu, S.K., A. Jindal, and G.K. Kshatriya. 1994. "Perception of Health and Pattern of Health Seeking Behaviour among the Selected Tribal Population Groups of Madhya Pradesh and Orissa," in S. Basu (ed.), *Tribal Health in India*. New Delhi: Manak Publication Ltd.

Carstairs, G.M. 1955. Medicine and Faith in Rural Rajasthan," in B.D. Paul (ed.), *Health, Culture and Community*. New York: Russel Sage.

Chaudhuri, B. 1986. Medical Anthropology in India with Special Reference to Tribal Population," in B. Chaudhuri (ed.), *Tribal Health: Socio-Cultural Dimensions*. New Delhi: Inter-India Publication.

Gupta, S.P. 1986. "Tribal Concepts of Health, Disease and Remedy," in B. Chaudhuri (ed.), *op. cit.*

Khan, Gorachand. 1986. "Tribal Health: Jmpact of Rural Development Programme," in B. Chaudhuri (ed.), *op.cit.*

Kapoor, A.K. 1998. "The Anthropologist as Bio-social Hero: Health, Medicine and Faith in a Scheduled Tribe of Himalayas," paper presented at the National Seminar on *Health and Hygiene among the Tribal Communities in India*. December 15-17, 1998. Andhra University, Visakhapatnam.

Mahapatra, L.K. 1994. "Concept of Health among the Tribal Population Groups of India and Its Socio-economic and Socio-cultural Correlates," in Salil Basu (ed.), *op.cit.*

Mann, R.S. and K. Mann. 1986. "Religious Attributes and Cure in Tribal India," in B. Chaudhuri (ed.), *op. cit.*

Marriott, M. 1955. "Western Medicine in a Village of Northern India," in B.D. Paul (ed.), *op.cit.*

Roy, S.C. 1984. "Magic and Witchcraft on the Chotanagpur Plateau: A Study in the Philosophy of Primitive Life," *Man in India*, 64: 91-120.

Sachidananda. 1978. Socio-Cultural Dimensions of Tribal Health," in S. Basu (ed.), *op. cit.*

Swain, S. 1994. "Health, Disease and Health Seeking Behaviour of Tribal People of India," in S. Basu (ed.), *op. cit.*

SEVENTEEN

BIOMEDICAL ANTHROPOLOGY IN CONTEMPORARY TRIBAL SOCIETY OF INDIA

R.S. BALGIR

Introduction

Anthropology, the science of human beings, endeavours to study man in totality. It has a colonial heritage in India, as the colonial administration tried to know the manners and customs of the people whom they wanted to subjugate and rule. Anthropology helps understand people, society, various social relationships and aspects of contacts, which have been occurring even today in the contemporary society throughout the world. Such anthropological concepts and methods, which became structured in due course of time and helped the colonial administrators for the better management of the people and their affairs, the science of man (Anthropology) became a separate discipline (Bhowmick, 1987).

In the colonial period, ethnographers generated information about people and their customs for the benefit of the rulers of the time. Some of them also spoke for the indigenous communities (Tribes and Tribal) and suggested measures for their welfare. The science of man became the service of man. Immediately after Independence in 1947, anthropologists have got together frequently to explore the relevance of their studies to the growing challenge of development (Singh, 1987). Thus, practical or applied anthropology and, later on, action anthropology became the watchword of the day as the social engineers or architects of India.

After Independence, the Government of India took the responsibility for the upliftment of the weaker sections (including the tribal) of the society and a number of departments were established, advisory committees or evaluation committees constituted; institutes were organized for research work and action was taken up relating to problems, constrains and compatibilities (Bhowmick, 1987). This type of involvement of anthropologists at the advisory level of the administration is needed to have a smooth functioning of the administration. A few of the anthropologists are posted at the advisory level too. In the Anthropological Survey of India, the Planning Commission Wing of the Ministry of Welfare, Department of Women and Child Development, District Welfare Department, various cultural institutes and Departments of Anthropology at university and college level, and the anthropologists got themselves acquainted with the problems, and in some instances became an integral part of the administration and planning in India. At present, there are more than 35 departments of Anthropology at university level in India.

In India, we have Community Development, National Extension Service and many other projects relating to overall development of the people. The Tribal concentrated areas are/were marked and special Multipurpose Tribal Blocks or Modified Area Development Agency (MADA) are/were created for the quick development of people and regions in India during the 2nd half of the 20th century.

In recent years, path-breaking researches have been under-taken which are immensely relevant to the task of upgrading the status of health and nutrition for a vast number of people (Sharma, 1987: 1992). Similarly, in social and cultural anthropology, a good deal of work has been done (Danda, 1981; Behera, 1998) that offers a valuable insight into people's traditions, attitude and behaviour which are now considered as an essential social input in planning and development process in India.

Biological Anthropology in Contemporary Tribal Society

The various channels made available to the Indian physical anthropologists range in their contents from the classic evolutionary studies to the biological welfare of the people including understanding the genetic structure and variability of the Indian populations. Morphological structure of Indian castes, communities and tribes is rather widely studied by various anthropologists (Reddy et al., 1993). It does not undermine the usefulness of the study of genetic structures by the physical anthropologists of the nation. India is a nation with the large genetic and morphological diversity of her people, living in the most diversified geographical localities. This compact structure provides a comprehensive scale for measuring the biological well-being of the people and planning for their improvement and welfare.

Earlier studies on human variations were of topological nature, hence looked for racial composition of Indian population and later were stressed for identification of an endogamous group (Rao, 1998). These studies emphasized on the local variation in population groups (caste, sub-caste, tribe, etc.) with an attempt to delineate the process of change (Basu and Biswas, 1980). The major findings of these studies were that, there were more intra-group variations than the inter-group variations, thereby, indicating the importance of looking for processes of change within population.

One of the major concerns of anthropology in India has been the determination of the physical status of the Indian populations. It started with racial classification of the Indian populations and shifted to the study of morphological variations (Singh, 1987). Mere description of intra-group and inter-group variations is of little value without the proper logic, philosophy or purpose of the study (Balgir, 2002). There has to be a correlation of anthropometric data to such variables as climate, ecology, nutrition or environmental stress or demand (Balgir, 1999a). The relevance of bio-anthropological data at the All India Level would be the exploration of the demographic profile in terms of fertility, food security, health status, mating practices, morbidity and mortality, besides the environmental factors (Balgir, 1999b).

During the last 2-3 decades of 20th century, the role of anthropologists in India has begun to change in the contemporary society (Reddy et al., 1993). The poverty stared the poor villagers. Neither sanitation, nor medical facilities, not even supply of safe drinking water is easily available. Illiteracy, superstition, prejudice and narrow worldview retarded the pace of rationalization and all these enveloped the minds of the majority of the people. Misunderstanding among the minor/major castes and tribal communities is manifested through the sporadic outbursts of riots and massacres and this is the go of the day. Over-population and pressure on land created acute unemployment problems and, as a result, people are becoming restive and tense. Non-availability of food, clothing and shelter constitute the major part of the problems among the tribal, which should be tackled on priority basis in India. Moreover, the current way of developing and assisting the tribal has made them dependent upon the Government funds and funding agencies from India and abroad for various hidden motives and missionary intentions.

The development sums up and designates the most important aspects of change concerning the well-being or upliftment of the people and ensures stability and comfort in living conditions (Balgir, 1999b). It is the utilization of resources of the region and, at the same time, removes the distressing conditions or poverty of the people. Sometimes, it refers primarily to economic backwardness causing malnutrition, ill health, little awareness of the cause of disease, high mortality rate and high birth rate (Balgir, 1997). Besides these, there are many contributory factors, causing more problems like housing, education, unemployment, etc. There are diversities and hierarchy among the tribal people and these bring social or economic deprivations through exploitation. All these constellate together and reflect the acute problem related to backwardness and under developed conditions of tribal in India (Balgir, 1996a).

To commit more explicitly, it is desirable to provide anthropological input for the study and evaluation of planned programmes relating to conservation of environment, poverty alleviation, combating malnutrition, welfare of women and children, development of weaker sections, and physical fitness (Balgir, 1995; 1996a). There is a concern for backward communities and tribes for their welfare and development and protection of minorities, their involvement in the formulation and evaluation of development programmes and various ways to articulate their fears and aspirations (Balgir, 1999b).

Emergence of Biomedical Anthropology

What makes anthropology immensely relevant to the development process is its concern for the upgradation of the status of those sections (including the tribal) of the society which suffer from genetic disorders, incidences of malnutrition and disabilities of all kinds, particularly of the women and children (Balgir, 1995). It is important to study the genetic structures in terms of distribution of genetic markers, level of genetic relationship between and among different regions, genetic distances among populations, probable and discernible effects of the ongoing human evolution (Rao, 1998).

With the recent advancements in biotechnology and the use of recombinant DNA technology, the basic theme at molecular level of the discipline of Anthropology has revolutionized the extent of applicability for human warfare and welfare in terms of population specific gene expression, disease susceptibility, evolution of diseases, ageing, adaptation, etc. In this perspective, it is high time to reorganize ourselves, our priorities of research and development, potential avenues in the light of our rich human genetic diversity particularly of the Indian tribes (Balgir, 2002).

Except the earlier few studies based on anthropometry, a comprehensive study on All India level of the tribal of India is lacking in the country. The various genetic studies conducted on Indian (tribal) populations are mostly of ad hoc nature. Later on, serological and electrophoretic techniques were adopted to study human variation in terms of distribution of genetic markers like blood groups, red cell enzymes and serum proteins (Balgir, 1986; 1995; 1996a; 1999a). As a result, the data being generated are highly non-compatible with the number of markers studied. In view of the recent biotechnological advancement, there is an urgent need to generate the database of genomic diversity of the people especially of the tribal of this country.

There is an urgent need to collect blood samples from most primitive, isolated tribal groups representing various biological types on priority basis to create a DNA bank or cell lines in the case of most primitive tribal populations, which are under threat of extinction. Such DNA banks also need to be generated on earliest human skeletal materials, which are available with various organizations/museums in this country (Balgir, 2002).

From the march of Indian Anthropology starting from Colonial exploitation, racial discrimination, evolutionary and diversity studies, and human growth, development and welfare to frustration, it is apparent that there is a lack of development of Biomedical Anthropology in the contemporary tribal society in India.

Biomedical anthropology is a newly emerging discipline, which combines the theoretical and methodological concepts of physical anthropology and medical anthropology in the study of disease and health of human populations (Balgir, 1996a; 1997; 1999a; 2002). This includes the integral approaches of physical anthropologist with interests in human biology, human genetics, molecular medicine, human growth, development and nutrition, and human being as physical entity, and of a medical anthropologist whose interests are in the areas of health behaviour, medical care (intervention) systems, health planning, psychosomatic illness including mental health, and correlation of demographic variables. The contention is that a biomedical anthropological approach is best suited when it emphasizes the biological basis of health and disease, while at the same time actively incorporating and understanding the socio-cultural nature of the sickness process in the society.

The study of genetics of various human traits especially of tribal is still a virgin area in anthropology. Deciphering and mapping of genes along with identification of various characters in human genome is a vast unexplored reservoir in India, with particular reference to Indian tribal lineage. Distribution and spread of various genetic diseases among the tribal in the world through migrations, admixture and genetic drift, and explaining their concentration in particular geographical and ecological niches is still a challenging task for a biomedical anthropologist in India.

Biomedical anthropologist should move into the design and provision of health care services for the intervention in improving the health status of certain at risk tribal population groups, extending their life expectancies, lowering morbidity, mortality, arson, sexually transmitted diseases, excessive drinking, and the other like public health issues. The entry of such unique expertise is not only welcomed in India, but is imperative also. Thus, the strength of anthropology lies in its analytical potentials, constructive suggestions and practical applications in the tribal society. A biomedical anthropologist has the responsibility to identify himself with the cause and pursue his role and goal with commitment and dedication wherever he is entrusted for the betterment of the contemporary tribal communities in India.

The subsistence economy of a tribal population has obvious effects on its population density, population size, marriage pattern, age at marriage, sex ratio, fertility, mortality, migration or social mobility and such other factors of population structure, which directly affect the hereditary characters in successive generations, and propagation and selection of particular characters (Balgir, 1986, 1999a). A tribe is also influenced by the level and type of nutrition, incidence and types of diseases and disorders, sanitation, personal hygiene and therapeutic practices. These variables ultimately bring about biological as well as socio-cultural variability in the tribe.

The tribes, mainly depending upon hunting and gathering economy and living near the forests maintain low density and small size of the population. These people are often fragmented into smaller food groups because of scanty and sporadic distribution of resources, which become the root cause of conflict, enmity and diversity. Marriage with close relatives occur in a relatively high frequency with several genetic consequences, such as loss of variations in the offspring, combination of undesirable genes carried by both parents leading to severe disorders of health, excelleration/diminition of body size and so on. In a small tribal group, there is a loss of variety in each generation and natural selection has very little to select from and may operate against the entire group, leading to impairment of the growth and declination of the tribe. The practice of polyandry or polygyny in some tribal communities is an adjustment system for sex ratio in addition to economic viability in India.

The relatively lower level of agricultural development in tribal areas, and smaller holdings, poor soil, soil erosion, simple technology and indebtedness, all reflect the poor physical dimensions and poor health and nutritional status of majority of the tribal in India.

Nutrition is a prime concern of all living organisms. The quality and quantity of food available play an important role in determining the health and well-being of an individual and tribal population. Its application involves the physical, social, biological and medical sciences. These encompass from food production, procurement and consumption, to cultural practices and beliefs associated with food to biological needs of food, sanitation of food (free from toxins, bacteria and contamination including adulteration), nutritional deficiencies affecting growth and development, fertility, mortality, morbidity, health and disease, nutritional variations as consequence of adaptation, natural selection and, in short, the whole process of biological evolution (Sharma, 1987).

It has been observed that the tribal unlike the general populations in India are vulnerable as well as have major threat of three major categories of biomedical health problems:

Genetical Diseases: Hereditary disorders of blood like hemoglobinopathy and thalassemia (Balgir and Sharma, 1988, Balgir, 1996b), glucose-6-phosphate dehydrogenase enzyme deficiency (Balgir, 1989) and hemophilia, and colour blindness (Balgir, 1999c), chromosomal aberrations, congenital malformations, inborn errors of metabolism, etc. among others. The preventive and control strategies along with remedies for some of these hereditary disorders have also been highlighted elsewhere (Balgir, 1999c, 1998, 1999d).

Non-communicable Diseases: Liver cirrhosis due to excessive drinking of country made alcohol, Hypertension due to excessive salt intake, Chronic respiratory diseases due to excessive smoking, oral cancer, Malnutrition, nutritional deficiency disorders like iron deficiency anemia, iodine deficiency (Goitre), Vitamins deficiencies, etc. Cardio-vascular diseases are very uncommon among the tribal in India.

Communicable Diseases: There are several communicable diseases prevalent among the tribal of India. These are: Tuberculosis, Hepatitis, STDs., Malaria, Filariasis, Diarrhoea and Dysentry, Jaundice, Parasitic infestation, Viral and Fungal infections, Conjunctivitis, Yaws, Scabies, Measles, Leprosy, Cough and Cold, HIV/AIDS, which is spreading like wild fire, etc. due to lack of sanitation and unhygienic living. They frequently become victims of repeated epidemics of above-mentioned contagious diseases.

There are several other environmentally caused health hazards due to poor sanitation, poor disposable facilities for human excreta, animal waste, sewerage and sullage, etc. associated with illiteracy, extreme exploitation by the elites, etc. However, their indigenous way of treatment for some common ailments using herbs and other forest flora or fauna products is much more advanced than the allopathic in some cases.

Here the role of a Biomedical Anthropologist is not only assertive but demanding dedicated efforts for amelioration, improving and promoting the health of the fair sex in the contemporary society, not only for the under-privileged, backward and tribal communities but also of the general people for the better perspective, purpose and promise in India.

Acknowledgements

Author is grateful to the Director General, Indian Council of Medical Research, New Delhi for providing the necessary facilities and all the authors whose work has been quoted in this article.

REFERENCES

Balgir, R.S. 1986. "Serogenetic Studies in the Gypsy Sikligars of North-Western India," *Human Biology*, 58: 171-87.

____. 1989. "Ethnic and Regional Variations in the Red Cell Glucose-6-Phosphate Dehydrogenase Deficiency in India," *Indian Journal of Hematology*, 7 (3): 101-109.

____. 1995. "Genetic Markers in the Tribal Health, Development and Welfare with special reference to North Eastern India," (pp.151-171) in J.C. Sharma (ed), *Anthropology, Population and Development*. New Delhi: Inter-India Publications.

____. 1996a. "Biomedical Anthropological Approaches in North Eastern India: A Synthesis of the Tea Garden Population of Assam," (pp.91-104) in Sarthak Sengupta (ed.), *Peoples of North East India: Anthropological Perspective*. New Delhi: Gyan Publishing House.

____. 1996b. "The Prevalence of Sickle Cell Hemoglobinopathy in India," (pp.21-29) in T Madhava Menon, C. Sivathanu, K.P. Prasanth, M. Sasikumar and P.R.G. Mathur (eds.), *The Encyclopedia of Dravidian Tribes*. Vol. I. Trivandrum: The International School of Dravidian Linguistics.

____. 1996c. "Preventive Genetic Strategies for Hemoglobinopathy and Thalassemia in India," *Indian Practitioner*, 49 (3): 219-226.

____. 1997. "Khonds-Health Status," (pp.160-63) in T Madhava Menon, C. Sivathanu, K.P. Prasanth, M. Sasikumar and P.R.G. Mathur (eds.), *The*

Encyclopedia of Dravidian Tribes. Vol. II. Trivandrum: The International School of Dravidian Linguistics.

____. 1998. "Prevention of Genetic Load of Thalassemia in India," *Current Medical Trends*, 2 (1): 269-274.

____. 1999a. "Biomedical Anthropology and Health Status of the Tribal Muslim Gujjars of Himachal Pradesh, India," (pp.1-19) in Sarthak Sengupta (ed.), *Health, Healers and Healing: Studies in Medical Anthropology*. Dibrugarh: National Library Publishers.

____. 1999b. "Human Genetics, Health and Tribal Development in Orissa," (pp. 87-104) in P. Dash Sharma (ed.), *Environment, Health and Development: Anthropological Perspectives*. Ranchi: S.C.Roy Institute of Anthropological Studies.

____. 1999c. "The Prevalence of Colour Impairment Disorders in India," *Indian Practitioner*, 52 (4): 256-268.

____. 1999d. "Control and Prevention of Genetic Load of Hemoglobinopathies in India," *The National Medical Journal of India*, 12 (5): 234-238.

____. 2002. "Biomedical Anthropology in the Service of Mankind in the New Millennium: Are We Ready?" (pp.141-147) in M.K. Bhasin and S.L Malik (eds.), *Anthropology: Trends and Applications*. New Delhi: Kamala Raj Enterprises.

Balgir, R.S. and S.K. Sharma. 1988. "Distribution of Sickle Cell Hemoglobin in India," *Indian Journal of Hematology*, 6: 1-14.

Basu, A. and S.K. Biswas. 1980. "Is Indian Anthropology Dead/Dying?" *Journal of Indian Anthropological Society*, 15: 1-14.

Behera, D.K. 1998. *Children and Childhood in our Contemporary Societies*. New Delhi: Kamala-Raj Enterprises.

Bhowmick, P.K. 1987. "Development and Anthropology: Rebuilding Rural and Tribal India," (pp.157-64) in A.K. Kalla and K.S. Singh (ed.), *Anthropology, Development and Nation Building*. New Delhi: Concept Publishing Company.

Danda, A.K. 1981. "On the Future for Anthropology in India," *Journal of Indian Anthropological Society*, 16: 221-30.

Rao, V.R. 1998. "Physical Anthropological Research in India and Recent Advances in Recombinant DNA Technology: An Approach Paper," *South Asian Anthropologist*, 19: 45-50.

Reddy, B.M., T.S. Vasulu, and K.C. Malhotra. 1993. "Physical Anthropology as a Science: A Commentary," *Current Science*, 64: 17-21.

Sharma, J.C. 1987. "Role of Nutrition in Physical Growth and Development," (pp.175-88) in A.K. Kalla and K.S. Singh (ed.), *Anthropology, Development and Nation Building*. New Delhi: Concept Publishing Company.

____. 1992. "Nutrition Factor in Health, Physical Growth and Development and Politics," Presidential Address in 79th Session of the Indian *Science Congress* held during January 8-12, 1992, Baroda.

Singh, K.S. 1987. "Anthropology, Culture and Development," (pp.13-36) in A.K. Kalla and K.S. Singh (eds.), *Anthropology, Development and Nation Building*. New Delhi: Concept Publishing Company.

NOTES ON CONTRIBUTORS

Balgir, R.S. (born 1952) post-graduated himself in Anthropology from Panjab University in 1976. Received his Ph.D. (Human Genetics) degree from the same University in 1984. Dr. Balgir served Anthropological Survey of India as Junior Research Fellow during 1978-80 and later joined Post-Graduate Institute of Medical Education and Research, Chandigarh, where he was pioneer for research work in Biological Psychiatry, Congenital Cleft Lip and Palate Anomalies. He joined the Indian Council of Medical Research as Senior Research Officer at Dibrugarh (Assam) in 1985 and, at present, serving as Deputy Director (Sr. Grade) and Head, Division of Human Genetics at Regional Medical Research Centre, Bhubaneswar, Orissa. Dr. Balgir is a Fellow of several International Scientific Organisations like Human Biology Council (USA), Fellow of American Dermatoglyphics Association, Fellow of International Dermatoglyphics Association, and active member of the New York Academy of Sciences. Dr. R.S. Balgir is a recipient of several awards, prizes and honours for his outstanding research contributions to Biomedical Sciences. Here mention may be made of Dr. B.C. Mehta Diamond Jubilee Endowment Fund Award 1990, 1993; Excellence Award 1994; Vishisht Chikitsak Award 1996; Excellence Award in Medicine 1997; International Gold Medal Award 1999, Manorama Sapre Oration Award 2000 and Bharat Excellence Award and Gold Medal 2003. Dr. Balgir has over 175 research publications in the international and national indexed journals of repute. He has successfully guided several M.D./Ph.D. theses.

Mailing Address: Deputy Director (Senior Grade) and
Head, Division of Human Genetics
Regional Medical Research Centre
Chandrasekharpur
Nandan Kanan Road
Bhubneswar-23
Orissa, India
E-mail: <balgirrs@yahoo.co.in>

Behera, Deepak Kumar is Professor and Head of the Department of Anthropology, Sambalpur University. He obtained his Master's degree (Gold Medallist) and Ph.D. from Sambalpur University, where he has been teaching anthropology since 1985. He has more than *60* research publications in reputed journals and edited volumes. Prof. Behera has authored/edited *fourteen* volumes. Of those seven are jointly with Prof. Georg Pfeffer of Institute of Ethnology of Free University of Berlin (Germany). He has successfully completed a dozen of research projects funded by national bodies like UGC, ICSSR, Ministry of Welfare, National Literacy Mission Authorities, Winrock International, Shastri Foundation Fellowship etc. Dr. Behera has participated in more than a dozen international conferences held in Mexico, Germany, Belgium, Sweden, Israel, Denmark, USA, South Africa, China, Japan, Italy, UK, Bangladesh and has lectured at different universities and research institutes there. He is the editor of the international journal - *Journal of Social Sciences.* Prof. Behera is a member of the Executive Board of International Union of Anthropological and Ethnological Sciences (IUAES) for the period 1998-2008. He is the Chairperson of the IUAES Commission on Anthropology of Children, Youth and Childhood. He is also the Officer-at-Large of the International Sociological Association Research Committee-53 - Sociology of Childhood for the session 1998-2005. He is a member of the International Advisory Board of the Journal - *Sociological Analysis* (North Carolina, USA) and also a member of the Editorial Board of Global Gutter Press (Cambridge, UK). He has successfully guided 6 Ph.D. and more than thirty M.Phil scholars. Prof. Behera is the Director of the Institute of Evaluation, Research, Documentation and Training. His current interests in research are tribal studies, childhood matters, inter-ethnic relations, gender and displacement issues.

Mailing Address: Head, Department of Anthropology
Sambalpur University
Jyoti Vihar, Burla
Sambalpur - 768 019
Orissa, India
E-mail: <dkbehera@sancharnet.in>

Behura, N.K. is a retired Professor of Anthropology from Utkal University. Prof. Behura is a recipient of Rai Bahadur P.R. Chanda medal from the Asiatic Society of India. Prof. Behura is the *ex*-President of Anthropology and Archaeology Section of Indian Science Congress Association. *Fourteen* scholars have been awarded with Ph.D. degrees in anthropology, sociology and home science under the supervision of Prof. Behura. He has also guided thirty M.Phil dissertations. He has published *five* books and *ninety* articles. The major areas of interest of Prof. Behura include development anthropology, linguistic anthropology, social systems and theoretical anthropology.

Mailing Address: A-147, Saheed Nagar
Bhubaneswar - 751 007
Orissa, India

Bhasin, Veena (born. 1964) secured first division in her M.Sc. courses in anthropology and was awarded Ph.D. in 1982 from University of Delhi on Ecological Anthropology. She worked as Research Fellow of Indian Council of Medical Research Center and later joined UNESCO MAB (Man and Biosphere) Project. Currently Prof. Bhasin is working as Research Scientists "C" UGC in the Department of Anthropology, University of Delhi. She has done extensive field and research work in the Himalayan region (Jammu and Kashmir, Himachal Pradesh and Sikkim) and has published five books, namely, (1) *Himalayan Ecology, Trancehumance and Social Organisation-Gaddis of Himachal Pradesh,* (2) *Ecology, Culture and Change: Tribal of Sikkim Himalayas,* (3) *Habitat, Habitation and Health in the Himalayas: A Comparative Study of the People's of Sikkim and Gaddis of Himachal Pradesh,* (4) *Sikkim Himalayas-Ecology and Resources Development,* (5) *People, Health and Disease: The Indian Scenario.* Her major interests in research are ecological anthropology and medical anthropology.

Mailing Address: U. G. C. Research Scientist 'C' (Professor)
Department of Anthropology
University of Delhi
Delhi 110 007, India
E-mail: <kre@vsnl.com>

Bhattacharya, Kumkum (born 1955) is professor of psychology in the Department of Social Work in Visva-Bharati University, Santiniketan, West Bengal. She is interested in minority groups and her research is in the area of socialization in a pluralistic society. She has a number of publications on this area of study. She has presented her papers in a number of international conferences.

Mailing Address: Deer Park, Santiniketan
West Bengal -731235, India
E-mail: <ranjit@cal2.vsnl.net.in>

Biswal, Nandini is a UGC NET qualified research scholar in the Department of Anthropology, Sambalpur University, Orissa. She completed her M.A and M.Phil degrees in anthropology from Sambalpur University. Her M.Phil work is in the field of industrial anthropology. She has presented papers in many national conferences. She has a good number of publications in edited volumes and journals. She has worked in different projects funded by national and international agencies. She is doing an ethnographic research on a dominant caste of Western Orissa for her doctoral degree. Her areas of interests are women studies and tribal studies.

Mailing Address: Department of Anthropology
Sambalpur University
Jyoti Vihar, Burla
Sambalpur-768 019
Orissa, India.

Fernandes, Walter (born 1939) is the Director of North Eastern Social Research Center, Guwahati and the Former Director, Indian Social Institute, New Delhi. He was the Editor of the journal - *Social Action.* He obtained his L.ph. Aloisianum, Gallarate, Italy; Post Graduate, Sociology of Religion, EHESS, Paris; Ph.D. Institute Catholique, Paris. He is a member of Indienhilfe, Hersching, Germany and Asian Studies Association, Chicago, General Body

MARG and CSE; Governing Body, NLLA. He is the author/co-author/editor of *20* books and *60* professional articles, including People's Participation in Development: Experiments in Non-formal Education (1980); Participatory Research and Evaluation: Experiments in Research as a Process of Liberation (1981); Caste and Conversion Movements in India (1981); Towards a New Forest Policy: People's Right and Environmental Needs (1983); Forests, Environment and People (1983); Trade Unions and Workers' Rights (1984); Social Activists and People's Movements (1985), Development with People (1985); Participatory and Conventional Methodologies: An Experiment with Integration as an Alternate Form of Action and Governmental Control (1986); Tribal Women and Forest Economy: Deforestation, Exploitation and Status Change (1987); Forests, Environment and Tribal Economy: Deforestation, Impoverishment and Marginalization in Orissa (1988); Development, Displacement and Rehabilitation: Questions for a National Debate (1989); National Development and Tribal Deprivation (1992); The Indigenous Question Search for an Identity (1993). His major interests in research are displacement and rehabilitation, tribal studies, dalit studies and action anthropology.

Mailing Address: Director:
North Eastern Social Research Center
C/o. Dr. G.C. Sharma
Khargguli Road
Guwahati-781004
Assam, India

Guru, S.S. obtained his M.Sc., M.Phil and Ph.D. degrees in anthropology from Sambalpur University. He also holds a diploma in Labour Laws and Personnel Management. He was the Associate Director of two TLC evaluation projects sponsored by National Literacy Mission Authority, New Delhi. Dr. Guru was a Lecturer in the Department of Anthropology and Tribal Studies, G.G. University, Bilaspur, M.P. He has got more than twelve years of post-graduate teaching experience. He has also successfully guided three M.Phil dissertations. Dr. Guru is the Associate Editor of two volumes - Contemporary Society: Tribal Studies (Vols. I, II New Delhi: Concept Publications) and Contemporary Society: Childhood and Complex Order (New Delhi: Manak Pvt. Ltd.). He is also the Associate Editor of the international journal - *Journal of Social Sciences.* Dr. Guru has presented papers at various national conferences and published a number of research papers in different journals and edited volumes. His areas of interest include tribal demography, anthropology of children and childhood and women studies.

Mailing Address: Department of Anthropology
Sambalpur University
Sambalpur-768 019
Orissa, India

Hota, Snigdha obtained her Master's and M.Phil degrees from Sambalpur University, Orissa. As a JRF qualified researcher, she plans to conduct her doctoral research on inter-ethnic relations. She has presented papers in many national seminars. She has a good number of publications in edited volumes and journals. She has worked in different projects funded by national and international agencies. Her areas of research interest are children and childhood, women studies and tribal studies.

Mailing Address: Department of Anthropology
Sambalpur University
Sambalpur-768 019
Orissa, India
E-mail: <snigdha_hota@yahoo.co.in>

Kapoor, A.K. did his Ph.D. in anthropology from University of Delhi, India. He has carried out extensive fieldwork on various ethnic groups of India with reference to health, genetics and socio-cultural aspects. Presently he is Professor at Department of Anthropology, University of Delhi.

Mailing Address: Department of Anthropology
University of Delhi
Delhi-110 007
India

Mishra, Arima obtained her Ph.D. from the Department of Sociology, Delhi School of Economics, University of Delhi. The title of her thesis was "Famine and Scarcities: A Sociological Study of Two Villages in Orissa". She is presently a faculty member of Dept. of Sociology, Delhi School of Economics, Delhi University. Dr. Mishra worked at the Centre for the Study of Administration of Relief and the Economic and Social Council of the United Nations as a visiting fellow and coordinator from 1993 -1999. She worked as a consultant to the UNICEF sponsored project on "Orissa Household Food Security" from August-November 1999. She also served as a consultant to the project on "Local Initiatives in the Rehabilitation of Common Property Resources" during February-May 1996. The project was jointly sponsored by the World Bank, World Wild Life Fund for Nature and the Ford Foundation. She was also a recipient of a national scholarship under the Centre for Advanced Studies Scheme, University of Delhi. She has also qualified UGC NET. She is a member of the International Sociological Association. Dr. Mishra's research interests include food security, CRP and land alienation.

Mailing Address: 53-G-23/7
Rohini
Delhi-110085
India
E-mail: <abhi_345@yahoo.com>

Mishra, Kamal K. is a Professor in the Department of Anthropology, University of Hyderabad, India. He was a lecturer at the Department of Anthropology, Utkal University, Bhubaneswar, prior to his tenure at the University of Hyderabad. He had his anthropological training at Utkal University, Jawaharlal Nehru University and University of Kent at Canterbury. His publications include three books, viz. *Social Structure and Change among the Ho of Orissa* (1987), *Tribal Elite and Social Transformation* (1994), and *Textbook of Anthropological Linguistics* (2000), and over *50* research papers in journals of repute. His forthcoming publication is an edited volume on People and Environment in India with Professor M. L. K. Murty as co-editor. His current research areas include environment, culture and development, language, culture and thought, and theories in anthropology.

Mailing Address: Department of Anthropology
University of Hyderabad
Hyderabad, India

Mishra, Pramod did M.Sc. in Anthropology from University of Delhi, Delhi. He secured first class at the master's level. He has carried out extensive fieldwork among the Meenas and Saharias of Rajasthan. He is at present ICSSR doctoral fellow at Department of Anthropology, University of Delhi.

Mailing Address: ICSSR doctoral fellow
Department of Anthropology,
University of Delhi,
Delhi-110 007, India

Nath, Nibedita is an ICSSR research fellow in the Department of Anthropology, Sambalpur University. As an ICSSR fellow. She is working on slum children for her doctoral degree. She was a part-time lecturer in the Department of Anthropology, Sambalpur University. She has obtained her B.A, M.A. and M.Phil degrees in anthropology under Sambalpur University, Orissa. She topped the merit lists by securing first class first position at B.A., M.A. and M.Phil levels. She was the recipient of OSANY AWARD for being the best graduate of humanities under Sambalpur University for the year 1999. Ms. Nath has qualified UGC NET. She has worked in projects funded by Winrock International and WHO. Recently she presented a paper in the international conference on "Dialogues with Gods" organized jointly by the Department of Anthropology, Sambalpur University and Institute for Ethnology, Free University of Berlin. She has own several prizes in Chancellor's Cup Debate and Governor's Cup Debate and Essay Competitions. She has delivered several popular lectures in All India Radio/Prasar Bharati. Her current areas of interest are children and childhood and tribal studies.

Mailing Address: Department of Anthropology
Sambalpur University
Sambalpur-768 019
Orissa, India
E-mail: <nn_nath @yahoo.co.in>

Padhi, Kanchan completed her M.A. and M. Phil degrees in Anthropology from Sambalpur University. She got first class both at M.A. and M.Phil levels. She has presented papers in many national level seminars. She has a good number of publications in journals and edited volumes. Her area of interest is tribal studies.

Mailing Address: Department of Anthropology
Sambalpur University
Sambalpur-768 019
Orissa, India

Panda, Bharati is a full-time Professor in the Department of Home Science, Sambalpur University. She obtained her Ph.D. degree under the Sambalpur University. She has presented many papers in national seminars. She has a good number of publications in many reputed journals and edited volumes. She has attended a number of refresher courses and workshops. She has acted as resource persons in many refresher and orientation programmes. Many scholars are working for their doctoral dissertation under the supervision of Prof. Panda. She has successfully guided many M.Phil scholars. Her areas of interest are family studies, health and nutrition.

Mailing Address: Department of Home Science
Sambalpur University
Sambalpur-768 019
Orissa, India

Pandya, Vishvajit is a Senior Lecturer of Anthropology at Victoria University of Wellington. He obtained his M.A and M.Phil from University of Delhi (1979) and Jawaharlal Nehru University (1981) respectively. Dr. Pandya got his Ph.D. from University of Chicago in the year 1987. He has done extensive fieldwork among the Jarwa hunters and gatherers in the Andaman Islands, nomadic groups in the desert of Kutch Malasia, Rathwas of Southern Gujurat funded by the American Institute for Indian Studies, Wenner Gren Foundation and Bushman Grants, Victoria University of Wellington. He has done researches in the following areas: museum collections and colonial administrators; nomadic groups in the desert of Kutch; ethno-aesthetics and architecture; study of design culture; ethno history of the Andaman and Nicobar Islands involving points of contact between tribes and colonizers during the 1800s and 1900s; comparative study of systems of classification of Negrito hunters and gatherers in Southeast Asia; study of visual anthropology and anthropological visualization; anthropology of chaos, smell and emotions; anthropology and art with special reference to Rathwas in Southern Gujurat; Naga Culture in North-east India; and Chinese minority groups.

Mailing Address: Department of Anthropology
Victoria University of Wellington
P.O.Box 600
Wellington
New Zealand
E-mail <PANDYA@matai.vuw.ac.nz>

Pfeffer, Georg is Professor of social anthropology in the Institute of Ethnology at the Free University of Berlin since 1985. He studied ethnology, sociology and history of religions at Freiburg University, Germany, where he obtained his doctoral degree in 1970 with a thesis on Paria groups of the Panjab. His postdoctoral thesis of Habilitation at the University of Heidelberg bore the title: Puri's Sasana Villages: Basis of a Regional Elite. In 1971 he was appointed Assistant Professor at the South Asia Institute of University of Heidelberg where he was promoted to the position of an Associate Professor in 1979. He has conducted fieldwork for several years in various parts of India and Pakistan. Since 1980 Prof. Pfeffer has undertaken numerous extended excursions to the middle India tribes. In addition to his teaching and research obligations in Berlin, he is an active member of several national and international academic societies and on the editorial board of the German Zeitschrift Fur Ethnologie. Prof. Pfeffer has published a number of articles in reputed international journals. He has brought out six edited volumes on tribal studies jointly with Prof. D.K. Behera of Sambalpur University, India. Religious cults and kinship structures of the Scheduled Tribes in the Koraput and Phulbani districts of Orissa (India) are Prof. Pfeffer's key areas of interest.

Mailing Address: Institute of Ethnology
Free University of Berlin
Drosselweg 1-3
14195 Berlin
Germany
E-mail: <gpfeffer@gmx.net>

Pradhan, Manto completed his M.A. and M.Phil degrees in anthropology from Sambalpur University. He has got a brilliant academic record. He is now attached to the AIDS Cell of Headquarters Hospital, Jharsuguda (Orissa). He has done many empirical studies in tribal areas of Koraput while working in Orissa Research Projects funded by German Research Council. He has attended many national and international seminars and presented many papers in national seminars. His areas of research interest are tribal studies and studies on children and childhood.

Mailing Address: Department of Anthropology
Sambalpur University
Sambalpur-768 019
Orissa, India
E-mail: <mantopradhan@rediffmail.com>

Ratha, S.N. (born 1936) got his Ph.D. degree from Gauhati University. He served Gauhati University as a Lecturer/Reader. from 1963 to 1976. He joined as Professor in Department of Anthropology, Sambalpur University and continued there till his retirement. He was also the vice-president of Ethnographic Folk Culture Society and Institute of Social Research and Applied Anthropology, Calcutta. He is the life member of Indian Science Congress Association, Indian Sociological Association, Indian Anthropological Association, Anthropological Society of North-East India, North-East Council for Social Science Research, Institute of Applied Anthropology and Social Research, Ethnographic and Folk Culture Society of India, Orissa Environmental Consciousness Society, Indian Anthropological Society and associate of Current Anthropology and member of Editorial Board of the journal *Man and Life.* He has successfully completed a number of projects funded by National Institute of Urban Affairs, New Delhi (NUA) and ICSSR. He has successfully guided *16* Ph.D. dissertations. He has authored two books and edited *two* Volumes. He has published more than 60 research papers in different edited volumes and journals on topics like caste, community and village studies, marriage and kinship, applied and development anthropology and paleo-anthropology. He has presented papers and chaired various sessions in many national and international conferences. He was the Chairman P.G. Council, Dean of Faculty of Arts and Director of Employment Bureau, member of Senate, Syndicate, and Advisory Council of Sambalpur University. He is the member of Advisory Board of Tribal and Harijan Research-cum-Training Institute, Orissa, State Advisory Board of Prison Administration, Board of Governors, REC, Rourkela, Board of Management, UCE, Burla and Advisory Council, Academy of tribal Dialects and Culture, Bhubneswar. At the national level he is the member of National Committee to Assess the Impact of Industrialization in Tribal Areas, Advisory Board, Department of Special Assistance in Anthropology, Ranchi, Advisory Committee to Review the Progress of Bench Mark Survey of Socio-economic Conditions of Bihar and Orissa, Advisory Committee, Anthropological Survey of India, Educational, Research and Innovations Committee (National Council of Educational

Research and Training). His areas of interest are caste studies, village studies, tribal studies and development studies.

Mailing Address: B 101 Solanki's Gul Mohar
Brahmanwada
Begunpeet
Hyderabad, 500 016
E-mail: <snratha@rediffmail.com>

Reddy, Sunita Bharati is an Associate Professor at the Centre for Social Medicine and Community Health. Jawaharlal Nehru University, Delhi. She has done extensive research on women and children's health, tribal health higher education and dalit studies. Prof. Reddy ha spresented papers at national and international conferences and published papers in reputed journals and magazines. She is an *"associate board member"* of an online publication "Citizens News" of Hindustan Times, New Delhi.

Mailing Address: Dr. Sunita Reddy
Assistant Professor
Centre for Social Medicine and Community Health
Jawaharlal Nehru University
Delhi

Sahay, Vijoy S. is a full-time Professor of anthropology at Allahbad University. He secured first-class first position both at B.A. and M.A levels. Prof. Sahay was awarded Ph.D. for his fascinating research work on the Nicobar Archipelago from Ranchi University. He is the co-author of the books, *Nature-Man-Spirit Complex in Tribal India* (1981), *Sanskritik Manavshastra: Sidhant Evam Uplabdhiyan* (1996), *Sparks From Bidisa* Land Forest and Twin Tribal Problems (1997) and Indian Anthropology (1998). Prof. Sahay has presented a number of papers in national and international conferences in India and abroad. He is the author of several research papers. Prof. Sahay has been interested in teaching history of anthropological theories and conducting field researches among the most primitive and isolated tribal groups of India, including that of Andamans and Bastar. His forthcoming publications are, Dramatis Personae of Indian Anthropology, An Anthropologist Looks at History, Gharwas of Bastar: A Study in Anthropology of Art and The Nicobar Islanders.

Mailing Address: Vijoy S. Sahay
Department of Anthropology
University of Allahabad
Allahabad-211 002, India
E-mail: < vijoys@yahoo.com>

Suzuki, Peter T. born in Seattle, Washington, U.S.A., studied anthropology at Columbia University (B.A., M.A.), Yale University (doctoral studies), and Leiden University, Holland (M.Phil and Ph.D. degrees). His post-doctoral work includes studies at Heidelberg University, Germany, and Louvain La Neuve, Belgium. Prof. Suzuki has conducted fieldwork in Turkey, and has done research among Turks in Germany, American Indians in Nebraska, American Blacks in Omaha, and Asian Americans, human relations in eastern Berlin, the Omaha, Winnebago, and Santee Sioux Reservations in Nebraska. He is the Frederick W. Kayser Professor at the University of Nebraska at Omaha, Nebraska.

Mailing Address: Department of Public Administration
University of Nebraska at Omaha
Omaha
Nebraska-68182-0276
USA
E-mail: <psuzuki@FA-CPACS.UNOMAHA.EDU>

Vashum, R. obtained his post-graduate degree from the University of Delhi. He was awarded the degree of Doctor of Philosophy by the University of Delhi (Department of Anthropology) for the research work - Nagas and the Question of Self-Determination. He has authored one book - *Nagas Right to Self-Determination: Anthropological-Historical Perspective* (2000), and co-edited the book - *Nagas at Work* (1996). He has participated in many conferences at the national level. He has to his credit several articles and book reviews published in leading journals. Since mid-1999, he has been actively engaged with a project entitled, "Indo-Naga Conflict: Problem and Resolution" under the aegis of the Indian Social Institute, New Delhi. He is currently Research Fellow, Indian Social Institute, New Delhi.

Mailing Address: Research Fellow
Indian Social Institute
Lodi Road
New Delhi, India

Venkateswar, Sita has been a Lecturer/Associate Professor in social anthropology at Massey University since 1997 and has been involved in research on child labour in Nepal since 1999. She has been conducting field research in Nepal since August 2000. Dr. Venkateswar's earlier dissertation research was conducted in the Andaman Islands over an 18-month period between 1989-1992, and was funded by a dissertation improvement grant from the National Science Foundation. She obtained her Ph.D. from Rutgers University in 1997.

Mailing Address: Social Anthropology Programme
School of Global Studies
Massey University
New Zealand
E-mail: <S.Venkateswar@massey.ac.nz>

INDEX